Protestant Empire

Protestant Empire

Religion and the Making of the British Atlantic World

Carla Gardina Pestana

PENN

UNIVERSITY OF PENNSYLVANIA PRESS

PHILADELPHIA

Published by
University of Pennsylvania Press
Philadelphia, Pennsylvania 19104-4112

Printed in the United States of America on acid-free paper

10 9 8 7 6 5 4 3 2 1

Library of Congress Cataloging-in-Publication Data

Pestana, Carla Gardina.
  Protestant Empire : Religion and the Making of the British Atlantic World / Carla Gardina Pestana.
    p. cm.
  Includes bibliographical references (p.   ) and index.
  ISBN 978-0-8122-4150-1 (alk. paper)
    1. Great Britain—Church history.   2. Great Britain—Colonies—Africa—Religion.   3. Great Britain—Colonies—America—Religion.   I. Title.
BR757.P47   2009
270.09171′241—dc22

                                                                    2008042299

To the memory of my father, Ray Gardina

CONTENTS

Introduction   1

ONE
Religion before English Expansion   15

TWO
Reformation and the Politicization of Religious Expansion   33

THREE
Exporting the Religious Tensions of the Three Kingdoms   66

FOUR
Restoration Settlement and the Growth of Diversity   100

FIVE
Battling over Religious Identity in the Late Seventeenth Century   128

SIX
Religious Encounters and the Making of a British Atlantic   159

SEVEN
Revivalism and the Growth of Evangelical Christianity   187

EIGHT
Revolutionary Divisions, Continuing Bonds   218

CONCLUSION
The British Atlantic World in Perspective   256

SUGGESTIONS FOR FURTHER READING   267
NOTES   277
INDEX   287
ACKNOWLEDGMENTS   301

INTRODUCTION

THE EXPANSION OF Europe from its peninsula into other parts of the globe was one of the most significant events to shape the modern world. Among the many effects of this cataclysmic movement of people and institutions was the intermixture of cultures that occurred in the colonies that Europeans created. Europeans crossed oceans, encountered native inhabitants, and interacted with them in a myriad of ways. What emerged from these encounters was, as historians James H. Merrell and Colin G. Calloway have pointed out, a new world for everyone involved.[1] Central to the creation of this new world was a clash of religious beliefs and practices. As a result of cultural encounters, all religions were changed—European Christianity no less than Native American spirituality. When Europeans moved out into the Atlantic basin, they brought together the diverse religious traditions and experiences of people from three continents.

By 1800 Christianity had reached into sub-Saharan Africa, both in the Kongo, where Portuguese Catholics had introduced Catholicism centuries before, and more recently in Sierra Leone, a new colony under British authority peopled by Protestant settlers of African descent who were strongly committed to the Christian faith. Native religions had been reshaped by the introduction of Christianity in vast areas of North and South America. Roman Catholicism had become an indigenous religion over centuries of adaptation in Latin America to the south and in Quebec to the north, while Protestant Christianity had made serious inroads in some communities in the broad central swath of North America. The movement of peoples with their beliefs and practices had spread not just Christianity generally but competing versions of that faith, so that in Anglophone areas of the Atlantic world a variety of Christian faiths were flourishing and vying for adherents, from Baptists and Methodists to Moravians and Quakers, by 1800. Though Christianity was dominant among the new religions, the other Old World

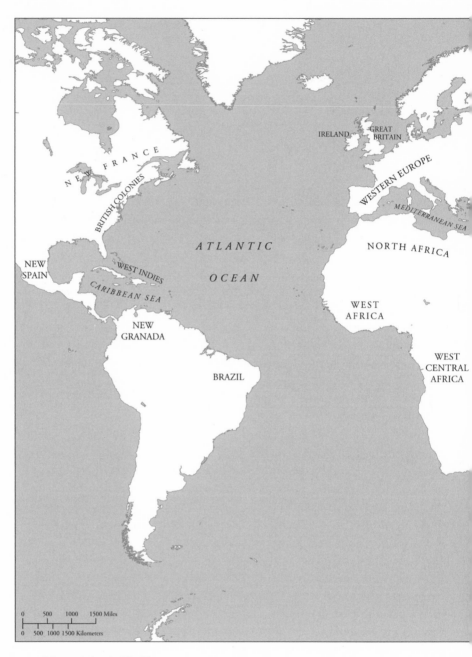

Map 1. Atlantic World

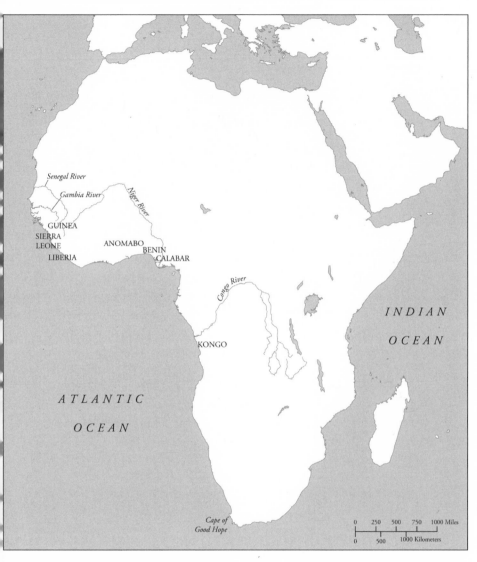

Senegal River
Gambia River
Niger River
GUINEA
SIERRA
LEONE
ANOMABO
BENIN
LIBERIA
CALABAR
Congo River
KONGO
INDIAN
OCEAN
ATLANTIC
OCEAN
Cape of
Good Hope

| 0 | 250 | 500 | 750 | 1000 Miles |
| 0 | 500 | 1000 Kilometers |

Map 2. Atlantic Africa

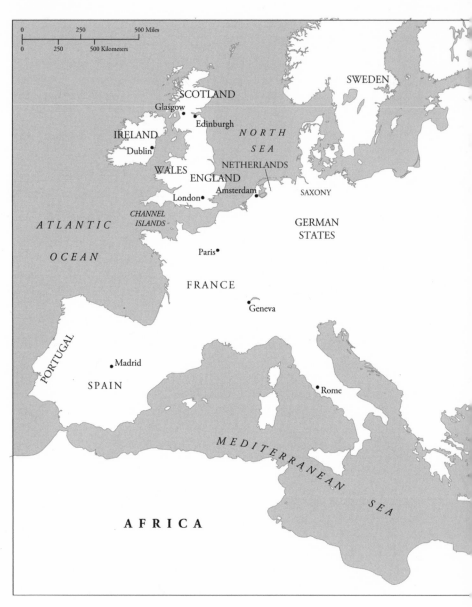

Map 3. Atlantic Europe

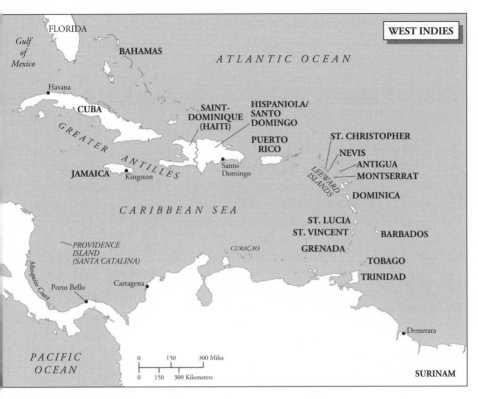

Map 4. West Indies

monotheistic faiths—Judaism and Islam—were also represented in the Atlantic world of 1800, while the traditions of many nonmonotheists continued to be practiced, whether by enslaved Africans or by native peoples of the Americas.

Although it made a late and unpromising start in the bid for colonies, England contributed profoundly to the religious history of the North Atlantic. As one of the principal sources of Protestant colonization in the Americas (along with the Dutch), England was often at odds with the Roman Catholic empires of Spain, France, and Portugal. In the British colonies, a diverse array of Protestant groups, along with a smattering of Catholics, participated—from England, Wales, Scotland, Ireland, and the northern reaches of Western Europe. Native Americans in the mainland colonies and Africans everywhere further complicated the religious assortment. The mixing of peoples that occurred in the English and British colonies was arguably more complicated than in any other colonial setting, with the possible exception of that of the Dutch. The English failed almost completely in asserting the level of control over religious practice that the Spanish achieved in New Spain. Only weakly establishing the Church of England, they oversaw an increasingly diverse religious landscape. Yet, despite this failure to create a uniformly Anglican Atlantic world under English purview, expansion established a broadly shared culture that united believers from different Protestant churches (and different ethnic and racial backgrounds) into a common Anglophone spiritual orientation. Revolution at the end of the eighteenth century would split the British Atlantic politically but the ties that bound it religiously would remain, shaping faith in western Europe, parts of West Africa, northern North America, and the Caribbean.

More than any other cultural practice, religion had a far-reaching impact on the very process of colonization and the world that resulted. Religion fueled expansion, justifying conquest and the authority that was established in the wake of those conquests. To a great extent, it sorted people into migration streams, so that Protestants generally went to the colonies of specific countries, Catholics largely to others. Given the variety of spiritual options available in Protestant Europe, diversity came quickly to those colonies opened to migration from England and the United Provinces. That variety would become their most startling feature and would prompt the eventual separation of church and state in the United States. Although religious liberty had intellectual justifications, drawn from the Enlightenment or older ideas about freedom of conscience, the social reality of a complex and contested religious scene propelled those ideas to the fore. Freedom of religion, though heralded in histories of the United States as one of the great accomplishments of the revolutionary era, was adopted reluctantly by most of those who oversaw colonial expansion in British North America.

Viewing religion within the framework of the Atlantic highlights a number of significant processes that shaped that history. As with many other works of Atlantic history, this book considers circulation—the movement not only of people but also of ideas and the books that carried those ideas. European expansion brought people, with their religious ideas and assumptions, into contact with others. In turn, this contact prompted innumerable religious encounters, not only among inhabitants from the four continents bordering the Atlantic basin but also among Europeans of different faiths. People moved in every conceivable direction: Africans who converted to Christianity in the Americas traveled widely as sailors, including manning slave ships that transported cargos from West Africa; Native Americans, sometimes kidnapped and sometimes voluntary visitors, were displayed in European capitals, feted in royal courts, and baptized into state churches; Jews who had been driven from Spain settled in the Netherlands, where their descendants participated in colonization and founded communities in both Dutch and British outposts. The very act of moving around changed people and their beliefs. Change occurred not only in the places that Europeans went but also in Europe itself, as people came to terms with the existence of the lands, faiths, and cultures that encounter brought together.

Particularly among the Protestants who played a leading role in the British Atlantic, books that circulated were important carriers of ideas and markers of identity. For Protestant Europeans, literacy was seen as fundamental to civility and to one's ability to function successfully as a converted Christian. A believer needed to be conversant with the Bible, and while familiarity with the Good Book was by no means limited to those who were literate, the ability to read was widely perceived as significant—by those doing the converting and by converts themselves. This emphasis on literacy affected the way Europeans went about the project of converting those they encountered. It would also provide one reason many masters feared the prospect of slave conversion. On one level, books were commodities that circulated like any other; but they were also repositories for ideas and potential sources of power.

A second process that shaped the history of religion on this scale is that of transplantation. Early colonizers used the term "plantation" to refer to actual settlements as well as to the process of creating them. The term connoted carefully uprooting and replanting people and institutions in a new setting. Sometimes whole communities were literally transplanted, such as the Baptist church of Swansea in Wales, which removed to Plymouth Plantation in the 1660s. On a broader scale, monarchs expected that the religious institutions of their kingdoms would be transplanted to distant colonies, there to bolster state authority just as they did in the Old World. English monarchs not only assumed that planters (as early settlers were frequently called) would introduce Protestant Christianity to far-flung Atlantic locations but also that their adherence to England's state church would help to make them loyal and effective representatives of the crown. This initial expectation was based on their observation of Iberian successes as well as on commonly held assumptions about the necessity for religious unity in a political polity, particularly a geographically dispersed one. Spanish rulers, working from a similar assumption about the centrality of Catholicism to their imperial agenda, organized Spain's movement into the New World to achieve a degree of religious uniformity that English monarchs would envy. Having previously banished Muslims and Jews from Spain, they worked from a more homogenous context.

For the English, this assumption of easily transplanted religious institutions proved not only a chimera but a problematic goal. As much as the common wisdom of the era dictated religious uniformity, England after the Protestant Reformation never achieved the ideal, having always a Catholic minority at the very least with which to contend. With England, Scotland, and Ireland all ruled by the same king from 1603, the religious diversity of that monarch's realm was remarkably complicated. Events of the mid-seventeenth century also drastically increased the complexity and contention of the religious landscape under the later Stuart rulers. Diversity within and among kingdoms made the simple transplantation of a uniform religious framework impossible. The unlikelihood of colonies being anymore homogenous than the metropolitan core was exacerbated by the impulse—at all levels, from rulers to the ordinary prospective colonist—that the Atlantic settlements might offer opportunities for the religiously marginal. Diversity at the center—remarkable as it gradually became—offered only a pale reflection of the multiplicity of religious faiths and practices that eventually characterized life at the margins. The institutional weakness of the Church of England in the colonies, the diversity of Protestant (and other) options everywhere, and the rising commitment to toleration all ensured that any plan to make the state church a central pillar of the British Atlantic was doomed. The planting of religious institutions was never limited to the official faith but was in fact a process participated in by many of those outside the established church—like the Swansea Baptists—and even beyond European Christianity. It therefore complicated the religious milieu rather than, as had been anticipated, helping to keep it simple.

The challenge of transplantation affected ordinary people's ability to carry their faiths and practices with them too. Some of the people in motion were able to travel with their community and its leaders—the puritan migrants to New England who included more clergymen per capita than any other English group come to mind—whereas others were cut loose from some or all of their previous relationships. European Catholics, for instance, left their shrines and holy places. For African captives, the religious disruption that enslavement entailed arose from leaving behind the small-scale, intimate social landscape in which their beliefs and practices had flourished. For the original residents of the Americas, the arrival of Europeans set into motion massive epidemics and repeated displacement of populations, both of which severed ties to spiritually significant communities and locations.

Even as a religious environment in its entirety proved difficult to transplant, everyone brought their interpretive frameworks, and these frameworks shaped interactions that would take place in colonies and other Atlantic outposts. For the Protestant English majority, their understanding of the purpose and meaning of their move into the wider Atlantic world was molded by their anti-Catholicism. The long and painful sundering of the ties that initially bound Tudor England to Roman Catholicism left a bitter legacy of suspicion and fear among many English Protestants, and this fear was perpetuated by seventeenth-century events such as the Catholic plot to blow up Parliament in 1605.

If anti-popery was a uniquely Protestant viewpoint, other interpretive schemes were more widely held. The idea that spiritually powerful beings had to be respected in order for believers to remain safe manifested itself in different ways among those of various traditions; whether it was Christians asking God for forgiveness or Africans honoring spirits of the dead, a common impulse to respect the wishes of the spiritually powerful animated many believers. Another framework involved witchcraft, in which spiritual power could be yielded by an ill-intentioned individual. This understanding often came into play in the context of encounter, such as when native peoples in New France suspected Jesuit missionaries of witchcraft after many of their companions mysteriously died. These interpretive frameworks—which touched on many aspects of life—were key components of the encounters that occurred in the Atlantic world.

A final process that characterized the meeting of religions in the British Atlantic was negotiation. Religious encounters involved an ongoing transaction of give and take. As people encountered new ideas and practices and worked to make sense of them in relation to what they already knew, they negotiated between the familiar and the unfamiliar. If the new appeared to have value, it could be incorporated, often creating a hybrid—a version that blended elements of two traditions into something new. When Christianity was brought to Europe initially, the process unfolded in this way, so that, for instance, older community celebrations and rituals were subsumed into the Christian calendar. Native Americans who gradually altered the way they envisioned the afterlife while doing so in the context of their long-held belief system participated in a version of this process. As historian John Thornton has described this development in the African context, they "naturalized" the unfamiliar, making sense of it in terms of the familiar.[2] That concepts and practices from various traditions might be melded into some new whole made sense in the context of the Native American or West African attitudes toward the potential usefulness of new beliefs or practices. Their religious systems tended to be more open to borrowing to create something both new and recognizably old. Even though they too participated in the blending process, European Christians officially rejected it intellectually, assuming that other traditions were by definition incorrect.

Europeans entering the Atlantic arena in the aftermath of the Protestant Reformation expected to convert the heathens of America, Africa, and the Caribbean to their version of Christianity—whether it was Iberian Catholicism, English Protestantism, or another option. They anticipated that a person confronting Christianity would undergo a dramatic and life-changing alteration. Conversion was a concept deeply ingrained in the Christian tradition, and it carried with it certain expectations about how the process would occur. As the word suggests, it was supposed to change the individual completely. When they carried Christianity to new places and encountered new peoples, Europeans sought to spark a drastic alteration in that individual as he or she embraced the new (and, in their view, superior) faith. Europeans who set about converting Africans, Indians, or, for that matter, one another expected that experience to proceed in a proscribed and predictable way. Christian missionaries were shocked to learn that this all-or-nothing understanding of the conversion process did not hold true for some converts. To incorporate former practices or beliefs into a new religion was anathema to their view of the transformative nature of this event.

Whether absorbing new into old ways, retaining some of the old while ostensibly embracing the new, or converting wholeheartedly to a new faith, all of these variations on the encounter necessitated negotiation. Within this larger context of continuity, change, and negotiation, individual choices occurred. A colonist who converted to a new belief system might do so because he was alienated from his community's dominant faith, found a spiritual option that reminded him of the practices he had experienced in childhood, or saw some benefit to his loved ones. Fear—whether of the spiritual power of others or their ability to do harm in more prosaic ways—was often central to these interactions too.[3] Individual, cultural, and situational contexts shaped encounter, in which negotiation of opportunities, hopes, and fears all played a role. Thinking of the negotiation process on such a large scale helps us to get a sense of the dynamic and multifaceted nature of the meeting of peoples and beliefs that occurred in these centuries.

If the British Atlantic ultimately took shape out of the decisions of many people—to migrate, to convert, to accept selectively or in full, to proselytize, or to remain silent—we must also consider that migration or conversion could be forced, while individual voices could be silenced. It is clear that no person worked as a wholly free agent, totally unencumbered and able to act as he or she pleased. The frustration of kings when they tried to implement new religious policies—and on one occasion thereby sparking a war—offers a dramatic case of the limits of individual purposive action to shape religion. Choices were often constrained, by the options that were available or by the power relations that prevailed. Like circulation and transplantation, negotiation was a contested process.

Protestant Empire: Religion and the Making of the British Atlantic World is intended for any reader interested in religion, the expansion of Europe, and New World cultural encounters. Religion has not been studied on such a broad canvas before, but specialized work produced by many scholars makes this wider-ranging account possible. Without detailed treatments of specific religious communities, of religious institutions, and of interfaith encounters, this book could not have been written. While something is lost when working on such a scale, much is gained as well. At this extent we can see connections and trends that might escape the close observer of one aspect or another of this history. Perhaps reading about the broad sweep of these religious encounters and the change they brought will encourage readers to look into specific incidents or groups in more detail. Readers interested to learn more should see the suggestions for further reading at the end of this volume.

Definitions of some key terms identify the scope of this book. "Religion" is used here to designate any shared understanding of what modern western-ers think of as the supernatural world (although that idea of a supernatural world separate from the natural world makes more sense in some religious contexts than others). The shared understanding shapes a community's be-liefs about its relationship to the spiritual, whether the spiritual is understood to be interwoven with or distinct from the natural world. Commonly held views serve as the basis of a community's religious system, providing a set of institutional practices and relationships that structure the social world in which people operate. Looking at how religion worked in the lives of individ-uals opens up a common ground among different faiths. Native American beliefs about spirit in animals and objects structured that community's worldview in a way that was broadly analogous to the English use of the idea that God shaped even the most minor occurrence in the life of the Christian.

The term "British Atlantic" designates those lands bordering on the Atlantic Ocean that were controlled by England or, after the 1707 Union of England and Scotland, by the newly named "Britain." It also encompasses those places where British people had a presence even when they were not in control, such as chaplains in trading forts on the coast of Africa or visitors to the continental interior who recorded their observations of native peoples. The English were the first subjects of their monarch to become actively engaged in Atlantic endeavors, and they migrated in the largest numbers of any residents in the first decades of colonization. What began as a largely (although never exclusively) English endeavor came to involve a large number of Scots as well as some Irish and Welsh, so that eventually the Atlantic world controlled from the seat of government at Westminster was indeed British—ethnically, politically, and, in some senses, religiously as well.

This book is organized chronologically, moving around the Atlantic world to lay out major trends and events. It begins with a sketch of the religious beliefs and practices in West Africa, western Europe, and eastern North America in 1500. This comparative treatment aims, first, to establish a baseline against which the change wrought by expansion can be measured and, second, to demonstrate the centrality of religion in the lives of all the peoples on the edges of the Atlantic at that time. The story then turns to Europe to explore the Protestant Reformation—the rupture in western European Christianity that led to the creation of many new versions of that faith, all of them outside the authority of the Roman Catholic Church. The Reformation split western Europe into Protestant and Catholic camps, which immediately went to war (literally and figuratively). The rivalry between them further fueled the geographic expansion that was already under way. The book's focus then narrows to the English case, charting the outward movement of Protestant England as well as the complexity of the religious situation prevailing in the three kingdoms of England, Ireland, and Scotland. Complications within that composite monarchy (as these multiple kingdoms under a single sovereign are called) greatly influenced the colonies that the English began to plant in earnest after 1600, as did revolutionary events in those kingdoms in the first half of the seventeenth century. It was not until the second half of the seventeenth century that the English first began to grapple seriously with the immense diversity of their colonies. Not only did the variety of Protestant alternatives increase in this era, but the large-scale importation of enslaved Africans, the arrival of Jews, and the first sustained missions to the Indians created a varied and complex religious scene. After a century of expansion, the end of the seventeenth century witnessed a number of crises—political revolution in England, Indian wars in the mainland colonies, and witchcraft scares in New England and Scotland—all of which had religious causes and consequences. The account then moves into the early eighteenth century, during which the reverberations of revolution continued while, at the same time, a number of contradictory trends began to reshape British Atlantic religion. Religious revivals at mid-century affected Britain and many of its colonies, introducing to Christianity notable numbers of captive Africans for the first time. Evangelical Christianity thus became a strong presence on both sides of the Atlantic. The era of the American and French revolutions marked a watershed, as political events redefined the contours of the British Empire and drastically altered the religious configuration within it and in the new United States. Despite such political rupture, continuities remained in the shared religious culture.

In focusing on the English and British experience I only occasionally glance at encounters that occurred among Africans, Native Americans, and the Europeans living in colonies founded by Spain, Portugal, France, and the Dutch United Provinces, to name only the most prominent. The religious history of European expansion into the Atlantic includes a number of chapters, of which the Protestant and British story is but one. A significant chapter, it is a story that has not been told except in fragments. Although I draw occasional connections with and contrasts to other Europeans in their encounters with the religions of America and Africa, a sustained treatment of their religious histories represents chapters that are beyond the scope of this book. Taking the Western Hemisphere as a whole, the Spanish encounter with native America had an enormous effect, bringing to much of North and South America an Iberian form of Catholicism that combined with various indigenous belief systems. Protestants who came to the Atlantic arena later were well aware that their entrée was both little and late. The major Protestant rival of the British, the Dutch, for a time provided competition by overseeing another set of colonies—especially Suriname and, until 1664, New Netherland (which in that year became New York)—to which Protestants might migrate. Although geographically more limited than the Spanish case, the British encounter had an impact that was both far-reaching and sustained, shaping not only the United States but also Canada, portions of the Caribbean, sectors of Atlantic Africa, Ireland, and Britain itself. As the first post-

Reformation empire in the Atlantic world, British expansion embodied features tied to its Protestant character.

I learned a great deal while working on this book, which had the usual result of making me aware of how much I do not know. Some of my lack is no doubt the result of personal failing, in which a smarter, more tenacious, or more imaginative person could have done better. Some of the holes in my knowledge arise from the limits to what can be known. Uncovering the experiences, worldviews, and even the actions of past peoples, all of whom were participants in cultures and societies drastically different from my own, is not simple. Understanding beliefs that may never have been expressed in any form that would have survived or plumbing the motives for actions that were never explained is more difficult still. Why did a particular enslaved African adopt Christianity? Did he understand his conversion in the same way as the white missionary who left a record explaining it? What did Squanto, who had been to Europe, think of the passengers on the *Mayflower* once he learned of their religion? Did he understand enough about the religious divisions within Europe to place this group of separatists in a Protestant framework? Had his sojourn in Catholic and Protestant Europe as both a slave and a free man affected his own religious faith? Why did some colonists choose to become Quakers in violation of brutal local laws? I do not know the answers to these questions, which could be multiplied almost endlessly, and I am not sure anyone can know. Conscious of this book's and of my own limitations, I hope readers will still find it enlightening.

ONE

Religion before English Expansion

IN 1500, THE three regions of West Africa, eastern North America, and western Europe were only beginning to come into contact. As the new century dawned (by the calculation of the western European calendar), both Spain and Portugal sent ships to ply the Atlantic. Each had previously conquered islands off the coast of Africa, the Madeira, the Azores (Portugal, 1418, 1432), and the Canary Islands (Spain, 1479). The Portuguese first visited the Kongo, in West Central Africa, in 1483, and eight years later missionaries administered Roman Catholic baptism to both the ruler and one of his sons (the future Afonso I, 1460–1542). Meanwhile Bartholomeu Dias had rounded the Cape of Good Hope, at the southern tip of Africa, in 1488, opening the sea route from Europe to Asia. Christopher Columbus, in the employ of the monarchs of Aragon and Castile (kingdoms that would unite to create Spain), had by 1500 made three voyages to the Caribbean and finally discovered the land mass that would prove to be South America, although he still hoped—or at least claimed—that his discoveries were part of Asia. Western Europe remained Roman Catholic, untroubled as yet by the schism that would erupt after Martin Luther's protest; his posting of a long list of criticisms of the church (the famous *Ninety-five Theses*) on the door of his church was still seventeen years in the future. Europeans had yet to visit North America beyond the occasional foray to Newfoundland, but European expansion and the increased intercontinental contacts it brought were under way by this time. The future accessibility of these far-flung places could not yet be guessed, but these regions were already becoming less isolated.

To all the peoples bordering the Atlantic in 1500, religion mattered.

Whether they lived in West Africa, western Europe, or eastern North America, everyone believed that the world they could not see—that of gods, spirits, saints, and other forces—affected their lives every day. In each region, communities used rituals to ensure that they would be kept safe from threatening forces, whether disastrous harvests, diseases, accidental injuries, or wars. With the world full of unseen powers, people assiduously followed ritual calendars of ceremonies intended to ensure good relations with the supernatural. Each community had spiritually powerful individuals who assisted other members in negotiating the challenges of dealing with these forces and the questions that surrounded them. Spiritual adepts assisted others in coming to terms with both the past and the future. People living around the Atlantic basin feared too that spiritual power could be used to do harm, and they relied on local experts to stave off that harm. Religious beliefs and practices addressed not just the mysteries associated with death but also basic questions about how to live a gratifying life. Origin stories explained both how the world came to be as it was and how believers ought to act within it. Despite variations in the specific aspects of each tradition, all the peoples bordering the Atlantic found reassurance and guidance in their religious life. For this reason, religion mattered profoundly to all peoples on the eve of the expansion of Europe.

Surveying western European, West African, and eastern North American religion in 1500, we might be inclined to think in terms of a radical disconnection between the faiths of the three continents. Europe was predominantly Roman Catholic, living under the authority of the pope in Rome and adhering to Christianity, one of the three great monotheistic religions that arose out of the Mediterranean basin centuries before. Jews and Muslims, adherents of the other two, also resided in western Europe, although in far smaller numbers. Indeed the Spanish had recently driven the Moors—North African adherents of Islam—out of the Iberian peninsula they had ruled for centuries, thereby drastically reducing the presence of Islam in western Europe. At the same time, they banished all Jews who refused to convert to Christianity. West Africa too included some Islamic faithful, usually traders with ties to North Africa, but the vast majority of inhabitants held traditional beliefs that had structured local life long before the importation of this relatively new system along continental trade routes. North Americans, entirely untouched by the impulses originating in the Mediterranean, held to alternative cosmologies developed in their communities over many centuries.

Europeans who met Africans or Native Americans after 1500 usually emphasized the differences between their own religious system and those of the people they encountered. A visitor to Guinea in 1554, for instance, came home to report that people living there were either "Moores," by which he meant Muslims, or "a people of beastly living, without a God, law, religion, or common wealth." Another typical comment, from the pen of a man known as Leo Africanus, a convert from Islam who wrote the most influential account of Africa circulating in early modern Europe, declared that the sub-Saharan Africans "embrace no religion at all, being neither Christians, Mahumetans [Muslims], or Jewes, nor of any other profession, but living after a brutish manner."[1] In North America, early visitors invariably opined on the question of whether the Indians had a religion at all; when they recognized the outlines of one, they sometimes concluded it was a form of devil worship. Cavalier dismissals of this sort helped justify the enslavement of both West Africans and American Indians, processes that would shortly be under way in the Iberian world. Christians, primed by their attitudes toward alternative religions, expected that "pagans" would eagerly accept their own system. These assumptions led them to think in terms of conversion or conquest. They were also disinclined to take seriously the beliefs of those nonmonotheists they encountered.

This impulse to sort belief into Christian and pagan, religion versus no religion—although it makes sense when we are primarily interested in theology or ideologies of Christian conquest—ignores the shared ways that belief and practice worked in people's own lives. The vast majority of European Christians did not understand either the theology or the hierarchy of the Roman Catholic Church in the way it might be presented in a Western Civilization textbook. Instead they understood that the world was alive with spiritual forces with which they needed to contend. Just like their pagan counterparts elsewhere, they turned to their faith to fulfill common needs for comfort and understanding. In this respect, religion served similar, and fundamentally important, purposes everywhere. While the differences among these traditions would matter enormously, the basic fact that all attached importance to this aspect of life established a context in which people and their ideas would begin circulating through the Atlantic basin. After 1500, the peoples living around the Atlantic would meet in American and Caribbean colonies, and they would carry with them their understandings of the way the human and spiritual world interrelated.

The lands abutting the Atlantic Ocean were permeated with spiritual forces, which affected daily life. In North America, the world was thoroughly imbued with spirit. For the inhabitants of the eastern woodlands, spirit infused people, animals, natural objects, and waterways. With spirit everywhere, native peoples interacted with it constantly. Their world was completely saturated with "other-than-human persons," and humans worked to remain in balance with them.[2] Any journey undertaken, any crop planted, any wild plant gathered, any animal killed had to be approached with proper reverence for this balance. Rituals marked these transitions, noting the interdependence of the human community with the rest of the world. North Americans often carried protective items that helped to keep them safe within the complicated world they inhabited. These amulets, which guarded their wearers, might be collected into a small pouch containing a variety of significant objects. Americans had a sense of sacred place, as they moved through a landscape suffused with the spiritual.

Africans also lived in a densely occupied spiritual landscape. Various spiritual beings influenced their daily lives. Family compounds included a shrine to deceased ancestors. Families looked to these honored spirits for aid and protection. Rituals around the ancestors, including leaving small offerings at their shrines, were a routine part of life. Shrines were also placed around a village; later they would become more common along the roads. Outside of the household space, other spirits resided. Some were associated with specific places, especially rivers or groves of trees. Other spiritual forces were unattached to households or places, and many communities had local deities that were more widely shared than the ancestor figures of each household. In some places these gods were associated with snakes, and temples housing huge snakes stood as ritual centers of their cults. Later visiting Europeans would remark on these snake cults, warning other visitors not to offend a snake for fear of earning the wrath of its devotees. In other locations the local deities came in different forms. In all locations, however, the spiritual landscape was complex and heavily populated. Believers there too wore amulets or other spiritually imbued objects that helped to keep them safe from the forces surrounding them. They made figurines to represent a specific spiritual entity, placing these in their shrines or at the entrances to public places.[3]

Western Europe of 1500 was a similarly densely populated spiritual world. The Christian cosmology of spiritual beings included a supreme being, known as God, who was thought to include three essences—a father, a son (who had once taken human form), and a more vaguely personified holy spirit. In addition to this complex figure, the cosmos was home to angels (powerful spiritual beings who resided with God and worked for good) and to devils (similarly powerful beings who worked for evil). Both kinds of beings might intervene in human affairs, and believers feared demons for their power to torment and tempt them into sin.

The spiritual panoply also included a host of saints—dead individuals who were honored for having lived exceptionally holy lives. Saints played an especially large part in the religious experience of lay faithful. Relating to them, Christians sought assistance in a way that was broadly analogous to the Native American appeal to the spirits of their ancestors or to the totems of their clans. While some saints were broadly venerated, having been sanctioned by the Catholic Church, others—whether officially recognized as saints or not—had local followings. Towns, cities, and sometimes even isolated rural communities venerated a neighborhood saint or other deceased person. They dedicated churches, shrines, and holy relics to these figures. The faithful prayed to them, seeking aid and comfort. Specific saints specialized in helping with certain aspects of life; so Saint Anne, mother of Mary, who was in turn mother of Jesus, aided women in childbirth. Many people wore medallions dedicated to a particular saint. Like the objects carried by the faithful of North America, these protective items gave comfort and minimized worry. Sometimes Christians made pilgrimages to specific holy places in order to ask for special aid or to give thanks for assistance previously given. Certain places were holy, and believers valued them accordingly. Throughout the lands bordering the Atlantic, such practices and the ideas behind them were common.

Every community had rituals for contending with the spiritual realm and the human obligation toward it. Rituals could respond to a specific crisis, such as the need to reveal and disarm witches. Ritual observance marked the major life transitions that all individuals experienced, and every culture marked coming of age and other transitions with ceremonies. Since all of these societies were primarily agricultural, many rituals conformed to a seasonal calendar marking the cycles of nature. Native American celebrations marked different transitions of the year, from the winter hunt to spring planting, and from the summer time of gathering to the fall harvest. Rituals punctuated these different seasonal shifts, and periodic large-scale community celebrations were held. One later participant recorded five regularly scheduled rituals among the Seneca people.[4] Most were tied to events in the agricultural cycle, the time for collecting sap from the maple trees, for planting, for harvest, and the moment when green corn appeared on the stalk. A final festival, which lasted nine days, was held at midwinter. This celebration symbolically put aside all strife and division within the community; all the fires were put out and relit, marking the opening of a new year. Among the Iroquois, this festival was timed to the appearance of the Pleiades in the winter sky. Legend has it that the Seven Sisters of the star constellation came down to teach the Turtle Island people to dance, thereby establishing the festival. In addition to the regular calendar of ritual observances, celebrations could also be staged to respond to a specific event, such as a young hunter's success in taking his first large game animal. Many communities also had rituals of condolence for lost members; the Great League of the Iroquois understood its origins to be rooted in a condolence ritual that included ceremonial gift exchange and mourning for dead leaders. The Native American calendar was full of ritual days.

In Africa, celebrations similarly dotted the annual calendar. A festival dedicated to the yam harvest was celebrated all over West and West Central Africa, where the yam was a staple. Special days commemorating the dead or other spirits were common too—in West Africa as elsewhere. One later visitor to the kingdom of Benin likened what he considered the excessive number of festivals marking the ritual calendar to Roman Catholic practice: "they have so many, and different ones, that they ought not to give place to the Romanists." While he was able to observe one such festival, "the Coral Feast," he could not find anyone to explain its origins or purpose. Despite participants' unwillingness to inform this outsider about the details of their practice, he could see that it was a day of great rejoicing.[5] The same observer noted an annual celebration given over to the ancestors, presumably of the royal family's deceased kinfolk, since the ancestors of the powerful would be the most likely subject of a widespread celebration. Families would have honored their own particular ancestor spirits without the public ritual. Whereas daily life was filled with an awareness of these spiritual beings and various gestures acknowledging it, occasional community events gave an opportunity for a collective expression of local belief and satisfied the sense of obligation to honor that world. Everywhere people offered thanksgiving for a good harvest, whether to the Christian God, a local patron saint, the spirit of the corn, or the local deity who had charge of the rain and a successful crop.

The European ritual calendar might at first glance appear less closely tied to seasonal change. The major communal ritual in Europe was the Mass, a symbolic recreation of the central tenets of the Christian faith, which was celebrated daily but required of believers weekly and special feast day observances. Community festivals centered on significant saints days, when feasting and celebration offered a break from the daily routine and an opportunity to join together as a community. Yet seasonal rhythms were also apparent. The calendar of the Christian church incorporated older celebrations into Easter—a springtime celebration of new life—and Christmas—a festival emphasizing light at the darkest time of the year. A season of fasting preceded Easter, and it fell at the time of the year of the greatest dearth, as the community awaited the spring and the new growing season. The calendar may reveal the continuity of older, pre-Christian rituals related to the earth's rhythms, but Europeans in 1500 were just as closely bound to the earth and its cycles as any other peoples of their time. By 1600 some (but not all) western Europeans who embraced Protestantism would move away from this aspect of their older Christian tradition, as the most radical groups rejected the liturgical calendar. In 1500, however, such observance was ubiquitous.

Every community boasted residents who were especially skilled in dealing with the spiritual world and often orchestrated communal events related to it. Whether in Europe, West Africa, or North America, believers turned to these experts for assistance and guidance. North American communities honored men and women who were adept at the ceremonial practices that needed to be performed to keep the world in balance. They helped with sickness, warded off misfortune, oversaw life's transitions (including birth, coming of age, and death), and aided believers in the interpretations of their dreams. In Africa each local deity had particularly adept followers who oversaw its worship and attended to its needs. Communities also looked to local experts who orchestrated rituals, uncovered malicious witchcraft, and guided major life transitions. Europeans turned first to the local priests who led the community in its primary collective worship ritual, known as the Mass; oversaw the major transitions of birth, marriage, and death; and counseled inhabitants on how to keep their relationship with God on the right track (especially through the ritual confession of sins). Other spiritually adroit persons included members of religious orders, who were sometimes cloistered away from the larger community but in other instances might work among the populace offering various services and spiritual support; healers who often combined midwifery and herbal lore with the creation of amulets and other protective devices; and cunning men and women who were believed capable of using magic to heal and protect.

In all three locations individuals looked to those with special abilities to help them foresee the future. In many locations dreams were a source of

Fig. 1. John White, governor of the ill-fated Roanoke colony, drew this figure, which his fellow colonist, the scientist and linguist Thomas Harriot, referred to as a Native American spiritual expert, or "Conjurer." White's illustrations were widely disseminated in engravings like this one by Theodore de Bry (1590). Courtesy of John Carter Brown Library at Brown University.

prognostication. They played a central role in North America. Dreams might predict the future or give the dreamer a task that had to be performed. Individuals remembered, discussed, and interpreted their dreams, often with the help of others. Africans also had access to diviners who cast palm kernels or cowries as well as using other means to foretell the future. These spiritual powers gave people information that they could use to try to keep themselves from harm or to plan a course of action. Europeans also attended to their dreams in the hope of understanding their fate and their duty. They might go outside of the structure of the church for assistance, turning to a resident healer or fortune-teller for guidance. Astrologers were widely consulted to determine a propitious day for a specific event, such as the start of a war or the crowning of a new ruler. Officially Christians did not believe that God continued to speak directly to individuals. They did generally accept that mystics might receive visions that had spiritual import. Saints or other significant figures might appear even to ordinary people and convey messages to them. Church officials would check these accounts and decide on their veracity. Regardless of the church's decision, local communities might accept a mystic or other seemingly able person as an adept. The desire to know drove people everywhere to seek help in prognosticating the future.

All the peoples of the Atlantic basin believed that in death they would continue to exist, albeit in a different form than they had gone through life. Among the people of eastern North America, death was understood to involve a journey to another place, a place of spirits. The dead were prepared for burial, interred with items they would need later or that had special spiritual importance. In the Chesapeake region the bodies of dead leaders received special treatment: first their corpses were placed on a scaffold, where they remained until the flesh decayed; then in a second ceremony the spiritual leader of the community collected the bones and transferred them to a special building that contained the bones of their predecessors as well. These temples were spiritually powerful places, which only the priests entered. Most woodland peoples of the northeast were buried in the ground, along with a number of possessions dictated by their status in life. Mourning took place for an extended period, with the bereaved painting their faces and wailing to show their loss. The spirit of a person who had been murdered could not rest until the death had been avenged; victims of such deaths remained unsettled, much as they did in West Africa, compelling their relations to resolve the matter. Native communities engaged in warfare in part to avenge such deaths, with the family members having the choice of adopting or executing a captive who had been seized in place of the dead. These "mourning wars" helped to put the spiritual world back into the necessary balance.

West Africans thought of death as a journey to another place, and they prepared their dead accordingly. Bodies, washed and dressed, were often buried with essential items symbolic of what the dead would need on the journey to this other place. In many communities the dead had to be returned to the place of birth for final burial, a requirement that took on special significance in the event that someone died far from home. Long-distance migration within Africa challenged believers to maintain these practices, challenges that became nearly insurmountable with transatlantic enslavement. Rivers were often symbolically significant in the death journey, and some believed that the dead crossed a river into the land of the spirits where he or she would then reside. West Africans celebrated the death of a loved one with a boisterous party (which some European observers would later liken to an Irish wake) to send the dead along their way. Community celebration of a life also helped those who had lost someone to deal with their grief. Families set up shrines for ancestors who had died, and they could draw upon the aid of these ancestor spirits in time of need. They also might set aside a day to celebrate that spirit, an annual remembrance of the ancestor who had died and of his or her spirit's continued role in the community. Those who died by violence or who could not be properly buried might remain as an unsettled spiritual presence, and they could cause problems for the living. The living therefore sought to bury the dead properly and to see that justice had been done to them. Spiritual experts could find out from the dead whether they had been murdered and that information would be used to avenge the death. By properly attending to these matters, villagers could ensure that the only spirits in their area were benign and at least potentially supportive forces. With the coming of the slave trade, the sense that spiritual forces threatened the community would increase, but apparently in this early period there was an enormous preponderance in favor of benevolent spirits.

Europeans too believed that the dead lived on, going to another place to continue their existence. They conceived of the dead as being dispatched to one of a number of destinations, depending on how they had lived their lives. Evil persons were consigned to a place of punishment (hell), while those who had been good went to another place (heaven), where they would be happy. By 1500 western European Christians also believed that some of the dead—those who did not deserve eternal torment but had not yet earned bliss—went to an in-between space to await the future resolution of their case. Called "purgatory" to invoke the idea that some of the dead might be purged of their sins and subsequently allowed to enter heaven, the concept offered the loved ones of the dead person the solace of being able to work for the salvation of the deceased by offering prayers on their behalf. Critics of the church would say it abused this concern, selling indulgences that were said to absolve sins. A day of celebration of the lives of the dead was held every year in the autumn, and the community gathered to remember those who had died and to pray for them. Ritual preparation of the dead was also part of this tradition. Although the dead were not buried with objects in the expectation that they could use these items later, they were interned in specially prepared ground, preferably in the yard of a church. Churchyards and the tombs in the interior of the church connected the living members of the community to the dead; continuity across time was visibly represented as the descendants of those buried in the grounds gathered for worship in their assigned pews each week. Believers anticipated that the dead would rise on the last day of human history, undergoing a judgment that would send them eternally to heaven or to hell. In tending the graves, family members awaited the reappearance of their ancestors and wondered if they would join them first in the grave before the end of time. Where the dead had been improperly buried—such as at a crossroads where suicides were interned—Europeans feared that their spirits might haunt the place and disturb the living. Folktales of the dissatisfied dead who disturbed the place of their death were common, and such stories might surface around a location where a person was thought to have died under suspicious circumstances.

Witchcraft beliefs—though they too varied across cultures—offered another commonality. In all three regions, community members might abuse spiritual power to harm others, and other spiritual adepts could respond to their threat by marshaling a countervailing force. Everywhere a witch might do harm by causing sickness or death. Regional variations existed in the understanding of the ways in which witches performed their malevolent work. North American witches caused illness by magically intruding a small object (or charm) into the victim's body or by capturing the victim's soul in a dream. They were thought to be motivated by envy or some grievance. With an emphasis on community harmony, witches were greatly feared and, when found out, aggressively confronted. West Africans thought witches harmed their victims by capturing some or even all of their soul. A person without an intact soul became vulnerable, so the witchcraft had to be discovered and reversed in order to save the victim. The western European church declared the devil to be the source of a witch's power. Yet lay people seemed to believe that magical powers might arise from a morally ambiguous source, rather than always originating in and therefore performing evil. Thinking that local healers might be able to draw upon a similar source of power to combat witchcraft, they responded in ways that often had more in common with the beliefs prevalent in other areas than with the official position of the church. For all, a spiritually dense landscape presented opportunities to those who could harness its power to do good or ill to others.

The church's official position on witchcraft departed markedly from the more widespread view. Understanding the origins of witchcraft as arising from a pact with Satan, the church's interpretive framework led it to expect witchcraft to be recognizably anti-Christian. Authorities questioned suspected witches to discover if they staged blasphemous counter rituals that inverted those of the Christian community, such as drinking the blood of sacrificed infants in place of the wine turned into blood that the celebrant consumed in the Eucharist. The church sought out witches, used torture to unmask them, and executed those it found. According to the official policy, believers who feared a witch were to go immediately to the authorities for aid. Yet the laity often turned instead to local healers, sometimes known as "wise women," violating the proscriptions of their church while acting more like an African or Native American might. Witches in all Atlantic communities were punishable by death, but outside Christian Europe they might instead be healed and reincorporated into the community. From the perspective of people everywhere, the chief goal was to prevent the harm that witches might do. Witchcraft was one of a number of similar interpretive frameworks—like a sacred landscape or a belief in powerful superhuman forces—that these cultures shared.

All of these societies told stories of the origins of humans and of the world in which they live, stories that arose from and shaped their religious beliefs. An Iroquois origin story (to take one North American example) features multiple powerful beings who created and populated the world. In one version of the tale, the Iroquois traced the origins of human life back to Sky Woman. One of the Sky People who lived in the sky before the creation of the earth, she fell and was rescued by animals. These creatures created land on a turtle's back as a place for her to live. She soon gave birth to a daughter, and they began the creation of the earth on their Turtle Island. Her daughter became pregnant by an Earth Spirit, the North Wind, and gave birth to twins. Dying in childbirth, she was buried on the island, becoming Mother Earth. The twins' grandmother, grieving for her daughter, was estranged from the twins, one of whom was more like the Sky spirits, while the other took after the Earth. The two boys carried on the creation of the world, although their differences lead them to creations that varied widely; they sometimes also caused disagreements. Eventually the two brothers battled, the younger Earth brother was defeated, and the creation process slowed. The Iroquois people thought that the natural world was structured by the different natures of the two brothers and that difficulties people contended with in their daily lives arose from the complicated contest that had shaped the creation.

The tale, featuring multiple powerful spirits (not only Sky Woman, her daughter, and her grandsons but also the animals who rescued her) explained why the world was heavily populated by all sorts of powerful beings with whom humans needed to negotiate in order to survive and prosper. Sky Woman's centrality to the beginning bespoke a significant role for women and their reproductive powers in the Iroquoian cosmology. The political and social power of native women flowed naturally from such religious traditions. When Englishman Thomas Harriot spoke with the native residents in the region of present-day North Carolina, he thought it especially remarkable that "they say a woman was made first."[6] Powerful women with a central role in creation differed markedly from his own understanding of the organization of the cosmos.

In Atlantic Africa, stories of origins shared some elements with the stories told in North America. A compilation of Yoruba myths[7] includes a number of origin accounts. The Yoruba lived in what is now Nigeria. In their tradition and in others, the creator or creators were typically described as coming from elsewhere, from some otherworldly place. In many versions of the story, a spirit, or *orisha,* was named Oduduwa, and in some versions he set out with his older brother Obatala, who became distracted along the way. Oduduwa had a bag of dirt or sand, which he formed into the land. Some stories feature a supreme deity more powerful than the others. In one from the Yoruba tradition, pieces of a supreme deity were scattered about the earth and most, but not all, of the pieces were collected. This tale suggested that multiple deities owed their existence to the one supreme divine force that had been scattered at the beginning of time. A scattering of this divine essence might also help to explain the belief that various places and things were sacred. On the so-called Slave Coast, that region that today ranges from Ghana to western Nigeria, the supreme being was not a male god at all, but rather a goddess, paired with a male consort who was also a deity.

These stories posited the existence of two worlds, the created world and another, never-created world that deities emerged from at the beginning of human time. The world of the dead may represent a third locus of activity, one that did not come into this account. African beliefs in the continuity of life after death fit well into this idea that there was another place to which the dead (some of them venerated as powerful figures, just as they had been in life) retired after their life in this world was over. The tales also reflected the existence of multiple deities, some of which had a special relationship to a particular place. Rivers and waterways were especially associated with spiritual beings, as powerful sites that were both dangerous and life-giving. Deities could be female as well as male, and in some cases when a supreme god was mentioned, she was figured as female. Traditional African beliefs divided this

origin stories

world from the next but did not draw so sharp a line between the spiritual and temporal worlds.

Christians too had an origin story. Found in the Christian Old Testament, which also served as a holy text for the other monotheistic faiths of Judaism and Islam, it assumed the existence of one all-powerful creator God. Christian creation distinguished the spiritual from the temporal, and it emphasized the unique nature of the human creation. In the Judeo-Christian stories of creation, as contained in Genesis 1 and 2, the one God created the natural world and humanity. The most detailed biblical account stated that God created man first and then, out of man, created woman; the first creation was therefore of the male human, with the female appearing later and as a derivative of man. Man was told that he was master of the other creatures on earth, and he was granted dominion over them. The intercessions of an evil spirit persuaded woman to sin against God; she in turn swayed man. As a result, the first pair of humans was forced out of paradise, a bountiful place in which they had lived without hardship. They were banished to a life on earth that would be full of trouble and strife. In the Christian creation the starring role for a nonhuman is profoundly negative—the snake brings about all the problems of humanity through deceit and malice. Other creatures take only a passive or supporting role, as the animals named by and subordinate to the first man.

An examination of the origin stories of these three traditions—traditional West African, Native American, and Judeo-Christian—reveals illuminating general characteristics of each belief system. All the stories included powerful superhuman forces in the face of which human beings were comparatively weak. Dependent on these forces, people found possibilities for fulfillment or at least benefit through cooperation with them. Sources of spiritual power were more or less focused in these tales. The Christian version presented a dominant deity, although the tempter Satan represented a rival (and ultimately weaker) source of authority. God was nonetheless a rather remote figure for most western European Christians in 1500—although some mystics communed closely with Christ—and his remoteness helped to explain the recourse to saints as spiritual intermediaries when aid was needed. The other versions conveyed a more diffuse sense of spiritual potency, with a variety of deities, venerated ancestors, and animals each playing a part. The place for women in the cosmology of each ranged from the subordination of Eve to the centrality of Sky Woman. According to the Genesis creation account, the spiritual world eventually became more sharply separated from material life, once the first man and woman were banished from God's presence and sent out into a harsher reality. The other accounts provided less of a sharp separation, so that continued intercourse back and forth (as in the African case) or a spiritually infused landscape (as in the American version) remained real possibilities. The Judeo-Christian view that man should dominate the natural world represented the polar opposite of the American and African concern to respect animal or water spirits in the hope of enjoying their bounty and protection. Yet in all cases the beliefs about creation shaped the practices and attitudes of the society that held them.

As these stories demonstrate, religious beliefs bolstered the social and political system in each location. Christians in Europe learned that God had ordained human society to be organized as it was and that each person had to accept his or her place. Obedience was enjoined as a virtue that all should cultivate. Rulers were thought to have divine sanction for their authority, and religious leaders consecrated kings with oils to invoke biblical images of divine selection. Religious beliefs that extolled the ancestors of local African rulers similarly helped to reinforce the social system. Those who were dissatisfied with their situation and sought the power to harm others were understood in religious terms, and the community called upon spiritual experts to control the harm they might do. In North America as well the spiritual shaped relations among people. The worldview emphasized the need to maintain balance by fulfilling one's obligations to the community, which included humans and other-than-humans. All societies looked to religion to keep their worlds under control—or in balance, as the Native American viewpoint would have it.

We tend to think—and the discussion here has emphasized—that the major categories at work in the early Atlantic meetings were continental—African, American, and European. These broad classifications obscure as much as they reveal. It is well to remember that sometimes the "other" was not from another continent but rather from a distant region or another religious tradition within one's own continent of origin. In Europe and West Africa, the Islamic tradition represented one version of the other; for European Christians, Jews were similarly identified. In Native America, prior to the arrival of Europeans, difference pivoted on the variety of local spirits or ancestors. The intermixing that would occur as people and ideas circulated included encounters of Europeans with other Europeans, Africans with others from Africa, and Native Americans with others from different parts of the Americas. Indeed the tendency to categorize people according to such broad geographical units as "European" or "African" was a later development, arguably arising out of the meeting of peoples in the Atlantic world. In 1500 people did not think in those terms about themselves. Europeans may have come closest, with their idea of "Christendom," but this concept was not continental by any means: it did not include all of Europe while at the same time it extended well beyond Europe's boundaries to such areas as Ethiopia.

If Christendom was not equated with Europe, however, it did carry great interpretive weight. The Christian tendency to think in dichotomous terms—Christian and pagan—shaped expectations for their forays into the Atlantic. Western Europeans who stayed at home might encounter Jews (although not in England in 1500, as they had been banished centuries before), Muslims (which was increasingly likely, given rising English involvement in Mediterranean trade and diplomacy), and pagans (whom the English would meet only on the margins of Europe or beyond). Yet the idea of paganism had wide currency and deep cultural significance. Unlike Jews, Muslims, and Christians, pagans were not monotheists: they did not accept the idea of a supreme deity. Historically Christians had understood pagans as likely objects of conversion. As they moved out beyond the confines of Europe and the Mediterranean world generally, European Christians interpreted the religions they encountered in terms of this pagan-Christian dichotomy. Whereas non-Islamic Africans or Native Americans might be open to the prospect of learning from the carriers of a strange belief system, Christians were inclined to understand difference as error. If this was true when they dealt with Muslims or Jews, it was all the more so when they confronted the prospect of paganism. Although some Europeans would look at the strange people they encountered for signs that West Africans or North Americans had an inkling of the truth—such as an awareness of a supreme deity or knowledge of an afterlife—they thought of these similarities as, at best, vaguely perceived hints of true religion. This interpretive framework would influence how European Christians approached the encounter, as they anticipated it unfolding in terms of Christian conversion of pagans who would reject their old and ill-informed ways to embrace the truth that Christians brought.

All religious believers assume, however, that their beliefs about the seen and unseen world are correct, and those beliefs clearly served similar functions in all these societies. They helped people to navigate through their world, to understand how they ought to behave, and to comprehend ill fortune and death. Religion—or the beliefs and practices that made sense of the human place in the larger scheme of things—was vitally important to all these cultures. In each it served many of the same needs. In all it helped to define what it meant to be human and to dictate how one ought to act within a community. When religions met subsequently, the differences would often appear more obvious than the common characteristics. The nature of the encounter, which connected people who had previously been separated by vast distances, brought out the strangeness of the religions of others. Those involved did sometimes search out shared beliefs and practices, attempting to find common ground. But more important than specific areas of overlap was the more general fact that religion was significant to everyone, shaping their understanding of what they saw as well as of their own role and responsibilities. Central to individual and communal self-understanding, religion explained reality, supported people through challenging moments, and guided right actions.

Encounter would create a new world for all participants, as the meeting of cultures helped to bring about a wide variety of changes. The expansion out of western Europe brought those people and their religious beliefs and practices into contact with a host of others, including natives of the Americas and captive and transported Africans. All those involved with the encounters brought with them their traditions and ways of understanding, transplanting these as best they were able into their new circumstances. While institutions would not be easily transplanted, the cultural baggage of attitudes and expectations came on every ship that plied the Atlantic. The meeting of peoples that resulted brought endless negotiations between older traditions and newer realities, among individuals and groups with widely different views. If the explorers, traders, missionaries, and settlers who came from Europe intended to remake the New World in the image of Christendom, they would find that the process was neither as straightforward nor as transparent as they anticipated. Englishmen would find that the truth of their own beliefs was not as self-evident to those they encountered as they assumed, that they themselves were often less interested in spreading their faith than in pursuing other agendas, and that recreating familiar institutions was not a simple task.

Before those realizations could be reached, however, Europe would first undergo radical changes that in some respects foreshadowed the dramatic transformation in the wider Atlantic world. As we shall see, the Protestant Reformation wrenched the Europeans of England, Scotland, and Ireland out of their traditional world, challenging many of the beliefs and practices that their societies had held for centuries. Expansion, by the time it involved the

English, catapulted out of a Europe divided between Catholic and Protestant as well as increasingly subdivided within Protestantism itself. The sundering of western Christendom would school Christians on both sides of the new divide that their faith was best and that they were obligated to spread it to others in the competition for souls that expansion represented.

TWO

Reformation and the Politicization of Religious Expansion

THE SIXTEENTH CENTURY witnessed two developments of enormous significance to religion in the British Atlantic world. The Spanish and (later) the Portuguese, having begun to conquer large stretches of the Western Hemisphere, launched a massive effort to convert the native peoples of the Americas to Roman Catholicism. At the same time, England and Scotland joined the Protestant Reformation that was circulating through much of northern Europe, removing their churches from the Catholic community they had been part of for centuries. Scotland and England each moved independently to impose a version of Protestantism on their national churches, and England pulled Wales, although not Ireland, in its wake. Protestant Reformation not only undercut the common religious ground in Europe but also reduced the areas of intersection that Christians shared with peoples elsewhere in the Atlantic world.

With so many Europeans rejecting the Catholic faith, Iberian (Spanish and Portuguese) Catholics understood their campaigns to convert Americans as an opportunity to replenish a church that had been ravished by attrition caused by the Reformation. When they later undertook their own missions among the Indians, English Protestants would understand their efforts in a similar way, as an effort to reverse the Iberian work of transplanting Catholicism, and to bring to the Americans their own version of Christianity. Expansion thus extended European religious battles of the sixteenth century into another hemisphere. For both Catholics in Spain and Portugal and for those who promoted a Protestant agenda in Europe, evangelism and religious polarization marked the sixteenth century. By disrupting the long-established religious patterns of English, Scottish, and Welsh people, the Reformation thrust them all into a new world.

Prior to the Protestant Reformation of the sixteenth century, western Europe had been united in its allegiance to Roman Catholicism. While political leaders differed on many matters and engaged in wars against their co-religionists, they all adhered to the same variant of Christianity: the Roman Catholic Church, headquartered in Rome and organized under the authority of the pope. Other Christians, especially those who belonged to various Eastern Orthodox churches, did not reside in western Europe in noticeable numbers. Catholicism was an ancient and venerable institution, with an elaborate hierarchy that included some of the most powerful men in Europe and a reach into every village throughout the land. As adherents of Catholicism, believers attended Mass, participated in a number of church rituals known as sacraments, and looked to the church for guidance about their obligations and hopes for salvation. Catholics believed that the way to salvation—an eternal life spent in heaven rather than in the torments of hell—lay with the church. It structured ritual observance, explained the human condition, and shaped the believers' relationship to God. Every community had at least one priest, and larger towns or cities had religious houses of monks or nuns who took vows to devote their lives to God. Some of these people lived cloistered from the world, engaging in a life dedicated to prayer. Others served the larger community with acts of charity or other contributions.

Of the seven sacraments, six of them commonly ordered the life of the laity. Baptism brought the infant into the church, whereas Confirmation marked full membership for the young person who had by that age some knowledge of the faith; Holy Eucharist gave an opportunity to participate in the mystical body of Christ by eating bread that had been transformed into his body; Confession to a priest allowed forgiveness of sins; Marriage bound believers into an indissoluble union said to last into the next life; and Extreme Unction prepared the individual's soul for an impending death. The seventh sacrament was offered only to those who became priests, whether a parish priest or a member of a religious order. The sacraments brought individual believers into active participation in the life of the church on a regular basis as well as ensuring that all of life's major transitions would be overseen by the religious representatives in the local community.

Beginning in the second decade of the sixteenth century, the Reformation split western Christendom into Roman Catholic and Protestant camps. The split arose from within the church, as disgruntled members attempted to reform it. Martin Luther, a monk living in the German state of Saxony, proposed changes that would curb abuses and make the church more accessible to laypeople. When the Roman Catholic hierarchy rejected his efforts, he faced a choice of conforming or rebelling. With the backing of local political leaders and rising support in his region, he persisted in his criticism. This confrontation launched the Protestant Reformation. As the reform impulse began to spread, a number of religious leaders—including Luther's associate Philip Melanchthon (1498–1560) in the German states, Huldrych Zwingli (1484–1531) in Switzerland, and John Calvin (1509–64) in France—advocated plans for replacing the Roman Catholic Church with a new system.

Out of this diversity arose competing versions of Protestantism. On the European continent, the primary variations were Lutheranism (which owed its beginnings to Martin Luther and which spread through German-speaking areas and Scandinavia), Calvinism (launched by John Calvin, who reorganized the city-state of Geneva according to his vision of a godly society), and Anabaptism (which did not have a single founder, gained little governmental support, and was also largely a phenomenon in the German-speaking regions). All agreed that the Catholic Church had to be rejected in favor of a Christianity that hewed more closely to the Bible and that church rituals and beliefs had to be challenged to some extent. Luther was most famous for emphasizing the priesthood of all believers, a radically democratic idea that everyone ought to approach God directly, through reading and prayer, rather than through the church. Calvin was best known for his idea that the individual sinner deserved eternal life in hell, but that God in his goodness had predestined some for salvation. This doctrine of predestination directed Calvin not to religious despair but to a conviction that the saved were an elected group who had a responsibility to see that the rest of society lived in a godly fashion. The Anabaptists believed that anyone could be saved and that once a sinner had found salvation he or she should be baptized. Anabaptists envisioned the Christian believer as separated from the larger society, either by withdrawing into communities of like-minded believers or by purging the nonbelievers from their midst. Anabaptists gained a reputation as radicals, and the authorities tried to suppress them but without complete success.

England, Scotland, and Wales, like other parts of northern Europe, participated in the Reformation. Separate countries at this time, England and Scotland moved into the Protestant ranks independently of each other. England's reformation was initially the work of the king, Henry VIII, who wanted freedom from papal control. He sought an annulment of his marriage to his brother's widow, Catherine of Aragon, which the pope would not grant. Propelled by this circumstance, Henry unsurprisingly launched a fairly limited reformation. He proclaimed himself head of the church in England, thereafter renamed the "Church of England." In the process, he seized much church property, which he distributed to his supporters, thereby committing many landowners to the Reformation. But he also left intact many Roman Catholic practices. At his death in 1547, he left a nominally reformed church as well as three children—two of them Protestant and one, his older daughter, a Catholic.

As each of Henry's three children and heirs came to the throne in turn, England was buffeted back and forth between faiths, finally emerging as more staunchly Protestant than Henry had intended. Under Henry's young son, Edward (who ruled from 1547 until 1553), first his counselors and then the king himself moved the Church of England more decisively in a Protestant direction. After his untimely death in 1553, the older of Edward's sisters, Mary, assumed the throne and attempted to bring England back into the Catholic fold. Her willingness to exploit violent tactics resulted in the deaths of nearly three hundred at the stake, punishment that became possible only once Parliament reinstated medieval heresy laws. Her opponents labeled her with the sobriquet "Bloody Mary," to emphasize her willingness to employ violence to return the kingdom to Catholicism. These executions—and the killings that occurred when Protestants resorted to force—echoed the religious wars on the European continent, although England's Reformation never reached the extremes that Europe suffered in this period.

Gruesome tales of martyrdom circulated widely, by word of mouth and in print, so that the faithful could revel in the tales of faith tested and found strong. One of the martyr tales involved Hugh Latimer (c. 1485–1555); as bishop of Winchester he helped to create the Church of England under Edward and died for the cause during the reign of Edward's sister Mary. The hapless Mary's own death in 1558 brought another sister, Elizabeth, Henry's final heir, to the throne. With her Protestant orientation, England conclusively embraced a Protestant national church.

By the end of the sixteenth century, the Church of England was organized into England's own variant of the Protestantism that had reshaped religion in northern Europe. It had its own catechism enumerating and explicating church doctrines as well as an authorized version of the Bible in English and a church service that no longer closely resembled a Roman Catholic Mass. The authorities forcibly closed all the religious houses in England and Wales, dispersed the monks and nuns, and seized the often extensive property. The church did remain hierarchical in its structure, although not to the same extent as under Catholicism. The monarch served as its head, while bishops oversaw the liturgy, the appointment of clergy, and discipline of wayward members. Because the principality of Wales was ruled by the English monarch, it officially followed the state church of England. The Welsh in fact energetically embraced reform, seeing it not as imposed from without but as a return to their own traditional faith. Wales willingly accompanied England into Protestant reform. To a lesser extent it also experienced the efforts to re-impose Catholicism, and many Welsh men and women were relieved to return to Protestantism.

Scotland's Reformation proceeded on its own trajectory, independent of that in England and Wales. Reforming Scotland was not the work of the reigning monarch. Rather the ruler, Mary (who ruled as "Queen of Scots" from 1542 to 1567), was herself a Catholic. Reformers took advantage of the instability of dynastic succession after the death of her father, James V, when Mary was only a few months old. They seized the initiative and attempted reformation but failed to implement it fully. Mary herself spent much of her childhood and early adulthood in France, which left her mother, the French noblewoman, Mary of Guise (also a Catholic), ruling Scotland as regent. The death of the regent in 1560 destabilized the situation in Scotland, and the moment was propitious to force Scottish Reformation. By that time, England's Queen Mary had died, and England was swinging back toward reform. One Scottish religious reformer had written a screed against female rulers when Catholics Mary of Guise and Mary I had ruled Scotland and England, but an embarrassed John Knox then had to face Elizabeth's wrath when the young Protestant queen gained the throne. Scottish leaders were divided as to whether Scotland should move with England in that direction or remain in the orbit of France as a Catholic kingdom. Catholics did not accept Elizabeth, recently crowned queen of England, as the rightful heir, since they questioned the validity of her parents' marriage: If her father's marriage to his first wife was legal and the pope had not sanctioned a divorce, then Elizabeth was what contemporaries labeled "a bastard child" and could not take the throne. If Elizabeth was illegitimate, then Mary, the Scottish queen, was also the queen of England as next in the line of succession. The new queen Mary exacerbated the tensions by beginning to style herself monarch over both Scotland and England at Mary Tudor's death, a challenge to Elizabeth's authority. This claim encouraged Elizabeth to support Mary's opponents in Scotland in their drive to seize power and complete the Protestant Reformation there.

With Elizabeth's backing, in 1560 the Scottish Protestants gained control of the political situation, and parliament voted to proscribe the Mass. They created a Protestant church, known as the "kirk," patterned on Calvin's Geneva. Legislated into existence in the 1570s, the kirk's triumph was only gradually achieved. The Catholic Mary, who had perhaps unwisely lived in France much of her life, finally returned to Scotland to rule her own kingdom directly the following year. She reached an accommodation with the new kirk, allowing it to develop while she continued to practice Catholicism within her household. This negotiated compromise was not universally popular, and a mob had to be kept from trashing her chapel the first time Mass was celebrated there. Guards were posted permanently to shield the queen from popular ire over her adherence to "popery," as Catholicism was derisively dubbed by its critics.

Scotland thereby found itself in the anomalous position of implementing reformation while ruled by a Catholic monarch. The split between the faith of the ruler and that promoted by the state temporarily put the kingdom at odds with a new trend on the European continent. Leaders meeting in Augsburg in 1555 had agreed that each state should follow the faith of the local ruler. Intended to put an end to decades of religious wars, the Peace of Augsburg, had its provisions prevailed in Scotland, would have stopped the reformation of the kirk.

Mary herself seems not to have been personally very devout, which is ironic given that she emerged as a symbol of Catholicism for her own people as well as in the international context. Her close ties to France—her mother was French, she had spent much of her own life in France, and she had been married to a French prince—associated her with French Catholicism in the popular imagination. Reformers sought to establish a new church order not only because they considered it more pleasing to God, but also because it represented a way to break the link to France, which many elites had come to resent. The next decade was increasingly contentious.

Reformation was secured politically only after the defeat of Mary in a minor civil war (1568–73). She was forced to abdicate her throne and soon fled to England. She would spend many years as Elizabeth's prisoner, until finally Elizabeth was persuaded to set aside her distaste for the idea of executing a fellow monarch, signing Mary's death warrant in 1583. With Mary's removal from the scene, Protestants around her infant son (James VI) were finally able to complete the religious and political settlement. Scotland became officially and conclusively Protestant at that time.

The Protestants of Scotland themselves divided into two factions, one favoring an Episcopal church, the other advocating a Presbyterian option. Episcopacy organized under a hierarchy of bishops was the church form adopted in England, whereas the Presbyterian system was somewhat more egalitarian, giving authority over the church to presbyteries, bodies made up of clergy and leading laymen. Presbyterianism used a central "presbytery" of clerical and lay leaders to control the individual churches, ministerial appointments, and discipline. Although the latter faction would eventually emerge victorious, the strict adherence of the Scottish church to Presbyterianism was a long time in coming. One historian states that "it is only in the 1580s and after that the reformed kirk of Scotland can properly be called 'presbyterian.'"[1] Not only did an Episcopal church order continue to have its advocates, but also the government occasionally appointed bishops in apparent violation of the Presbyterian church structure. Rulers did this as a way to establish their own appointees in positions of influence in the church. Furthermore in its earliest form the kirk included an office of superintendent, held by a leading minister in a given region, which did not conform precisely to the presbyterian model as it would later be accepted.

More so than the other reformation in these islands, the Scottish Reformation was influenced by continental European reformers. Ideas from the continental Reformation circulated through both England and Scotland, influencing both reformations. The link between Scotland and the Continental reformation was direct and decisive, and the resulting church order was recognizably similar to that of John Calvin's Geneva. Clerical leader in the Presbyterian faction John Knox was guided by Calvin's example, having associated with the reformer during a period in exile. Knox promoted the Calvinist theology of predestination—that those who were to be saved had been chosen by God before creation—along with Calvin's heavy emphasis on discipline. Church discipline played a key role in Scottish local society, which had not developed secular institutions to control the population comparable to the English Justices of the Peace. The kirk functioned in the local arena to fill a gap that made it and its disciplinary work more pervasive than might have otherwise been the case. At the highest level in Scotland, James VI cultivated the image of himself as a godly prince and tried to project it into the wider European Christian community. Although Catholicism remained a minor presence within Scotland, especially prevalent in the Highland region, that faith never seriously threatened the Protestant establishment again after Mary's reign ended.

However prickly the relationship in other ways, during the sixteenth and for the first decades of the seventeenth century, the English and Scottish church orders were largely in agreement on key theological issues. Both the Church of England and the Scottish kirk embraced an understanding common among Reformed churches that salvation was limited to those who had been predestined to be saved by God before the beginning of time. *The Thirty-Nine Articles* stating the doctrine of the Church of England explain this position (Article 11) and work out some of its implications (Articles 12–18). According to this theology, only a select few would be saved and people's own actions (such as the good works that Catholics emphasized) did not affect the outcome. This negative assessment of human nature and the heavy emphasis on the need to receive divine grace encouraged preaching that would turn the hearer toward God. It could also create a heightened emphasis on discipline because reformers felt compelled to prevent sin in their communities, even sins committed by those with no hope of salvation. Fearing that some sinners might decide that since their fate was sealed they might as well sin wantonly, Christian leaders resolved to prevent such misbehavior even on the part of the damned. So, for example, the church authorities would police sexual morality, punishing sexual relations outside of marriage among those they considered to be damned anyway.

Converting an entire kingdom to Protestantism was a two-part process, in Scotland as in Wales and England. First, the Roman Catholic Church had to be rooted out and a new Christianity based on Reformed precepts and practices planted in its place. Second, the laity had to be brought into the new faith, which involved persuasion, re-education, and sometimes coercion. In the first area, the institution of the church had to be altered to replace its Catholic structure, practices, and doctrines with those that were distinctly Protestant. Monasteries and convents closed, English priests were asked to become Church of England clergymen (which meant they might marry but had to renounce their vows of celibacy as well as their adherence to Rome), the sacraments were eliminated or redefined, and the liturgy was altered to accommodate the changing theology. In the English case, the transformation of the church hierarchy, liturgy, and the like occurred slowly and unevenly.

Henry VIII made relatively modest changes beyond sundering the tie to the pope, taking church property, and closing the religious houses to which that property had belonged. Most students of the early Tudor reformation see Henry as focused on his immediate needs, including a divorce the pope would not grant (hence he made himself head of the church so he could arrange a divorce) and income (so he sold monastic property that had been in the church for centuries to fill his treasury). Translating the Bible into the vernacular (or the spoken language of the local population, in which more common people would have been literate) was a hallmark of the Protestant Reformation. Yet after Henry endorsed an English version of the Bible in 1537, popular enthusiasm for it made the king so nervous that he tried to limit access to the elite. The king further attempted to retain the previously Catholic clergy within the church by asking them to keep their posts after swearing allegiance to him. He made relatively modest alterations in liturgy. His reformation was a negotiated and fairly modest affair, in which he tried to avoid direct confrontation but instead sought to carry the populace along with the changes that he promoted. Those of his subjects who enthusiastically supported his plan for a reformation in the hope of a radical alteration of the religion of England and Wales viewed the changes Henry accepted as inadequate.

The story of the great translator William Tyndale well captures the ambivalent relationship Henry had with the more thorough Reformation on the Continent. Born in Gloucester in about 1494, Tyndale attended Oxford University, where he entered the priesthood and began the study of languages. He worked to translate the New Testament into English, eventually seeking official sponsorship for his efforts from the bishop of London in 1523. Rebuffed in that effort he decided he would be safer living on the Continent, given his increasingly radical views regarding the necessity of making the scriptures available to all. He is reported to have said to a learned opponent of his agenda that "if God spare my life ere many years, I will cause a boy that driveth the plough, shall know more of the Scripture than thou dost."[2] For the next thirteen years he worked on his translations and his own writings, publishing the first New Testament in English and a defense of duty to one's ruler alongside adherence to the Scriptures. The reform-minded court lady Anne Boleyn supposedly showed the latter tract to Henry prior to their marriage, and Tyndale's defense of royal authority was said to have pleased the monarch.

Still, in 1535 the English authorities ordered Tyndale arrested. The king seems to have tried to intervene to prevent his execution, but his underlings in Europe apparently stopped his order long enough to permit the sentence to be carried out. Tyndale was brought before the Inquisition, convicted of heresy, and executed in Antwerp in August 1536. Out of respect for his great learning, he was strangled to death and then his body burned at the stake (the latter alone being the usual punishment for heresy). Within a short time of his death, a version of the Bible in English that was composed largely of Tyndale's translation but which did not name him on the title page was for sale openly in England, and it carried the king's official endorsement.

Although he was defrocked from the Catholic priesthood and executed for heresy, Tyndale's work translating the Bible was (and is) widely admired. Much of his translation was taken verbatim for the King James Version of the Bible that is still in use in many English-speaking communities today. That Tyndale had to flee to the Continent to continue his work and that those who opposed it could use English royal authority to have him arrested indicated the contested nature of the process of Protestantization during Henry's reign. Yet Tyndale's translation was also ultimately accepted by the king, despite his concern that a wider readership would learn radical lessons in their Bibles.

When the young Edward VI came to the throne in 1547, dedicated reformers had an opportunity to pursue their more ambitious agenda. It was under his reign that a new liturgy, popularly known as the Book of Common Prayer, was produced (1549). Reformers eliminated the Latin Mass in England, Wales, and (officially at least) much of Ireland, incongruously replacing it with services in English regardless of the local vernacular language. They sanctioned clerical marriages (which were officially proscribed in the Roman Catholic Church). Although parish priests had often lived openly with women, a practice that was seemingly accepted, the laity initially objected vehemently to official clerical marriage. Whereas Henry had made changes slowly and only after engineering local consent, the men who instituted reforms during Edward's reign acted more forcefully. Edwardian reform had its limits as well, however: it did not eliminate the episcopal structure of the church, for instance, and it continued as it had under Henry with bishops and church courts to punish wayward parishioners.

Later, after the Catholic interlude under her sister Mary, Elizabeth (reigned 1558–1603) reinstated the church more or less as it had developed in Edward's time. In deference to those who objected to a woman as "supreme head" of the church, she adopted the title of "supreme governor" to describe her position vis-à-vis the Church of England. Elizabeth was herself somewhat conservative in her Protestantism, and she chose to go only as far as her brother had gone before her. She hung a cross in her private chapel, which was anathema to serious reformers, and she enjoyed a rich liturgy more than the preaching that was a telltale sign of a more extreme Protestantism.

A second aspect of the process of remaking a state church in a Protestant mode involved persuading the laity to accept the new faith and educating laypeople to understand it. When Henry VIII broke with Rome, he concentrated on maintaining the obedience of the populace. Although the king was not personally concerned about the need to re-educate his subjects as Protestants, he appointed men who were more dedicated to that task. Fear and habits of obedience probably did more to smooth the transition under his reign than any genuine change of heart among most English Catholics. Only after his son Edward became king did the real effort to educate and persuade the laity commence. The prayer book produced during his reign had a lasting impact on lay belief within the Church of England.

Even though considerable opposition existed to the changes Edward's reign brought, the return to Catholicism under Mary did not satisfy those who longed for the old ways. When some religious houses reopened, some former residents returned to them eagerly. The laity that longed for the whole Mass and sacraments willingly participated in them once they resumed. But Mary was not able to restore the church as it had been when her father was crowned, despite the persecution of committed Protestants. Efforts to arrange the recantation of a principal architect of the English Protestant Reformation backfired when former archbishop Thomas Cranmer made a dramatic and public renunciation of his recantation. While he was being burned at the stake, he thrust his writing hand into the flames to punish it for signing the documents that had momentarily returned him to the Catholic fold.

Spectacles of Protestant martyrdom undermined Mary's efforts, but more than her subjects' religious affinities stood in the way of the restoration of the Catholic Church. Too much had changed in the interim, not the least Catholicism itself. In response to the Reformation and the splintering of the church that resulted, the church at Rome heeded internal calls for reform and embarked on a sustained movement to improve the church from within. This movement is variously known as the "Counter Reformation," to emphasize the response to Protestantism, or the "Catholic Reformation," to underscore continuities with earlier reform impulses emanating from within the church itself. It intended both to answer the criticisms leveled against the church, such as corruption and failure to teach the laity about the faith, and to strengthen it in its fight against its critics. As the church remade itself, any return to the old faith was complicated by that fact. In addition, the swing from a Reformed polity under Edward to conservative Catholicism under Mary politicized religious choices. The middle ground once cultivated by Henry vanished.

Elizabeth inherited this polarized situation when she took the throne. She cleverly used the Church of England as a rallying point. By identifying England as a Protestant nation besieged by predatory Catholic states, especially the powerful Spain, Elizabeth was able to unite many of her subjects in support of her rule and the reinstated church of her father and brother. Mary I had married the future king of Spain, who, by the time she died, had become Philip II. He intended to resist England's shift back to Protestantism, trying various means to keep it in the Catholic camp. Elizabeth benefited from the fear of what Philip might do, relying on the fact that many English men and women opposed the idea of coming under the thumb of Spain. She even had her portrait painted in martial regalia to communicate to her subjects that she was a fit ruler to fight off the Catholic menace. She sent troops to complete the conquest of Ireland, which she feared would be used as a staging ground for an invasion by Spain.

In addition to citing the danger of foreign assault, Elizabeth also emphasized the threat of an enemy within. Denunciations of popery became an exercise in identifying what it meant to be English and Protestant. One such stealthy enemy was the newly founded Society of Jesus, which dispatched Jesuit priests to England to re-convert the population and undermine the regime. Elizabeth's government ordered the death of Jesuits captured in England, treating them as traitors. In 1570 the pope excommunicated Elizabeth and enjoined Catholics to disobey her commands. This policy put England's Catholics in an awkward situation even as it enhanced the queen's ability to rally the nation to a Protestant and anti-Catholic cause.

Elizabeth was aided in her efforts to remake England in a Protestant image by John Foxe's enormously influential *Actes and Monuments*, popularly known as the "Book of Martyrs." This tome placed the persecution of Protestants under Mary within a long history of Christian martyrdom. It began recounting those who had died in the early Christian church, spreading the gospel message after the death of Jesus, and carried the story all the way forward to those who were executed for their faith during Mary's reign. Among the more famous of the recent martyrs was the gentlewoman Anne Askew, whose Protestant conversion during the reign of Henry VIII alienated her from her husband. An account of her torture and death was first published in German and later translated into English in Foxe's book, thereby securing her a place in the tradition of English Protestant martyrs. All were treated as martyrs who died for their faith, an inspiring idea that connected believers in their own time to those in the early Christian church. By the time of Elizabeth's death in 1603, England embraced a mythology that identified it as Protestant and liberty-loving in contrast to "popish" tyranny and oppression. ("Popish," like "popery," was an insulting term for Catholics, emphasizing the church's allegiance to the pope.)

Elizabeth succeeded in depicting herself as a leader of international Protestantism, but the church she created represented a conservative version of the Reformed faith. It had a hierarchy that was fairly elaborate by Protestant standards of the time, it had a set liturgy rather than a strong emphasis on extemporaneous prayer, and it doled out discipline with less energy than a Scottish presbytery. Elizabeth embraced this middle way in part because it seemed suited to the variety of views present among her subjects and in part because she was herself of a somewhat conservative Protestant stripe. As much as Protestants in England and Wales embraced the view of the queen as a militant advocate of the Protestant cause, Elizabeth was not especially radical in her faith. Her Church of England did not go far enough for some of her subjects, who argued openly from the 1570s for additional changes to bring it closer to some of the more reformed churches in Europe. This group, known derisively as "puritans," worshipped within the national church even as they sought to reform it. Since Elizabeth was more concerned with unity than with uniformity, she was able to hold together a somewhat heterogeneous worshipping community under the banner of a godly Protestant and English nation. Doing so may have been her greatest achievement.

The Scottish Reformation was also gradual, and the triumph of the presbyterian church order—even after the Protestant political victory—was not a foregone conclusion. The most ardent reformers in Scotland favored a church order that placed responsibility on ministers and members of the local elites. Unlike their neighbors to the south, the Scots initially did away with bishops and permanently eliminated church courts. In their more decentralized model, the local congregation was governed by the kirk session, which meted out discipline; and presbyteries made up of clergy and leading laymen appointed ministers and took up more far-ranging disciplinary matters. This approach depended upon an informed and committed populace. Reformers thus aimed to educate the laity to understand and accept the changes that

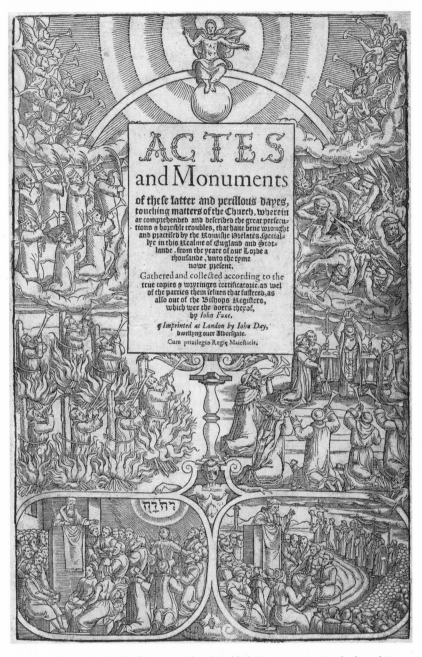

Fig. 2. John Foxe's Book of Martyrs placed English Protestantism in the long history of Christians dying for their faith. Elizabeth ordered copies of the work, officially entitled *Actes and Monuments*, prominently displayed in all churches in England and Wales. In some editions, the image on the left is labeled "the persecuted Church," and that on the right, "the persecuting Church." From the 1584 edition. Courtesy of the Huntington Library, San Marino, California.

came with the move toward Protestantism. Ministers preached sermons designed to educate believers about predestination and the need to examine the state of one's soul for signs of election. They held catechism sessions for both children and adults to school their communities in the new ideas. They advocated increased literacy in order that all would be able to read the Bible, and they produced Bibles in the vernacular to facilitate that process.

Even as these reformers gradually engineered a widespread commitment to reformation, the process spilt far less blood than was the case in England. The number of martyrs in Scotland—twenty-five Protestants and two Catholics—was minor in comparison to those killed south of the border. Yet Scotland's Protestants were particularly vehement in their anti-Catholicism, sacking monasteries and indulging in other acts of aggression. There was some truth to James's later complaint that the church there had been reformed through "populaire tumulte & rebellion . . . & not proceeding from the princes ordoure as it did in englande."[3] His insistence on appointing some bishops and his willingness to accept the Church of England when he later became ruler of that kingdom have to be understood in the context of his dismay over the idea of anyone below the level of the prince deciding religious policy.

Within Scotland itself regional variations in the reach of the new Protestantism were apparent. The laity in the Lowlands regions of the country, especially urban areas like Edinburgh, responded eagerly to these changes. Lowlands dwellers were more likely to be literate and to live in towns. Experiencing social changes, on one hand, may have made them more open to accepting new ideas, including religious reform, while, on the other, it may have encouraged a sense that strict discipline was necessary to address developing social ills. This region became committed to the new Protestant order and willing to defend it. In the Highlands, perhaps because society was more traditional and continued to be organized along clan lines, the older religious forms often survived. (Lowlands residents were somewhat more likely to live outside the clan structure.) To the extent that Protestant worship caught on in the Highlands, it tended to be concentrated in elite households, much as residual Catholic practice would be in the north of England. Some important early converts to Protestantism were, however, Highlands clan leaders, and since clans might follow the proclivities of their heads, this change could have a ripple effect through a community. This strategy of converting the elite on the assumption that others would follow would be attempted in other circumstances later.

By 1600, Scotland's Reformation, where it had taken firm hold, looked somewhat more extreme than that which prevailed in England and Wales. Not only had priestly celibacy been eliminated, along with the monasteries and convents (as in the neighboring kingdom), but also the structure that included cardinals and bishops had been, at least theoretically, eradicated. These had been replaced by married clergymen and by a church governance structure that drew upon the talents of ministers and leading laity. The Scottish Presbyterian Church was a remarkably intrusive institution in those locations where it was most fully developed. Here the inspiration from Calvin's Geneva was most strongly felt. In addition to more sweeping reforms of its ecclesiastical structure, the Scottish kirk had moved more decisively away from some of the liturgical aspects of traditional Christianity, such as the choral music loved by Queen Elizabeth. Church services emphasized preaching by the ministers (rather than a set liturgy repeated each time), and this preaching was aimed to convert and educate the congregation. That the churches north of the border took such vigorous positions on these issues caused the "hotter sort of Protestants" in England to gaze upon Scotland with some envy. The distance between the two churches would grow and take on added significance in the seventeenth century.

Although by 1600 Scotland as well as England and Wales were officially Protestant, that transformation did not entirely obliterate Catholicism. Advocates of reform labored to wipe away all vestiges of Catholic worship, in a process that scholar Eamon Duffy has described as "the stripping of the altars."[4] As the government seized the wealth of the church and as overzealous reformers smashed art objects such as stained glass and statuary or desecrated saints' relics, they seemed intent on destroying every symbol of the old way of worship. The physical infrastructure of the church was not fully destroyed, since many buildings and some of their less obnoxious accoutrements were simply transferred to the use of the Protestants.

Despite the obvious obstacles, laypeople might cling to older beliefs and, to the extent that conditions allowed, to older practices as well. Reformers swept away the monasteries, convents, and collections of saintly relics that had helped to structure worship in previous generations. While a woman who had grown up propitiating a specific saint for aid often continued to do so once neighboring reformers pulled down the local shrine, her daughter, never having seen the shrine or only dimly remembering it from childhood, could not participate in that ritual in the same way that her mother had. Her own daughter would be even more pressed to understand her grandmother's devotions.

The elimination of public spaces where age-old sacred rituals were practiced undermined those rituals or pushed them indoors. Even though Protestants often argued for more emphasis on household worship, Catholics in a reformed kingdom were forced to rely on the household as a new site for the sacred, an unintended consequence of the Protestant Reformation. Bans on Catholic priests—especially in Elizabethan England, where priests were popularly associated with opposition to the monarch—made it difficult for the faithful to participate in the Mass or to receive the sacraments. Elite families were able to shelter priests who then ministered to the household, thereby further increasing the centrality of domestic spaces in their worship. In some cases, especially where the elite Catholic family was very powerful, priests might be able to move about the local community as well.

Other Catholics resisted the new Protestantism even though local options for the practice of their own faith were limited to their private family worship. They struggled with whether to conform outwardly, by attending and nominally participating in the state-sanctioned church, or to risk punishment for their failure to do so. Catholics often attempted to hide their continued adherence to the old religion, which makes it difficult for later historians to document their numbers and to understand the nature of their practice. Women upheld the old faith within many households, while their male relatives publicly associated themselves with Protestantism in order to escape punishments—such as fines—that fell more heavily on men. Catholicism became both domesticated and feminized as a result of the Reformation and aggressive suppression. Public worship spaces were destroyed, creating wrenching cultural change that believers coped with the best they could.

Within England, Wales, and Scotland, the Roman Catholic faith was gradually changed by the shift from its initial status as an established church of the realm to its eventual position as a minority and even pariah faith. Although religious allegiance is often discussed as an either-or proposition—one was either Protestant or Catholic—that binary construction may be too simplistic. In all likelihood, many people participated in a slow process of religious change that resulted, over generations, in the creation of a recognizably Protestant identity. It was an incremental "process of assimilation, by which a new language and ideology were to become normative, the stuff of everyday experience and exchange."[5] Conversion as a process of negotiation rather than a sudden shift becomes a recurrent theme as the religion of these islands moved out into the wider Atlantic. Dramatic conversions to the new ways or clear-sighted insistence on older forms are idealized versions of religious change rather than a reflection of a common reality. In this era of change it is more helpful to think in terms of a tipping point, with a particular community moving gradually but decisively in one direction or the other. That seems to have happened in Ireland as the majority of the Irish and Old English (descendents of early Anglo-Norman settlers) eventually became committed to continuing as Catholics. In other areas the move toward Protestantism often occurred in a similarly gradual way.

As the political context for religious differences became more polarized, the Protestant population of England became increasingly fearful of Catholics. One anti-Catholic tract repeated the common view that the goal of the "impious policy" of the "papists" was "to gull, terrifie, and amaze the simple ignorant people" and "to inchant and bewitch their innocent simple soules, and so to offer them up for prey to their Idol of Rome."[6] Catholic missionary priests working in England were subject to execution during Elizabeth's reign, and martyrologies recounting their deaths for the Catholic cause made for popular reading in such Catholic countries as Spain and France. In England occasional Protestant scares about papist plotting erupted, leading to an upsurge in the persecution of Catholics. In the Gunpowder Plot of 1605, a group of Catholics was caught planning to blow up Parliament during a session that would have included the king in attendance. Had it succeeded, the plot would have wiped out much of England's ruling elite in one moment. The foiled plot became a symbol of deliverance from a popish threat. To this day, Guy Fawkes Day (November 5) celebrates the discovery of the plot, although currently festivities in most locations tend to minimize the anti-Catholic message of the commemoration. For the first few centuries that November 5 was a public holiday, however, the message was hammered home, with effigies representing Fawkes burned in huge bonfires and local Catholics (or suspected Catholics) harassed. Fear often focused on Jesuit missionaries, who were considered highly capable and especially sneaky. The idea that such men were working secretly in England to re-convert the people to Catholicism was a terrifying thought.

Ireland did not ultimately participate to any great extent in the Protestant Reformation that reshaped the religious landscape of Scotland, England, and Wales. A small Irish Protestant church was created at the behest of the English government, but, despite being the official church of the kingdom, it did not succeed in attracting many Irish people to Protestantism. By the time the English government was trying to impose the Reformation on Ireland, the population was made up of the Irish people and two groups of English: the "Old English," who had come to Ireland long before the Reformation; and newly arrived soldiers, settlers, and officials who were in Ireland as a result of the ongoing English work of conquest. The vast majority of the Irish and Old English residents ultimately chose to remain Catholic. One major exception among the Old English was the influential James Ussher (1581–1656), who was appointed archbishop of Armagh in the Protestant Church of Ireland. His influence spread far, in fact, because his scholarly study of the Bible established a widely accepted date for the creation of the world, setting it at about four thousand years before the birth of Christ.

Scholars have debated the reasons that Ireland remained predominantly Catholic. Some have tried to uncover an essentially different nature to Irish Catholicism prior to the efforts at reform. On the eve of the Reformation, Ireland was well served by friars, members of religious orders who took vows of poverty and celibacy and worked among the population. They made up a highly regarded clerical elite already engaged in evangelical outreach. They used the vernacular language, which gave them an unusual advantage. The clergy, many of them descended from Anglo-Norman immigrants, thought of themselves as the defenders of the Catholic Church, and they were committed to protecting it. Even though their Old English status might have inclined them to support changes coming from England, their profound commitment to the Church and their role in it prevented most of them from doing so. Another explanation blames the manner in which the Reformation was undertaken. Elementary programs aimed at educating the laity, such as the translation of the Bible or the catechism into the vernacular language, were not as readily employed in Ireland. Appreciating the importance of the Bible and the liturgy in the vernacular, Elizabeth ordered the preparation of Welsh and Irish language books. The New Testament and the Prayer Book appeared in Welsh in 1567, and William Morgan's Welsh Bible, widely acknowledged as a literary masterpiece, was published in 1588. In Ireland, an apparent lack of enthusiasm for the project slowed the production of liturgical and scriptural publications in Gaelic. For a time, in fact, Gaelic speakers interested in learning about Protestantism read the Scottish books prepared for use in the Highlands. During this time written Gaelic in both kingdoms was a classical early modern Irish, so the language was equally appropriate to Irish or Scottish readers. Yet the circulation of these books gave the English officials pause, since they feared the possible infiltration of Ireland by its neighbor (and rival) to the north, whose Protestantism was moving in another direction from that in England. These factors, and the financing and structure of the Irish church, all worked against its success.

One obvious explanation for Ireland's refusal to convert was the nature of the relationship between the native Irish and those who sought their conversion. In other locations, the drive toward Protestantism was led by local advocates. The monarchs who ruled England and Wales pushed for Protestantism, and the Welsh elite embraced reform as its own. A Scottish elite and clerical faction similarly promoted the project in that country. But English intruders brought Protestantism to Ireland. Resisting conversion to this new faith was a way to shun full cooperation with a conquering power. In Ireland local lords continued to exercise great authority, creating an alternative, indigenous power structure that competed with that of the invading English. Whereas Wales (which might seem to have been in a broadly analogous position to Ireland) had participated in the reform of government under the early Tudors, Ireland had then been independent and had consequently remained decentralized, with power more diffused. Resistance was easier in such circumstances. This circumstance would later prevail in British America, where a diffuse political structure undermined the strategy of persuading a small group of elites to convert in order to reach a whole community. In Ireland, local leaders and the lay community upheld the church in spite of opposition from the English government. Even in Dublin the laity maintained the church in the decades after 1560 when the Catholic ecclesiastical structure was disrupted. As historian Nicholas Canny has noted, two cultures gradually emerged in Ireland, with religion as the primary distinction among them.[7] Although the Irish assimilated other aspects of English cultural practices and were brought under English governance, they held on to the difference represented by their own commitment to Catholicism.

In another interesting variation on the theme of refusing to negotiate with proponents of religious change as a form of resistance, the Channel Islands avoided not Protestantization in general but only full identification with the Church of England. Located in the channel between England and France, these islands were ruled by England but populated by an ethnically French people. When presented with Reformation, residents chose, after debate, to follow the Presbyterianism common among the minority group of Protestants in largely Catholic France rather than joining England's official church.

Ireland (as well as the Channel Islands to an extent) moved against a general trend in Europe. Over the seventeenth century, Europeans embraced the general principle that the ruler of a given region ought to dictate its faith without outside interference. This concession to local control over religious institutions had been developed first on the Continent with the Peace of Augsburg in 1555. When Mary Queen of Scots ruled a Protestant kingdom while remaining Catholic, she was at odds with this emerging principle. Later the concept would be applied to put an end to another series of continental wars and enshrined in the 1648 Peace of Westphalia. The principle would thenceforth be followed with few exceptions by most European states. Despite the intentions of those who ruled Ireland after the Elizabethan conquest was completed in 1603, Ireland remained, by and large, defiantly Catholic. The Channel Islands turned, with less insolence, to a variant strain of Protestantism, one that linked them more closely to French Protestants than to their English rulers.

While the Irish majority held to its Catholic beliefs, the larger religious context in which Irish Catholicism functioned underwent changes during this century of transformation. Most significantly Ireland's state-sanctioned established church by 1600 was Protestant. Elizabeth continued to work for the military conquest of Gaelic Ireland and finally brought the island fully under England's control for the first time in the last year of her reign. Ireland was a separate kingdom that shared a ruler with the combined kingdom of England and Wales, so Elizabeth granted it a separate Protestant Church of Ireland. That church, like the Church of England, was also headed by the English monarch but it had a distinctive hierarchy with its own bishops. More puritan than the Church of England, the Church of Ireland eventually provided employment opportunities for Scottish Presbyterians and for English nonconformists who were critical of the Church of England. These ministers saw to the spiritual needs of only the small portion of the population that was part of the official church. The majority of inhabitants remained Catholic.

Roman Catholicism, once it ceased to be the official church of the realm, experienced changes as well. When state support for Catholicism was withdrawn, the institutional structure of the church was shaken. Throughout Europe, the church had sought to counter the affects of Protestantism by promoting a reformation of its own. In Ireland, where papal authority was undermined by state opposition to the church's presence and work, this internal reform movement had a limited impact. The Catholic Church during this period increased its emphasis on the catechism of the church. Yet the drive to educate Irish laity was hampered by a shortage of priests and. the difficult conditions under which they worked. A renewed emphasis on the majesty of the church and the importance of sacred spaces within church buildings and on the grounds also had relatively little effect on Ireland, thwarted by the church's comparative poverty and its pariah status. Irish Catholics were relatively unaffected by changes in the church, focused as they were on maintaining a traditional Catholicism in a Protestant and therefore hostile political atmosphere.

In all these places, religion was both national and tinged by localism. As new forms of faith were transplanting into a given location, they took root in and were shaped by the local situation. In Scotland the political context, in particular the drive for autonomy, affected the church. The Scots equated political autonomy with their own established church, having succeeded at eliminating the French influence, strong in the 1540s and 1550s, and minimizing English intervention by entering into their own Reformation. Where Protestantism succeeded, it was identified with local custom. In England, Foxe's martyrs reached back before the time of Bloody Mary, making connections to earlier dissenting movements as well as to the primitive Christian church. In Wales, reformers presented the Church of England as a return to early Welsh Christian tradition. Enamored of the Tudor monarchs because of their one Welsh ancestor, the Welsh were ready to see changes inaugurated under them—whether in governance or in church order—as arising from their own community rather than as imposed from outside. The Scots similarly claimed that their Reformed kirk marked a return to an earlier faith. In contrast to our modern fascination with the new, intellectuals of this era believed that ancient ways were generally superior. Demonstrating that something was old helped to make it more acceptable, especially if it was old enough to make a link beyond the recent history of Roman Catholicism, against which Protestantism revolted. In this context the idea of a return to earlier practice had great allure. Ethnic or proto-nationalist sentiments were tapped to foster support for a new faith claiming to be old. In Ireland alone, that link to an earlier time was not successfully forged by Protestants. There Gaelic traditionalism continued to be associated with Catholicism and its local saints, shrines, and liturgy.

The magnitude of the change that the shift from Catholicism to Protestantism represented can be seen in the transformation of the sacred landscape. All over medieval Europe, shrines and holy places had dotted the land. Lay piety was strongly identified with local saints and holy people, to whom lay believers turned for help. Churches often held saintly relics, and pilgrims traveled to visit significant holy sites. Religious houses—monasteries, convents, abbeys—were ubiquitous, and they housed religious communities dedicated to prayer and good works. Martin Luther had himself been a monk in the Catholic Church before his break with Rome. The Reformation, especially in its more extreme forms, derided the older sacred practices as gross superstition and idolatry. Although Anglicans acknowledged some Catholic holy figures, they turned away from the veneration of Mary and other saints. The Protestants of Ireland and Scotland, as well as the more radical among the English and Welsh, strenuously objected to these beliefs and to the existence of religious orders. Radical Protestants desecrated shrines and smashed the religious art that adorned churches. This iconoclasm was especially frequent in Scotland.

In England attention to the religious houses and shrines rose and fell until finally all were destroyed. Henry's government made an initial effort in the early 1530s, closing some of the smaller religious houses and dismantling some shrines. In 1536, an uprising in Lincolnshire and York attempted to end the dissolution of monasteries and to bring England back into the Catholic fold. After this northern rising, known as the Pilgrimage of Grace, was suppressed, the government launched a more systematic destruction of both religious houses and shrines. In Winchester the team sent to pull down a shrine to Saint Swithun decided to "sweep away al the rotten bones" so as not to give the impression that "we came more for the treasure than for avoiding of the abomination of idolatry."[8] Popular perceptions understood the dissolution as arising from the king's greed for the wealth of these institutions but the more ardent reformers who worked for him were at least equally dedicated to ridding the land of idols. As a result of this campaign, the monasteries of England had surrendered to the king's officials by 1540. Some of the buildings were converted to college houses and others continued as cathedrals for the new Church of England but without a religious community any longer attached to them, while others were destroyed. The residents of these houses who cooperated with the changes were given small pensions; a few who resisted entirely were executed for treason. Under Elizabeth I the government collected fines from practicing Catholics for resisting reform, while at the same time paying out pensions to former monks and nuns to compensate for the livelihoods lost in the closing of the religious houses.

The idea of holy places or of holy individuals who might assist the living was alien to Reformed Protestants, which set their beliefs apart from not only

Catholicism but also all the faiths that were about to undergo encounter in the wider Atlantic world. Radical Protestants insisted that the Bible was the source of all authority, an insistence that desacralized nonbiblical places. This shift was only slowly (and sometimes not thoroughly) accomplished, but as the Scottish Lowlands, most of England, and much of Wales moved toward Protestantism, it was gradually carried out. The change would have enormous significance for the daily lives of lay believers. Accomplishing the de-sacralization of the landscape was a major goal of the Protestant re-education effort. In Ireland, where the effort at Protestant conversion ultimately failed, the Catholic population placed a new emphasis on local Irish saints. Protestant efforts to eradicate saints seemed to have invigorated local support for them among those who remained Catholic. To maintain a sacred landscape and all that went with it was one way to reject the offer of Protestantism.

With the Reformation, the lay religion of much of the British Isles was moving away from some common ground that Roman Catholicism shared with the faiths of Native Americans or traditional West Africans. Just as the English prepared to move out into the wider Atlantic world, they rejected long-held beliefs that created a common ground with other religious systems in the Atlantic world. In this respect the English men and women who became Protestant had already entered a new world before they ever left England. In this world, believers looked to the Bible and inward to the state of their own souls rather than outward to a larger community of faithful—made up of both the living and the dead—for religious guidance. They relied less on spiritual adepts to help them, instead embracing the idea of a "priesthood of all believers" that emphasized the individual faith tradition. Their ritual lives were less rich and full than they had been before, as they jettisoned many sacraments. The more radical reformers rejected saints' days and the church calendar of Lenten and Christmas observance. Protestants varied among themselves as to how much of this tradition they dropped, but all of them abandoned at least some of the religious elements that had been broadly analogous with those in use elsewhere. That Protestants would enjoy less success as missionaries in the Americas and Africa than their Catholic rivals should come as no surprise, given how Reformation altered the Protestant religious sensibility.

Even as Protestant reformers worked to communicate a new faith to the laypeople of the British Isles and Ireland, Catholic missionaries were undertaking the same work among Native Americans in the Americas. European expansion during the sixteenth century was largely a Catholic affair.

Spain and Portugal, but especially Spain, dominated on the western side of the Atlantic, while the Portuguese were most active along the coast of Africa and, eventually, in Asia. Remaining staunch supporters of the traditional church during the Protestant Reformation, both were also affected by the subsequent currents of reform within Catholicism.

The church in Spain had been reinvigorated on the eve of the Protestant Reformation, a development related to the drive to expel the Muslim Moors and the Jews from the Iberian Peninsula. The kingdoms that eventually coalesced into the entities we know as Spain and Portugal had been ruled by Islamic invaders who had conquered the peninsula centuries before. During that time, Muslims, Catholics, and Jews had lived in the region, the latter two groups tolerated by their Muslim rulers. The Catholics eventually organized an effort to drive the Moors back to North Africa. Once it succeeded they also banished (or forced the conversion to Catholicism) of the Jews. This move sparked another Jewish diaspora, sending Sephardic (Iberian) Jews into other parts of Europe and elsewhere in the Mediterranean world. These changes were just completed as the Spanish monarchs learned of the existence of the Americas and launched their plans to bring the Western Hemisphere under Spanish authority. Spanish Catholicism was better situated than the church in Portugal to expand into the wider world as it pushed out into America and Asia.

A major component of the Reformation movement within Catholicism was an emphasis on catechetical instruction and education, which helped to clarify specific Catholic positions and communicate them clearly to the laity. Hence Catholics in Europe (as well as new converts in Africa and the Americas) were subjected to a new level of religious instruction. Portugal's missionary work in Africa in this early period was a largely top-down affair, and it saw the greatest success in the kingdom of Kongo. There missionaries undertook to convert the society's leaders, with the idea that others would follow in their stead. The ruler and other elites did convert to Catholicism, but how far the change spread through the kingdom and how thorough those conversions were are matters of some debate. The Portuguese traded with and opened missions to the Kongolese, but they did not conquer that kingdom, which remained independent for centuries.

Spain would have greater success in its missions in the Americas. In the western Atlantic, the church was central to the Iberian agenda of conquest. Catholicism provided compelling justifications for expansion, especially the need to bring salvation to the benighted souls of the native peoples of the

Americas. Drawing on their history of subjugation to Islam, the church adapted a Muslim practice of offering pagan populations the option of allegiance to the faith or death. According to this practice, employed first as Spanish moved from the Caribbean to conquering the mainland, Spanish conquistadors read a statement (in Spanish, a language the people of the Americas did not understand) called the "Requirimiento" (or Requirement) when they invaded. The statement offered a choice between submitting "voluntarily" to the church or being warred upon "everywhere and however."[9] Once the natives indicated their acceptance of the Requirimiento, priests staged mass baptisms. One account mentions 1,500 brought into the church in one day. With this ritual, the conquered people were accepted as neophytes—or initial converts still learning the ways of the faith—into the Catholic Church. Early records abound with instances in which so many were baptized at one time that the religious personnel performing these ceremonies complained of exhaustion or even sunburn and calluses. One priest, Pedro de Gante, described in a letter of 1529 a day in which fourteen thousand baptisms took place.[10] Believing that theirs was the one true church, proponents of expansion often asserted that any brutality attendant on conquest of the Americas was ameliorated by the gift of salvation. This perspective could be used to justify despicable practices in the name of spreading Christianity.

Yet church officials also questioned the morality of colonial practices. Bartolomé de las Casas, a Dominican priest who wrote extensively against mistreatment of Indians, earned widespread fame (or infamy) for his advocacy. His *Brief Account of the Devastation of the Indies* described the Spanish arrival on the island of Hispaniola (today Haiti and the Dominican Republic):

> Yet into this sheepfold, into this land of meek outcasts there came some Spaniards who immediately behaved like ravening wild beasts . . . Spaniards have behaved in no other way during the past forty years, down to the present time, for they are still acting like ravening beasts, killing, terrorizing, afflicting, torturing, and destroying the native peoples, doing all this with the strangest and most varied new methods of cruelty, never seen or heard of before.[11]

Criticisms of such cruelty helped to bring an end to some of the worst abuses of the Native Americans. Although forced labor of the native inhabitants continued, especially in the mines, their circumstances were assuaged by the

Fig. 3. Bartolomé de las Casas wrote of the cruel treatment of the Indians in order to change Spanish policy. Protestant Europeans who hated Spain, especially the Dutch and English, reprinted las Casas's text, adding horrific illustrations, in order to drive home the point that the Spanish were inhumane. This engraving by Theodore de Bry appeared in Bartolomé de las Casas, *Narratio regionum indicarum per Hispanos quosdam deuastatarum verissima* (Frankfurt, 1598), 92. Courtesy of John Carter Brown Library at Brown University.

intervention of these critics. The church, in other words, was central to the creation of an Iberian empire, both in justifying the initial move into the hemisphere and in shaping the impact of colonization on the native peoples.

The major focus of the church in Latin America was the work of conversion rather than justifying conquest or ameliorating its effects. Iberian expansion into the Americas included a missionary component from the very first, and the role of the church expanded with the European presence in the Caribbean and on the mainland. The Spanish and Portuguese monarchs took control of the missionary campaign immediately, making it an extension of their role with regard to the churches within their realms. The pope later struggled to exert his authority over the missions, attempting to bring them under his direct control, but he had only limited success in Portuguese America and failed altogether in Spanish America. Much of the missionary work in the Americas was undertaken by members of separate religious orders, such as mendicant friars. The Dominicans and Franciscans (two of these older orders) were the most energetic early missionaries in the Spanish colonies. Franciscans dominated in New Spain, where they began arriving in the 1520s. Dominicans along with Franciscans labored in Peru. A newer preaching order, the Society of Jesus (or Jesuits), had been founded partly in response to the Protestant Reformation, and it included missionary work, both in Europe and elsewhere, as part of its call. The Jesuits would eventually play a large role, after they came to the American missions beginning in 1568. Dominican and Franciscan friars worked to convert Native Americans throughout Spanish and Portuguese America. They founded hundreds of local missions to do so, while the Jesuits added the additional project of opening a number of schools that were attended by Indian boys as well as their Spanish and creole (or American born but of European descent) counterparts.

As in the areas subjected to Protestant evangelizing in Europe after 1530, Catholic missionaries in Africa and the Americas sought to educate and persuade the native populace. In order to communicate Catholic beliefs, the friars and later the Jesuits had to address the problem of language. Anything beyond rudimentary communication necessitated either learning the native language, locating an interpreter with fairly sophisticated language skills, or teaching Spanish to the indigenous population. The missionaries generally favored instruction in the native languages of those they attempted to convert, and this approach required that they learn these languages and produce catechisms and other teaching aids to support their instruction. Between 1546 and 1556, missionaries issued at least seven catechisms in the local languages of Mexico, Chiapa, and Guatemala. In producing these catechetical works, their authors struggled to convey novel concepts in indigenous languages and debated whether to adapt indigenous terms to Christian concepts or to import Spanish terminology into the catechisms. Franciscans believed that new (non-native) terms were needed to communicate the differences that distinguished Christianity from local beliefs, whereas the Dominican missionaries thought it best to use native terms to designate such central concepts as the supreme deity.

When these friars labored to put instructional texts in the vernacular languages, their efforts paralleled the Protestant agenda of making religious texts available in accessible form for the populations they sought to convert. Among the Catholics, however, there were limits to the use of the vernacular: the Mass continued to be said in Latin and no effort was made to translate the Bible into native languages. Catholic Bibles in the vernacular, though they existed throughout Europe, were not central to the church's practice in the way Protestant Bibles tended to be. Sections of the Bible were rendered in the Spanish language for use in the Americas as early as 1579, but the Catholic missionaries placed more emphasis on catechisms. Both orders of friars staged Passion Plays and other dramatic presentations of biblical stories using indigenous casts. These performances educated both the players and their audiences. In contrast, Protestant missionaries produced not only catechisms and guides for worship services (such as the Book of Common Prayer), but also the Bible in local languages. The centrality of the Bible to the Protestant faith promoted biblical literacy as a goal of all Protestant outreach. Religious texts circulated in both colonial contexts, yet ultimately played a more central role among Protestants. The Catholics, however, were the first to attempt to cross the linguistic and cultural divide to communicate unfamiliar concepts.

As Christian missionaries reaching out to peoples they considered "heathens," Catholic religious leaders worked to replace one spiritual system (that of the indigenous peoples they encountered) with their own (in this case, Roman Catholicism). The crown and the church undertook a massive effort to transplant the faith to the Iberian colonies. In doing so, they interpreted local beliefs in one of two ways. Either they saw in pagan practices a hint of the "true" faith (that is, their own faith), or they saw local religion as the work of the devil and therefore diametrically opposed to Catholicism. In Iberian America, these views were adopted sequentially to an extent. Initially missionaries highlighted commonalities between American and European religions, such as a similar belief in a supreme deity, where that existed, only later to replace this idea of complementarity with the conviction that native belief came from Satan.

This shift took place often after missionaries discovered that Indians they had instructed (and whom they thought of as fully converted Christians) maintained their older beliefs along with their newer Catholic ones. Having been exposed to the true faith, these Native Americans seemed to have rejected it as they continued to give attention to their traditional gods and beliefs. Expecting conversion to bring transformation, missionaries interpreted evidence of hybridity as utter rejection of the faith. The first bishop of the Yucatan, for instance, was appalled to learn that supposedly converted Indians continued to venerate the "idols" of their traditional religion. The bishop assumed that the traditional gods and spirits had been entirely supplanted by the Catholic panoply of saints and the Trinity of the Father, Son, and Holy Ghost. When he learned otherwise, he had over four thousand alleged offenders brought before the Inquisition in a short time, using torture to bring about confessions. When resident Spaniards complained, he ordered them examined as well. About 160 Indians died in this incident, which only ended when the overzealous bishop was sent back to Spain. Church leaders imported the Inquisition to the Spanish colonies as a mechanism to police heresy and extirpate lingering older practices. The Portuguese relied instead on the powers of the local bishop and occasional inquisitorial visits from Portugal to the same end.

Yet the religious hybridity of the American peoples was not easily eliminated. It is likely that the veneration of Our Lady of Guadalupe has pagan as well as Catholic roots, with her shrine located at a site with spiritual significance that predated the arrival of Catholics in Mexico. She certainly became a symbol of indigenous Christianity, preferred over competing European images of the Virgin, such as the Virgin of Remedios brought by the conquistadors. In this and other instances, Catholic holy places replaced pagan sacred sites, as the landscape itself was converted to Catholicism. As in Europe, the process of converting people and places involved negotiation and selection. Never was one system entirely and instantly replaced with another. When in the twentieth century Pope Pius XII named Our Lady of Guadalupe the official "patroness" of the Americas, he made an appropriate selection for capturing the contested process that remade the American landscape into a Roman Catholic sacred space.

During the sixteenth century, Catholicism both contracted and expanded. The contraction resulted from the exodus of church members into the newly founded Protestant churches of northern Europe. At the same time, Roman Catholicism expanded into the Americas and the Caribbean as part of the Iberian conquest of those regions and to Atlantic Africa as a result of Portuguese trading activity there. Western Christendom was divided into Protestant and Catholic camps even as its message was transplanted into new locations and communicated to new groups of potential converts. Indeed Catholic missionaries framed their own endeavors in terms of a push to replace the souls lost to the Protestant "heresy" by converting the heathens in these newly discovered lands. That Christendom's expansion occurred simultaneously with its division into literally warring camps would have enormous consequences for religion in the Atlantic settlements.

When the English subsequently entered into conquest and colonization of the Caribbean and the Americas, they justified their own activity in terms of countering the Spanish Catholic threat. They objected that the Spanish had captured so many souls for an erroneous religious faith. They also saw that the great wealth that the Spanish extracted from their American possessions not only exalted Spain but also supported the papacy. With the competition for souls with Spain in the foreground, every English colonial charter spoke of the need to proselytize the natives as one reason for settling in the Americas. Early colonial promoter Richard Hakluyt objected that English men who went to trade in the Spanish dominions were "dryven to flinge their bibles and prayer bookes into the sea, and to forsweare and renownce their relligion and conscience, and consequently their obedience to her Majesty."[12] Hakluyt saw the books of the new Protestantism as emblematic of that faith, and he hoped to see these move with English men as they circulated through the Atlantic. He also equated religious adherence to political allegiance, so that a man who renounced his church also rejected his queen. The perception that religious and civil obedience were intimately linked was shared by many, and it helps to explain the high level of suspicion that was manifested across confessional lines in this era. The division of Europe into Protestant and Catholic provided one motivation that propelled Europe into the wider Atlantic world.

England moved toward expansion within a context of religious divisions. The experiences in the sixteenth century, and especially during the reign of Elizabeth, had helped the English and Welsh to think of theirs as a Protestant nation. Their religious worldview had been transformed. Threatened by papist Spain—famously with the planned attack by its fleet of ships, or "Armada," in 1588—and by a much exaggerated internal Catholic menace, they rallied around their Protestant identity and the idea that they had a special role to play in the world. More militant Protestants wanted not only to stand up to Spain in Europe but also to attack it in the Americas. Sir Walter Ralegh was never an especially devout man. Like most early colonial advocates, he assumed that English conquests in the Americas created conditions in which "infinite nombers of soules may bee brought from theyr idolatry, bloody sacrifices, ignoraunce, and incivility to the worshipping of the true god."[13] But his own piety seems to have been of a fairly routine sort. Nonetheless, when he was executed by James VI and I to appease the Spanish—whose colonies he had repeatedly attacked—Protestant boosters enshrined him as a godly martyr to England's cause. One motivation for a greater English role in the Americas was the perceived need to challenge Catholic power and to create a Protestant presence there.

Ireland's place in these developments was a difficult one. By the seventeenth century, Ireland was almost entirely controlled by England. Just at the end of Elizabeth's reign, her military forces completed the conquest. Yet Ireland, although physically subdued, never relinquished its control over its spiritual choices, by and large rejecting the Protestantism of the other kingdoms under Tudor and later Stuart rule. Obviously, that Ireland was newly conquered had something to do with its intransigence: continuing in its Catholicism represented a form of resistance to English rule. English authorities also did less than they might have to evangelize the Irish population—their failure to produce the usual catechetical materials for Irish targets of conversion efforts being one case in point. Whatever the reasons, Ireland remained largely Catholic, and this reality affected the politics of expansion. Far from being seen as a co-kingdom joined in the effort of Protestant colonization, Ireland was viewed as a likely subject of colonization itself. An energetic effort to bring Protestantism to Ireland involved a campaign to displace Irish Catholics and replace them with Protestant English or, later, Scots.

In adopting this strategy, the Protestants figured the Irish Catholics as outside of their imperial agenda. Sometimes seen as barbarous and backward, the Irish stubbornly refused to embrace the "true religion" of Protestantism. As part of this polarizing attitude, English Protestants associated the Irish with Spain or with Rome, seeing them as allied against the Protestantism of the other kingdoms. Indeed, after 1600, some Irish left Ireland to take up residence in Catholic countries on the Continent. By 1700, those Irish Catholics who remained, and Ireland itself, were at odds religiously with neighboring islands. Ireland's subordinate position, combined with these acrimonious religious differences, all but ensured that it would not be integrated into the polity ruled by England's new Stuart kings on anything like an equal footing. The seeds of Ireland's second-class status had been sown in the sixteenth-century reformations that protestantized the neighboring kingdoms but left it relatively unaffected by these religious changes. Conquered by its powerful

Protestant neighbor, Ireland's position was unenviable even if its unwilling-ness to take up the conqueror's faith was understandable.

On the eve of expansion into the wider Atlantic world, recent religious changes shaped the English perception of itself and of its place within Eu-rope. England (and Wales) had emerged as a Protestant state, with a reformed church headed by its monarch. As Foxe's Book of Martyrs reminded its nu-merous avid readers, the English had suffered and died for their Protestant-ism, placing them in a long tradition of Christian martyrdom. Their heroic Protestant advocacy put them in conflict with powerful Spain as well as with the papacy itself. Hostility to Spain led easily to resentment about its vast New World possessions and the great wealth it extracted from them. The great age of English piracy in the Spanish Caribbean was launched in this atmosphere of religious animosity and envy. Although Catholicism domi-nated the European conquests in the Americas in 1600, a Europe religiously polarized between Catholic and Protestant was prepared to export its divi-sions into the wider Atlantic world. The entry of England into the coloniza-tion business was framed in terms of confronting and displacing papist Spain. The English sense of its own superiority arose out of its Protestantism, and that Protestantism—with its emphasis on literacy and individual faith—made the English less prepared to negotiate with others in the cultural en-counter they were about to experience. Their commitment to Protestantism and the heightened political tensions around religious issues in Europe sent them out into the Atlantic determined to defend and promote their own faith and ready to perceive alternatives in the worst possible light. Militant and uncompromising English Protestantism prepared to enter the Atlantic arena.

THREE

Exporting the Religious Tensions of the Three Kingdoms

THE ENGLISH MOVED tentatively into the wider Atlantic world in the late sixteenth century and entered more decisively into the colonization in the first decades of the seventeenth century, shortly after King James of Scotland assumed his cousin Elizabeth's throne. In doing so, James became James VI and I, ruler over three kingdoms—his native Scotland, as well as England and Wales, and Ireland—each with its own disparate religious situation. Each kingdom had a different church established by law, a situation that created tensions that would become obvious when James's son Charles I tried to force uniformity upon them in the 1630s. The multiplicity among established churches, along with the large number of Catholics and a smattering of more radical Protestants, meant that James's subjects held a wide variety of religious positions. In each case, however, a legally established faith held precedence over all others. Alternatives operated under legal disabilities and sometimes faced outright persecution.

Despite its complexity, this situation did not lead to an acceptance of diversity, which was seen as both highly problematic and anomalous. Religious choices would proliferate in the Stuart kingdoms between 1640 and 1660, as political upheaval opened the way for religious experimentation and undermined the established religions in both Ireland and England and Wales. English expansion into the wider Atlantic world was undertaken,. therefore, under a monarch who ruled over subjects of various religious orientations and at a time when diversity and openness to it would shortly be on the rise.

As they moved outward, the English, along with the Welsh, Scots, and Irish, were also contending over religious issues. Even as these fights battered the Stuart kings' corner of Europe, they would also shape the plantations that were established across the Atlantic.

The English were not the only Protestants to become active in the wider Atlantic world in the seventeenth century. Other Protestant states that undertook colonizing projects were Lutheran Sweden and the Dutch Reformed Netherlands. Sweden's project was modest, resulting in one short-lived colony on the banks of the Delaware River (1638–55) and the more lasting presence of a small number of transplanted Lutherans whose numbers would be augmented in the eighteenth century. A minister stationed in the colony in the 1640s produced the first Protestant catechism in an Indian language.[1] The Dutch effort was more sustained and far-reaching, and in the Atlantic included the colonies of New Netherland (1624), Curaçao (1634), and Suriname (1667). The Dutch West India Company officially sanctioned a Reformed Dutch church establishment in its colonies and made some effort to transplant that church, but in reality permitted religious pluralism. Sephardic Jews were the most conspicuous minority but many variants of Protestantism were also represented. Curaçao was important as a trading center, but none of the Dutch colonies was very populous.

Anticipating the arrival of the Swedes and the Dutch, the English were the first Protestants to gain a foothold in the Atlantic. Their efforts in the Western Hemisphere would have the most extensive religious effects of any of its Protestant rivals. As subjects of a composite monarchy that brought together different Christian faiths under one ruler, the people who colonized the New World under the authority of the early Stuart kings were especially affected by the post-Reformation fragmentation of Western Christendom. They would carry the tensions inherent in the Stuart kingdoms—tensions that would subsequently be exacerbated by the revolution against Charles I—with them into the wider Atlantic world.

When James became ruler of three kingdoms in 1603, each had its own peculiar religious establishment. Scotland's church, erected by Protestant elites who controlled the kingdom before James came of age, was basically Presbyterian. Although the Scottish kirk (as its established church was called) vacillated on whether to grant a role for bishops, in its pure form the Presbyterian system was run by ministers and lay elders meeting in presbyteries. Sections of the Scottish Highlands were not fully incorporated into the established church, and non-Presbyterians tended to be either Catholic or Episcopal in their orientations. In England and Wales, the church organization was Episcopal, with clerical appointments and discipline handled by bishops and church courts. The theological emphasis within the Church of England at the start of James's reign ranged from orthodox Calvinism to a newer anti-Calvinist emphasis on the universality of divine grace and the free will of the sinner. The small established church in Ireland straddled the two extremes: its theology and preaching was staunchly Calvinist (like the main Scottish church) but it was also fully organized under bishops appointed by the crown (following the Church of England). Most Irish, though, remained Catholic. Each of the kingdoms included Catholic populations of indeterminate size and composition, despite widespread suspicion surrounding Catholicism and official efforts to use the legal system to push it out of existence. Roman Catholics living in London might attend Mass at one of the ambassador's chapels, and even during the height of the anti-Catholic sentiment at mid-century attendees were only sporadically arrested. An occasional dramatic conversion to Catholicism shook some Protestant families, as was the case when the son of puritan preacher William Crashaw embraced the church of Rome. Remembered as a metaphysical poet, Richard Crashaw wrote numerous verses about the Spanish mystic and martyr Saint Teresa. The incongruities between the religious organizations of the three kingdoms were largely allowed to stand under James, although his son would combat them in the 1630s.

In spite of this confused situation, both James and his son and successor Charles assumed that uniformity would prevail in the colonies with the establishment of the Church of England. European elites of this era (regardless of confessional affiliation) agreed that religious uniformity was necessary to peace and good order, and the early Stuarts shared that view. As a result, the first nine English colonies were organized with the assumption that the Church of England would be transplanted to serve as a legally established church in each of them.[2] Even the religious dissenters who established Massachusetts Bay at least said they were establishing the Church of England in their colony, since to say otherwise in the 1630s would have provoked royal displeasure. The exception to this rule was the tenth colony, Maryland; it was anomalous in that it did not attempt a religious establishment, a strategy intended to make space for the practice of Catholicism. In Virginia, James instructed the early governors to ensure that "the true word, and service of God and Christian faith be preached, planted, and used, not only within the said several colonies, and plantations, but alsoe as much as they may amongst the salvage people which doe or shall adjoine unto them, or border upon them, according to the doctrine, rights, and religion now professed and established within our realme of England."[3] Although raised under the less hierarchical Presbyterian system in his native Scotland, James advocated the Church of England establishment for his colonies. Preferring the greater power the English church granted the monarch, he also disappointed reform-minded English clergy who hoped he would turn the Church of England in a Presbyterian direction once he took the throne. Regardless of the faith of his natal kingdom, James anticipated that his colonies would hew to the Church of England.

In addition to the transplantation of the Church of England, the Stuart monarch also assumed his colonizing subjects would convert Native Americans to Protestantism. By the time the first lasting English colony was founded at Jamestown in 1607, the Spanish already boasted extensive missions as close to Virginia as Florida. They were launching another missionary campaign into New Mexico at the time. To the English kings and others, the Spanish example suggested that expansion and missionary work could and should go hand in hand. Every early charter granting royal permission to establish a colony mentioned the need for the conversion of native peoples as a justification behind colonization. The indigenous residents of the Americas were often referred to as the "poor" Indians, the pity arising from the fact that they had no knowledge of Christianity or of the other advantages associated (in the minds of Europeans) with European civilization. Colonization would, it was assumed, introduce them to these benefits and would therefore be welcomed as well as justified.

English settlers never readily embraced the work of conversion, however. The first colonies were not supplied with missionaries (as the Spanish colonies had been) so whatever work was to have been undertaken fell to the settlers themselves. No Protestant missionary organizations existed at this time, the founding of the first one occurring only in 1649, after four decades of neglect of this project.[4] Prejudices they brought with them were one cause of the hesitation to attempt conversion. For example, when William Shakespeare imaged an indigenous person in his play *The Tempest* (1611), he created Caliban—the son of a witch, whom he depicted as monstrously ugly and not especially intelligent. Having probably never met a native of the Americas—although a number of them had been kidnapped and brought to England for exhibition by this time—Shakespeare conveyed in Caliban one image of difference that was common in his culture. Colonists also feared the native peoples whose lands they were invading, which put a damper on any impulse to undertake missionary work.

Some settlers, less fearful and more open-minded, did discuss religion with Native Americans they encountered. Those who visited early and wrote about their experiences for an English audience often surveyed the native beliefs they encountered, early examples of a nascent anthropology at work in the English colonies. Thomas Harriot, a highly learned man who studied the inhabitants of the Carolina Outer Banks whom he met at Roanoke in the 1580s, recorded their creation story, which included the idea that the first human was a woman. Roger Williams, a New England settler who learned to speak a native dialect, conversed frequently with Narragansett Bay–area Indians about their beliefs. William Wood published his own observations in *New England's Prospect* (1634), offering his opinion that the original inhabitants of the region believed in a heaven that was much like that of the Muslims. Both expected that good people would go to a bountiful land full of all earthly joys. Such accounts were fascinating to English readers who stayed at home, since they gave insight into an exotic and intriguing culture.

The most famous exception to this general disinterest in converting Native Americans to Christianity occurred in first-generation Virginia. Early settler John Rolfe agonized over the decision to marry an Indian woman, fearing that he was motivated out of lust rather than obedience to God. Just as any Native American might do, Rolfe received confirmation for his desire to wed in a dream, in which God came to him in his sleep, "pulling mee by the eare, and crying: why does thou not endevour to make her a Christian?" He finally persuaded himself to wed the young Pocahontas on the grounds that her Christianization would be good for her as well for her people and the struggling English colony. Baptized and married to Rolfe by a Church of England clergyman, Pocahontas, now renamed Rebecca, would prove the most famous native North American convert of the century. When the couple and their young son visited England in 1616, she was feted at court and throughout London society. Her portrait depicted a fashionably dressed native lady. The visit would cut her life short, leaving John Rolfe a widower for a second time, with an Anglo-Powhatan son who would grow up to be a major colonial landowner.[5] Lady Rebecca's death ended plans that she and her husband would return to her native land to open a mission, since her linguistic expertise and standing were central to the scheme as it had been conceived in England. Rolfe was exceptional, however, in that English colonists neither married nor attempted to convert native peoples as a general rule.

Marriages like that of Rebecca and John Rolfe as well as English efforts to convert Native Americans in the first years were both extremely rare, and their rarity begs for explanation. In contrast to both the Spanish and the French, who married native peoples and worked for their conversion, the English seemed at first almost completely uninterested in either creating marital alliances or bringing native peoples into the Christian fold. One major difference separating the English from these other colonizers was their Protestantism: the more successful evangelizers and the willing marriage partners were Catholics. The Protestant faith of the English may have made them less willing or able to participate in one or both of these forms of outreach. Protestant churches lacked the priests or friars who could be sent to work for the conversion of the natives. Catholic missions gained from the existence of religious orders (like the Jesuits) that provided priests for the work. Protestant churches included neither separate communities dedicated to such efforts that could take up the project nor institutional structures that facilitated the organization and funding of evangelical outreach. Such was largely the case for the first century and a half of British Protestantism, until various missionary organizations emerged around the turn of the eighteenth century.

Beyond this structural difference, however, it may be that something about the Protestant faith made the English less open to the idea of a native person as either a legitimate convert or an acceptable spouse. Protestantism, with its emphasis on deep knowledge of Scripture and (in some cases) its insistence on the need of believers to convey a conversion experience to gain access to church membership, raised the bar for conversion. Then, too, in the Protestant way of thinking, marriage was spiritually a more important institution. Having rejected celibacy as a superior moral state (the Catholic position), Reformed clergy instructed believers that marriage was the ideal institution in which all the faithful were expected to live. This idea may have put more emphasis on marriage in a way that made cross-cultural unions less acceptable. Catholicism was understood as a universal church, which was supposed to unite all the peoples of the world, and that understanding may have made church officials and lay people more open to accepting the native people they encountered both as church members and as marriage partners. This difference, which was so important for the development of the societies being created in the New World, defies easy explanation.

Among many English people, rivalry with the Spanish and other Catholics

Fig. 4. By the time the young Powhatan woman Pocahontas traveled to England as the wife of John Rolfe, she had converted to Christianity and adopted English-style dress. While in England, this likeness was produced; it identified her by her native name (Matoaka) and her baptismal name (Rebecca). The name Pocahontas was most likely a childhood nickname. Engraved in 1616 by Simon van de Passe and reproduced in John Smith's *The Generall Histoire of Virginia, New England, and the Summer Isles* (1624). Courtesy of John Carter Brown Library at Brown University.

was central to their ideas about expansion. From the first English forays into the wider Atlantic world, hostility toward Catholicism and the major Catholic power, Spain, motivated many. Under Elizabeth, piracy against Spanish colonies and ships was often presented as a religiously inspired assault on papists. Promoters of colonization used similar language to justify expansion, framing it in terms of combating Catholic (especially Spanish) gains. By the early seventeenth century, Portugal and Spain had extensive colonial holdings, and the two kingdoms were united under the Spanish monarch from 1580 to 1640. Conversion of the conquered populations to Catholicism was part of their program from New Spain south to Brazil. English Protestants viewed these conversions as illegitimate; if forced to choose between leaving the Indians in their heathen state and converting them to the false religion of popery, many would be hard pressed to decide which constituted the worse fate. By conquering and converting numerous natives, the Iberian Catholics not only increased the ranks of Catholics worldwide, but also (objectionably) captured wealth that would be used in support of Catholic causes. Both for its direct religious effects and its financing of popery, Spanish colonization had to be combated. Those who held these views most vehemently were "the hotter sort of Protestants," those within the Church of England who wanted to turn it in a more reformed direction.[6] For them expansion took on a more partisan political edge.

The affinity of this group for the project of expansion meant that disproportionately more reform-minded individuals got involved in the early colonies. Virginia, for instance, included a sizeable number of the godly sort, whom we know as puritans, both on the company board and in the ranks of the colonists themselves. Others were active in the colonies of Providence Island and Massachusetts Bay, both founded in the year 1629, the former with a particularly anti-Spanish agenda. To the extent that colonization was endowed with a religiopolitical mission, it was one that was especially dear to the hearts of the puritans within the Church of England.

As the discussion of anti-popery's role in expansion suggests, tensions within the Stuart kingdoms were exported into the wider Atlantic world as part of the colonization process. In retrospect we might wonder how it could have been otherwise. Despite the official prejudice in favor of sending settlers who were loyal Church of England adherents, the diversity within and among the kingdoms was soon re-created in the colonies. During the first decades the majority of migrants were English, as opposed to Welsh, Scottish, or Irish. But they included the entire range of religious positions in England:

Church of England members content with it, puritan critics of the church who had heretofore continued within it, more radical critics who had separated themselves from it (called at the time "separatists" but known in American history as "Pilgrims"), and Catholics. A "Great Migration" in the 1630s moved individuals not only to colonial New England (where the phrase is most often applied) but also into all the colonies in the Atlantic basin as well as to Ireland and other locations in Europe, such as the Netherlands. The plan to ensure loyalty by limiting migration only to mainstream Church of England members was never successful, and a sizeable minority of all migrants did not enthusiastically support the state church.

Indeed potential migrants might see colonization as a means of attaining a religious liberty that they could not experience in England itself. Settlers who were unsupportive of the established church (whether they were Catholics, members of Protestant alternatives to the Church of England like the separatists, or critics nominally within the church) might migrate to escape religious restrictions and possible persecution. By the 1630s Charles I was concerned that the migration of potentially disloyal non-Anglicans represented a danger, and he ordered the port authorities to interview every departing passenger to check his or her religious orientation and loyalty to the monarchy. This strategy did not prevent critics of both church and king from moving to a colony. Numerous migrants are known to have sworn allegiance in spite of having serious reservations. A few, such as radical Hugh Peter, sneaked out of the kingdom disguised as servants. Other tensions also existed. While some migrants were Catholics (especially those who went to the colonies of Maryland and Montserrat), the anti-Catholic prejudices that were so much a part of English popular culture were exported to the colonies as well.

The problems with planting a uniform church order in all the colonies was exacerbated by the difficulty of transferring religious institutions from England to the Atlantic plantations. Unlike the colonies of Catholic kingdoms such as Spain, Portugal, and France, the colonies of England were not the beneficiaries of a highly structured and well-staffed religious institution like the Roman Catholic Church. Lacking the religious orders—especially the Dominicans, Franciscans, and Jesuits—the Church of England did not have the mechanisms in place for sending clergymen to their colonies. Each man for a colonial pulpit had to be recruited and sent separately. Staffing colonial Church of England posts proved a challenge, first in attracting candidates to fill the posts and then in replacing those who died during the "seasoning" period, when migrants adjusted to a new disease environment.

Colonial churches were subsumed under the hierarchy in England, and as a result no bishops were sent to the colonies and no church courts were erected. This fateful decision was made without much apparent discussion, although at the height of his ambition to regularize church affairs everywhere Charles did agree to send a bishop to Sir Ferdinando Gorges's colony in northern New England. The appointment was never made, and the idea of dispatching a bishop quietly faded. The subsequent failure to assign a bishop to the colonies seems to have been related to a general expectation that colonial affairs could be effectively managed from England. The episcopal hierarchy was not re-created in the wider Atlantic world in the early colonial period; neither did the disciplinary arm of the church function there.

The Church of England in the colonies lacked the very features that defined it against the other religious options at play in the three kingdoms. In the Atlantic Church of England, therefore, the worship service, based on the prayer book, became its distinguishing characteristic. Virginia, the first permanent colony, immediately ordered ministers to read from the Church of England prayer book at Sunday services. Going beyond that proved daunting, however. Even in the simplified colonial environment, churches needed buildings, books, and the various accoutrements of the Church of England service, such as the communion plate and clerical vestments. These represented sizeable investments. It took time for the Church of England to be transplanted in a semblance of itself. Arguably it never achieved more than that semblance prior to the American Revolution.

What was true of the difficulty with importing Anglican institutions was equally true of the other churches that made their way across the Atlantic. In the early English colonies, Catholic churches were erected only in Maryland. There Catholicism was openly practiced under the protection of the proprietor Cecil Lord Baltimore (1605–75). The Roman Catholic hierarchy considered Maryland to be a mission church, a categorization that allowed the ecclesiastical organization there to function without bishops. Jesuit missionaries staffed the Maryland churches initially. Baltimore battled with the Jesuits over the division of authority between proprietor and priests, a controversy that no doubt undermined the latter's effectiveness.

Intra-Catholic debates were never as significant as tensions between the relatively few resident Catholics and the province's Protestant majority. To prevent hostilities from multiplying and to protect Catholic interest in the colony, Baltimore adopted a policy of religious toleration. His policy was eventually enshrined in a 1649 act. It contained a long list of religious slurs that were proscribed—a list that suggests the insults colonists were inclined to throw around: "heritick, Scismatick, Idolator, puritan, Independant, Prespiterian popish priest, Jesuite, Jesuited papist, Lutheran, Calvenist Anabaptist, Brownist, Antinomian, Barrowist, Roundhead, Separatist."[7] Later famous as an early move toward religious freedom, the act actually limited that freedom to those who were Christian and believed in the Trinity, that is, the three-in-one God. At the time the practical effect of this limitation was to prevent Jews and any radical Christians who questioned the Trinity from worshiping openly in the colony. Moreover, the act enjoyed only limited success at preventing religious animosities from flaring out of control. A battle was fought in 1654 that arrayed two political factions in the colony against each other, one that upheld toleration and a continuing role for Catholics against one that advocated Protestantism and exclusivity.

Catholics living in other English colonies often subsisted without priests. On the heavily Catholic island of Montserrat, the faithful were bereft of the Mass and the sacraments until French priests surreptitiously visited the island to minister to people there. Although many Montserrat Catholics haled from Ireland, they may not have been predominantly ethnically Irish. Many of the initial migrants were apparently Old English Catholics who had migrated to Ireland prior to the Reformation. Others were not Catholic at all but Protestant migrants to Ireland who had been there for a generation or more. English or Irish Catholics on Saint Christopher (an island divided between English and French zones) could sneak over to the French sector for an occasional Mass. Catholics were a clear presence but the community was underserved in the seventeenth-century climate of Protestant suspicion against their faith.

Those who fared best in transferring their institutions adhered to more decentralized versions of Protestantism. Since the puritans and separatists of New England were opposed to bishops and church courts, not to mention priestly vestments and the idea that buildings ought to be dedicated solely to worship, their task of transplantation was made easier. They favored a Congregationalist church order that vested control over ecclesiastical business in the local congregation. These radical Protestants expected the local congregation to discipline wayward members and to call its own minister. The act of being called made the man a minister; ordination by a bishop was not necessary nor was it deemed proper. This decentralized system was much more easily erected, and the process was helped enormously in New England by a very high proportion of clergy among the settler population. As clergymen in England began to lose their positions if they insisted on adhering to

Reformed principles in their preaching and practices, many men decided to migrate rather than to conform. As many as ninety ministers migrated to New England in the 1630s, a startlingly high number in contrast to the numbers in other colonies.[8] This phenomenon gave early New England the benefit of many well-educated and dedicated ministers, almost more than the churches there could reasonably employ. Congregationalism in New England was more rapidly and completely organized than other ecclesiastical systems elsewhere, such as the Church of England in Virginia or Barbados. It represented an alternative orthodoxy, a fact New Englanders were loath to admit while King Charles remained secure on his throne.

Being a remarkably inflexible man, Charles I objected to the disjointed ecclesiastical situation he inherited in 1625, and in the 1630s he set about to change it. The new king had two goals: to make the churches uniform across his kingdoms and to require greater conformity within both Ireland and England. In the Church of England he worked through his archbishop, William Laud. They began requiring ministers to read the Prayer Book, wear their vestments, elevate the host in the communion ritual, and forswear extemporaneous preaching. All these reforms were aimed at the puritan dissenters within the church who had been avoiding those aspects of the prescribed worship they found objectionable.

Besides choosing to neglect these various forms, they were also inclined to deliver powerful and occasionally critical sermons. Preaching was so popular with puritans, in fact, that they were described as "gadding" after sermons by their critics. Charles I, unlike his father James, was not a fan of sermonizing. In this, he was closer to Elizabeth I, who was similarly disinterested in preaching. Unlike Elizabeth, however, he wanted to put an end to the practices he disliked and force a conformity that Elizabeth had never insisted upon. Ministers who would not conform lost their positions, so that those church members who had sought out the preaching of these men found their access blocked. Both the ministers and their disgruntled former parishioners opposed the changes. One puritan woman bemoaned "such prosedings as will greve any christien hart to hear: that in so short a time so many of Gods faithfull ministers should be silenced; and that which is wors, many that semed to be zeleous doe yeld obedence to the inventions of men."[9] Some would participate in the migration into the Atlantic world in the hope of finding churches that could accommodate their own religious preferences.

Others parishioners welcomed the changes, preferring an emphasis on church ritual and the liturgy of the Prayer Book. While Laud was extremely strict on conformity to church ritual and liturgy, he and the king saw little need to discipline communities for Sabbath amusements like sports and festivals, to which the godly sort that attended puritan preaching strenuously objected. The godly hated Laud as much for allowing lawn bowling on the Sabbath as for making ministers use the sign of the cross in baptism. Those who loved the traditional amusements and did not care for the strictures of fiery preachers were perfectly happy with these changes. Popular religious culture polarized over these issues in the 1630s.

In his other kingdoms, Charles worked to impose a church settlement that would bring Ireland and Scotland into closer conformity with his religious and ecclesiastical ideal. The Church of Ireland had been organized similarly to the Church of England: the monarch was its head and its organization was episcopal (or run by bishops). Despite its bishops, however, the Church of Ireland before 1634 had a marked Reformed style that made it more to the liking of the dissenters within the Church of England than to the mainstream in that church which Laud was seeking to encourage. Thus, in Ireland Charles's challenge was much like that which he faced in England: to rid the church of radicals and force ministers and laypeople to follow the prescribed practices. Laud, with the help of Charles's Lord Lieutenant of Ireland, Thomas Wentworth, the first earl of Stafford, largely succeeded in forcing obedience on the small Irish church in 1634.

The challenge in Scotland was broader, for Charles found the church there unacceptable ecclesiastically, liturgically, and doctrinally. The Scottish Presbyterian system would have to be replaced with a system that boasted powerful bishops as well as church courts, while the liturgy and preaching would have to be remade as well. Charles tried to force the Church of Scotland into his Church of England mold but with disastrous results. Scottish Presbyterians so vehemently opposed the policy changes that they fought a series of minor wars against their sovereign in the late 1630s. The controversy is said to have been sparked when a group of women in an Edinburgh church interrupted the reading of the order to alter church practice. Because those of lesser social status did not have seats in the church—the pews were assigned to wealthier church members who were able to pay for them—one young woman had a stool that she had brought into the church to serve as her seat; so outraged was she by what she heard that she threw the stool at the official reading the royal proclamation. The wars this policy sparked, called "the Bishops' Wars," led directly to the outbreak of the first civil war in England and indirectly to the collapse of Charles's government. During the same period, the Presbyterian churches of the Channel Island of Guernsey were slated for renovation, as were the independent churches of much of colonial New England. Both managed to hold onto their customary practices until Charles I and Laud were distracted by wars and other matters closer to home.

Charles's policy of enforced religious conformity contributed to crises in his three kingdoms and eventually to the collapse of his government as well as of the established church in England. The Bishops' Wars forced Charles to call a parliament, which he had avoided for the previous eleven years of "Personal Rule." The men elected brought multiple grievances about governmental policy—religious, fiscal, and otherwise—and they used the king's need for financial support to push through reforms. Charles objected to the activities of this Parliament. The resulting impasse eventually led to civil war between the king and his supporters, on one side, and the parliamentary opposition with its backers, on the other. In the midst of the brewing crises in England and Scotland, a group of Irish Catholics rose up in rebellion in 1641, attacking the Protestants living in their midst. Possibly three thousand died, more from deprivation than murder, but Protestant reporting in England inflated the figure to ten thousand. Parliamentarians suspected that the king had a hand in this uprising, for they understood it as part of his assault on true religion. When he was later caught considering the use of Irish (Catholic) troops to suppress his rebellious (Protestant) opponents in England and Scotland, his godly Protestant subjects became convinced that he would go to any lengths to punish and destroy them. In two civil wars fought in England (1642–1646 and 1648), Parliament was twice victorious.

In January 1649, Parliament tried and executed Charles for crimes against his subjects. The spectators at his execution reportedly let out a huge groan as his head fell from his shoulders, shocked at the idea of killing a king whom some saw as anointed by God. A supporter wrote an account claiming to be Charles's own pious reflections on his fate, and the book stalls were soon filled with this tract, *Eikon Basilike*. It would prove a runaway best seller not only in England but also elsewhere in Europe. Support for the killing of the king was not as widespread as the revolutionaries would have liked. Nonetheless, a faction within Parliament then created a new government, a republic, ruled by the remnant of the parliament elected in 1640, "without king or house of Lords."[10] In 1653, this government was replaced by the protectorate of army general Oliver Cromwell and, at his death (1658), briefly by that of his son, Richard. A period of indecision followed, with Parliament nominally in control of the government. In 1660, Charles II, the son of the executed king, regained the throne, in an event known in British history as "the Restoration." Two decades of major political and social upheaval were brought to an end only with this Restoration.

These two decades had major consequences for the development of religion in the three kingdoms and in the wider Atlantic world. For a time Charles's ecclesiastical projects were overturned. The church in Scotland was able to return to its former practices. For England and Wales, Parliament declared the Church of England illegal. A similar fate met the Protestant Church of Ireland. Church courts were closed, the office of bishop ceased to function, and the Prayer Book rite was proscribed. In some areas, crowds of local residents or soldiers engaged in acts of iconoclasm, destroying symbols of the church that violated their Reformed expectations. Attacking aspects of worship that reminded them of popery, they continued the work of a previous generation of destructive reformers, pulling down communion rails, smashing stained glass, and defacing religious statuary. Reforms that the puritan dissenters within the church had wanted for decades were brought about in these years.

Smashing the established church would prove easier than erecting a new one in its stead. The vast majority of concerned individuals in England, Wales, and Scotland would have agreed that an established church was desirable. Permitting complete religious freedom and a plethora of competing options was a radical path that did not have widespread support. The difficulty came with the need to agree on what the new establishment would look like, not to mention the challenges of erecting it once agreement was achieved. The Westminster Assembly of Divines, a group of clergy (or "divines") appointed by Parliament, worked to create a new national church for England and Wales. The assembly endorsed a Presbyterian plan, which had support from some of the former puritan faction in the old Church of England. In allying with the Scots in the war against Charles, Parliament's agents had agreed to the Solemn League and Covenant. According to the Scots, the covenant committed Parliament to create a uniform church in both kingdoms based on the Scottish model. This interpretation was controversial, however, and some complained that the Scots were trying to foist their faith on England. The recommendations of the Westminster Assembly were not universally popular among parliamentary supporters, in part because they did not accommodate those who wanted a decentralized church order, more along the lines of that being erected in Congregationalist New England. The proposed church establishment also disadvantaged anyone adhering to any of the new sects that were springing up all over the three kingdoms in this time of upheaval. The assembly and those in Parliament who supported its work wanted to keep a lid on religious experimentation.

Ultimately no comprehensive national system was put into place. Rather, an effort was made to examine current and prospective clergy for doctrinal and ecclesiastical acceptability. This system used the titles (rather humorous to modern ears) of tryers, for those who interviewed prospective clergy, and ejectors, for those who dismissed sitting clergy who proved unacceptable. In both England and Wales, Church of England clergy who had supported Charles's policies lost their positions, and the new ministers generally endorsed extemporaneous preaching and congregational discipline while rejecting the established church liturgy and the wearing of vestments. But, despite its prohibited status, the Church of England rite was still practiced, not always surreptitiously. John Evelyn reported in his diary that he attended a Church of England service held in a church building in London in the 1650s.[11] The rite was also banned in all the colonies in the early 1650s, with equally incomplete results. Church of England practice continued there as well, sometimes quietly and in other cases quite openly.

In the meantime, religious diversity rose sharply. With church courts and the Church of England pulled down, people felt free to engage in religious experimentation. Baptists, who had been members of a small and illegal sect prior to 1642, won numerous converts to their gathered churches of baptized believers. A new movement, its members derisively dubbed "Quakers" for their tendency to express their spirituality with physical movement, grew at a great rate from about 1650. Quakers preached that salvation was potentially available to all, that an educated ministry and even the office of minister were offensive, and that anyone who felt a call could preach. With their unstructured meetings and often confrontational style, they were seen as extremely radical. Other, ultimately more ephemeral, movements also developed. The Muggletonians followed prophecies delivered by two "witnesses," John Reeve and Lodowick Muggleton. Scholars long thought the movement faded in the seventeenth century, but it was not until the mid-twentieth century that the last Muggletonian died. Soldiers in the parliamentary army—the New Model Army—were often quite radical, both religiously and politically. Once the reconquest of Ireland was complete, for instance, New Model Army soldiers introduced the Baptist faith there: ten churches limiting admission to baptized adult believers founded by 1653 had risen to 130 by 1660. Radical ideas and movements were in wide circulation in the former kingdoms and in the colonies as well.

While the sheer diversity of beliefs and practices that emerged in this period makes it difficult to characterize the movements as a whole, they shared some common features that contributed to their radicalism. None of the sects or movements that came into existence or moved out of hiding in this period endorsed a church hierarchy; all were decentralized. None upheld the idea of an educated ministry; all looked to uneducated but gifted individuals to lead them, in some cases even accepting the idea (shocking at the time) that women might preach. Some, like the Muggletonians, believed that particular individuals of modest backgrounds were receiving messages directly from God; many prophetic voices were raised in this period. Their beliefs covered a wide range, from the Calvinism of some Baptist churches to the belief in the possibility of universal salvation that characterized the Quakers and others. Numerous groups believed the end was near, anticipating the appearance of Christ to render a last judgment or, in the views of some, the beginning of a thousand years of peace and plenty ruled over by the godly few prior to the arrival of Christ for the judgment. Civil wars and regicide seemed to portend these changes, and not just to those radicals on the fringes either. The two decades of revolution were an exciting or terrifying time, depending on one's perspective on the regicide and rising radicalism of the era.

One man who symbolized for his enemies the excesses of this period was a minister named Hugh Peter. Born in about 1598, Peter received a degree at the University of Cambridge and sought a position in the Church of England. One of the great puritan aristocrats, the Earl of Warwick, promoted Peter's career and protected him when his criticism of royal policy landed him in trouble. Eventually Peter fled to the Continent, where he became the pastor of the English church at Rotterdam. In 1635, that church was forced to conform to the Church of England, so Peter and his wife returned briefly to England before joining the migration to Massachusetts Bay. There he accepted the call to serve as minister to the church of Salem, where he stayed until the colonial government sent him to England in 1641 as one of three agents that were to represent its interests to Parliament. Peter soon took a post as military chaplain, and his zeal for the godly (and antiroyal) cause combined with his persuasive preaching brought him to a prominent place in the movement. Increasingly involved in politics, Peter favored radical solutions to the problems besetting his native England. When the king was executed in 1649, Peter—although at home sick in bed—was rumored to be the masked executioner who lobbed off the king's head. This rumor demonstrated the man's reputation for radicalism. Later, when his friend Oliver Cromwell was Lord Protector of all of England, Scotland, Ireland and the colonies, he appointed Peter one of his personal chaplains. A New Englander visiting him at that time found him residing in the lavish apartments that had once belonged to Archbishop Laud, which both men considered a lovely joke. From the harassment he first experienced to his prominence during the revolutionary years, Peter's life indicated the drastic nature of the transformation England underwent from 1640 to 1660.

In this climate of freedom and experimentation, pamphlets on religious subjects poured from the presses. These printed materials, addressing a great variety of religious topics, circulated widely. Some of the books were relatively innocuous guides to piety for the Christian believer, while others debated doctrine or argued over the proper church order. Some were sensational, laying out prophecies or advocating practices, such as lay preaching or easily arranged divorce, which had recently been illegal. Books and tracts of all description passed into colonies throughout the Atlantic world, despite efforts of authorities in some locales to prevent their circulation. The leaders of most of the New England colonies were apoplectic at the prospect that a Quaker book might come into the hands of anyone living there. Only a minority of the texts published, however, were provocative or partisan, whether raising novel or controversial ideas or simply advocating for a particular approach to questions of faith. The mere fact that the general public was invited to consider such questions was a new—and to conservatives frightening—change. Views were publicly debated that had never been freely articulated before, ranging from anticlericalism to the possibility of living free of sin. The massive heresiography—or study of heresies—compiled by Presbyterian minister Thomas Edwards, *Gangraena*, provides a glimpse into the worry that the outpouring of new ideas and practices caused in certain circles. Many reformers who would be happy to see the Church of England renovated were appalled at the religious questioning that occurred in the context of the revolution.

Radicalism was a transatlantic phenomenon. Before the Restoration every one of the former Stuart kingdoms boasted Baptist churches and Quaker meetings. Baptists, Quakers, and other radicals also made their way to the Atlantic colonies. When Oliver Cromwell in 1655 sent out a fleet to attack Spanish America, it sailed with numerous radicals on board. Barbadian planters voiced complaints that they were infecting and converting the populace, when the fleet paused on that island for some months. Quaker missionaries traveled through Europe as well as throughout the English Atlantic, making converts as they went. Barbados and Rhode Island became early centers of Quakerism, although by 1660 only one or two colonies had not yet received missionary visits. Some colonists shuttled back and forth between England and the plantations, bringing back new ideas and occasionally new affiliations when they returned to a colony. Samuel Gorton, for instance, a leader of the settlement at Warwick, Rhode Island, frequented radical London circles when he traveled to England. (He named the town to honor the Earl of Warwick, who protected him from punishment for his radicalism at one point in his career.) Others joined new groups—like the Quakers—on visits to England, bringing their views home with them when they returned. If the initial migration had sent English and Irish Catholics as well as English puritans and separatists into Atlantic settlements that the authorities had intended would host only Church of England adherents, then the circulation of people and ideas during the two decades after 1640 introduced further diversity.

In both England and the colonies, the collapse of the established church and the rise in diversity were accompanied by a discussion of the benefits of liberty of conscience. The idea was an extremely radical one—going far beyond toleration, which assumes that the minority position is wrong but may be permitted to exist. Liberty posits that each person ought to find his or her own way to the truth and that no one ought to punish anyone else for their religious views. Advocates of liberty, such as Rhode Island founder Roger Williams, might uphold it on the grounds that people were likely to arrive at erroneous positions and that the important thing was to stop them (and the state) from interfering in the devotions of the godly few. Others, like the Quakers, believed that people would arrive at the truth if left free to do so, and they advocated liberty as a way to make their own specific message widely available. Oliver Cromwell believed that a range of religious positions was essentially godly—including those of the various radical groups active in the New Model Army that he led for years—and that liberty, by allowing them freedom to voice their views, represented a positive good. Cromwell sought to combine limited liberty with a strenuous educational and evangelical program that would eventually bring all to embrace Reformed Protestantism.

Often those who spoke in favor of liberty wanted to grant it only to like-minded Protestants, seeing Roman Catholic and, especially in the current political context, Church of England adherents as beyond the pale. Two colonies in this period made such limited liberty their set policy—neither Rhode Island nor Maryland constrained the consciences of those whose views fell within broad parameters. In Maryland at least these parameters explicitly included Catholics, whereas Rhode Islanders were probably thinking in terms of granting liberty only to Protestant Christians.[12] Although never the dominant viewpoint, liberty of conscience was openly discussed and debated in these decades, expanding the range of publicly expressed positions on this controversial issue.

With the explosion of sectarianism, the collapse of the national Church of England, and the debate over liberty, some ministers struggled to maintain a parish-based church against the drift away from geographically defined religious communities. The sectarian solution to the problem was to opt into the group of one's choice, thereby turning one's back on neighbors and even family members. These exclusive groups then saw to their own intragroup needs without regard for those beyond their boundaries.

On the island colony of Bermuda, this approach was adopted when the island's ministers decided to reform the churches. In concert, they quit serving the entire population but instead gathered an exclusive church with membership limited to those they deemed godly. To qualify for church membership individuals had to persuade the ministers and their fellow believers that they had experienced conversion. Those who had not enjoyed the requisite experience or who could not persuade others that they had done so were not granted the privileges of membership. The ministers urged those who were excluded to receive instruction and hear their preaching in the hope that they would someday qualify for membership. This move effectively "unchurched" the majority of the islanders, who were left without clergy to administer baptism or communion. This group vehemently objected that the clergy, having adopted the puritan view that marriage ought to be a civil ceremony, would no longer perform marriages. A highly unpopular policy change with many Bermudans, the introduction of a congregational order became the focus of a major political struggle on the island. It ended only when the Independent faction was banished, and the remaining islanders returned to a parish-based church order.

Some clergy wanted to keep the parish structure, which drew the entire local community into the church, but at the same time they wanted to remake the churches in a Reformed direction. They endorsed effective church discipline, even though they had opposed the ecclesiastical courts that had

Mr, Richard Mather,

Fig. 5. Richard Mather migrated to Massachusetts with his family in 1635 and served the Dorchester Church as its minister until his death in 1669. This 1670 woodcut by John Foster, the first such image produced in English America, revealed the austere style of the puritan movement. Mather holds a book, indicating the importance of literacy and a learned ministry to pious Protestants. Courtesy of the American Antiquarian Society, Worcester, Massachusetts.

enforced discipline under Charles I. In the new religious environment at mid-century, discipline that was too aggressive could drive away members who felt unfairly censured, while lax control might force the godly sort to leave in order to gather a pure church. Richard Baxter, minister at Kiddermis-ter, England, struggled during these years with this issue, finally refusing to administer communion for fear of offending one faction or the other. He knew some of his parishioners would object if he included those who did not appear to be stellar Christians but that excluding such persons would alienate them instead. What clergy like Baxter wanted was what the Massachusetts Bay clergy enjoyed: state support for their parish-based churches that only granted full membership privileges to the godly but prevented disgruntled parishioners from leaving altogether. Effective discipline on the parish level was well-nigh impossible without coercive mechanisms in place to enforce unpopular policies.

The central change in religion throughout the English Atlantic world in this era might be described as puritanization. The puritans, as opponents of Charles's efforts to impose religious conformity, had fought to bring about a number of reforms that became the official policy of the English government in these decades. They wanted an end to the office of bishop, which effec-tively ceased to exist during this era. They also wanted to see the church embrace Reformed preaching, intensive instruction, and effective discipline. Men with these views gained control of the public expression of religion in England, Wales, and many of the colonies (and regained control of the churches in Scotland and Protestant Ireland). The most puritan-inclined col-onies were generally those that had gone into the civil wars with a commit-ment to reformation, including all the New England colonies save for Rhode Island—in this era, that included Massachusetts and Connecticut but also New Haven and Plymouth, both separate colonies. Other places, such as Bermuda, Maryland, Virginia, Barbados, and, once it was conquered by Cromwell's fleet in 1656, Jamaica, also moved in this direction. Reformers throughout the Atlantic basin pulled down the Church of England and put into place programs to pursue their agenda. They made efforts, eventually through the formal system of tryers and ejectors, to verify the acceptability of any minister holding a parish pulpit. The Scottish Presbyterians launched a campaign to convert Gaelic-speaking Highlanders to their church, unsuc-cessfully attempting to produce a Gaelic Bible for use in the project. The Commission for the Propagation of the Gospel in Wales (established in 1650) collected tithes, using the money to fund itinerant ministers. That program was vigorous and fairly successful. Sabbath laws and other legislation associated with the puritan movement were enacted in colonies that had not previously had them. Bermuda's clergy were so taken with the prospects for puritanization that they founded an Independent church on the island against the wishes of a majority of settlers, at least for a time.

The heightened concern for discipline may also have led to an increase in witchcraft prosecutions. The belief in witchcraft was widespread and, in theory at least, any confessional group might conduct a witch prosecution. But in the mid-1640s an upsurge in witch-hunting occurred, not only in the traditionally puritan region of East Anglia (in England) but also in New England and Bermuda. In Massachusetts witches and strange religious opinions were collapsed together in a call for a special day of fasting and prayer, asking God for protection from these two evils. One of the rare men to be executed for witchcraft was John Middletown, a long-time Bermuda resident who had participated in a host of illegal activities, from sex with a cow to harming his neighbors through witchcraft. Scotland similarly experienced witchcraft prosecutions, and it did so when the more militant Presbyterians (known as the "Covenanters") regained control of the church and its disciplinary arm. Since witches were understood to be linked to Satan's battle against the godly, a heightened sense of embattlement and an increase in the power of the most vigorous disciplinarians sparked a hunt for witches in various locations.

The triumph of puritanism shaped the religious politics of the wider Atlantic world. As the new settlements were drawn into the religious battles of the center, positions that had once coexisted peacefully—such as mainstream and puritan factions in the Church of England—became polarized. During the 1650s, hewing to the older form of the Church of England made a royalist statement in favor of monarchy. After the Restoration in 1660, continued adherence to puritan positions would be seen as opposition to the monarchy. Confessional identity, or the church an individual joined, came to be read as a sign of political position in a way that had not been true in the period before 1640. Anti-Catholicism continued as a major force in the English Atlantic, even given a boost by the rise to power of those who had been the strongest advocates of an antipapist agenda. Two dramatic expressions of this impulse were civil war in Maryland between Protestant and Catholic settlers and the 1655 invasion of the Spanish colonies in the West Indies. In Maryland colonists hostile to proprietor Baltimore's Catholicism hoped that political shifts in England would result in his ouster. When they did not, his opponents went on the offensive, seizing power away from his appointees and routing Catholic forces at the Battle of the Severn. According to their highly partisan account, the battlefield was strewn with religious medals and other objects of popish idolatry, information that was intended to scandalize Protestants.

The decision on the part of England's leaders to invade the Spanish West Indies drew upon the long-standing opposition to Spanish wealth and power. The war itself was framed in part as a religious war against the popery and cruelty of the Spanish in the Americas. Scholars have seen this rhetoric as a throwback to Elizabethan conceptions of international politics, but in fact Oliver Cromwell and those around him had always held views similar to their Elizabethan forbearers. English printers published translations of the works of the sixteenth-century Spanish Dominican Bartolomé de las Casas, broadcasting his attacks on Spanish cruelty to the Indians in order to encourage support for war against Spain. In doing so they were following a practice that had been started by the Protestant Dutch, and used by the English previously as well, of trotting out the Dominican's testimony whenever feelings against Spain were running especially high. At the conquest of Jamaica, the army's offer of terms for the surrender required all Catholics to leave the island at once; in this the English went further than the Dutch, who, despite fighting a long and devastating war against the Spanish to gain their independence, did not drive all Catholics off Curaçao when they conquered it in 1634. They expected to convert the Spanish, along with the Portuguese, their children, and "also the blacks and Indians," to Reformed Protestant Christianity, but in the meantime they permitted them to remain.[13] England's more extreme anti-Catholicism was both consistent with the triumph of puritan politics and another result of the heightened religious tensions of this era.

For a time, certain New England colonies had the only viable religious establishments in the entire British Atlantic world, launched by those who had been considered outliers only a few years before. After the abolition of the Church of England, only those colonies that had never embraced it in the first place were free to continue conducting their ecclesiastical affairs as they had prior to the Parliament's rise to power. Plymouth, Massachusetts Bay, Connecticut, and New Haven colonies had all legislated their own religious establishments that supported a Congregational church order. Under Charles I, they had found it necessary to be circumspect about the nature of those religious establishments, but once others who also opposed the Church of England triumphed in England, they publicized their system as a possible model for a revised ecclesiastical system there. Church and state in each of these colonies were intimately intertwined. Their societies were shaped by the precepts of godly order, so that it was, for instance, a capital offense in Massachusetts for a son to talk back to his father. Although the most extreme laws were rarely invoked, they demonstrated the concern to follow biblical precedents in many areas of life. The authorities encouraged community watchfulness, in which neighbor kept an eye on neighbor, in order to ensure that social discipline was enforced. Only in New England did church and state work so closely and effectively.

In this altered context, the governments of New England attacked the spread of Quakerism in a way that no other elites felt able to do. While Quakers encountered mild opposition or even limited toleration in other parts of the Atlantic world, Massachusetts authorities aggressively suppressed them. They banned Quaker literature and blocked any Quaker from entering the colony. Despite these efforts, Quaker preachers traveled throughout New England spreading their views until Massachusetts legislated banishment on pain of death. Four people, including one elderly woman, defied the order of banishment. They were executed. Quakers would accuse New Englanders of having fled persecution in England only to turn into persecutors themselves in America. They responded that they had migrated in order to practice the one true faith, a faith they were defending by preventing Quakers from spreading pernicious doctrines.

Heightened millennial expectations were another aspect of religion during these years. Millennialism is the belief in the imminent end of the present world as foretold in the biblical book Revelation, and the creation of a long era of peace and righteousness before the final return of Christ or after his return. Promoters of the Virginia Company explored these themes, seeing the colony as a harbinger of dramatic change. Seventeenth-century radical Protestants were particularly interested in biblical prophecy, and they tended to interpret extraordinary events (such as revolution and regicide) as signs pointing toward their fulfillment. Many people wondered if they were living at the dawn of a new era. Those who fought against Charles I saw their victory as resulting from God's providential intervention in human affairs. Some also interpreted it in terms of eschatology, as a sign of the coming end of the world. Numerous publications discussing prophecy and linking it to current events issued from the London presses.

Some of the energy behind the explosion of sectarianism was millenarian. The Quakers were propelled by this excitement. Another group was the Fifth

Monarchists who hoped that Oliver Cromwell would provide leadership in bringing about the millennium. When he failed to do so, a minority in the movement, led by former New Englander Thomas Venner, rose up, trying to rally their fellow English men and women to fight the government in a last desperate attempt to inaugurate Christ's reign on earth. Colonists in New England and elsewhere, watching with amazement the upheavals in their homelands, speculated about the meaning of events, often putting them in a millennial framework. Efforts to catechize Indians for the first time and discussion of whether to permit Jews to reside in England once again were both fueled by millennial understandings of the necessary preconditions for Christ's second coming. Millennial hopes coursed powerfully through the English Atlantic during the two decades from 1640 to 1660.

The radical Protestants who controlled England in the 1640s and 1650s readmitted the Jews, who had been banished from the country in 1290. One motivation for this was millennial. Eschatological thinkers expected Christian conversion of the Jews to herald the end of time. This conviction fostered support for readmitting the Jews, which would supposedly encourage their conversion by exposing them to English Christianity. Newly created Protestant churches in England emphasized the Old Testament in a way that fostered an affinity for Judaism. Hugh Peter sought to alter English law by basing it on biblical law conveyed by the prophet Moses. New England legal codes in this period departed from English law in numerous instances, almost always by opting for the Mosaic alternative. This system proscribed the death penalty for rebellious sons as well as for adulterous spouses. Moreover, the popular belief that the English were God's chosen people, encouraged by John Foxe's Book of Martyrs, connected contemporary English Christians to the Jews of the Old Testament. New England preachers made this connection. Leaders in English Protestant churches—Baptists and Independents especially—developed relations with leaders of European Jewry, such as Menasseh Ben Israel, the Amsterdam rabbi who worked for the return of the Jews to England. He and his brother-in-law, another Dutch Jew, traveled repeatedly to England to appeal directly to Cromwell for readmission. Their appeals succeeded. Even before this decision had been reached, Jews resided in a number of English colonies, having been driven out of Brazil when the Portuguese recaptured Pernambuco from the Dutch (1654). Brazil, Surinam (then an English colony), Jamaica, and Rhode Island as well as London all boasted Sephardic Jewish inhabitants by 1660.

Interest was also piqued on the question of the conversion of Native

Americans during these decades, for some similar reasons. For the first time since colonization began in 1607, a few English settlers seriously attempted to convert the Indians to Christianity. Missionary work had supposedly always been central to colonization, but little discussion and almost no action had occurred in the first decades of settlement. Pocahontas's transformation into Rebecca Rolfe was the dramatic exception to the general rule. In the 1640s a handful of New Englanders engaged in the work. By this time the French had established missions and two female religious orders in Quebec, while the Spanish had organized missions in New Mexico and Florida, not to mention their extensive activity farther south.

Among the English missionaries, Roxbury pastor John Eliot took the lead. Cotton Mather would later dub him "Apostle to the Indians." Eliot studied Massachusett, a southern New England Algonquian language, and he published a Bible in that language with the aid of native interpreters in 1663. For decades from the 1640s he preached to various Indian groups and educated select native men to preach as well. He conceived a system of Praying Indian Villages in which neophytes would learn to live as Christians with an English lifestyle. Eliot and other Protestants assumed that to become Christian, native peoples had to live as Europeans did, in settled towns with farms and family dwellings. These European missionaries could not envision an Indian person living in a traditional way—hunting, gathering, planting, and moving about seasonally to accommodate these activities—while at the same time worshiping as a Christian. They equated English civility—by which they meant all the social practices that they associated with a civilized life—as a prerequisite to Christian conversion. Native Americans were asked not simply to change their beliefs and religious practices but to change everything about their lives. Given that Native American life was entirely permeated with the spiritual, the missionaries were perhaps as astute about as they were prejudiced against Indian ways.

Eliot and others wrote accounts of the mission that were published in England to generate support for the project, and, in 1649, Parliament created a corporation empowered to collect funds to sustain the effort. Support was widespread in England and Wales, partly a continuation of the earlier expectation that such activity would be integral to the establishment of plantations. In some circles, speculation that the native peoples of the Americas descended from the biblical "lost Tribes of Israel" was taken to indicate that their conversion should be a high priority. If the Jews had to be converted before the end of the world, then Indians (who at this time were widely thought to be descendants of the Jews) would be among those targeted. Some people thought the discovery of the Americas was part of God's plan to bring Christianity to these benighted natives in preparation for the end of time. Support for the praying villages and the entire missionary campaign was decidedly lower among settlers themselves, who were either hostile to Indians in general or doubted the efficacy of conversion efforts. Eliot himself said that keeping native neophytes away from hostile colonists by segregating them into villages of their own was one reason for the structure of the program. Roger Williams, who had relatively positive relations with the indigenous residents of the Narragansett Bay region, thought little of the conversion efforts. He argued that more energy should be put into converting those in the "darke corners of the land" in England and Wales instead. Others, including Hugh Peter, voiced similar views.

Indian missions were not easily sold to native peoples either. The most successful conversion effort in New England occurred on the island of Martha's Vineyard. There the settler population was small, and the original inhabitants were able to maintain largely autonomous communities. On the mainland, the group that first approached the Massachusetts Bay government to indicate its willingness to receive missionaries was propelled by the need to squelch tensions brewing with the encroaching English settlers. Accepting missionaries was expected to bring protection, both from rival Indians and from hostile colonists. Forming a Praying Indian Village also helped to carve out some land for a native community, land that would have been otherwise absorbed by a new colonial town. This strategy to protect native land worked for a time.

With the emphasis in the praying towns on anglicizing as well as Christianizing, the decision to join one had wide-ranging implications. Published accounts describing Indian converts' questions and concerns as they went through the process of education and offered themselves for church membership reveal that native peoples struggled with the drastic changes that conversion entailed. One tract recorded the concern that God might not understand Native American languages. If that were the case, then prayers from an Indian person would go unheeded. This worry arose, interestingly, when an unconverted man taunted a convert with this argument. Others raised complicated theological issues about how to square traditional practices with the requirements of Christian living. A man with an infertile first wife from whom he had parted and a second wife who had borne numerous children sparked the query: if the Christian ethos found only his first marriage valid, what became of the children of the second union? Such exchanges suggest some of the debates that occurred within native communities over the introduction of a new god and a new religious system.

Native Americans seem to have engaged with missionaries and joined Praying Indian Villages because, in doing so, they saw an opportunity to protect aspects of their traditional culture and to keep their communities intact. Indeed, the Congregationalist church structure that fostered a high level of local autonomy probably made that option especially attractive to Indian converts who were gathering all-native churches. Despite the best efforts of missionaries, Indians did not abandon all their former beliefs and practices. The native ability to blend new and old allowed them to maintain much of their former perspective while adding Christian elements to it. For instance, among the Wampanoags of Martha's Vineyard, Satan was equated with a local deity associated with death. The identification of such similarities amounted to an act of "religious translation" across a cultural divide.[14]

Native peoples who retained traditional burial practices did so while incorporating artifacts associated with the new Christian faith. One grave site in Rhode Island contained a medal given by French Jesuits to converts or potential converts in New France. Apparently via trade networks, the object made its way to southern New England where it was sufficiently prized to be placed in a grave. Its final owner probably did not understand the medal in precisely the way the Jesuit priests had intended—if he knew of its origins at all—but Christian missionaries could never control the ways in which their message (or their artifacts) were received. Possibly the inclusion of a page of an Indian-language Bible in another grave indicated a greater appreciation of the import of that religious icon, although the use of it as a powerful object did not quite suit the Reformed Protestant sensibility, which opposed relics of any kind. In the Reformed view, the word had power but not as an artifact. Still the native convert who took the page into the afterlife valued it according to his own understanding. Such cultural blending, which involved a reformulation of Christian and traditional beliefs to emphasize commonalities between them, shaped the Native American encounter with Protestantism, as it already had in the Catholic French and Spanish colonies.

Of more widespread impact in the short run was the way in which the presence of Europeans in North America altered native practices separate from the introduction of Christianity. The Iroquois tradition of the mourning wars offers a good example of how the changed circumstances brought by the invasion from Europe affected ritual and its functionality in native lives. According to Iroquoian belief, a death diminished the spiritual power of a community and especially of the clan that suffered the loss. In order to replenish that lost power and to assuage the grief of those who did not find healing in less dramatic therapies, a practice developed for incorporating a new person into the community in the place of the one who had been lost. War captives could serve that function—either by being adopted into the bereaved family as a sort of replacement or by being ritually killed at the behest of the mourners. Either approach, adoption or torture and death, was expected to heal the wounds of the bereaved and to replace the lost spiritual power. The bodies of those who died in these ceremonies might be consumed by an entire village in a ritual that had a symbolic and religious significance that horrified European observers failed to grasp. These practices, which dated from long before 1500, continued into the eighteenth century. As the death rate among the Iroquois rose dramatically with the influx of illnesses and sharp upturn in warfare resulting from the arrival of Europeans, the community found it had to limit the practice. It did so in part by creating alliances that reduced the number of potential enemies to be confronted in mourning wars. At the same time, however, the practice continued. In the face of European objections and demographic pressures, the Iroquois adapted but maintained this ritual practice.[15]

This blending of Christian and non-Christian belief and practice was apparent among Africans as well. Slave traders brought large numbers of Africans to some English colonies during these years, and this influx of laborers raised the question among colonial slave masters of the proper religious identity of their slaves. By 1660, Barbados, which had led the way for the English colonies in this shift to slave labor, had twenty thousand African slaves. The other Anglo-Caribbean islands had twenty-five hundred between them, and Virginia had about one thousand.[16] It was not clear what relationship these laborers were to have to the churches of their respective colonies. Although millennial expectations might encourage conversion efforts aimed at Indians because of the perceived connections between the coming of the millennium, the conversion of the Jews, and the alleged identity of Indians as Jews, no such reasoning linked Africans to biblical prophecy.

Not only did they lack this religious motivation to convert Africans; colonists also worried that conversion might strengthen a slave's claim for freedom. Two theoretical justifications existed for slavery: slaves should be either captives in a just war, who had forfeited their lives and so could have the sentence commuted to enslavement, or non-Christians. In the early mod-

ern Mediterranean region, Christians enslaved Muslims and Muslims enslaved Christians using these justifications. After a person enslaved on these
grounds converted, theoretically freedom would result. Fully half of the Barbary pirates preying on European shipping in this era were so-called renegade
Christians, having converted to Islam and gained their liberty after their
capture. Although European Christian slave masters worried that freedom
might be the result of conversion, evidence suggests that they never adopted
the practice. In the Spanish colonies, slaves were baptized without earning
their freedom, and a number of slaves sold in the early English colonies were
already Christian but of the Roman Catholic variety. Nevertheless, in the
colonies masters occasionally cited worries that conversion might mean freedom for their chattel as a reason to oppose their Christianization.

They also worried that slaves would use either the literacy that was typically a part of the Protestant conversion process or the very message of Christianity against their masters. Richard Ligon, who resided in Barbados in the
late 1640s, was not permitted to catechize a slave owned by another for these
reasons. William Penn, father of the founder of Pennsylvania, purchased a
slave because the man desired Christian instruction that his master denied
him. We do not know if the slave Anthony eventually became a Christian or,
if he did, whether Penn had any compunction about continuing to hold him
as a slave. The hesitation of Anthony's original master offered further evidence that masters in the seventeenth-century English Atlantic often opposed
the conversion of their chattel. As a result, little effort was made during this
period to convert the newly imported slaves who were especially numerous
in Barbados. In contrast, Africans living in England as servants in elite households seem to have been routinely baptized into the Church of England.
They were also regularly painted in portraits waiting upon their master or
mistress, a common artistic practice in portraiture of the English elite in the
seventeenth century. One early planter who had the audacity to suggest another link between Christianity and slavery—that Christians should not hold
slaves, regardless of the religion of the enslaved—got no hearing for his views.
Indeed he temporarily lost his position on the governor's Council in the
Providence Island Colony for expressing them.

In spite of these prohibitions, European observers could not help wondering about the religious beliefs of these exotic people, much as they did
about those of Native Americans. Their records offered early examples of
amateur anthropology, that impulse to record the different religious systems
prevailing among peoples met in the course of travel. Their observations,

made across barriers of language and culture, were not particularly astute, which makes it difficult for historians to use the evidence. For instance, Barbados resident Richard Ligon offered this assessment: "Religion they know none: yet most of them acknowledge a God, as appears by their motions and gestures; for, if one of them do another wrong, and he cannot revenge himself, he looks up to Heaven for vengeance, and holds up both his hands, as if the power must come from thence, that must do him right."[17]

That said, it is apparent that early captive Africans developed a blended religious culture. Brought together in the Caribbean, enslaved West Africans found common ground around certain concepts and practices with other slaves who came from similar backgrounds. A practice called Obeah offers one example of this phenomenon. In this case, various West African traditional beliefs were incorporated into a new system that allowed Africans to maintain previous religious identities while dealing with new physical circumstances. Obeah is a system of beliefs about the supernatural world and the ways in which people can intervene in it that draws upon West African roots but probably represents a melding of various traditions that occurred in the Atlantic colonies. Obeah practitioners were always natives of Africa, men or women who were African-born rather than children born in the colonies to enslaved parents. These specialists performed functions they may have first performed in their native Africa, although the range of services they provided seemed to have been much wider, encompassing those of healer, diviner, and spiritual guide. They cared for the ill and also foretold the future or uncovered the source of an illness or injury. Obeah practitioners provided objects, which Europeans called "fetishes," that were intended to keep the wearers safe. Slave rebels sometimes used such objects in order to protect themselves from death or capture. Their clients believed that Obeah men and women could discover witches and put an end to the harm they caused. As a result slaves often went to them for help in dealing with masters, and the Obeah specialists intervened to assist in coping with these oppressive relationships. Europeans therefore feared them. As one observed, after describing a dance that culminated in a trance-like state: "Whatever the prophetess orders to be done during this paroxysm, is most sacredly performed by the surrounding multitude; which renders these meetings extremely dangerous, as she frequently enjoins them to murder their masters, or desert to the woods."[18] In this case, traditional West African practices and beliefs had been adapted to the needs of a slave community, one that included a disparate population from numerous African locations.

A few Africans were already at least nominally Christian at the time of their enslavement. Some had been converted in the Kongolese region where Portuguese Catholic missionary efforts dated back over a century. Others had been exposed to Christian teachings in the colonies of Catholic Europeans, whether Spanish, Portuguese, or French. When Father Antoine Biet visited Barbados in 1654, he encountered slaves who had been converted in other colonies before being sold to the English Protestant masters. Biet reported that these slaves objected to having heretics as masters, although we might wonder whether it was the masters' status as heretics or simply as oppressors that was most objectionable.[19] Muslims, converted or born into Muslim families in Africa prior to capture, were also scattered among this early slave population. For this early period in particular, it is difficult to uncover details of the religious lives of these transported Africans.

The revolution that fueled religious diversity and cross-cultural conversation in the British Atlantic world between 1640 and 1660 came to an abrupt end with the Restoration of the Stuart monarchy in 1660. English support for the revolutionary republic declined until those who were willing to welcome the king's return arranged for Charles II to assume his executed father's place on the throne. This political counter-revolution halted the conditions that had allowed radicalism to flourish, putting on the defensive the religious and political groups that had arisen in the previous two decades. Among the small number of men who would be executed for their roles in the events of the previous two decades was the charismatic preacher Hugh Peter. The unfounded rumors that he had wielded the ax that had severed the head of Charles I came back to haunt Peter at this time, though he was officially killed for encouraging those who had ordered the regicide. The changed political climate pushed radical faiths underground or out of existence altogether.

The Restoration brought back the Church of England, but with differences. Writings about the "martyrdom" of Charles I offered the church its own hagiography, an account of a saint's life, similar to those in the Roman Catholic tradition. The link between loyalty to the church and to the monarchy, so recently a political liability, became a positive good, and the obverse—disloyalty and support for a religious alternative—a liability. Restoring the Church of England and addressing the various religious issues raised by revolution was the work of the next decade or more (and will be discussed in a subsequent chapter).

The Atlantic empire that Charles II regained in 1660 differed markedly

from the one his father had ruled over in 1640, and changes that had over-
taken it in the interim would not be reversed. This revolutionary interlude
had a particularly significant impact on British Atlantic religion by increasing
diversity within and beyond the Christian community, politicizing religious
positions, and sparking discussion of religious liberty in distant colonies not
so quickly influenced by political changes at home. By 1660 the newly instated monarch held a far-flung collection of colonies in the Atlantic world,
and controlled England, Wales, Scotland, and Ireland. Much of what had
been wrought in the decades of revolution since the founding of the first
successful English colony would remain as it was. The diversity among and
within kingdoms had been transferred into the wider Atlantic world and
exacerbated by the increased fragmentation of the revolutionary era. The
transplantation of religious institutions to the new plantations had ironically
been most successful in the case of New England congregationalism, a system
that necessitated the local control that an Atlantic setting encouraged. Hence
the first successful religious establishment in the English colonies had no
direct equivalent as an establishment in England or the other Stuart kingdoms.

Of necessity religious observance in the wider Atlantic was often a personal affair since individuals and families were bereft of institutional supports
for their faith. Thrown back on their own resources, believers acted on their
adherence to any one of a wide variety of faith traditions at work in the
region, including various forms of Christianity as well as Judaism, Islam, and
traditional Native American and African faiths. Believers navigated a complex
and variegated religious reality that had emerged by 1660, with profound
implications for the future of religion in the British Atlantic world.

FOUR

Restoration Settlement and the Growth
of Diversity

THE YEAR 1660 marks a traditional divide in the political history of Britain and the British Atlantic world. It brought an end to twenty years of revolutionary upheaval and a return of the Stuart dynasty to the throne. The political restoration of monarchy had predictable religious consequences, since, as a matter of course, the Church of England returned as the official state religion. Yet, the events of the previous two decades made it impossible to return to the status quo of 1640, a time when each of the three kingdoms had a distinctive established church, and diversity (save for the residual Catholicism) was comparatively rare. Since then, religious options had increased drastically. New approaches to religious difference had to be developed, and in the negotiation between old expectations and new realities, the colonies often led the way. By 1660, the English presence in the Atlantic had strengthened, with local governance structures that had largely survived the test of revolutionary upheaval, a colonial population of perhaps two hundred thousand; emerging regional differences; and a nascent imperial policy. Events of 1640 to 1660 had, to a large extent, shaped the religious culture of the plantations, and because of this the Restoration of 1660 did not herald a sharp reversal. Such changes as the rise of African slavery and the related influx of new beliefs, the first serious effort to convert Indians, the rising numbers of Europeans adhering to diverse versions of Christianity, and the novel presence of Jews continued. Changes in the institutional infrastructure furthered more than they hampered these trends, so that the two—official policy changes and long-term trends—tended to be mutually reinforcing. From 1660 to the end of the century, people at the imperial center and those on the periphery adjusted to this complex environment in which the one ruler–one faith model was overthrown.

The English colonial world was well on its way to becoming noteworthy for its religious multiplicity, a trend that was furthered by the rising number of African slaves after mid-century. The majority of the Africans who were imported into the English-controlled colonies before 1690 were adherents of traditional West African faiths. Where large numbers of slaves were imported—such as the Caribbean islands—these captive Africans melded various traditions into a shared system of belief and practices. In such settings, Europeans observed "Idolatrous dances" and other "Heathen rites" among Africans; one minister who criticized such practices argued that they ought to be eradicated by proselytizing slaves in the Christian faith.[1] Most masters left communal practices alone, however, unless they perceived them as threatening their own interests.

They evinced little concern for the salvation of their slaves, a neglect that was also reflected in the utter lack of attention to this issue that prevailed in the trading posts in West Africa itself. Whereas charters to establish colonies invariably mentioned the conversion of Indians, those granted to trading companies in Africa skirted the topic of religious mission. These trading forts were purely economic endeavors, and they eschewed any pretense of an evangelical role. Indeed, Charles II's charter of 1672 mentioned God only in laying out the wording of the oath that company officers were required to take—a clear indication that conversion was not an aspect of these endeavors.[2] Trading forts were analogous to royal naval ships in that they ideally had a chaplain to conduct services for the crew or, in this case, the company employees. Such was the outward limit of the English religious presence in Africa for generations.

With more frequent interactions with the Africans they purchased and employed, English planters had the means and the possible motive to Christianize their slaves; but only a few advocated that captive Africans receive instruction in these years. William Berkeley, long-time governor of Virginia, reportedly encouraged the conversion of three "Mahometan" (or Muslim) slaves, offering them freedom and a plantation if they would convert to the Church of England. According to a story later circulating in Virginia, he succeeded with two of the men, while the third held out, receiving baptism only at the age of eighty.[3] A handful of English or Welsh religious leaders advocated the Christianization of slaves. Traveling Quaker missionaries, such as George Fox, urged slave owners to teach their slaves about Christianity in Barbados and other colonies. Presbyterian Richard Baxter and Church of England clergyman Morgan Godwyn also went on record advocating missionary work among slaves. In 1669 Bermuda minister Samuel Smith requested permission of the governor's Council to baptize "Mulattoes, Indians, (and more especiallie) Negroes," but the Council unanimously agreed not to settle the question at that time. Eighteen years later the assembly was absolutely opposed to the practice.[4] Although the Bermuda Council may have been willing to consider the idea at one time, generally the pleas of the ministers interested in catechizing slaves fell on deaf ears. Masters continued to oppose their arguments and their efforts during the seventeenth century.

Given this modest advocacy, a handful of Africans converted to Christianity in the Restoration period. Generally these individuals lived in locations where few Africans resided. Low numbers of Africans reduced fears of mass revolt arising from unmediated access to literacy and to the message of Christianity, and encouraged closer contact between slaves and European colonists. In New England but also occasionally in early Virginia, slaves were often instructed within the households where they worked and lived, as masters extended to their slaves their traditional obligation to teach scriptures and the basic tenets of the Christian faith to their servants. In Virginia, while the slave population remained small (and the rate of manumission relatively high), Africans might become part of the local Christian culture. Wills from the mid-seventeenth century written by free blacks in Virginia were similar to those produced by other small landowners, regardless of race. That of Francis Payne, who died in 1673, opened with standard Protestant phrasing: "I bequethe my Soule to my almighty father . . . and to Jesus Christ who by his blessed and perfect suffering redeemed his servant [meaning Payne himself]."[5] Other last testaments include similar preambles, indicating the extent to which these first African Virginians took part in the Protestantism of the larger society.

A similar situation prevailed in seventeenth-century New England, where a handful of Africans became church members. That this was the case in spite of the relatively rigorous admission requirements that these Calvinist churches had in place demonstrated a deep commitment to the Christian faith on the part of these men and women. With at most only one or two slaves to a household, masters tended to include their bonds people in household religious practices of scripture reading and catechizing, as they did their servants. Because they lived in some isolation from their fellow Africans, these slaves could not create an exclusively African spiritual community. They also experienced greater exposure to Christianity as practiced among the local European population. Under the circumstances, they became incorporated into the churches of their masters, at least in small numbers during this era. In locations where slave imports were few prior to 1690, the possibilities for Africans to create a blending of traditional elements brought from their homeland were concomitantly limited, at least in the short term.

Despite the Christianization of few Africans in the seventeenth-century English colonies, many masters fretted over the issue, inclined to oppose the practice. Among owners with many slaves or in regions with a heavy concentration of slaves, fears that conversion would make bondsmen and bondwomen eligible for freedom worked against evangelization, as did worries that slaves could use literacy skills associated with catechizing or the very message of Christianity itself to combat their enslavement. Slaves and freed Africans had joined the Dutch Reformed Church in New Netherland. At least with the colony's conquest by English forces in 1664, and perhaps somewhat earlier, however, the church dropped the practice of converting slaves. As the numbers of slaves grew and as owners became nervous about the implications of Christianization for freedom, they ceased catechizing or permitting the baptism of their chattel. After 1664, no more black couples were married in the Dutch church, although over two dozen such unions had been recognized in the twenty-three years before that date.

In other locations, English masters often made no effort to catechize their slaves. Frequently they prohibited preachers from gaining access to them. Clergymen of the Church of England occasionally spoke in favor of the evangelization of Africans, but they had little success in persuading masters. With vestries (committees of elite male parishioners) managing the Church of England ecclesiastical apparatus in the colonies, ministers relied on local leaders for their appointment, their salary, and help disciplining wayward members. This reliance reduced the ministers' ability to act independently. Beholden to slave masters, ministers generally did their bidding on the issue of slave conversion as on other matters.

The Society of Friends—although it would later lead the fight against slavery—did not take an unequivocal stance on Christianization, much less abolition, in the seventeenth century. After Quaker leader George Fox visited the Caribbean in the early 1670s and advocated that masters teach their slaves about Christianity, the Quaker community in Barbados apparently heeded his advice. In 1676, the governor's Council declared it illegal for slaves to attend Quaker meetings; at the same time the Council members also barred any stranger from preaching on the island, in an effort to reduce Quaker outreach generally and among slaves in particular. In this instance Friends had to be forcibly stopped from catechizing their slaves by the authorities. As far as surviving records suggest, this was the high point of the sect's catechical efforts. It would never take a lead in that work again, and few Africans became members of the Society of Friends.

The Society's later commitment to ending the slave trade and eventually the institution of slavery itself was not much in evidence in this era. On the North American mainland, Quakers took a few small steps in opposition to slavery, but they hesitated to fight it aggressively at this time. In 1688 four German-speaking Quaker men living in Germantown, Pennsylvania petitioned against the practice, advocating that their co-religionists end their association with the institution. They argued that slavery encouraged slaves to commit adultery (by tearing apart their families) and to rebel; it sullied the reputation of the sect; and it violated the golden rule of "do unto others as you would have them do unto you." The local Quaker community took no action on the petition, citing its inability to act on such an important issue without gaining the agreement of all of the other Friends' meetings in America and Britain. By the end of the next decade, however, the Pennsylvania Friends advised members to exercise caution in their involvement in the institution. The meeting further asked that members at least provide a religious education to any slaves they did own. With the Society's diffused structure and its emphasis on decision-making through consensus, a strong stance on this issue would be a long time in coming. As a result no group in the seventeenth-century Atlantic world publicly offered a compelling, religiously based critique of the practice of enslavement.

The encounter of Native Americans with European religion occurred in a different context than did the African encounter. Occasionally Native Americans worked as slaves or servants in the households of colonists and therefore might be catechized (or not) as local practice dictated. But they were more likely to continue to live in their traditional communities, which had been altered but not destroyed by the ravages of war, disease, and increased migration. Touring the Middle Colonies in 1679 and 1680, two Dutch men met numerous native peoples living in close proximity to settlers and upholding their traditional beliefs. Fascinated by the Indian viewpoint, they discussed theology (including the sources of evil and punishment for it) and heard various creation stories. In one community near the Delaware River they learned that a woman possessed by the devil had been liberated through a traditional ritual; and they found the account they heard of the incident to be persuasive, sharing as they did a belief in the possibility of such possession. In one conversation with Hans their Indian guide they learned his view of the cause of sickness and other troubles within the native community: the Europeans had "taught the people debauchery and excess; they are, therefore, much more miserable than they were before. The devil who is wicked, instigates and urges them on, to all kinds of evil, drunkenness and excess, to fighting and war, and to strife and violence."[6] Another man explained that only those who were literate had access to the distant Christian God, and native peoples who remained illiterate had to deal with Maneto, who concerned himself more directly in the daily lives of humans. These encounters reveal Native Americans maintaining their traditional beliefs and drawing on them to make sense of the presence and ideas of Europeans.

Those who lived in closest proximity to whites theoretically had the greatest exposure to Christianity, but, since few missionary efforts were undertaken, Indian peoples usually had little direct contact with the Protestant faith prior to 1690. This situation contrasted sharply with Catholic successes in Florida and Quebec. Martha's Vineyard had a long-standing mission, and the Praying Indian Villages of eastern central New England organized by missionary John Eliot were at their height in the decades after the Restoration. A handful of other colonists contemplated a missionary calling among Native Americans, but not much came of these plans. John Oxenbridge, while serving as a minister in Surinam (an English colony before it was taken by the Dutch in 1667), proposed a large-scale mission, but the English presence there came to an end without the plan ever being implemented.[7] Morgan Godwyn had similar intentions with regard to Native Americans as well as African slaves in Virginia a decade later, again with scant results.

The weakness of Protestant English efforts contrasted sharply with those undertaken by the French on behalf of Roman Catholicism. During the seventeenth century French Catholics outpaced the English in their missionary efforts, working with the Caribs of the West Indies as well as with the Hurons and others in New France. Catholic missionaries converted native peoples in the North American interior, far from any French settlements. They endured great hardship to do so, occasionally earning martyrdom for their efforts. On the English side, the minor headway that was made in converting the Indian population involved only those who lived close to

English settlements. For example, the Indian population on Martha's Vineyard largely embraced Christianity. The native community's conversion resulted from a small but focused campaign launched by the leading English family on the island. Indians living among the English had either to make their peace with the invaders—which might include accepting Christianity—or to leave the area, hoping to find a more distant location where they could live without regular contact with settler society. The geography of conversion differed greatly between the French and English cases.

The preeminent English effort to convert Native Americans in the decades after 1660 was tied up with the struggle of one man to come to terms with the fact of the failed "puritan revolution" and the Restoration of the Stuart monarchy. As a result of this connection, the Praying Indian Villages may be more revealing about John Eliot's struggle to give up his millennial hopes than about native experiences. This era saw the praying villages reach the height of their success, with nearly one quarter of the native population remaining in New England living in fourteen different towns. Reflecting the peculiar ideas of their founder, the towns were organized around the assumption that native converts should embrace English civility (which the English held to be a precondition of legitimate conversion), and the less common idea that every society should be organized according to a scheme that Eliot drew from the Bible. Inspired by the revolution of the 1640s and 1650s to envision a biblically based government (drawing on Exodus 18—in which Jethro proposes to Moses a system of governance using judges placed over segments of the population), Eliot laid out his proposal in *The Christian Commonwealth*. By the time it was published in England, the king was on the throne and the moment for utopian schemes had passed. Forced by the king's displeasure to renounce his ideas as a model for England, Eliot showed his continued adherence to them by implementing it in the Praying Indian Villages. In an ironic turn a relatively small group of Native Americans lived according to radical ideals associated with the mid-century revolution after its demise. Ruled by Old Testament–inspired elected leaders of tens, fifties, and hundreds, the praying Indians living in these villages were able to carry on with their accustomed leaders. From the native point of view the Mosaic governing structure created a space for Native American autonomy. The radical vision of Eliot helped the residents of these villages maintain traditional practices and beliefs, as they negotiated between their own customary spirituality and the Christianity they were taught by missionaries.

Even as the colonists made only very limited headway in the project of evangelizing the native peoples, the European Christian community was becoming more diverse. In one rather odd case, believers drew together aspects of various churches and movements to create something new. The Rogerenes were a uniquely American sect founded in the Rhode Island–Connecticut region in the late 1670s. John Rogers, although a wealthy Connecticut resident, joined the Westerly (Rhode Island) Seventh-Day Baptist Church in the mid-1670s. He did so in the company of his father's Indian servant, Japhet. Seventh-Day Baptists followed other Baptists in the practice of adult baptism but differed with them over the dating of the Sabbath; they upheld the Jewish tradition of a Saturday Sabbath. With radical religious groups severely circumscribed in Connecticut, Rogers initially sojourned to Rhode Island to find a community of like-minded believers. He soon parted ways with the Seventh-Day Baptists, however, as his views became more extreme. As he received his own revelations and began to construct his own version of Christianity, Rogers's new co-religionists were not willing to follow his lead. Breaking with the Westerly church, he founded a new sect that came to be known as the Rogerenes. His wife, a member of the established (Congregational) church of the colony of Connecticut, divorced him on the grounds of his defection from the orthodox faith.

The Rogerenes and their views are somewhat obscure. Some contemporaries described John Rogers's ideas as "Quaker-like." The sect may have embraced pacifism (a position that the Quakers were associated with increasingly after 1660). They certainly advocated less formal worship practices than were common in Connecticut churches at the time. Eventually, and probably somewhat unfairly, the group was likened to the Ranters, an anarchic English civil-war-era sect.[8] Although Rogers eventually claimed to receive communications directly from God, much of his writing revealed a strong streak of biblical literalism. He opposed an educated ministry. Publishing his views in a series of strident tracts, Rogers drew upon the language of prophecy to convey his message. He gathered a small band of followers, and his sect continued in existence after his death in 1721. Boasting an unusual blend of views drawn from various radical groups, the Rogerenes were heavily influenced by English and New English radicalism. In their eclectic blending from numerous traditions, they showed a flexibility reminiscent of the native peoples and the Africans who drew from multiple traditions as they confronted the intermixture that occurred in the seventeenth-century Atlantic world. If we consider the Rogerenes the first distinctive religious community born in English North America, that may only be because they left recognizable traces in the records, such as published tracts, that help us follow their history. Charting the blending that was occurring in Indian and African communities is more challenging, given the paucity of sources.

Rather than the creation of new movements, the circulation of peoples from various traditions was the more likely cause of rising diversity. Through migration, the various churches and sects in England, Wales, Scotland, and Ireland contributed individuals to other kingdoms as well as to the settlements in the wider Atlantic world. Another growing source of spiritual variation was Christians from other parts of Europe, who were incorporated in the British Atlantic world through conquest as well as migration. In 1664 the English conquered the Dutch colony of New Netherland, which thereby became New York. Prior to its conquest the colony included a diverse population: not only the Calvinist members of the established Dutch Reformed Church but also Jews, Swedish or German Lutherans, Walloon Calvinists (from the area of Europe today known as Belgium), English Congregationalists, and Scots or English Presbyterians. All of these settlers along with a fairly numerous African slave population were allowed to remain in the colony; those who were Christians were permitted to continue to practice their faiths as well. Additional English settlers—many of them Church of England adherents—migrated to the newly conquered colony, adding to the local variety. By 1680, New York was probably the most religiously (and ethnically) diverse of any English colony.

Migrants from Europe enhanced English, Irish, and colonial diversity. French Protestants (or Huguenots) constituted another continental European group introduced into the British Atlantic world in this era. They began leaving France even before the Revocation of the Edict of Nantes, which had permitted limited Protestant worship, in 1685. Ireland received its first Huguenots in the early 1660s. Saint Christopher (now known as Saint Kitts) reportedly had a French Huguenot church by 1685. After toleration was withdrawn in their native France, French Protestants already living in the French West Indies moved to English or Dutch Caribbean islands, where they would be welcomed as fellow Protestants. Others arrived in the British Atlantic from France, often first migrating to England and then on to a colony. Although the Church of England eventually absorbed a number of Huguenots, especially the elite, French-speaking Protestants formed a distinctive religious and linguistic community for a time.

The French were not the only such group. Very soon after the opening of Pennsylvania to settlement in 1682, German-speaking migrants, including such pietist groups as the Mennonites, began entering that colony. Their numbers and influence would grow over time. Another group to find its way to colonial North America was the Labadists, who opened a community in Maryland in 1683. Followers of Jean de Labadie, they combined mysticism with a Calvinist emphasis on the limited numbers of people likely to be among the elect. They lived communally on land they acquired from a sympathetic settler—whose father opposed his son's association with the sect—in a Dutch-speaking enclave within the colony of Maryland. New Bohemia, as it was called, was apparently the first example of a separatist, communal experiment, this one transplanted from Europe into the Anglo-American setting. Although it did not long survive—it would collapse in the first decades of the eighteenth century—the Labadist commune would be the first of many such attempts. Labadists, Dutch Reformed, Huguenots, and German pietists all added to the varied religious landscape of the late seventeenth-century Atlantic world.

Continued migration from the kingdoms of Charles II and James II also complicated the mixture. The great rise in religious variety within the Stuart kingdoms in the period prior to 1660 left a legacy of dissenter churches as well as Quaker meetings in each of the kingdoms. Members of these religious communities joined the migration stream into the wider Atlantic world. Baptists had been a recognized (although illegal) religious alternative in England prior to the outbreak of the civil wars. Over the course of the 1640s and 1650s, the number of Baptist churches in England and Wales jumped dramatically. The numbers rose as well in Scotland and Ireland, although not as sharply. Baptist churches were also founded in the colonies. Rhode Island hosted a Baptist church from 1639, and new churches were steadily added there in the decades that followed. A Welsh Baptist church migrated more or less in its entirety in the 1660s, under the continued guidance of minister John Myles. Transplanted to Plymouth Plantation, the church founded the town of Swansea, named for the Welsh town it had left behind. Before the end of the century, a group of Wampanoags gathered a Baptist church on Martha's Vineyard. In 1683 a Scottish settlement in the new colony of Carolina exhibited "Baptist leanings," and another community of Baptists eventually relocated there from Maine.[9] Other Baptists migrated or were transported to various colonies but their numbers seem to have been too small to make much of an impact on the records.

Quakers far outnumbered Baptist migrants, especially from the 1670s when the first Quaker colonization effort got under way. Quakers probably resided in every colony in the British Atlantic by the mid-1660s. Barbados had a sizeable Quaker community, as did Rhode Island, and there is also evidence of Quaker activity in Nevis, Antigua, Saint Christopher, Jamaica, the Chesapeake colonies, Massachusetts, Plymouth, Maine, and eventually Bermuda, Newfoundland, and Carolina. Quakers often came into conflict with the authorities, especially over their refusal to perform militia duty or to swear oaths. In the Caribbean colonies where slaves were increasingly employed, every able-bodied free man was needed for military service. When Quakers refused to serve, the government looked askance upon their peace testimony. In one decade the Barbados Quaker community faced fines totaling £7,000. Oath-taking occasionally became an issue as well. Quakers in Maryland routinely refused to swear oaths of office after 1680, and instances of office holding by members of the sect plummeted as a result. The colony of West Jersey, founded in 1674, and the ultimately more populous colony of Pennsylvania (1682) attracted large numbers of Quakers from England and Wales.

When their presence dramatically increased in the Middle Colonies, they were able to institute the full range of meetings that structured their organization in England—weekly, monthly, and yearly meetings. Interestingly the much older New England Quaker community first held its own yearly meetings in 1683, although whether they were directly influenced by the practices of the recently arrived Quakers in Pennsylvania is not clear. Men's and women's meetings throughout the transatlantic Quaker community kept an element of gender equality in the sect (one of its more radical traits in its early years), and women traveled between meetings as ministers crisscrossing the Atlantic. For all the continuity with early radical practices, the nature of the Quaker movement was beginning to change. From the 1660s it attracted more educated or elite converts, who helped to remake the sect in the Restoration era. With such men joining the sect, Quakers began to move away from the early practice of looking to preachers and other leaders of modest means and less education. The Society of Friends became somewhat less radical, perhaps, than it had been in its first decades, but it also systematized its commitment to some of its more unusual elements, like a relatively open system for identifying ministers and an ongoing commitment to social actions reflective of its beliefs. The growth of Quakerism since 1650 was a remarkable phenomenon: from a nonexistent faith, it had grown to a widely dispersed and relatively interconnected sect, with membership in every kingdom and nearly every outpost of the British Atlantic.

Among the important converts to the Society of Friends during the post-Restoration period were William Penn (1644–1718), son of an admiral, and the university-educated George Keith (1638?–1716) of Aberdeen, Scotland. Perhaps the leading Friend of his generation, Penn founded the colony of Pennsylvania, imagining it as a haven for his fellow Quakers but also for other persecuted groups. In the preface to the "First Frame of Government" for his new province, Penn felt called to justify government in religious terms. He considered "the divine right of government" a settled matter, for it worked "to terrify evil-doers . . . and to cherish those who do well." As a result, he added, "government seems to me a part of religion itself, a thing sacred in its institution and ends."[10] With his ideas about proper government, Penn pursued a policy of peace with the native peoples who resided in the region he had been granted for his colony. He made treaties with them and worked to prevent the bloodshed that was by this time a hallmark of early colonial history on mainland North America. His colony did not make him a fortune—indeed he spent some time in debtor's prison—but did serve as a haven for many members of the Society of Friends.

George Keith, who was converted in Scotland in the early 1660s, traveled widely in the British Isles and Ireland until 1684. In that year he accepted a post as surveyor in the new colonies of East and West Jersey. He would live in various colonies for the next decade. While in America he entered into controversies with various people, including a group he called "Ranters," after the civil-war-era sect, and a number of New England clergymen who refused to debate him. Eventually he would disrupt the Quaker community of the Middle Colonies with a religious schism caused by his efforts to create a structure for the Society more like that of a church than his fellow members were prepared to accept. He would return to England in 1693, there to continue his fight with the Society of Friends. By 1700 he had left the society and joined the Church of England. His trajectory from Presbyterian to Quaker to Anglican captured some of the range of options in the British Atlantic world in one man's religious meanderings. Although Keith may have been more combative than many others who similarly shifted their orientation, his various turns were not untypical.

Cutting against the grain of the religious politics of the Atlantic world was the fact that people of widely different faiths sometimes shared common assumptions. Dreams and dream interpretations, for instance, were widespread, and individuals from diverse communities and traditions believed dreams told the dreamer something important about themselves or their future. Quakers and Native Americans shared dream stories, occasionally using their dreams to persuade another to see a circumstance from their own perspective. Africans frequently interpreted their dreams or sought help from community experts in order to make sense of them. Believers as disparate as John Winthrop—early governor of Massachusetts—and Elizabeth Ashbridge—indentured servant without any particular religious orientation at the time—remarked on their dreams and tried to read in them hopeful or instructive signs. Eighteenth-century mariners, who are often considered a relatively irreligious lot, put great stock in dreams. One sailor dreamt "the girl [who] was the one I was to have" as a wife, and then spent his days looking until he found a young woman who fit the dreamed visage.[11] Such reliance on dream portents created one area of common ground that, even if it were not always recognized as such, cut across the diversity that marked the British Atlantic increasingly in this period.

As the variety and density of religious communities expanded after 1660, the religious infrastructure also shifted. One notable change at the Restoration of 1660 was the return of the Church of England as the officially established church. Charles II and his supporters in England agreed on the need to resurrect the church, seeing it as essential to the process of Restoration. In the very different context of the post-revolutionary era, how the church establishment would function vis-à-vis the many subjects who supported other spiritual options was a matter for some debate. Charles I had been determined to crush dissent and many royalists at the Restoration shared this goal, yet Charles II himself was personally inclined to toleration. He offered "liberty to tender consciences"[12] in a declaration he issued from Breda before crossing the Channel for his triumphal entry into England in May 1660. Although the Declaration of Breda might have been issued to ensure Charles's acceptance by a larger portion of his subjects, it seems to have been heartfelt, reflecting the new king's own preference. As events unfolded, he was only able to institute the promised policy partially and unevenly. The staunchest supporters of the Stuarts, sitting in the "Cavalier Parliament," refused to countenance their religious and political enemies by instituting toleration, much less liberty of conscience. The policy Parliament instituted did not achieve the full measure of coercion that many advocated, but it effectively foiled the king's attempt to revive the church without the older element of compulsion. The renewed Church of England was not the church Charles I had overseen, nor could it be, given his son's proclivities and the changed circumstances.

Throughout the kingdoms and in the dominions, the government worked to resurrect the church, to reappoint clergy, and to resume the various practices that had been moribund or, in some places, had gone underground. In Wales the church expanded its educational efforts, as indicated by a jump in the number of religious publications in the Welsh language. From 1564 to 1660, only 108 books were published, but from 1660 to 1730, a whopping 545 appeared.[13] The other kingdoms were brought more closely in line with the establishment in England. The Protestant Church of Ireland with the king at its head was revived through the appointment of bishops with links to the Laudian reforms of the 1630s. The Church of Scotland was established in a quasiepiscopal form, as Charles I had aimed to do in the late 1630s when he sparked the Bishops' Wars. This new system demoted Presbyterians, now known as "Covenanters," to the status of dissenters. Restoration-era reforms also forced Guernsey, one of the islands located in the Channel dividing England and Ireland from the European mainland, away from Presbyterianism and into the Episcopal fold. The Channel Islands churches had (like the Scottish churches) resisted Archbishop Laud's efforts to bring them into the Church of England in the 1630s. The religious establishments in the three kingdoms were more similar than they had ever been, since both the Church of Ireland and that of Scotland were forced into an Episcopal structure patterned on the Anglican hierarchy. In theory, Charles II achieved the uniformity that his father had sought but failed to secure. Yet this reestablished state church did not hold the same place it had once enjoyed, since the wide variety of religious options that had flourished in the period before 1660 created a new context for that establishment.

Advocates of the Church of England made an effort not only to reinstate it but also to invigorate it in the colonies. Those plantations that had previously boasted Church of England establishments—Virginia, Bermuda, the leeward Caribbean island colonies—revived them, and crown appointees in newly acquired Jamaica worked to transplant the Church of England there. The first new colonies founded after the Restoration, Carolina (chartered in 1663) and New York (conquered from the Dutch in 1664), did not start with full-blown establishments, reflecting the king's wish to avoid coercion; but they received Church of England clergymen who were assigned to create a church structure. Under Charles, the church was present but not mandatory in these colonies, a policy that would be reversed later in the century. Eventually, it would be more widely established, but that would take some time, institution building, and the replacement of Charles with other monarchs before it would be realized. Everywhere the institutional church had to be resurrected and strengthened. In Virginia, for instance, vestrymen—lay members who had charge in the absence of a well developed hierarchy—rebuilt the church. In one parish, new vestrymen took an oath that began "I doe Acknowledge my Selfe a True Sonne of the Church of England, Soe I doe believe The Articles of Faith there profess[ed] and do oblidge myselfe to be conformable to the Doctrine and Discipline There Taught and Established."[14] With such steps, local institutional growth occurred, if slowly and sporadically.

The Church of England was also introduced into the major New England colonies, where settlers now had the option of attending its services. To the defenders of New England orthodoxy, this change was cataclysmic. One local minister revealed his distaste for the thought of conforming to the Church of England when he related a rumor that a minister in England "read the services with a disturbed spirit, & was so smitted in it, that he took to his bed, & died."[15] Despite fears that their own churches would be undermined at the Restoration, the New England colonies of Connecticut, Massachusetts, and Plymouth maintained their congregational establishments under Charles II. Their charters were swept away only decades later, in the mid-1680s, in anticipation of the founding of the Dominion of New England. Officially inaugurated in the first years of the reign of his brother, James II (1686), the Dominion created a giant colony (stretching from New York to Maine) in which was mandated a Church of England establishment.

The church apparently became more firmly entrenched than it had been before in the Caribbean colonies after the Restoration. The West Indian church was brought under the direct authority of the Bishop of London after 1676, and a system of commissaries with ecclesiastical authority was instituted from the 1680s. A group of six ministers were sent to the Leeward Islands of the Caribbean in 1677, which one scholar asserts "marked the real beginning of serious and sustained efforts by the Church of England to establish itself in the Leeward Islands." This did not prevent the planters from occasionally resisting bids for greater authority by bishops, the king, or later the missionary arm of the established church. Laments about the lack of ministers were still voiced, both in the Caribbean and elsewhere, as were complaints about the quality of men who did get appointed. Sir Charles Wheler, who arrived in the Leeward Islands in 1671 to assume the post of governor, reportedly found "one drunken orthodox priest, one drunken sectary priest, and one drunken parson who had no orders."[16] Still, more sustained attention was paid to these matters than had been the case previously.

Problems that hampered the effective establishment of the Church of England in the colonies prior to 1640 remained in the Restoration era: problems of distance from episcopal authorities, staffing, and funding. The modest settlement effort in Newfoundland—where year-round colonists' numbers were annually augmented by the summer arrival of the fishing fleet—offered a particularly challenging case. With Catholic, Anglican, and puritan influences at work in various parts of Newfoundland, clergymen of any type were usually lacking. As John Thomas, a visiting ship's chaplain, noted, "Noe publicke prayers, nor sermons, noe sacraments, no holy wedlock, noe worship, nor praise to God all the year long, unless a chaplain in a man of warre comes in and happily marryes and baptizeth a very few in that harbour only when he resides."[17] He probably overstated the problem somewhat, for apparently a literate colonist often read aloud from the Prayer Book in the absence of a minister, a common strategy for maintaining an element of Church of England worship when no clergy was present. In Newfoundland all officers were ordered to have the service performed in this way on their ships as well. Colonists' religious practice may have remained somewhat simplified, but it did not follow that the extent of their devotion was lessened. On his death bed, planter John Kendall "blessed [his gathered children] severally and commanded them to serve god and to keep the Sabbath day holy and to bee dutifull to their mother."[18] With these words he outlined the components of a faith that he shared with many others in various locations. And for colonial Virginians as for others, headway in the institutional structures of the church was made between the Restoration and 1690.

As matters developed during the Restoration era, non-Anglican Protestants could not be entirely suppressed. Protestant dissenters within England and Wales were, however, reduced to a sort of second-class citizenship under the so-called Clarendon Codes (1661–65). The naming of the codes for the king's chief governmental minister, the Earl of Clarendon, was misleading, in that Clarendon did not favor a harsh policy aimed at dissenters any more than his master the king did. The new laws were also used to harass a small Jewish community in London. They aimed to drive the more radical or threatening sects out of existence. Muggletonians, followers of the prophet John Reeve and his cousin Lodowick Muggleton, went underground. The authorities succeeded in destroying the violent Fifth Monarchists, after they tried to bring about the reign of Christ on earth as foretold in the book of

Revelation through a violent uprising at the time of the Restoration. The codes did not entirely succeed in driving out of existence the less threatening churches, like the Presbyterians or Independents (the latter also known as Congregationalists). The Quakers and the Baptists, although considered far more radical than the other dissenters, were eventually but grudgingly covered under the laws. Their plight was eased only after members spent considerable time in prison and paid (or refused out of conscience to pay) numerous fines. During this period, many first-generation Quaker leaders died in jail. John Bunyan wrote his classic allegory of the Christian's struggle for salvation, *Pilgrim's Progress*, while imprisoned as a nonconformist. Having joined a Baptist church in 1653 at the age of twenty-five, Bunyan eventually became a preacher. Jailed at the Restoration, he spent twelve years behind bars until he was released in 1672 when statutes against dissenters were suspended. Later generations in various Christian churches embraced his *Pilgrim's Progress* as an inspirational spiritual text, reading it as an allegory of the journey to salvation. In its own time, it also made a plea for liberty of conscience.

Dissent beyond England and Wales was handled somewhat differently. Protestant dissenters in Ireland did not feel the full force of religious persecution, apparently because the Protestant-Catholic divide remained paramount to that kingdom's religious politics. They were occasionally considered suspect, especially when ties to Scotland, especially among those Presbyterians living in the Irish province of Ulster, seemed to threaten disloyalty to the monarch or instability in Irish politics. The presence of organized dissent in Britain and Ireland—notably Baptists, Quakers, Congregationalists, and Presbyterians—rendered the situation more complex and multivalent than it had been prior to the collapse of the Stuarts' ecclesiastical balancing act in the late 1630s. The situation in Scotland was especially odd, in that the Presbyterians, members of what had been the established church, became dissenters. In 1666 some of them rose in arms against the imposition of episcopacy. After the rising was easily quashed, a number of them were transported to the colonies as punishment. In Virginia and Barbados, these transported rebels assumed places working on plantations that had once been occupied by their countrymen, only that earlier wave of transportees were sent for their royalism rather than for their opposition to the king's church settlement. The practice of banishment and its contribution to the complex social and religious environment of early America remained, even as the subjects of the policy shifted from group to group.

Colonies generally enjoyed (or suffered, depending on one's perspective)

TRUTHS VICTORY,
AGAINST HERESIE;

All sorts comprehended under these ten mentioned:

1. Papists, 2. Familists, 3. Arrians, 4. Arminians, 5. Anabaptists, 6. Separatists, 7. Antinomists, 8. Monarchists. 9. Millenarists, 10. Independents.

As also a Description of the Truth, the Church of Christ, her present suffering estate for a short time yet to come; and the glory that followeth at the generall Resurrection.

By *I. G.* A faithfull lover and obeyer of the Truth.

Now I beseech you, Brethren, mark them which cause divisions and offences, contrary to the doctrine which you have learned, and avoid them, Rom. 16. 17.

Imprimatur, JOHN DOWNAME.

London, Printed for *H. R.* at the three Pigeons in *Pauls Church-yard,* 1645.

Fig. 6. Numerous new religious groups emerged during the 1640s and 1650s in England, when an end to censorship and the eradication of the church courts permitted open expression of various radical views. These developments horrified conservatives like John Graunt; the title page of his *Truth's Victory against Heresie* (1645) depicted some of the diversity that he so abhorred. This diversity, shocking when it first emerged, became increasingly commonplace after 1660. Courtesy of John Carter Brown Library at Brown University.

a greater degree of liberty and more toleration than was the case in Britain. Religious freedom developed in part because of the specific histories of individual colonies that had been founded with liberty of conscience. It also arose because of the difficulties in enforcing conformity in the Americas. Another factor was that Charles, who favored liberty more than his leading subjects did, had more direct and unmediated authority over the situation in the wider Atlantic world than in his own kingdoms. Distance made it possible to pursue policies in colonial settlements that could not be instated in England. As Charles noted in the 1663 Rhode Island charter, liberty there "will (as wee hope) bee noe breach of the unitie and unifformitie established in this nation."[19] Maryland, along with Rhode Island, continued to advance liberty within certain limits. Grants for new colonies included provisions for toleration, including New York (1664) and Carolina (1665). Pennsylvania (1682) promised complete religious liberty. Given the level of animosity some dissenters felt for the Church of England establishment in England, the authorities believed it necessary explicitly to require the Pennsylvania proprietor to permit Church of England clergy to minister in the colony in the event an Anglican population settled there.

From Virginia to Massachusetts, officials made efforts to suppress religious dissenters—especially the Quakers—and went to various ends in order to do so. Colonial governments that sought to harass those of alternative faiths used fines for failure to attend worship services or, in the case of the Quakers, for failure to participate in militia duties. Magistrates also ordered the imprisonment of traveling ministers, and in Maryland, Virginia, much of New England, and the Caribbean, Quaker proselytizers were incarcerated. The government of Massachusetts Bay, however, continued to react far more harshly to Quakers in the first years of the Restoration, using mutilation and even the death penalty in an unsuccessful effort to rid the colony of the sect.

Charles II's response to the execution of four Quakers in Massachusetts Bay (1659–61) demonstrated how his own personal proclivities in favor of liberty could carry the day in the colonies better than in England itself. At the Restoration, while hopes were still high that Charles would make good on the sweeping promises of liberty contained in the Declaration of Breda, Quakers in England approached Charles to protest mistreatment by the Massachusetts authorities. Leading Quakers obtained interviews with the newly instated monarch. They also published tracts protesting the use of the death penalty. The accounts of the executions cast the Quakers as martyrs for their faith and the colonists who executed them as hypocrites, people who had once migrated in search of religious freedom themselves but who subsequently denied it to others.

The king, unable to stop his Parliament from passing punishing laws against sectarians within England, came to the defense of the Quakers in New England. He sent a letter ordering an end to the more severe persecution, and his appointed messenger to the colony was Samuel Shattuck, a Salem resident who had been previously banished for his Quakerism. Shattuck and his fellows relished his triumphal return to the colony with the missive that prevented the magistrates from carrying out the execution that was the proscribed punishment for Shattuck or any other Quaker who returned from banishment. Charles told the Massachusetts authorities that if they thought any of his subjects had committed a capital offense, they should ship the culprit to England to stand trial. This suggestion, had it been followed, would have undermined the authority of the Bay Colony government generally at the same time that it would have stopped the execution of all Quakers. Massachusetts chose instead to reduce the punishments meted out to the sect in order to retain (a more limited) control of its own polity. They adopted the Cart and Whip Act, instructing the sheriff to tie the Quaker missionary to the back of a cart, and whip the offender to the borders of the colony. Though brutal, serial whipping was still an obvious improvement over capital execution. In Massachusetts, Charles could restrain his more zealous subjects, even as Parliament passed laws to persecute Quakers and others in England. Due to his intervention, the small resident community of Quakers founded in Salem in the previous decade was protected from the worst of the government's harassment.

The differential levels of liberty and toleration prevailing in different parts of the Atlantic world affected migration streams, although perhaps not to as great an extent as we might expect. Dissenters did leave England at the start of the Restoration, fearful of the punishing repression that seemed to be looming. The most famous exiles were three regicides, who had participated in the decision to kill King Charles. They escaped death by traveling to New England, where their co-religionists gave them shelter. New Haven lost its status as a separate colony, being forcibly absorbed into the colony of Connecticut, partly as punishment for harboring the regicides. Other migrants ranged from Henry Adis, a London artisan and radical, to John Oxenbridge, a university-trained Independent minister. Both went to Surinam. Rather more Presbyterians may have fled the imposition of episcopacy (or ecclesiastical rule by bishops) for the greater liberties available in the northern Ireland province of Ulster, joining co-religionists who had been migrating into the area since the early seventeenth century. By 1690, a synod had been organized there, comprising nine presbyteries and 120 congregations serving 150,000 Scots. One advisor to the king thought that Charles could encourage dissenters to leave old England for New England if he publicly vowed not to meddle with the non-Anglican religious establishments prevailing in most of the colonies in that region. Uncertain that he wanted New England fortified with yet more potentially hostile settlers, Charles ignored this advice. Quaker migration to the colonies or between kingdoms was apparently minimal prior to the 1676 founding of West Jersey as a Quaker enterprise. Until that time, most colonies—Rhode Island being the most dramatic exception—were inhospitable places for Quaker migrants, and most Friends chose to stay and cope with what came where they were. One exception was Mary Fisher, who had been one of the first two women to visit Massachusetts as a missionary. She lived out her life as a settler in the Chesapeake region.

Sometimes colonists migrated between colonies in search of an improved religious climate, although it is difficult to gauge the number that moved as a result of their religious circumstances. Clearly, however, anyone who migrated (whatever their initial motivation or their affiliation) selected a settlement that seemed amenable to them religiously as well as in other respects. When the English colony of Surinam collapsed in 1667, John Oxenbridge migrated to Massachusetts. The Bay colony was attractive because it was populated by like-minded Christians and ministerial colleagues with whom Oxenbridge had corresponded for decades. As the Church of England increased its hold on the Caribbean colonies, dissenters may have taken the opportunity to move to other outposts (either to those in New England or later to newer colonies that granted toleration or even liberty). Lewis Morris, who rose from Providence Island servant to leading Barbados planter, relocated in New York. The colony of Carolina (founded in 1665 and later divided into two) permitted religious freedom to all Christians and to Jews and made special provisions for the sensibilities of the Quakers. As a result, early settlers to Carolina who came from other North American or from Caribbean locations often considered the colony's provisions for toleration. Reshuffling by religious proclivity took place, as people sought out like-minded believers or at least a tolerant environment in which to practice their faith.

Catholicism continued to be a practiced if pariah faith. The position of Catholics in the Restoration era was problematic. Only in Ireland and the Irish-dominated Caribbean colony of Montserrat did the later Stuarts rule over a sizeable number of Catholics. In Ireland in particular the Catholic community was complex and multifaceted, with a sophisticated Counter Reformation culture flourishing alongside an older folk religion. These cultures overlapped in the Mass, which created a "sacramental community" that appealed to all.[20] Maryland, despite its Catholic proprietor, had an overwhelmingly Protestant population. One wealthy and powerful settler there, Mistress Margaret Brent, personified the authority of some Catholic laywomen in post-Reformation England. Catholics were also scattered through England, Wales, and Scotland. Their numbers were small, however (save in the Scottish Highlands and parts of the north of England), and the Catholic role in public life minimal.

Protestant public opinion was generally hostile toward Catholicism, less because of the actions of these resident Catholics and more because of the international situation that continued to pit Catholic against Protestant. Dissenting minister Richard Baxter expressed widespread fears when he wondered whether the Great Fire of London in 1666 was started as part of a popish plot. In direct conflict with the prejudices of their subjects, both Charles II and James II were sympathetic to Catholicism and tried to improve the position of their Catholic subjects. James eventually converted to Catholicism, and, because he was heir to his elder brother's throne, opposition to his popery led to a series of political crises in the last years of Charles II's reign. Once James became king (1685), he attempted to ease the disabilities placed upon nonconformists, including Catholics. James's subjects were often hostile to this policy. When the birth of a Catholic heir replaced James's Protestant daughters in the succession, a backlash against his faith occurred. It would lead directly to the so-called Glorious Revolution, which removed James in favor of his Protestant daughter and son-in-law, Mary and William (1688).

Anti-Catholic sentiments also played a role in the various settlements. Just as in the three kingdoms, Catholics were sporadically treated shabbily in the colonies, even in those where toleration was the official policy. In the West Indies, by 1680 papists were excluded from the benefits of toleration. During his short reign and in keeping with his efforts in England, James II granted full protection to Catholics in Jamaica; other islands followed suit. After the Glorious Revolution, though, these local governments would return to the former practice of exclusion. Deep suspicion against Catholics continued in New England, and Catholics were unlikely to settle there as a result. On the mainland, only Maryland had a sizeable Catholic population, but there the burgeoning Protestant community sporadically expressed hostility toward the power of Catholics in the province. The Catholic proprietor of the colony, Lord Baltimore, had appointed Protestant governors during the crisis of the 1650s to assuage hostility toward his charter both in England and in Maryland itself. At the Restoration, he resumed his previous practice of naming his kin and other co-religionists to the post. Protestant settlers were restive in this situation. In English North America both the northern-most and southern-most settlements abutted territory held by Catholics—in Carolina the awkward neighbors were in Spanish Florida; in New England, they were in French Quebec. As the distance separating Protestant and Catholic settlements slowly shrank, border rivalries encouraged the flare-up of historic religious animosities.

The anti-Spanish and anti-Catholic sentiment that had inspired the conquest of Jamaica and the attacks on Spanish settlements continued to motivate the privateers (those with a license to attack enemy ships, in the fashion of pirates, only with government sanction and therefore legal standing) who worked out of Jamaica. The famous Henry Morgan, sometimes governor of the colony, was a noteworthy example. Charles's and James's governments opposed Cromwell's policy of continued warfare in the region, however. They worked to shift from depredations on the Spanish to trade and peaceful coexistence, but they had trouble persuading their subjects to cooperate. Spanish unwillingness to open trade to the English did not help matters. Although open hostilities slowly abated over time, the Catholic-Protestant divide continued to mold the politics of religion in the Atlantic.

The extent of the diversity in colonial North America was clearly revealed in a journal kept by a European visitor of 1679 and 1680. Two members of the Labadist movement traveled on a reconnaissance mission looking for a place to start a community with other members of their sect, and one recorded their adventures in an account that illuminated colonial religious life in the later seventeenth century. Visiting New York and traveling as far south as Maryland and as far east as Massachusetts, Peter Schluter and Jaspar Danckaerts encountered Christians of various stripes, including French Catholics, Dutch Reformed, Quakers, Anglicans, and Congregationalists. Schluter and Danckaerts analyzed the spiritual state of everyone they met, and they frequently offered unsolicited advice to people about how they might improve. Asking so many questions and knowing various languages, they were feared to be Jesuits in disguise. Indeed one group of "French papists" living without a priest on Long Island tried to get them to perform sacraments, so convinced were they of the pairs' true identity. The two were highly censorious of one Quaker prophetess, describing her drinking and disputing into the wee hours. Everywhere they traveled, the two men distributed religious literature when they found anyone they thought would be receptive to their message. A high point of their tour of the colonies was meeting John Eliot, who deeply impressed them. The three men swapped books and enjoyed an edifying conversation. Less impressive by far was Harvard College, where the students smoked, drank, and learned little. The travelers found settlers living in a wide variety of circumstances, upholding numerous spiritual options and sometimes feeling cut off from organized religion altogether. Their tour offered a perspective on the complex and varied landscape that had grown up in the northern English colonies by 1680.

Of the many people they encountered, the two who most captivated them were a woman named Eltie and her nephew. She was born of a Mohawk mother and a European father but had been taken in by Christians and baptized. Being raised by her mother in a Mohawk community, Eltie encountered Dutch settlers who identified her as more like a European than an Indian, and they began to encourage her to come to them. The girl's interest in their offer eventually alienated her from her family, and she did finally move into a colonial home, where she was taught needlework, reading, and Christianity. As an adult she found the Christian Europeans among whom she lived to be impious, a view that Danckaerts wholeheartedly shared. She expressed her gladness at meeting the two Labadist travelers, saying that God had sent them to her so she would know that there were good Christians in the world. Through her they met her nephew, another convert, whom they found to be obsessed with God and persecuted for his faith by other Indians. This young man, Wouter, described a successful hunt in which God had sent him game to kill. He took this as a sign that God "loved him—a God whom the Indians did not know, but for whom he felt he had a greater hunger than his hunger for outward food." So taken were they by this young man that the two travelers wanted him to accompany them back to Europe, where he could enter their religious community. Wouter was unable to join them when they departed the colony and never appeared in Boston for their planned rendezvous, for reasons they never knew. Their account of the encounter with him and his aunt revealed how deeply the pair touched them.[21]

Although diversity was a reality throughout the British Atlantic world by 1690, accommodating it took a massive adjustment in thinking about the place of religion in the social and political order. The assumption that religious uniformity was necessary to a harmonious society continued to carry great weight. If anything, the experience of revolution, regicide, and religious experimentation in the 1640s and 1650s had proved to conservatives the necessity of tight control over religious dissent. Governments generally continued to act in support of a state establishment. Usually (as we would expect, given the ecclesiastical system prevailing in England) the Church of England was established, but four New England colonies had Congregationalist establishments in its stead. Whether one supported the Church of England in Barbados or the Congregational church in Connecticut, the assumption was widespread that all residents ought to adhere to the dominant church order.

In most places, including Britain, Ireland, and the majority of colonies, alternative religions were merely tolerated. Toleration meant that they were assumed to be wrong, in that they departed from the accepted church order, but the dominant group in society agreed to permit them anyway. Toleration usually came with some legal disability, as was the case in England, where dissenters were routinely fined, or in Massachusetts, where various restrictions were eventually used in an attempt to limit the first alternatives (Quaker and Baptist) organized there. Most contemporaries found diversity unsettling, and the limits of toleration reflected that fact. In all three kingdoms and in many colonies, religious differences that could not be eliminated pushed authorities toward toleration. They did not go down that path willingly. Diversity often seemed a problem that could not be resolved rather than a cause for celebration.

The Atlantic settlements tended to be more diverse than the Restoration kingdoms, a situation that was furthered by the changes occurring in this era. A few colonial polities embraced complete (or nearly complete) religious liberty, in which no faith was established and the logic that supported mere toleration did not apply. These places usually combined a past experience of persecution that engendered hostility toward state repression of religion with a high degree of variation or other practical problems that complicated the selection of a dominant faith. Many early Rhode Islanders, harried out of Massachusetts, opposed persecution on principle. At the same time inhabitants of Rhode Island shared no single common religious orientation that might serve as a basis for unity. Maryland might have become an officially Catholic colony, except that such a move would have been politically impossible, and so it permitted freedom to all Christians in order to ensure it for Catholics. William Penn was, as a Quaker, opposed to the coercion of conscience and therefore unwilling to force conformity in his new colony of

Pennsylvania. At the same time he was interested in attracting more settlers and so he recruited widely among all Protestants. Rhode Island, Maryland, and Pennsylvania were extreme cases, in which the government supported no specific church order.

At the same time that the Stuart dominions in the Atlantic basin became pluralistic, the idea that loyalty to the monarch was best expressed through membership in the Church of England grew stronger. The Restoration Church of England cultivated the imagery of martyrdom around the dead king Charles I. Whereas his opponents thought Charles died justly for shedding the blood of his subjects against God's will, his supporters saw his death as the unjust murder of a godly king. In this version of events, the king died not for his crimes against his people and against God but for his commitment to his faith. The officially liturgy of the church, published in the Book of Common Prayer, carried a frontispiece depicting a saintly Charles kneeling to receive a halo. The church made January 30, the date of Charles's execution, into a holy day, providing special readings on the martyrdom. This anniversary would remain on the church's calendar until 1859. After the English acquired Tangiers in a 1662 treaty, the chapel there was dedicated to Charles the Martyr. When Parliament launched its political assault on non-Anglicans, it framed its efforts in terms of punishing those who killed the king and tore apart the country.

Religious affiliation became shorthand for disloyalty (or, in the case of Church of England adherents, loyalty). In this climate, New England was deeply suspect, and many anticipated that the monarch would withdraw the charter privileges of those colonies (especially the bold and semi-autonomous Massachusetts Bay), as he finally did in the 1680s. Alternately Virginia became inordinately proud of its once and current governor, Sir William Berkeley, who had been ousted from the governorship by Charles's opponents and so became a symbol of the colony's loyalty to the king. The language used to describe the Restoration in Virginia and other Anglican outposts was heavily imbued with religious imagery, as relieved royalists saw God's hand in the monarchy's return. Those who could not partake of the easy equation of Church of England membership and loyalty struggled to present themselves as good subjects nonetheless. Those who were too openly associated with disloyalty and hostility to the monarchy (such as the Fifth Monarchists, who staged an unsuccessful uprising at the Restoration) were driven out of existence. Others, such as the Quakers and the leaders of New England, sought to prove their support for the king. Those without Anglican credentials had

Fig. 7. Revolutionaries in England executed Charles I (1600–1649) for crimes against his people. His supporters revered him as a martyr and produced this image showing him losing his earthly crown but receiving a heavenly one. After the revolution, when the Church of England was resurrected, the image appeared as the frontispiece to the new edition of the Book of Common Prayer (1662). Courtesy of John Carter Brown Library at Brown University.

to work hard to avoid association with regicide and murderous disloyalty. The idea that support for the state church was necessary to stability and the new suggestions that accommodating Protestant dissent could strengthen the social and political order coexisted uneasily in the Restoration Atlantic.

The decades after 1660 were shaped by two conflicting trends. On one hand, the Church of England and its episcopal equivalents in Scotland and Ireland gained new ground in the kingdoms and the plantations of the re-stored Stuarts. In this sense the effort to transplant religious establishment seemed to enjoy some success. On the other hand, the numbers of those who did not adhere to an Episcopal church rose. The non-Anglican population increased, through the creation of dissent as a distinctive category outside the Church of England fold within England, through migration of Christian adherents to other churches into the Stuart domains, and through the incorporation of non-Christians in the populations of the plantations. Alongside an established and expansive episcopal order were numerous other churches and faiths, ranging from traditional Native Americans to German pietists. The British Atlantic was predominantly Protestant and within that the Church of England probably had the majority of adherents, but both within the Protestant community and outside of it, pluralism was increasingly evident. While some actively supported this trend, others continued to think of diversity as a problem to be combated. It was a volatile state of affairs.

FIVE

Battling over Religious Identity in the Late Seventeenth Century

TENSION AND CONFLICT permeated the British Atlantic world during the last quarter of the seventeenth century. In 1675–76 an Indian war erupted in New England, while Virginians fought a combined Indian and civil war. In the broader Atlantic context, the period was dominated by the Glorious Revolution of 1688–89, which affected the religious histories of England, Wales, Scotland, and Ireland as well as the colonies. The ouster of the Catholic king James II in favor of his Protestant daughter and son-in-law, Mary and William of Orange, culminated a period of strife over the prospect of a Catholic on the throne. It also set into motion almost a century of war between the decisively Protestant Britain and the resolutely Roman Catholic France. The Glorious Revolution also planted the seeds of later conflicts, especially in Ireland and Scotland. In Massachusetts Bay political uncertainty created by the Glorious Revolution set the stage for the witch trials of 1692. Insecurities arising from the settlement seemed to have played a role in a spate of witch prosecutions in Scotland later in the decade as well. Religion was implicated in the various controversies of the late seventeenth century, including those that did not appear at first glance to be primarily concerned with religion. Canvassing these events permits us to explore the religious culture of the British Atlantic world, the nature of the tensions that divided it, and the prospect for creating at least a partial unity around anti-Catholicism. The late-century conflicts represent an opportunity to assess the affects upon religion of English expansion and everything that expansion had set into motion.

Wars between colonists and Indians were most obviously sparked by conflicts over settler encroachments on native lands. Given that the eastern woodland Indians of Virginia's hinterland as well as those of southern New England thought of the landscape as imbued with the sacred, protecting the land and maintaining their relationship with it could be a spiritual compulsion. On the European side religious views also informed attitudes toward the land. Settlers justified their very presence with biblical strictures to make the land fruitful, and they discounted modes of Indian land use as failing to fulfill that imperative. They also understood the colonization project in terms of spreading true religion to the Americas. Christianizing North America might entail converting natives—as many English commentators had long assumed—but it could just as easily (or perhaps more easily, in the minds of increasingly prejudiced settlers) involve physically replacing heathens with Christian migrants from Europe. Viewing the original residents of the region through a Christian–heathen dichotomy encouraged colonists to be suspicious of Native Americans, to question their right to the land, and to doubt their ability to enter fully into the Christian community. On both sides, then, religious attitudes about land helped to frame the war.

In both wars that broke out in 1675—King Philip's War in New England and Bacon's Rebellion in Virginia—Christianity was a polarizing issue. Colonists north and south spoke of the natives as vicious threats to poor defenseless Christians. The rhetoric denied any colonial responsibility for the tensions between the two groups. According to an anonymous New England author, who may have been the minister Increase Mather, the region's original inhabitants felt "causeless enmity" toward the settlers, and only that inexplicable hatred could explain the "malicious and revengefull spirit of these Heathens" which was expressed in the war.[1] In this view, Indians, far from being provoked, were by nature violent and aggressive. Despite the differences in the church establishments in the two areas, Church of England in Virginia and Congregationalism in New England, colonists in both drew upon this religiously inspired language to pin the blame for all hostilities on the Indians themselves.

In the New England conflagration in particular, ample evidence indicates that the Indians joined the war to resist not only the imposition of English sovereignty over their communities—especially the insistence that they be subjected to English justice in colonial courts—but also the encroachments of European Christianity. Native peoples who participated in war in New England occasionally targeted Christian objects, such as the Bible, for

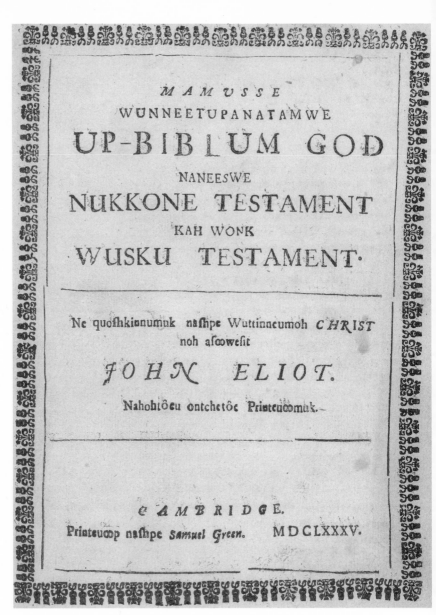

Fig. 8. With the help of native converts, John Eliot translated the Bible into an Algonquian dialect. This title page from the 1685 edition used a combination of native and English terms to convey its meaning. Copies of an earlier edition were destroyed during King Philip's War, but whether by colonists or Indians, we do not know. *Mamusse wunneetupanatamwe Up-Biblum God naneeswe Nukkone Testament kah wonk Wusku Testament. Ne quoshkinnumuk nashpe Wuttinneumoh Christ noh asoowesit John Eliot. Nahohtôeu ontchetôe printeuoomuk* (Cambridge, Mass., 1685). Courtesy of John Carter Brown Library at Brown University.

desecration in their attacks on settlements. By rejecting Christian symbols, these Native Americans indicated their defiance of the European God who would have been understood as the source of English power, and they rejected a faith that was used to promote expansion. In the aftermath of the war, John Eliot reported that "in the late Indian war, all the bibles and Testaments were carried away, and burnt or destroyed." At least some of these had been left behind by Praying Indians who were being hurriedly evacuated to an island in Boston Harbor; "only some few caryed their bibles," as Eliot noted, "the rest were spoyled & lost."[2] Whether this destruction was undertaken by natives eager to demonstrate their rejection of Christianity or by colonists equally bent on showing their hostility to Eliot's outreach to the Indians is not known. Perhaps most significant is how the Bible in an Algonquian language became a symbol of the failed accommodation between Indian and colonizer. Christianity explained the conflict to the English even as it became a focal point of Native American animosities.

The precipitating events leading to King Philip's War were linked to the Indian missions and tensions within Native American communities over how to relate to the invading Europeans. The war started in the wake of the trial of three Wampanoags for the murder of another native man named John Sassamon. Sassamon, who had lost his parents to smallpox when he was very young, may have been brought up in a colonial household. He certainly learned not only to speak but also to read English, and as a young man he assisted Eliot as an interpreter and translator and also worked as a school teacher among the Indians. He even briefly attended Harvard College. Withdrawing somewhat from the white community in the early 1670s, Sassamon nonetheless told the governor of Plymouth Plantation that Wampanoag leader, Philip or Metacom, was planning an attack on the settlers. When Sassamon's corpse was discovered in a frozen pond, colonial authorities concluded he had been murdered for betraying Philip's secret. Three men were accused of the murder and tried in the Plymouth court. The Wampanoags claimed that the three were innocent and deeply resented the intrusion of colonial justice into their community; colonists were persuaded that Philip intended to launch a war against them. With this added provocation, war broke out shortly thereafter, bringing a united force of numerous Indian tribes down on many settlements.

The war in New England was interpreted by the colonists through the religious lenses of a test and a punishment sent by God. This providential framework—which viewed the hand of God in every significant event—was a common line of thinking in New England but could be found throughout the British Atlantic world. A cataclysmic war—in which about 5 percent of the colonial population was killed and the line of settlement pushed back so dramatically that it would not recover for decades—was ripe for viewing in providential terms. Any suffering could be interpreted as a test: God's people were subjected to horrible distress so that they could respond with fortitude and continued faith. An appropriate response demonstrated that the colonists were still godly. According to this view, the experience of war, properly undertaken and understood, brought the English Christians of New England closer to God and reconfirmed their faith. Mary Rowlandson, captured from her Lancaster, Massachusetts, home in February, 1676, wrote a famous account of her captivity that placed it within this framework. The wife of a minister and herself a member of the Lancaster church, Rowlandson presented her ordeal in terms of her reliance on God. When an Indian man gave her a Bible taken from the home of another Christian family that had been attacked, Rowlandson saw this as a mercy from the Lord. She never considered the motives of the human agent who delivered the Good Book to her. After intensive contact with native culture during her three-month captivity, Rowlandson used her narrative to signal her continued commitment to the Christian God and to reintegrate herself into the community of English Christians.

The other providential construction for understanding the war—that it was a punishment—was especially popular among ministerial reformers. Public preaching in late-seventeenth-century New England—particularly that for political occasions like the annual opening of the General Court— often dwelled on the need for reform. Ministers frequently reminded colonists of the religious heritage of the region. Indeed they were the first to develop the idea that the early settlers suffered much in migrating to New England and they did so in order to be able to practice their religion. According to those preachers, the colonies had fallen away from their original mission, neglectful of the local churches, interested in worldly affairs, tolerant of religious dissenters, and generally less godly. Ministers such as Increase Mather used the occasion of the war to drive this message home. Mather published *An Earnest Exhortation to the Inhabitants of New-England* (1676), in which he argued that the war was a judgment on the sins of the colonists. After the war, responding to the idea that it had been sent to punish wayward settlers, ministers called a special meeting to discuss a reform agenda. They approached their task by issuing a list of the colonists' failings. Revealingly, the list did not mention ill treatment of the Native American inhabitants among the causes of God's wrath. Mather would later explain that the land of "the Heathen People" had been given by "the Lord God our Father" as the colonists' "rightfull Possession," but that the Indians, rather than accepting this outcome, began "plotting mischievous devices." God punished the "English Israel" for reasons focused on the internal dynamics of colonial society (such as acceptance of religious dissenters or disrespect for ministers) and not for relations with Indians.[3]

Explanations based on divine providence leave much room for interpretation. Virginia royalists, including Governor Berkeley, saw the war as a punishment for New England's opposition to Charles I during the revolutionary era. Berkeley believed that New England was implicated in the death of King Charles and that God sent war to punish the region for the regicide. Quakers angered by the Massachusetts government's execution of four of their fellows fifteen years before interpreted the war as punishment for persecution. During the war they attempted to erect a monument to their slain friends at the site of the gallows. Useful to royalist defenders of the Church of England, to godly opponents of that Church, and to sectarians lamenting persecution, providential interpretations cut across regional and confessional lines. They were also very much in vogue: historian Kenneth Murdock suggested that because New England minister William Hubbard declined to employ a providential construction, he got a cool response to his history of the war, *A Narrative of the Troubles with the Indians in New-England*.[4]

Whether viewing the war as a test or a punishment (or both), New Englanders frequently responded by reconfirming their faith in their local Congregational churches. During this crisis, the practice of covenant renewal took hold in New England. Ministers had been worrying about a decline in church membership for decades. As the first generation of settlers gradually passed from the scene (and it took a long time, as they were a remarkably long-lived lot) the proportion of church members within the overall population declined. Subsequent generations, though most of them had been baptized as the children of members, joined a church in full communion in relatively small numbers. This shift alarmed clergy, who eventually proposed a new policy that permitted the children of church members to have their own children baptized even if they had never become full members themselves. The change, later known as the Half Way Covenant, was not widely accepted initially, as some ministers and more church members opposed it. Those ministers who supported it (the majority) worked to gain its acceptance. One mechanism for integrating the unbaptized children of church members into the religious community was the mass covenant renewal. In these new community rituals, those affiliated with the church would participate in a ceremony in which they publicly and collectively stated their commitment to the church covenant. This practice, though suggested much earlier, was widely adopted only during King Philip's War. Feeling besieged by invading Indians, colonists flocked to reaffirm their commitment to the New England way in mass covenant renewal ceremonies. The renewals became a way for settlers to support their churches and communities in the face of the wrath of God and that of the Indians.

King Philip's War, besides sparking a spate of providential interpretations, caused a serious decline in the project of Christianizing the Indians. During the war itself, settler suspicion aimed at the praying Indians increased. Crowds harassed Indian commissioner Daniel Gookin for his support for the Indian missions. One settler was hauled before the court for "calling him an Irish dog that was never faithful to his country, the sonne of a whoare, a bitch, a rogue."[5] The authorities herded Praying Indian Village residents onto an inhospitable island in Boston Harbor to quell popular fears that even converted Indians would join the war against the colonists. Many died under the difficult conditions there. Other converts returned to their own people in the face of English hostility. Some fought on the side of the colonies, adding to the conflict an element of civil war among native peoples. Whether Christian Indians remained loyal to their English co-religionists or rejoined their native communities to fight against the settlers, colonists often hated and suspected them. Rowlandson's narrative of her captivity repeatedly asserted that any seemingly loyal praying Indians were false friends and had undoubtedly betrayed colonists when they could.

One way or another, the war brought much death to the Christian Indian community. At its end the number of Praying Indian Villages that could be reconstructed was drastically lower. More than two dozen villages extant on the mainland and the larger islands before the war fell to just a handful. The Christian Wampanoag communities on Nantucket and Martha's Vineyard were largely unaffected and remained intact, but on the mainland only four towns survived.[6] Amid the devastation, former residents of multiple villages were often consolidated into one. The population of Natick was lower at the end of the century than it had been in 1674, although survivors from three other villages had been combined with the original remnant. Whereas villages had once been made up of fairly coherent groups, the population decline and subsequent consolidation meant that the praying towns became less unified. Once-protected village land was increasingly vulnerable to the encroachments of English settlers who often succeeded in wresting it into their own hands. Though the Praying Indian Villages had never been generally popular with the New England settlers, King Philip's War sounded a death knell (though one that would ring for some time) on the concerted effort to Christianize Indians in southern New England.

As New England struggled with King Philip's War, Bacon's Rebellion—an Indian war compounded by an internal civil war—erupted in Virginia. As in New England, the series of interrelated crises in Virginia included a religious dimension and received religious interpretation. Named after its leader, Nathaniel Bacon, the rebellion began over settler hostility toward neighboring Indians and toward Virginia Governor Berkeley's conciliatory Indian policy. Bacon, a newly arrived and well-connected planter, wanted to depart from the governor's official policy and offered to lead a military force against neighboring Native American peoples. Bacon gathered men in spite of his lack of official sanction, attacking allies as well as "enemy Indians." His forces eventually turned on Berkeley and sacked Jamestown itself. The rebellion was finally put down with the help of the unhealthy environment, when the newly arrived and therefore not fully "seasoned" Bacon died of a fever and the "bloody flux" (or dysentery).

Those in Virginia who favored an aggressive anti-Indian policy used rhetoric very similar to that deployed in New England, referring to the Indians as violent and aggressive heathens and to their victims as "poor Christians." The political context of this rhetoric was different, however, for its use entailed a criticism of Berkeley's policies, the implication being that he was leaving poor helpless Christians to be wantonly massacred by his allies, the "barberous heathens."[7] Massachusetts residents responded to its Indian war with this language, whereas Virginians used it at first in order to justify starting a war in defiance of colonial policy. In neither colony did settlers seriously consider that colonial policy had contributed to the conflagrations. They overlooked the effects of the dramatic proliferation of settlements in New England that elicited an Indian attack and of the more modest but relentless Virginia expansion beyond the official line of settlement that led to frontier skirmishes and whetted colonial appetites for revenge. In both cases, the rhetoric placed all responsibility for the problems between settlers and Indians with the Native Americans. As in New England, Virginians writing about Bacon's Rebellion invariably figured the colonists as "Christians," underscoring the contrast to Indian "heathens."

In the course of the rebellion, religion shaped the construction of the English monarchy as sacred and of those who supported it as fulfilling their hallowed duty. Berkeley, as the king's appointed governor and long-time servant, referred to the king's "sacred majesty" and to his own role as the upholder of it. He described Bacon as launching a rebellion not only against Virginia policy and authorities but also against the monarch's divinely ordained position as king. Berkeley's "Declaration and Remonstrance" against the rebellion ended with the words "his most sacred majesties Raigne Charles the Second whome god grant long and prosperously to reign and let al his good subjects say amen Amen."[8]

Not to be outdone, Bacon enlisted the same imagery for his cause. Historians of Virginia once presented him as a heroic rebel anticipating the American revolutionaries, motivated by a desire to throw off English authority. Yet he laid claim to the same religiously inflected language of loyalty that Berkeley employed. In a proclamation in which he explained his position and tried to garner support, Bacon depicted himself as coming to the rescue of an ill-governed colony in hopes of saving it on behalf of the king. He repeatedly invoked the monarch and asserted his loyalty. In hoping for a hearing from the king in which he and his followers could justify their actions, he stated "we doe unanimously desire to represent our sad and heavy grievances to his most sacred Majestie as our Refuge and Sanctuary."[9] The struggle between Berkeley and Bacon revolved around these competing assertions that each side represented true loyalty, but both utilized the language of divine right kingship and personal fealty.

This language formed an interesting contrast to that utilized in New England, where defense of the region's religion might be seen as implicitly antiroyalist. The impression might be increased when we consider the legend in the town of Hadley, which recounted that the town was saved from Indian attack by the appearance of a powerful charismatic white-haired hermit, supposed to be one of the regicides who had been harbored in the region since the Restoration. Farther south, the legacy of the mid-century revolution and of regicide pointed the other way. Having become central to the construction of the Church of England generally and to the identity of Restoration-era Virginia, these events provided a religious vocabulary for discussing rebellion and loyalty.

While loyalty as a sacred trust was not mentioned in New England in reaction to King Philip's War, providential interpretations and especially the idea of war as punishment had currency in both regions. Berkeley concluded that calamity befell Virginia to punish it for the "Blood of King Charles the first." He assigned his troubles to the same cause that he had given for King Philip's War in New England. In coming to this conclusion, Berkeley ceased to blame the regicide only on his puritan foes and came to see it as the fault of "the Universal English Nation." Everyone was complicit in the death of Charles I. Berkeley's judgment offered a rare instance, as he stood back from the politics of providential name-calling, citing only the sins of others, in order to accept his own responsibility. The self-blaming potential within the providential scheme was not much in evidence as contemporaries debated the meaning of events, making Berkeley's remorse all the more striking. Still he was surprised that Virginia collapsed into crisis, for "this country would have beene the last that would have Expected Gods Anger for that wicked act for the whole Country was in a most serene and calme."[10] In Berkeley's view, all men had a sacred duty to support the king, which meant also the king's appointed governor, and God would punish those who did not do so—whether he exacted vengeance on the whole English nation for the killing of a king or on the rebels for defying the king's governor. In a similarly providential vein, Berkeley concluded that the successful seizure of Bacon's fleet was "a great and miraculous mercy" in which God showed his favor to the rebel's foes.

Others used providential imagery, laboring to read the prodigies and signs in this cataclysmic string of events. For instance, Thomas Matthews reported the story of an injured Indian boy, son of the Doeg leader, who was being held captive and lay in a coma for ten days. Finally a visitor to the home where he was being held suggested that baptism might cure him if his coma was the result of his being bewitched. After discussion about how to surmount the difficulty represented by the lack of a clergyman, it was concluded that the homeowner Captain Mason's clerk could legitimately perform the service. The child was then baptized according to the Church of England rite. He immediately "open'd the eyes, and breath'd, whereat [Mrs. Mason] ran for cordial [a liqueur, thought to have restorative properties] which he took from a spoon, gaping for more and so by degrees recovered, tho' before his baptism, they had often tried the same meanes but could not by no endeavours wrench open his teeth."[11] This rite was performed at the suggestion of Mr. Brent, "a papist," whose Catholicism might have aided him in thinking in terms of the healing powers of the sacraments. Yet the boy's rescuers employed the Church of England liturgy, and those present attributed the boy's recovery to its use. The story upheld that faith at a time when adherence to it and political loyalty were closely intertwined.

The opponents of Bacon attempted to present themselves as the representatives of true religion and Bacon as a dangerous threat to orthodoxy as well as to the social order. Berkeley himself utilized a large fund of spiritual language in this crisis, in addition to the vocabulary of divine kingship. He called upon God to witness the justice of his rule, for instance. When Bacon appeared ready to abandon his rebellious designs and submit to Berkeley's authority, Berkeley presented him to the gathered burgesses, saying, "If there be joy in the presence of the angels over one sinner that repenteth, there is joy now, for we have a penitent sinner come before us." Bacon's opponents repeatedly accused him of "atheisme." Berkeley stated that if Bacon was being quoted accurately, then he was guilty of "divers Expressions of Atheisme, tending to take away al Religion and lawes." Bacon and his fellows were also said to "drink Damnation to their Soules to be true to him." When Jamestown was burned to the ground, it was dubbed "this flagitious, and sacralidgious action." Philip Ludwell, who opposed Bacon, observed that the rebel leader made "such Dreadfull, new coyned oaths of which (as If he thought God was delighted with his Ingenuite in that kind) he was Very liberall."[12] Bacon's swearing to the damnation of his blood was thought to have been aptly rewarded when he died of the bloody flux, which was then understood as the result of an infection of the blood.

The twin crises in New England and the Chesapeake in 1675–76 reveal the religious sensibilities of the two regional cultures. Staunchly Anglican Virginia saw its commitment to the king as a sacred duty. Abhorrence of regicide and the continued expectation that divine wrath was owed to all those responsible shaped the religious culture. Devout Virginians, like their counterparts in Massachusetts Bay, employed a providential framework for understanding troubled times, and in both places local crisis was analyzed in such terms. In Virginia religion was understood as supportive of good order in society and politics, so that rebellion was thought to go hand in hand with atheism. In New England religion was no less central, but the cultural and political context differed. Virginians battled among themselves as well as fighting Indians, and they worked to lay blame within their own community and to discredit their opponents. New England settlers were united in their opposition to the Indians, and no civil war complicated the issue, so colonists in that region deployed religious language to explain the cause of the crisis or to demonize their Native American opponents. Placing blame within the settler community involved locating the sins that brought down God's wrath. While such finger pointing could get nasty, it never rose to the level of the accusations bandied about in Virginia. Indian-settler warfare may have been primarily about land and sovereignty issues, but religious language and interpretations reverberated through these crises.

While Virginia and New England were still reeling from the effects of King Philip's War and Bacon's Rebellion, a new crisis was brewing on the other side of the Atlantic. This one revolved around the long-standing fear of popery. The opening phase of the confrontation that would ultimately become the Glorious Revolution occurred in the late 1670s, during the so-called Exclusion Crisis. Exclusion referred to a political effort to exclude the king's brother, James, Duke of York, from inheriting the throne. Charles II, though he acknowledged paternity of a number of illegitimate children (notably his eldest son James Scott, Duke of Monmouth), had not sired a legal heir to the throne in over a decade of marriage to Catherine of Braganza. If this situation continued until his death, as seemed likely, the Duke of York, as Charles's younger brother, would become king. After James joined his second wife in open adherence to Catholicism, Charles's Protestant subjects began to fret over the succession. These worries were translated into fears when one Titus Oates spread unfounded rumors of a popish conspiracy to assassinate the king so that James would replace him on the throne. Oates was an obscure clergyman of no particular reputation and a background in Baptist circles. Yet the government and the public were taken in initially by his tales. Hysteria over the plot reached a fevered pitch. Authorities made many arrests and executed a dozen alleged conspirators in the frenzy. All went to their deaths claiming to be innocent, as historians have subsequently agreed they were. The allegations ultimately included one against the queen herself, averring that she intended to poison the king to make way for her co-religionist, in the person of his brother. Once word of the plot reached Maryland, local Protestants cited their own version of a popish plot, spreading rumors that the province's Catholics were in league with neighboring Indians to kill them all. Rumors to this effect had been circulating for at least a decade, but they suddenly seemed more compelling with the arrival of the news from England of papist conspiracy. In 1681, as a result of these rumors and an alleged rebellion planned against the government in response to them, the Maryland authorities ordered major instigator Josias Fendall to pay a fine and leave the colony. Before settling on that course, they seriously considered having his tongue bored or his ears cropped as well.

The controversy in England moved to a new level when Protestant political leaders broached the problem of a Catholic succession by offering a legislative solution. They perceived that a sure way to foil any popish plot against England's Protestantism was by blocking James's access to the crown. Parliament moved to do this in an Exclusion Bill, stating that any Catholic heir would be disqualified and the next Protestant in line would become the monarch instead. Charles viewed this bill and the movement behind it as a threat not just to his brother's claim but to the monarchy more generally. This impression was confirmed when republican theorists who supported exclusion attacked hereditary monarchy and the extent of the king's power. Charles therefore defended his brother with increasing determination and eventually foiled the bill. As part of the political maneuvering during this confrontation, the Duke of York neutralized the opposition of William Penn, a moderate supporter of exclusion, by promising him a proprietary grant in North America. The colony of Pennsylvania was chartered to reward Penn for dropping his support for exclusion at a key moment. Although it was a rather minor footnote to the political crisis as it unfolded within England, the chartering of a "Quaker colony" that would be dedicated to religious liberty and would foster religious pluralism had enormous implications for the history of British North America. Charles and James succeeded in staving off the Exclusion Crisis, but fear of popery and of the imminent succession of a Catholic ruler remained. These fears would resurface during James's short reign, finally bringing an end to rule by a Catholic in the Glorious Revolution.

The Protestant opponents of James's kingship lost the exclusion battle, but they won the war in 1688 by deposing him once he became king. A coup (bloodless at least in England and Wales), the Glorious Revolution brought in James's eldest daughter, Mary, and her Dutch husband, William of Orange (Protestants both), to rule in his stead. Upon Charles's death in 1685, when James became king, he did nothing to calm the fears of those subjects who believed he meant to impose Catholicism and to exercise a tyrannical power modeled on that of Louis XIV. No doubt reacting at least in part to the earlier exclusion move, James attempted to abrogate authority to himself and to limit the political role of his opponents. He affronted local elites by canceling customary privileges and rights, such as revoking corporate (including colonial) charters. In this way, Massachusetts Bay, Connecticut, and

Rhode Island all lost their charters and were subsumed under a new Dominion of New England ruled from New York. A demand that clergymen read James's "Declaration of Indulgences" (granting new freedoms to Catholics) from their pulpits was one of the last straws. It led a group of bishops to write to William to ask him to take the throne from his father-in-law. The birth of a Catholic heir to Mary of Modena and James was another straw. The nativity of a new Prince of Wales boded ill for the Protestant cause and led to rumors that the infant was not in fact the queen's child. Although many courtiers of both sexes and both religious parties were present at the royal birth, stories nonetheless flew that the baby had died and been replaced by another. Because this alleged substitution was said to have been made when the baby was smuggled into the birth room in a warming pan, the scandal was dubbed "the warming pan controversy." Its currency suggested how unwilling the kingdom's Protestants were to accept the legitimacy of another Catholic claimant to the throne. Protestant political and religious leaders united to invite William and Mary to England.

The Glorious Revolution was the result. William landed in England on November 5, 1688, having been carried by a "Protestant wind" that also bottled up James's ships in the Thames. The date was auspicious, the anniversary of the Gunpowder Plot, in which Guy Fawkes and others attempted to blow up Parliament and the Protestant king James I with it. The symbolism was not lost on William and Mary's supporters in England and Wales, as the day had long been commemorated with anti-Catholic festivities. William and his army marched to London unopposed, after James failed to rally his troops and instead escaped to France. When his departure became known, the City of London exploded into an orgy of anti-Catholic vandalism. Crowds set fire to the homes of Roman Catholics as well as to chapels attached to various embassies. Though those who invited William into England were motivated by anti-Catholic prejudice as much as anything else, William came from the far more tolerant and diverse Netherlands with an army that included Catholic soldiers and officers. Parliament met and passed a Declaration of Right intended to end Stuart abuses of power, and William and Mary agreed to assume the throne and become monarchs over the three kingdoms of England, Scotland, and Ireland.

James, having failed to galvanize his supporters in England, decided to take his stand to save his kingdoms in Ireland. In the meantime a supporter in Scotland, John Graham of Claverhouse, 1st Viscount of Dundee, led Highlanders into battle on behalf of the deposed king. Dundee's death at the

Battle of Killiecrankie on July 17, 1689, effectively ended the organized Scottish opposition to William and Mary. Only Ireland remained to fight on James's behalf. Contemporary observers were not surprised to find Ireland, long feared as a potential site of invasion by continental Catholics, serving as the battleground for William's and James's confrontation. Only Ireland among all his kingdoms had not deserted James, and it became the arena of a two-year-long war (1689–91) that ended in James's defeat.

The Glorious Revolution altered the religious settlement in the three kingdoms. The Church of England remained as the established church in England and Wales, but the government reversed the various concessions that James had made to accommodate his co-religionists. Roman Catholics would continue to live as second-class subjects for years to come. Restrictions on Protestant dissenters—including Presbyterians, Congregationalists, Quakers, and Baptists—were lifted, and their situation improved. In Scotland, the crown moved to disestablish the Episcopal Church, which had been the official state church since the Restoration, because of the support Episcopal leaders had offered James. The Episcopal Church not having succeeded in capturing the allegiance of most Scots, they supported a return to Presbyterianism, which was achieved after 1688. In Ireland, where Catholic leaders supported James in the hope of reversing years of discrimination against their faith, the settlement ultimately reached under William and Mary represented a major step backward. In particular Catholics were blocked from all positions of authority, so that the ruling elite of Ireland became effectively Protestant after 1691.

Decades of intermittent war with France were another result of the overthrow of James II. For some time prior to his landing in England, William had been the leader of a coalition against France. Indeed one motive for taking James's throne was the need to keep England out of the French camp in the wars then gathering force on the Continent. William's war with France of necessity involved the kingdoms (as well as the colonies) after William and Mary became rulers. These wars—fought by a Protestant Britain in alliance with the Dutch against a Catholic France—would mold the history of western Europe and the Atlantic world until the final British victory in 1763. They also kept alive the anti-Catholicism that was on display in the Glorious Revolution itself. Little wonder, then, that Irish soldiers who left Ireland after James's defeat at William's hands (1691) often volunteered to fight for France. Similarly, at the time of the Cromwellian reconquest in the 1650s, they had departed to support Cromwell's nemesis, Spain.

The Glorious Revolution resounded across the English Atlantic, sparking companion rebellions in numerous colonies, in all of which religion played a major role. As with all such abrupt changes at the imperial center, news was slow to arrive in the colonies, and official instructions about how to respond to the invasion of England and the overthrow of James were slower still. This lack of timely advice left colonial governments choosing whether to respond to rumors about events in England and wondering how best to do so. Settlers in Massachusetts, New York, and Maryland perceived the upheaval as an opportunity to pursue their own local agendas. In each location, colonists used the overthrow of James to remove an unpopular colonial government. The most successful efforts—those in Massachusetts and Maryland—had religious as well as political goals that they communicated fairly effectively to the authorities in England. In New York, the politics of the ouster were more divisive and complex, and rebels were ultimately unable to persuade William and Mary of the legitimacy of their cause. Support for the new government in Westminster was a common feature of these local coups, even though each played out in the context of specific colonial conditions. In the Leeward Islands of the eastern Caribbean the governor appointed by James II stepped down rather than declare allegiance to his successors. Otherwise the initiative was all with those who agreed that the events in England were indeed glorious.

Traditional colonial leaders had cause to be unhappy with James's rule. Massachusetts as well as New York had been subsumed under a new administrative unit, the Dominion of New England, in the late 1680s. The 1629 charter for Massachusetts was abrogated in 1685, toward the end of Charles II's reign, in a move that had been threatened sporadically for the previous half century. A new government meant an end to an unprecedented degree of local control. Henceforth governors would be appointed and (in theory at least) policy would be dictated from the metropole. Most New England colonies had a Congregational religious establishment that was out of step with the established church in England. For them, greater control by the crown was thought to mean the imposition of the Church of England. The leaders of Massachusetts liked to think of their colony as uniquely patterned upon God's word, and they had relished the control which had allowed them and their predecessors to create that system. The loss of the 1629 Massachusetts charter was therefore a serious blow. The colony's leaders perceived the creation of the Dominion of New England, which brought the colony under a regional government that eventually extended from New York to Maine, as a disaster.

Against this backdrop, Massachusetts was the first colony to respond to news of William's arrival in England by staging a coup of its own. A sizeable group of colonists gathered in arms and seized the appointed governor of the Dominion of New England, Sir Edmund Andros, who was then in Boston. Imprisoning Andros, the Massachusetts rebels declared the old charter government back in force until they could learn the new monarchs' pleasure. The leaders described their uprising in terms of bringing an end to James's tyranny and his attacks on their religion. On the other side, a proponent of the king's cause, Edward Randolph, used the language employed earlier by Berkeley to suggest that the rebels' disloyalty was irreligious. In spite of the accusations leveled against it, the Dominion government had not attempted to institute popery or even liberty for Catholics in the New England region. Its religious policies stopped at promoting the Church of England, which had previously held dissenter status vis-à-vis the established Congregational church.

While it might seem reasonable for the English monarch to promote a policy in which the national established church had at least neutral if not favored status, the Massachusetts rebels did not see it thus. Instead they framed their actions in terms of battling another popish plot. In this view, popery sought to undermine Protestantism and therefore pursued policies aimed to weaken religion in "a Countrey so remarkable for the true Profession and pure Exercise of the Protestant Religion."[13] Even though Catholicism was not being promoted, they argued that local churches were weakened as part of a long-term effort to destroy the foes of the papists. The rebels in Massachusetts presented themselves to William and Mary as dutiful subjects but also as allies in the battle against tyranny and popery. They hoped the new monarchs would officially reinstate their old charter and allow them to return to their old ways—using the government to support the "New England Way" of Congregational church order and all the practices that had developed to buttress its place in society.

Once the Massachusetts Bay colonists had imprisoned the governor of the Dominion, its foundations were shaken. Not only had questions about its legitimacy been raised by the revolution at home, but the Dominion was also undermined by the elimination of its governor and a number of the members of its appointed Council (also imprisoned in Boston). After the Massachusetts coup, the Dominion ceased to function within New England.

Other colonies followed Massachusetts' lead and resurrected their former governments. Connecticut, Rhode Island, and Plymouth all went back to their older patterns and habits of governance while awaiting word from England.

In New York, simple reversion to a pre-Dominion government was complicated by a number of factors. Prior to being absorbed into the Dominion, New York had been James's own colony. Charles had granted it to him at the time of the conquest of New Netherland, when he was Duke of York, and it became a royal colony (that is, a colony controlled directly by the crown) when he became king. Reversion to the old government took on a very different implication in this context. If the New Yorkers returned to their pre-Dominion government, they would be supporting rule by the ousted king James, to whom the colony had belonged. Such a move amounted to a break with England in favor of James. Returning to pre-Dominion status was also problematic, since to do so was to set aside James's own more recent instructions to join in the Dominion. New York might have functioned as an attenuated version of the Dominion (basically remaining in the position James had left it). Lieutenant Governor Francis Nicholson, whom Andros had left behind to govern during his absence in Boston, tried to affect this outcome by rallying the colonists when news of Andros's arrest arrived. Faced with rising tensions within the population, Nicholson expanded the appointed Council to a larger committee that included a cross section of local leaders. The situation gradually spun out of his control, and Nicholson eventually fled back to England to report on the collapse of government in New York as elsewhere.

New York, in addition to lacking an obvious earlier version of authority to which it could revert, was also riven by factionalism. How to replace the Dominion with a government that would have broad support was a much more difficult question in New York than it had been in the various New England colonies. The outcome in New York was more contested than elsewhere. Having been a Dutch colony until 1664 (and having been briefly retaken by the Dutch in 1673), New York maintained a majority Dutch population. The colony sheltered numerous English residents—some of whom had lived under Dutch rule but more of whom had come since the conquest. In addition it housed a variety of other European migrants and a fairly sizeable African and African American population, the last of these especially numerous in the principal town of New York. Given this ethnic (and related religious) diversity, the colony experienced social and political tensions beyond what any New England colony had known to date. Nicholson's Committee of Safety, an expanded version of his Council, took over initially when he departed. Colonial militia officer Jacob Leisler emerged as a leader, and he eventually took over the post of lieutenant governor with a Council to advise him.

Jacob Leisler interpreted events in the context of his own virulent anti-Catholicism. He had been born in Frankfurt am Main, the son of a French Reformed minister serving an immigrant church in that German-speaking city. He migrated to New Netherland in the employ of the Dutch West India Company in 1660, where he soon married into one of the leading merchant families. By 1674 he was among the wealthiest merchants in the city of New York. When Huguenot refugees fled France, Leisler made arrangements for the settlement of a number of communities within the bounds of New York. His work on their behalf and his fears of the policies of James, whom he saw as an absolutist papist, roused him to become involved in politics as the Dominion began to totter. With his European and American experiences of Catholicism as a powerful and predatory force, Leisler stood ready to support the Glorious Revolution in his own colony.

As in Massachusetts, New York insurgents also tried to justify their rebellion and present it to the authorities in England in the best possible light. For the New Yorkers who gathered around Leisler, fighting the Catholic threat was a major concern. Catholicism and arbitrary government were closely linked in the minds of these rebels—as they were elsewhere in the Atlantic world. The colonists emphasized that their own uprising against James's government had been part of a larger move against popery and tyranny. Although Leisler was of French background, born in the German lands, and married into a prominent local Dutch family, he still claimed to have acted in defense of the rights of "freeborn English men." In this he and his supporters used typical rhetoric, asserting that James's popery and arbitrary government threatened their rights. Like other English subjects in this period, Leislerians invoked the metaphor of slavery to describe their condition under James. Opponents of Leisler did not support James, especially once it became clear that William and Mary had successfully taken the throne. Rather, his foes only questioned Leisler's motives and goals. By dismissing him as a radical and a rabble-rouser, those who denounced Leisler to the authorities could associate themselves with the same antipopery and hostility to arbitrary government that Leisler sought to claim while dismissing his bid to be accepted as the man who could guide the colony toward Protestantism and liberty.

Anti-Catholicism played an even greater role in the rebellion of Marylanders than it had for New Yorkers. Founded by the Catholic aristocratic Calvert family, Maryland continued to boast a Catholic ruling elite and a largely Protestant populace in 1689. For reasons that have not been adequately explained, the government of Maryland did not proclaim the new king and queen even after neighboring Virginia had done so and Lord Baltimore had dispatched messengers instructing the colony to follow suit. (It is not clear that these messengers ever arrived.) As the Protestant rebels later put it, they expected Calvert's government to issue a declaration in support of William and Mary: "For as much as it has pleased Almighty God, by means of the great Prudence and Conduct of the best of Princes; Our most gracious King William, to put a Check to the great Innundation of Slavery and Popery, that had like to overwhelm Their Majesties Protestant Subjects in all their Territories and Dominions (of which none have suffered more, or are in greater Danger than our selves) we hope and expected in our particular Stations and Qualifications; a proportionable Share of so great a Blessing."[14] Yet the local authorities seemed bent on denying the colony's residents their "proportionable Share" of this good fortune. The proprietary's opponents had other concerns as well. As the government refrained from issuing a declaration in support of the revolution in England, rumors spread through the province that the Catholics were conspiring to enter into an alliance with local Indians in order to attack the Protestants within the population. Such rumors built on fears of Indian wars and exacerbated Protestant hostilities toward the ruling Catholic elite.

Baltimore's supporters eventually fell to a bloodless coup. After tense months, in July an armed contingent that came to be known as the Protestant Associators took the State House. Government officials had fled to the manor house of the Baltimore family and the rebels captured that as well. The victorious Associators led by John Coode issued a declaration complaining of the oppression of Protestants under the Catholic Baltimores and declaring the province's support for William and Mary. The rebels directly linked the uprising in Maryland to William's success in England, averring that both ended arbitrary rule by Catholics bent on oppressing Protestants. The Associators also revived the rumored Catholic-Indian conspiracy, which, although it was groundless as far as the accusations involving the Maryland elite were concerned, seemed justified by recent attacks on English colonies to the north by the French and their Indian allies. France and England had gone to war once William and Mary took the throne from France's ally James. These attacks were related to the Protestant-Catholic divide as it was playing out within Europe and spilling over from Europe into the French and English colonial possessions. In the continental colonies the already hated Catholicism began to be equated with Indian wartime atrocities, so that papists and savagery were linked in the rhetoric of these wars. Maryland rebels presented themselves as loyal Protestant subjects to William and Mary, fighting on their behalf in order to throw off their Catholic oppressors in Maryland and to regain their rights as freeborn English men. Maryland's new rulers immediately barred Catholics from office holding, citing English practice for doing so, and turned to William and Mary to back their coup.

Faced with these three rebellions, the king and queen had to decide what to do with their self-proclaimed supporters. Although the justifications differed somewhat in the three rebellious colonies, Massachusetts, New York, and Maryland all presented their uprisings in the context of antipopery, liberty, and loyalty to the new monarchs. All three hoped for the crown's support for what they had done. As royal policy developed in the aftermath of 1688, it became clear that the monarchs more or less accepted the rebellions in Massachusetts and Maryland, but not in New York. The reasons for this variable response had to do with local conditions in each colony. The Maryland Associators won confirmation for their effort to bring down the Baltimore proprietary. Maryland was made a royal colony, and the power of the Catholic proprietor was brought to an end. (The Calvert family would win back the colony in the eighteenth century, but only after giving up its Catholicism to conform to the Church of England.) Having Maryland as a royal colony suited the king's needs to prosecute a war with France that had already spilled over into America, so the crown was happy to go along with the rebels in this instance. Far from punishing Coode, the government rewarded him for his services. In a move that might have seemed aimed to satisfy the Protestant Associators, the crown instructed its new governor to establish the Church of England in the colony. Yet, because few Maryland Protestants were members (as opposed to Protestant dissenters of one sort or another), the legislature did not wholeheartedly embrace this proposal. It instead erected a weak establishment that did little to promote the official church.

The Massachusetts rebels, although they earned the crown's approbation for their actions, did not win all they hoped for out of their uprising. The colony was not returned to its original charter, but was granted a new royal charter that gave the monarch more direct control over the government. Boston minister Increase Mather, in England as the colony's agent, was permitted to propose the first royal governor—and at his suggestion Sir William Phipps of northern New England was named. Yet the change to an appointed rather than an elected governor had serious implications for the colony's ability to control its own governance. In addition the new charter eliminated the colony's favoritism toward Congregationalists, canceling the church membership requirement for voting, and promising religious freedom to all Protestants. Massachusetts Bay leaders would subsequently be challenged to keep the populace's commitment to its traditional church with little of the customary aid from the central government. Remaining an independent colony, since William and Mary dropped the policy that had created a large dominion out of numerous distinct colonies, Massachusetts did not return to its originally high level of local autonomy or its distinctive religious practices.

In New York the rebels fared worst of all. With New York more deeply divided than Massachusetts and the divisions less easily sorted out than the Protestant-Catholic divide in Maryland, the assertion that Jacob Leisler and his supporters represented the interests of the new monarchs was less apparent. Although Leislerians did their best to present themselves as the advocates for English liberty and Protestantism, their opponents in the factional fight within the colony made similar claims. The former lieutenant governor, Francis Nicholson, effectively turned William and Mary against Leisler, whose inept agents did him no good in the deliberations over how best to settle New York's government. Critics carried the day, persuading the crown that Leisler and his closest supporters did not represent its interests. Henry Sloughter, the royal governor dispatched to take control of the colony, arrived to find Leisler fighting against the military commander whom he had sent ahead of him because the officer had challenged Leisler's authority. This defiance sealed Leisler's fate, and he and a handful of other supporters were tried. In the end, the authorities executed Leisler and his brother-in-law Jacob Milbourne. Others were acquitted or pardoned. Despite this sorry end to Leisler's uprising, his professed goals were accomplished. New York returned to the status of a royal colony, with the Church of England established and other Protestants (but not Catholics) tolerated. William and Mary's policies agreed with those of their predecessor in that they expected to exercise fairly close control over their colonies, an imperative that was increased by the onset of decades of intermittent warfare with France. The worst abuses of English liberties of which James had been suspected were no longer feared. The Glorious Revolution could be seen as rescuing all freeborn English men from the threat of enslavement to popish tyranny.

The uneven outcome in various colonial locations should not be allowed to obscure the common themes of the Glorious Revolution in the wider Atlantic. As in Britain, events pivoted on fear of Catholicism. In this spirit, Presbyterian minister Francis Makemie would shortly call from Barbados for Protestant unity (encompassing Church of England members along with others) to combat popery in his *Truths in a True Light* (1699). Despite the fears sparked by Guy Fawkes's plot to blow up Parliament in 1605, dread of popery was usually directed at external enemies such as the Irish, French, or Spanish. The Irish rebellion of 1641, which targeted Protestants, brought the worries close to home. Still English and Welsh Protestants had generally tolerated Catholics in their midst. In the years leading up to 1688, however, Catholicism ceased to be seen as a largely external threat. A Catholic monarch with a son to whom the throne would eventually pass posed a grave danger. Coming together to defend Protestantism in England and Wales and in some colonies might serve to unify church members with dissenters in opposition to popery. In spite of references to the rights of freeborn English men, the largest context for understanding these events was not ethnic, pitting English against others. The use of the rhetoric by German and Dutch opponents of James in New York suggested as much, as did the arrival of an ethnically Dutch king on the throne. Protestantism rather than English rights could unite James's opponents across ethnic and confessional lines. While the rhetoric of antipopery obviously excluded Catholics, it could conceivably include all Protestants. Dissenter support for the coup in England and for the related uprisings in the colonies indicated the potentially unifying power of hating James for his Catholicism. Virginians in Bacon's Rebellion embraced a rhetoric that ostracized non-Anglicans as disloyal. In the Glorious Revolution, the language of antipopery and support for liberty had a power to unite. The Church of England was losing its grip on this power in the fragmentation of the Protestant community that had occurred over the preceding century. Protestantism broadly conceived held enormous potential as a transatlantic rallying point.

The tensions generated by these various crises contributed toward an upsurge in fears of witchcraft in both Massachusetts and Scotland in the last decade of the century. Witch belief was part of the culture of the British Atlantic, and the Europeans who lived under British rule were nearly unanimous in their conviction that witches posed a threat to individuals and the community. Few people were skeptical about the existence of witches, and their objections were viewed as irreligious. Africans living among the settler population similarly believed in the witch's ability to do harm, but their suspicions were not sparked by these tensions within British Atlantic society. Rather they focused their witch concerns on the cruelty of their masters, whom some saw as practicing witchcraft; Africans' concerns were more constant and less responsive to broader trends. Among Europeans, in contrast, witch scares such as had plagued Europe for centuries appeared to be in decline more generally, but they flared up in times of social stress.

No scholar has been able to come up with a perfectly satisfying explanation for the combination of circumstances that went into a witch hunt, but community anxiety helped to create conditions that could precipitate one. In Massachusetts the instability of the government compounded by fears that the local church order was being displaced set the stage, while in Scotland similar concerns over the traditional church were key. In both places a desire to combat atheism by proving that witches existed played a role, whereas in New England fear of Indian attack added to the sense of a community besieged. Both Massachusetts and Scotland were under the authority of a distant power—the crown in England—that seemed to threaten local control of religion, and both felt uncertain of their ability to maintain local commitment to a traditionally intrusive faith-based disciplinary system. In both instances such uncertainties created serious social strains that manifest themselves in witch-hunting.

Possibly the most infamous conflict of the late seventeenth century was the witchcraft scare that emanated out of the towns of Salem and Andover, Massachusetts, and enveloped the colony in 1692. In an event reminiscent of earlier scares that had periodically rocked one area after another in Europe, accusations against suspected witches spiraled out of control. Hundreds were accused, many jailed, some fled the colony, and nineteen were executed. A twentieth accused witch died, pressed to death under a board with rocks slowly piled on it in an attempt to force him to plead guilty or not guilty before the court. Without a plea, the court could not try him, so the justices sought to coerce his participation by using this ancient legal technique. New England had experienced witchcraft accusations, trials, and executions before, including one small-scale scare in the early 1660s. But the extent of accusations in 1692 was unprecedented in colonial America. Taking a broader geographical perspective, by the 1690s, mass scares and even isolated accusations were becoming a thing of the past. Indeed, the only later scare to occur in Europe took place in Scotland in 1697–1700. Otherwise major witch hunts were already over by the time Salem became ensnared in its crisis. The extent and the timing of the upsurge in witch fear both require explanation.

The aftermath of the Glorious Revolution in Massachusetts provided a context for sudden fear of "a plague of witches." Colonial religious leaders had been preaching about the loss of the charter and the need to recommit the colony to its former vision. They warned of what would happen to New England if the colonists failed to respond. Ministers tended to see political threats to the churches in cosmic terms. The loss of the charter was therefore a punishment or a test, just as King Philip's War had been. New Englanders were repeatedly warned to be vigilant against efforts to undermine their churches. The clergy promoted the belief that Satan was particularly bent on the destruction of the Massachusetts Bay Colony. Satanic conquest of such a godly region, they averred, would be worth more than if he were to succeed in a host of other places. By framing the situation in such terms, local clerics encouraged a climate of fear.

This apprehensiveness was exacerbated by the political situation. Since the arrest of Edmund Andros in 1689 the government had been organized on the questionable basis of its revoked charter. Until confirmation came from England, the government had no real legal foundation. That being the case, the Bay Colony government was ill prepared to deal with a crisis. When confronted with accusations of a satanic conspiracy to overturn the colony and its churches, the authorities reacted by jailing the alleged witches and waiting for word about the settlement of their government. If nervous accusers went to the authorities hoping for a resolution to their fears that witches threatened them, all they got was the confirmation of those fears in the jailing of the suspects. The answers a trial could bring had to be postponed, which did nothing to allay the suspicions of the nervous and may have led to further accusations. As more and more people were named, the jails in northeastern Massachusetts filled up. A skittish population awaited a resolution.

The scare was probably also aggravated by the Indian wars, which returned to the New England frontier with a vengeance after the Glorious Revolution. Initially witchcraft allegations arose among a group of girls and young women, servants, and others in the section of Salem known as the Village. Servant accusers were often refugees from the Indian wars on the northern frontier, where warriors attacked their family homes. Witnessing horrific sights, they lost not only relatives but also their place in society. Orphaned or at least impoverished, they were forced to take positions as servants in the homes of families living farther south. A number of them ended up in the north shore town of Salem. The trauma of their experiences or their resentment at their reduced prospects may have made them more open to participation in the witchcraft scare. Girls became bewitched or possessed: bewitchment involved torments imposed by a witch (often designed to force its victim to join with the devil), whereas a demon or Satan himself possessed the victim, taking over the body, sometimes speaking through the victim's mouth. The "afflicted girls" gave evidence that helped to propel the witch controversy forward.

Despite the apparent connection to the Indian wars and the tendency to describe enemy Indians as demonic, Indians themselves were not targets of witchcraft charges. Allegations were usually made between neighbors, people with long personal experience that could provide evidence of malice or supernatural abilities. The one exception proves the rule: Tituba, who may have been a South American Indian kidnapped into slavery in Barbados and later transported to Massachusetts by her master, was among the first incarcerated. Living as a slave in the household of a prominent English family, she had the sort of contact with prospective accusers that usually preceded suspicions of witchcraft. One scholar has suggested that the stories Tituba told, blending South American Indian, West Indian African, and English beliefs, terrified the authorities and escalated the crisis further.[15]

A much more typical victim of the scare was Sarah Good. Born in the colony some forty years earlier, Good had a reputation as a beggar and a nuisance in the village of Salem by the early 1690s. Her husband, a day laborer, did not earn enough to provide adequately for his family. Sarah therefore begged from house to house, and her irascible personality may have offended her neighbors. After numerous unpleasant encounters, the neighbors began swapping stories of difficulties that befell them after these exchanges. Misfortunes might be blamed on a variety of causes in seventeenth-century New England, but the idea that Sarah Good was a witch who was responsible for the misfortunes of her neighbors began to gain currency. As a result of her unfortunate reputation, Good was among the first accused. Even though her six-year-old daughter spoke out against her mother, the child herself was incarcerated as a suspected witch for over six months. Eventually the court released the girl but hanged the mother. Good's marginal status and her reportedly combative personality made her a likely candidate for a witch accusation. Most unusual about the Salem situation was that accusations did not stop with the likes of Tituba and Good but continued on to target other, less likely candidates. Events had left predictable paths.

Fig. 9. Belief in witches was widespread throughout Europe in the seventeenth century. Joseph Glanvil's book, first published in 1681, argued for the existence of witches and, in its second book or section, compiled evidence of their activities. This image served as the frontispiece to the second book. *Saducismus Triumphatus: or, Full and plain evidence concerning witches and apparitions* (1689/1726). Courtesy of John Carter Brown Library at Brown University.

Into this situation came the colony's newly appointed governor, Sir William Phipps, armed with a new charter and the authority to settle the dispute. Unfortunately, he acted in a way that worsened an already-tense situation. Arriving to find numerous suspected witches in jail, Phipps set up a special court with the power to dispatch cases quickly. In a court of oyer and terminer, a group of justices decided the guilt or innocence of the accused, passed sentence, and saw it executed. Phipps left for northern New England to handle business there, leaving the court to resolve the witchcraft problem on its own. In his absence the justices proceeded to deal with numerous pending cases. The trials resulted in many convictions, and some alleged witches confessed to having committed the crime of witchcraft. Suspecting a widespread witch conspiracy, the court postponed the executions of confessed witches in order to question them about other suspects slated to be tried subsequently. New accusations cascaded in, and those named included a growing number of elite colonists. Eventually a minister's wife and, finally, the wife of the governor were targeted.

The Quakers, a potentially suspicious group heavily concentrated in Salem, were not identified as witches. With few exceptions, accusers overlooked known Quakers. Similarly the Quakers did not usually lodge complaints. What Salem Quaker and general troublemaker Thomas Maule later said of the trials has been borne out by the evidence: God left the Quakers out of this crisis. Rather than policing boundaries between rival religious groups, the trials were an affair internal to the dominant, Congregationalist community. Particular people may have been fingered because, though members of the orthodox community themselves, they had close ties to their Quaker neighbors. Suspicions of divided loyalties may help explain the accusation of Rebecca Nurse. Her conviction as a witch was shocking because of her godly reputation and impeccable behavior. At her trial, she was able to recite the Lord's Prayer without stumbling, a sign that she was not in league with the devil. Two of Nurse's sons, however, had married into a Quaker family, which may have helped to taint her reputation. Quakers themselves, however, seem to have been immune from prosecution as witches. The Proctor family, made famous by Arthur Miller's somewhat fanciful use of its story as the basis for his play *The Crucible*, was not affiliated with the sect at the time of the accusations. Rather, some Proctors joined in the aftermath of the crisis. Deliverance Proctor, born of the pregnancy that saved her mother from hanging as a witch (and named Deliverance to commemorate that fact), would grow up to be a leader in the Salem meeting. Becoming Quakers allowed the Proctors to distance themselves from their orthodox neighbors who had accused and harassed them in 1692.

The plague of witches ended only when the colony's clerical elite joined together to challenge the judicial process and persuade the governor to bring it to a stop. The ministers focused on an aspect of the court's work that was especially controversial, the use of spectral evidence. Accusers often reported having seen the shape (or specter) of a person, perhaps accosting them in the night in their darkened house. This phenomenon raised a theological question with legal implications: did the devil need an individual's permission to send his or her specter out? In other words, was the person represented by the specter necessarily in league with Satan or could the apparition be a trick of the devil to bring about the accusation of the innocent? The judges proceeded as if the former were the case and used the specter to prove complicity. The ministers eventually decided the opposite, that such appearances could be a satanic trick. They advised the judges to use more caution. Upon his return to Boston, Phipps found his own wife accused and the colony's ministers (including Increase Mather who had nominated him as governor) opposed to the proceedings. Phipps called a temporary halt to the trials, put an end to the executions, and advised the judges to absolve all remaining suspects. The killings ended rather abruptly. The jails were emptied of both the convicted who had yet to be executed and others who had yet to face trial. By releasing so many confessed witches, the court seemed to indicate that it forgave and reprieved those who confessed. This outcome may have been more an inadvertent development than the result of official policy. The court had already ordered the execution of some confessed witches, and may well have done the same with the others if the proceedings had been allowed to take their bloody course.

Witches appeared in Scotland in the 1690s (or so residents feared), although the scare there ultimately resulted in fewer accusations and executions. As in Massachusetts, the courts concluded that young female victims were suffering at the hands of witches, and almost fifty people were accused in connection with these cases. In the end, seven of the accused were tried and executed, all of those involved with the earliest of the three possession cases. The other accused were released without trial after an extended period in jail, once the panic subsided. As in Massachusetts, religion in Scotland seemed under general attack. The Presbyterian kirk, which had been reestablished in the aftermath of the Glorious Revolution, was failing to garner the support of the populace in the way that its advocates desired. Atheism, believed to be on the rise, also caused concern. Presbyterians' proponents sought to reinvigorate the traditional supports of religion, from blasphemy laws to witch hunts. Rumors of a planned French invasion of western Scotland contributed to the sense that religion was tottering. The invasion was expected in the region that became caught up in the witch scare.

Western Scotland in the late 1690s, experiencing similar stresses to those that Massachusetts had endured earlier in the decade, manifested its fears in similar ways, hunting witches in its midst. Witch scares emerged in times of community stress, and these cases were no different. Economic and political conflicts combined with fears of foreign invasion and worries about the state of the local church created ripe conditions. With local residents already suspected by their neighbors and authorities newly willing to prosecute, the requisite constellation of factors existed in Scotland. In the end, however, the local leaders turned away from witchcraft as the answer to their community's problems, effectively ending the trials. Also as in New England, the Scottish cases seemed to have come to a close because the local authorities began to doubt the credibility of the evidence. In this case they worried that confessions had been forced and that some of the women involved were mentally ill. As the officials began to question the legitimacy of the proceedings, they quietly stopped them without further discussion. Authorities in both areas wanted to punish sin and support God's cause, and were willing to execute witches if that appeared necessary. The elites also began courting the idea that other issues—like the credulity of the populace or the mental illness of the accusers—might explain witch cases. These uncertainties would bring witch hunting to an end, even though belief in witches remained. Salem participants quickly came to recognize the excesses of their trials. They then explained the crisis by saying that the devil, rather than tempting individuals to take up witchcraft, had tricked the community into killing innocent people as witches. Satan continued as a force to be feared, especially in times of community stress, long after the last witch died.

Civil and Indian wars, political upheavals, and witch scares marked the last decades of the century in the crisis-filled British Atlantic world. In all cases, religion played a major role in bringing about and shaping events. In the Chesapeake and in New England hostilities with natives played out the religious tensions produced by cultural encounter. Colonists understood Indians as heathens whose land could be taken and who were ultimately at fault in the conflicts between settlers and the indigenous inhabitants. When Native Americans concluded that the presence of settlers was threatening the continued existence of their communities, they forcefully articulated their rejection of European culture by slighting its religious symbols. Negotiations between these different communities and cultures broke down in a spectacular orgy of violence. In the context of political crisis, loyalty was frequently presented as a religious duty, and disloyalty as an irreligious act. Indian war or other community crises were explained as divine retribution for regicide, just as witchcraft was seen as punishment for various community sins.

The Glorious Revolution and its lesser colonial manifestations had especially wide-ranging effects not only on religion but also on other aspects of life in the three kingdoms and in the Atlantic basin. The expulsion of James II prevented the throne from falling permanently into the hands of Catholics. This in turn halted the movement of the kingdoms toward a pro-Catholic domestic policy and a French alliance. The position of Catholics in the Stuart domains was weakened by the outcome of the revolution. Catholics were further marginalized in Ireland, and Catholic proprietors of Maryland were displaced. Foreign policy joined popular culture in being rigorously anti-Catholic, as England entered into a series of wars against France. These wars had far-flung effects, as invasion fears helped to spark witch accusations in Scotland and related Indian attacks influenced the language of witch fears in New England. In the colonies, dread of French Catholicism was increasingly conflated with fears of Indian attacks, a situation that would persist through almost three quarters of a century of warfare in North America. The Glorious Revolution also shifted the religious settlements in the three kingdoms.

Certain crises—Indian wars and witchcraft scares—were localized, even as they reflected problems that were widespread throughout the British Atlantic. Endemic warfare between displaced Indians and land-hungry settlers elicited language from colonists that revealed their attitudes toward both Indians and themselves. During Bacon's Rebellion, Virginians spoke reverently of the king's "Sacred Majesty," using religious imagery to underscore their own duty to be loyal. The descendants of puritan migrants in New England worried over their region's mission and their own ability to fulfill it in changing times. Their concerns were similar to those of their fellow Calvinists in Presbyterian Scotland. Both proved susceptible to witches, in part because their insecurities made them suspect a demonic plot against their churches. Indians too understood the centrality of religious beliefs and of spiritual power to the confrontation. They destroyed Christian religious symbols in their efforts to eliminate settlers from their homelands. The late seventeenth-century crises caught the British Atlantic world in a moment of transition, struggling over issues of identity and destiny, issues that would continue to shape religion for the next century and more.

SIX

Religious Encounters and the Making of a British Atlantic

THE EARLY EIGHTEENTH century in the British Atlantic world was shaped by two factors: the working out of the religious implications of the Glorious Revolution and a number of contradictory cultural trends. The first cluster of developments arose from shifts in religious politics in the aftermath of the Glorious Revolution. Following the dictates of William and Mary as well as the wishes of committed English Protestants, the kingdoms championed the Dutch and Protestant cause in a series of wars with Catholic France. The Protestant-Catholic divisions of an earlier era returned with a number of twists. First, the enemy of choice was now France, as opposed to the old foe, Spain. Second, Britain emerged as a major player in European politics and warfare. As a firmly Protestant state that benefited from being somewhat removed from continental warfare, Britain (and its colonies) received Protestant immigrants from throughout Europe. In the Middle Colonies, those lying between the Chesapeake and New England, diversity became an increasingly multiethnic phenomenon. In a related change, the circumstances for Catholics within Britain, Ireland, and the wider Atlantic empire deteriorated. Papists were associated, rightly or wrongly, with disloyalty to the new monarchs. In addition, the Church of England lost much of its coercive power after 1688. This apparent diminution rejuvenated the church's missionary impulse. Early eighteenth-century Anglicans worked to convert Britons rather than Africans or Indians, although the missionary groundwork was laid for more broad-based evangelical efforts later in the century.

Beyond the changes arising from the Glorious Revolution, broader shifts within European Christianity or religion in the Atlantic world also affected this history. A renewed interest in mysticism was partly imported by migrants from the Continent, including the French Prophets (accused of various radical views, including the ability to raise the dead and belief in the immediate return of Christ) and some German sectarian groups. Even while confessional variety increased, some thought seriously about how to pull down barriers between Protestants, exploring universalistic aspects of Christianity that might serve as a basis of unity. A widespread concern for the reformation of manners within the Church of England worked in tandem with the evangelical efforts of the church. The attention to this issue also spread well beyond that institution to affect the state church in Ireland, the mainstream churches in New England, and others. Intellectual currents that supported a rationalist approach to Christianity (in which all doctrine was expected to be reasonable, which challenged the mysterious elements of faith) and even deism (which entailed questioning revealed religion even while continuing to believe in the existence of the deity) also had an impact.

These trends could be contradictory. For instance, mysticism emphasized experience and a spiritual, even emotional, connection to the deity, while rationalism strove for an intellectual understanding that did not rely on biblical revelation or spiritual experience. These contradictions had great potential to create tensions within British Christianity. In general, during this era these occurrences were only trends within existing churches and did not lead to the founding of new movements. Working out the implications was left to a later period, to the extent that they would ever be fully resolved. The early decades of the eighteenth century saw negotiations over the new situation inherited from the Glorious Revolution but also the circulation of ideas that took religion in new directions, such as ethnic pluralism, rationalism, and mysticism.

Whereas James II had declined to oppose Louis XIV's expansionist plans, the new monarchs William and Mary brought Britain's foreign policy into direct opposition to the designs of France's Catholic king. As a leader in the Netherlands, William had stood against France. One of the main attractions of taking James's throne was the opportunity to throw England's support behind the Dutch cause. His commitment to countering Louis involved his new kingdoms in twenty-five years of almost continuous warfare: first, the Nine Years War (1689–97, known in the colonies as King William's War), and after a five-year break, the War of Spanish Succession (1702–14, also known as Queen Anne's War). In these wars, England, Wales, Scotland, Ireland, and the colonies fought alongside the Dutch against France. From the perspective of his opponents, Louis XIV's absolutism, his Catholicism, and his imperialist ambitions appeared to be consistent with a Catholic effort to take over Europe and crush Protestantism.

The struggle against Catholicism and all the fears it invoked were played out through these wars. For New Englanders fear of the popish French was blended with hostility to France's Indian allies, as international conflicts sparked border wars that included raids on villages and the capture of colonists. Native peoples of the Quebec region frequently converted to Catholicism, and this only aided the English colonists in their tendency to conflate popery and savagery. Various English settlers captured in colonial wars became Catholics as they built new lives in French or native communities in New France. Their apostasies caused grave alarm among their Protestant brethren. During this era, Eunice Williams, the young daughter of a New England minister, was carried into captivity in New France along with others from her town. There she converted to Catholicism, refused to return to her native Massachusetts, and eventually married a Mohawk man. The loss of this Protestant child, although not by any means unique, rankled because of her family connections. Her relatives made repeated efforts to win her return from what they saw as a papist, savage life to the godly Protestant society of her natal family. She preferred to remain a Catholic Mohawk woman in New France. Such conflicts kept alive older fears of Catholicism as a menacing force, and the Protestant subjects of England, Scotland, and Ireland united against it. A nascent sense of British identity converged around hostility to absolutist and expansionist Catholicism, positing it as the opposite of English rights and Protestantism.

As Britain became Europe's leading Protestant stronghold (and its colonies became the most prominent destination in the Atlantic world for a displaced Protestant), it attracted more migrants from other parts of Europe. "Strangers" had been migrating to England since the Reformation of the mid-sixteenth century. More recently that trend broadened to send migrants to Ireland and the colonies. In this era, Protestantism was under renewed pressures on the Continent, while the Dutch Republic was involved in nearly continual wars, rendering it a less attractive option. Britain and its colonies were among the few places in the Atlantic world to welcome Protestant migrants. Others were the small island colonies of St. Thomas (controlled by the Danes) and of Curaçao (Dutch) as well as the more sizeable plantation settlement of Dutch Suriname. British colonial destinations were more numerous and extensive than any other alternatives.

A variety of European Protestants took advantage of the opportunity that the British colonies offered. Huguenots (French Protestants) were driven from their homeland, seeking refuge where their Protestantism could be freely practiced. Some went to locations elsewhere in northern Europe, but many journeyed to England, others to Scotland and Ireland. A sizeable minority of these went, either initially or after a few years, to British colonies in North America or the Caribbean. Faneuil Hall, now a tourist attraction in the old section of Boston, was built in 1742 with money donated by one such Huguenot migrant, successful merchant Peter Faneuil. Separate Huguenot churches were established in various locations, particularly in colonial towns, although the urban-dwelling merchants among the migrant stream were just as likely to join the Church of England. Rural Huguenots and those less well off financially seemed to have been less inclined to assimilate into the local established church.

German speakers, propelled by war and agricultural crisis in Europe, were also drawn by a concerted campaign to attract settlers for the new colony of Pennsylvania. William Penn used agents in Europe to recruit migrants who came to North America in three waves beginning in 1683. This migration stream contained enormous religious variety (as did the German-speaking regions of Europe), although Lutheran and Reformed church members dominated. Even Catholics from German parts of Europe entered the Middle Colonies during this period, revealing the audacious extent of Penn's commitment of religious liberty. Palatines also transplanted a community into the south of Ireland in the early eighteenth century, remaining for decades "an unassimilated minority."[1] Reformation-era Anabaptists such as the Mennonites also joined the flow into Pennsylvania. Radical pietists including Moravians and Waldensians, although fewer in number, transplanted their distinctive faiths into the British Atlantic as well. They migrated in groups and established separate communities upon arrival. Members of these groups (notably the Moravians) traveled to the Caribbean and the Carolinas as well as the Middle Colonies. Numerous Protestant migrants chose to become subjects of the British crown.

In keeping with the religious politics of the era, the situation for Catholics deteriorated in the aftermath of the Glorious Revolution. Anti-Catholicism, which had long been part of British and Irish politics, was intensified by the events surrounding 1688. James's rule fostered fears of a

Catholic takeover of government, and anti-Catholic sentiment was correspondingly high during his short reign. Catholics, many of whom opposed the effort to depose him, were tainted as opponents of the new government. This tendency was especially marked in Ireland where a war was unsuccessfully fought to return James to the throne. In Ireland Catholics lost most of their remaining land and were subjected to legal penalties intended to keep them impoverished and marginalized. The early decades of the eighteenth century in Ireland were bad enough for Catholics that it was possible for at least one man to make a living in the profession of "priest catcher." John Garzia became notorious (in some circles at least) for his work revealing the identities of priests to the authorities for money. The highpoint of his career came with the successful 1718 conviction of six priests, found guilty of violating legislation ordering the banishment of most priests working in Ireland.[2]

Elsewhere, Catholics were inclined (or were at least suspected of being inclined) to support James's return to the throne. In Scotland, the brief military opposition to the Revolution had centered in the Catholic (and Episcopal) Highlands, suggesting convergence there too of religious orientation and political opposition. Jacobites or those suspected of being Jacobites, as James's supporters were dubbed, were subjected to occasional persecution, especially at moments of heightened concern over a possible invasion. Anti-Catholic panics related to Jacobite fears occurred in 1715, 1718, and 1722. In 1697 the Scottish Catholics gained the services of a resident bishop, and so ceased to be a mission church in the Roman Catholic system. Shortly thereafter, however, Scottish Protestants responded by founding a missionary organization aimed at quashing Catholicism. For Scottish Catholics, these changes might be described as one step forward and two steps backward. Catholics faced other troubles, like losing their protected status in the province of Maryland with the fall of the Baltimore proprietary in 1689. Despite small strides, the situation for Catholics generally became more difficult in the aftermath of 1688.

While Catholicism underwent the most dramatic changes, the post-1688 period also decisively affected the various church establishments within the British Atlantic world. In 1687 the various semiautonomous established churches in the kingdoms and the colonial dominions converged to a greater extent than had been the case previously. Not only England and Wales but a majority of colonies were officially under the Church of England during James's reign, and the establishments in Scotland and Ireland were broadly similar. Since the Restoration the Scottish and Irish establishments had moved closer to the Anglican norm, with Scotland forced to accept episcopacy and Ireland's church made less puritan in its theology and practice. More recently, under the Dominion of New England, New England's peculiar Congregational establishment was undone. From their founding until the 1680s, the churches in Connecticut, Massachusetts, and Plymouth were legally established. Yet all were organized on a congregationalist model, not the Church of England model that had legal endorsement in England. Congregationalists in England belonged to "dissenter churches" that did not have the support of the law. But in New England their position was legally analogous to that of the dominant Church of England at home. With the reforms started under the Dominion, the Church of England was clearly slated for establishment in the northern mainland colonies. During James II's brief reign, New York became a royal colony, with a new Church of England establishment. In 1687, only the infant colony of Pennsylvania, dominated by members of the Society of Friends but upholding no single church, did not grant the Church of England privileged status. The Glorious Revolution would partially undo that newly won (if not fully realized) Anglican dominance.

The Glorious Revolution brought Scotland back to its own Presbyterian establishment, reversing the policies of the later Stuarts. The longed-for return to Scotland's earlier church order was not without its tensions, however. Over the decades that followed, a split within the church developed. One group averred that the church had lost its purity and needed to return to its heroic Covenanter days. Worry about falling away from an earlier godly commitment helped fuel the brief spate of witch-hunting at the end of the seventeenth century. Its once hallmark Calvinism became a source of contention with time too. A divinity professor at Glasgow University lost his post because his theological views were seen as too liberal and therefore a violation of orthodoxy. While this outcome might suggest that the traditionalists retained the upper hand, John Simson's views became increasingly common among one sizeable faction within the church in spite of his two trials and his eventual dismissal. His case revealed how difficult some found it to navigate between the early Enlightenment and the customary theology of the newly reestablished kirk. Presbyterianism's privileged place in the post-revolutionary settlement, reaffirmed when England and Scotland united in 1707, was undermined somewhat in 1712. In that year, legislation took church appointments out of the hands of the presbytery and put them into those of the laity (the controversial Patronage Act) and enacted protections on episcopal worship. Divided by internal dissension and undermined by legislative fiat from Westminster, Presbyterianism declined somewhat in the early eighteenth century.

Colonies in New England also witnessed a partial reversal after the Glorious Revolution. Under the Dominion of New England the authority of Congregational orthodoxy had been seriously undermined. As the Dominion fell, more damage was feared from the imperious governor Andros and an expansive Church of England. The major effect of the Glorious Revolution in New England was to return most colonies to their pre-Dominion boundaries, so that Rhode Island, Connecticut, Massachusetts, and New Hampshire resumed their separate existences. Plymouth, ceasing to be a colony, was absorbed into Massachusetts Bay. At the same time, each reverted also to its earlier charter, with the religious circumstances enshrined within it, save for Massachusetts Bay. This, the largest of the New England colonies, had to await a new charter. That charter would not return it to its quasiautonomous status or to the ecclesiastical arrangements that had been worked out over the course of its earlier history. Property ownership rather than church membership became the basis of political participation—a reform unsuccessfully demanded by Robert Child and his fellow Remonstrants nearly a half century earlier.

In addition, throughout New England, the Church of England was placed on a stronger footing, with churches organized in all the colonies and preferential treatment often forthcoming from the (now appointed rather than elected) governors. The privileging of the Anglican church would receive added support when the staff of Yale College (formerly a bastion of New England Congregationalism) converted en masse to the Church of England in 1722—an event known as "the great apostasy."[3] After Connecticut officials staged a debate on the superiority of Congregational versus Episcopal practices—which the defenders of the local establishment lost—they removed the apostates from their posts. Henceforth employees of the college had to swear to uphold Congregational principles.

Even before this occurrence, which the defenders of New England tradition saw as a scandal, severe cracks had appeared in the commitment to Congregational orthodoxy. Brattle Street Church, founded in Boston in 1699, brought more lenient standards of membership and a Presbyterian-ordained minister into a prominent position in the heart of the Bay colony. Members of the merchant community in Boston joined Brattle Street or became Church of England members in the early eighteenth century. Although New Englanders often felt the traditional suspicion of the Church of

England, it had become not only a presence in the region, but one that was increasingly tied to respectability in commercial and college towns.

Maryland went toward a Church of England establishment for the first time, after its Protestant rebellion. That legal change pushed against the continued diversity in the colony. Maryland had not previously endorsed a religious establishment, and it contained a diverse population. William and Mary ultimately supported the rebels who ousted the Baltimores, making Maryland a royal colony (rather than the family's private preserve) with a Church of England establishment. Maryland's political elite henceforth excluded Catholic leaders who had governed under the lords Baltimore. While Catholics, Quakers, and others continued to reside and worship in the colony, they were now subordinated to those in the Church of England. The colony would eventually return to the Calvert family, but only after key members converted to the Church of England and made themselves politically acceptable colonial proprietors. The Episcopal church order was a presence everywhere throughout the British Atlantic by 1700 in a way that had not been the case twenty years earlier.

Within England and Wales, surprisingly, the Church of England was not decisively strengthened by the Glorious Revolution. Replacing James II with William and Mary necessarily involved shifting the leadership over the church to the new monarchs as well. Because officials in the church swore allegiance to the reigning monarch as both secular ruler and head of the church, the revolution required officials to abandon their expressed allegiance to James. Some bishops and clergy refused to take the oath of allegiance to William and Mary, since to do so would violate the oaths they had earlier sworn. Dubbed "non-jurors" ("juror" meant simply one who takes an oath, so "non-juror" referred to those who refused to do so), they split with the church. Although the non-juror controversy necessarily waned with time and the deaths of participants, it did cause a serious breach in the church structure temporarily. Even for those who remained within the Church of England itself, the events of 1688 contributed to divisiveness. Some clergy came to deemphasize apostolic succession and episcopacy, hallmarks of the so-called Low Church viewpoint. High churchmen endorsed the idea of an unbroken link back to the earliest Christian church through bishops, upheld a rigorous episcopacy, and emphasized ceremonialism. Low Church worshippers were more tolerant of dissenters, made less vaunted claims for the basis of church authority, and preferred a simpler style of worship.

As the coercive power of the church declined, disagreements over how to relate to dissenters continued. Before the Glorious Revolution as after, Low and High churchmen differed over whether to tolerate and work with dissenters or to persecute them in an attempt to drive them out of existence. With the ouster of James II, the upper hand shifted to the Low Church side, so that toleration and cooperation became the official policy. Whether as a result of these changes or for other reasons, at least for a time after 1688 the number of dissenters increased. Laypeople who favored the High Church position of intolerance sometimes attacked dissenters, and popular violence against them spiked upward. The split in the church echoed that between the Laudian and puritan factions within the Church of England of the 1630s. Archbishop Laud's efforts to create a more ceremonial church and a more obedient populace was entirely consistent with aspects of the High Church position, while the puritans of his day had points in common with Low Church advocates of the latter seventeenth century. At the same time, the split had parallels to the situation in the Scottish church after 1688, as various fissures over doctrine and style appeared there as well.

If anything, the established Church of Ireland became more narrowly based as a result of the events of 1688 to 1691. Ireland's official church was Episcopal, modeled more directly on the Church of England than had been the case in the early seventeenth century. Its membership was slight, since it did not include even the majority of Protestants. Presbyterians made up the biggest dissenting group, dominating the northern Ireland province of Ulster but with a presence elsewhere in the northern part of the kingdom. Other Protestant groups included a smattering of each of the other dissenter churches present in England (Congregationalist, Baptist, and Quaker) as well as eventually Huguenots and a small group of Protestant German speakers from the Palatine. Outside of the Christian ranks, a small Jewish community existed in Ireland by the early eighteenth century. Given that the Protestants in Ireland were a distinct minority, the established church might have joined together with other Protestants in solidarity against the majority Catholic population. Instead, it worked to marginalize and suppress other Protestants. The power and coercive practices of the Irish established church were referred to as the "Protestant Ascendancy."

Not all Protestants partook of this ascendancy. During the period in question, in fact, most were excluded from power. Ireland passed a Test Act in 1704 that made membership in the established church a requirement for political participation. The impact of this legislation was dramatic, narrowing the political nation to the small minority who were male established church members. Far from building bridges between Protestant communities to combat Catholicism, the Church of Ireland punished its fellow Protestants and remained narrow and parochial in its thinking. Ulster Presbyterians found the opening decades of the eighteenth century trying on a number of counts. A schism divided the local church into Old and New Lights, based on theological differences as well as disagreements over how to deal with their second-class status within Ireland. Persecution from the established church, economic pressures, and perhaps these internal fissures contributed toward a massive outflow of Ulster Presbyterians in 1718. Ireland lost Protestant population in part due to the narrow definition of Protestant orthodoxy promoted by the established church.

Looking at the British Atlantic overall, the Church of England's presence expanded but then so did that of the Presbyterian Church. Born out of the Scottish Reformation, Presbyterianism nonetheless fought an often uphill battle in its efforts to maintain its position and its purity within Scotland itself. The challenges posed by the imposition of episcopacy by James VI and I and the demotion of the church to dissenter status under Charles II were finally overcome in this era. By the time Presbyterianism was securely established in Scotland (1690), Presbyterian churches were also worshipping in Ireland (especially Ulster), in England, and in some colonies. Migration into the wider Atlantic world in the early eighteenth century catapulted the Presbyterian Church to the status of the second most substantial institutional presence in the religious landscape, a position it would hold until the American Revolution set other changes into motion. Presbyterians apparently resided in every colony by the 1730s, and a sufficiently sizeable population in the Middle Colonies existed by 1716 to create a synod to unite the three presbyteries there.

The confessional community experienced some divisions over doctrine and practice, as might be expected of a fairly decentralized church order. Colonial Presbyterian leaders hammered out an agreement (the Adopting Act of 1729) that allowed them to avoid arguing over doctrine, but its benefits would prove only temporary. Common features of colonial Presbyterianism were its emphasis on preaching and its willingness to impose discipline. Presbyterians in Scotland, Ulster, and some colonies practiced lavish communion rituals intended to bind the worshipping community together, events that one scholar dubbed "Holy Fairs."[4] Occurring in late summer or early autumn, these rituals involved feasting as well as preaching and sorting out the saved from the rest of the community. To an extent they set the stage for later revivals in both the United States and Britain. At this time, however, Presbyterianism was simply one notable but far-flung church order within the larger British Atlantic world.

If the royal brothers Charles II and James II had attempted to broaden the reach of the Church of England (by imposing episcopacy on Scotland and expanding into various dissenter-dominated colonies), the Glorious Revolution limited that reach. But the revolution did not entirely turn back the clock either, as the Church of England entered the post-1688 period with a more widespread presence than had been the case during the reign of Charles I. The first Anglican college in a colony was founded in 1693, named for those saviors of British Protestantism, William and Mary. It was fittingly located in Virginia, which housed the oldest American Church of England establishment, and, perhaps less fittingly, was financed with a tax on tobacco. Anglican churches existed in every colony by 1707 and were established by law in about half of them.[5] The three kingdoms either upheld an Episcopal establishment (Ireland, England, and Wales) or enforced protections of Episcopalians against a dominant Protestant church of another type (Scotland). Some colonies that had been originally founded without a Church of England establishment, such as Maryland and South Carolina, had one in place by the early eighteenth century. In North Carolina a faction attempted to erect such an establishment, but the effort was foiled by a rebellion of Quakers and others in 1711. Establishment status would not be achieved for another three decades. The Church of England (or its equivalent in Ireland) had become fairly ubiquitous.

Yet, at the same time, the church was less able to force individuals and communities to embrace it. The government's willingness to compel conformity to the church had been drastically reduced in England and Wales. Ireland became more coercive in the years after 1690, while the renewed Presbyterian establishment in Scotland attempted to force allegiances but was thwarted by the 1712 law protecting Episcopalians. Colonial churches varied in their ability to demand adherence, but in general the ability of those governments to exact conformity was seriously hampered by relatively high levels of diversity and weak coercive mechanisms. If the Church of England was everywhere, no where was its hold on the religious allegiances of the population exclusive: everywhere alternatives existed. Even Virginia hosted two Presbyterian and three Quaker meetings in the early eighteenth century.

As established churches lost any power they had ever had to intimidate believers, they turned toward persuasion as a means to increase their influence. Missionary efforts burgeoned within the Church of England, as new societies to propagate the gospel sprang up. Although we tend to think of mission as working in foreign lands and aiming to convert non-Christians, these early efforts sought mainly to convert the inhabitants of England, Wales, and Scotland. Eventually they turned their attention to the colonial churches as well. In seeking to Christianize the British Isles, missionaries resumed a project that had engaged the attentions of mid-seventeenth-century godly revolutionaries. As with other projects undertaken then, Anglicans picked up where their foes had left off without acknowledging any continuity between earlier schemes and their own.

The first priority of reformers was promoting piety and increasing levels of religious observance among nominally Christian Europeans. The problem of understaffed churches—often associated with the West Indies or the mainland south, not to mention Newfoundland—was far more widespread. Reformers were eager to rectify the situation. They sought to educate and convert men, women, and children who were either unchurched—that is uninvolved in any organized faith—or who were members of rival churches. Dissenting Protestants were a main target of the Church of England missions, while the Scottish missionaries sought to convert Catholics. The Anglican Society for the Promoting of Christian Knowledge (SPCK, founded 1698) was active in Wales, erecting schools and issuing Welsh-language publications. The Scottish Society for the Propagating of Christian Knowledge (SSPCK, 1709) began as a cooperative effort among Episcopal and Presbyterian Scots, but dropped its ecumenical bent to become Presbyterian-dominated with time. With that emphasis, it functioned within Scotland in much the way that the English missions functioned within England and Wales: as a promotional arm of the official church.

Although the Church of Ireland retained (and even extended) its ability to punish opposition in this era, it also followed the Church of England's lead in developing organizations for Christian outreach. Charity schools aimed to educate as well as convert the poor, while missionary societies sought to spread the Protestant faith in Ireland. Among Catholics in Ireland legal sanctions compelled men in particular to conform to the established church to protect family property, but conformity was neither widespread nor, apparently, heartfelt. The Church of Ireland focused instead on the resident Protestant community and did not use its missionary energy to convert Catholics. For their part, Catholics ignored the new charity schools, sending their children instead to illegal but widespread hedge schools for Catholic youth.

Reformers saw the colonies as another terrain ripe for the promotion of Christianity, as they were often plagued with chronic problems staffing pulpits. Only New England (where Harvard and, after 1701, Yale produced a steady flow of ministers) avoided these difficulties in the early eighteenth century. Indeed New England Congregationalists were able to launch their own missions, attempting unsuccessfully the conversion of French Catholics in Acadia after that colony was conquered (again) in 1713. Although the Church of England had the College of William and Mary, that institution was hampered in its ability to furnish clergy by the fact that graduates had to go to England for ordination. This requirement discouraged men from taking orders, and disproportionately fewer of them entered the ministry than was the case among Congregationalist college graduates in schools farther north. Under that system a call from a congregation was sufficient to make a young man into a minister.

The Society for the Propagation of the Gospel in Foreign Parts (SPG), founded in 1701, concentrated its efforts initially on filling Church of England pulpits in the colonies. Its agenda was to strengthen the transplantation of the church by other means. When the Church of England did send missionaries with instructions to convert Native Americans, more often than not the clergy ignored these instructions. Once ministers arrived in a colony, empty parish pulpits beckoned, and the men rarely managed to make it to an Indian mission. The first SPG missionary to South Carolina remained in the capital, resided in the governor's home, and never approached a single Native American. The first clergyman dispatched to New York to convert the Mohawks (in the early eighteenth century) never once preached to the Indians there. His successors would do better, making that mission an exception that helped to prove a general rule. When the Scottish missionary organization arranged to provide missionaries to Native Americans in the 1730s, the first three clergymen were stationed at frontier forts where they served as chaplains to the soldiers. They had little interchange with the local Indians. When the Church of England won the brilliant and combative George Keith from the ranks of the Society of Friends, it appointed him to the SPG to counter Protestant challenges to the church's hegemony in the colonies. Dispatched to preach to his former co-religionists, Keith offered to debate Congregational ministers in New England and, after they refused to join battle with him directly, engaged in pamphlet wars with them. Whether he changed anyone's mind was not recorded. Although shocking to the defenders of New England's heritage, the dramatic conversion of Yale staff and students was not typical of the small, incremental successes the church compiled in these years. Still, at least with regard to dissenters in Britain and the colonies, the demise of its power to coerce had rejuvenated the sense of mission.

Some time would pass before this missionary impulse expanded from converting and educating already ostensibly Christian European populations to reaching out to the non-Christian residence of North American and the Caribbean colonies. In a 1724 survey conducted by the Bishop of London on the state of the colonial churches, fewer than half of all ministers surveyed had baptized at least several and occasionally more blacks. This relative disregard for the souls of non-Europeans within the British Atlantic did not arise from a dearth of Africans (not to mention Indians): during this period the numbers of enslaved Africans under the sway of British authority skyrocketed. English involvement in the African slave trade brought huge numbers of Africans into the British colonies, especially Jamaica, where the slave population grew at a phenomenal pace. Well before the end of the seventeenth century, the major English Caribbean colonies had majority populations of Africans and African Americans. In Jamaica a provision in the 1696 slave code favoring the Christianization of slaves went unheeded. Christopher Codrington's 1710 bequest to the SPG to establish a Christian school and mission to the slaves on his Barbados plantation was similarly ignored for years. The first baptisms did not take place until 1728, and the level of instruction accompanying them was deemed modest at best.

On the mainland, the turn toward large-scale slave importation began toward the end of the seventeenth century in the Chesapeake. Annual imports into all mainland colonies in the first three decades of the new century held steady at about ten thousand, shooting up after 1730 to reach almost sixty thousand a decade by mid-century. While the Caribbean had long had many slaves to convert (or ignore), large scale slaveholding came to those mainland colonies with monoculture agricultural regimens only after 1700. Once again, high numbers of Africans or African Americans in the population worked against conversion efforts. As slave populations rose, masters became more nervous about insurrection and less willing to have their slaves catechized as a result. The early incidents of slaves and former slaves professing Christianity fell off with the rise in slave imports. In the early eighteenth century, some slaves already worked as lay preachers in their communities, holding secret religious meetings attended by fellow slaves. These gatherings occurred outside of official notice and without official support.

That slavery complicated the relationship of Africans to Christianity was well demonstrated in the story of William Ansah Sessarakoo, also known as "the Royal African." The son of a Fanti chief in Ghana, he learned to speak English in the trading fort there. Consistent with the lack of missionary outreach emanating from these trading posts, no one apparently bothered to introduce the boy to Christianity along with the English language in these visits. His father, desirous of furthering his relations with various European states active in Ghana, sent one son to France and another to England in the 1730s. On its way to England, the ship carrying William put in at Barbados with a cargo of slaves, where its duplicitous captain sold William as well. Subsequently, his father refused to aid the English in a local dispute until his son was rescued, so the boy was redeemed from his enslavement. He then traveled on to England in the company of another Fanti boy. The two were educated for a time in England, and William authored a pamphlet entitled *The Royal African: or, Memoirs of the Young Prince of Annamaboe*. He eventually made it home to his native Africa, where he was employed by the newly appointed SPG missionary to instruct local children.

William might well have lived out his life as a Barbados slave if his father had not had the power to force his rescue, in which case he would have gained neither an English education nor the facility to assist the Ghanaian missionary.[6] Such tales of elite Africans caught up in the slave trading net offer a recurrent theme. For all the stories that have come down to us because they were in circulation in some form at the time—such as that of the "Two Princes" of Calabar in the later eighteenth century or the "African Prince sold into Slavery in the American South" in the nineteenth century—many others presumably were never able to parlay their status into release from bondage, as William Ansah had been.[7]

Despite the obstacles, some slaves sought out Christianity during these years, but on their own terms. An unknown number arrived in English colonies already exposed to Christianity, either in their native Africa or elsewhere. In either instance the version of Christianity the slaves would have brought with them was likely to have been Roman Catholicism. In the vast majority of cases, this religious orientation would have separated them from the faith of their new master or mistress when they were sold in the British Atlantic. The first SPG missionary in South Carolina with any interest in converting non-Europeans was Francis Le Jau, whose efforts may have sparked the passage of a 1712 law declaring that conversion did not gain a slave freedom. Le Jau recognized that some of the slaves he encountered were already tainted with popery.

Fig. 10. William Ansah Sessarakoo was one of a number of elite West Africans who traveled to Europe in this period. Sent by his father to cement ties with England, he was temporarily sold into slavery in Barbados. After being redeemed, William Ansah lived in London for a time (where he was baptized), before returning to his native Anomabo. English society feted him as a celebrity, Gabriel Mathias painted his portrait, and an account of his life, *The Royal African: or, Memoirs of the Young Prince Annamaboe,* was published ([1750]). This mezzotint by John Faber, Jr. was based on Gabriel Mathias's portrait. Courtesy of the National Portrait Gallery, London.

Catholicism and perhaps specifically devotion to the Virgin Mary may have shaped the 1739 Stono Rebellion in South Carolina. Africans involved in the rebellion seem to have been drawn especially from the Kongo. These rebels may have used Catholic religious symbols (including flags in colors associated with Mary), and they staged the uprising on an auspicious day for Catholics (one of a number of days in the church calendar dedicated to Mary). The rebels were planning to flee to Florida, attracted by the Spanish offer to grant freedom to any escaped British slave who converted to Catholicism. Although the chance to gain their freedom was no doubt the most attractive aspect of this offer, an opportunity to return to their former faith seems to have given added motivation to some. Although the Stono Rebellion was put down, other slaves did escape to the Spanish. An entire town of escapees would be founded in the Florida colony, where the men among them formed a militia prepared to defend the Spanish outpost from invasion by their (British and Protestant) former masters.

Evidence of the Catholic inspiration behind the rebellion notwithstanding, most slaves continued to participate in various traditional African practices. The Commissary of the Anglican church in the Leeward Islands, James Knox, wrote to the Bishop of London in 1732: "There are about 25,000 [Africans] in Antigua; and in the other three islands together, there must be that or probably a greater number. They are all heathens, and like to continue so; there are no means used for their conversion, nor I believe ever will: That is a thing rather to be wished for than hoped or expected."[8] As Knox's assessment suggests, the Church of England paid little heed to the project of converting slaves at this time. His description of them as "heathen" referred to the multitude of practices that Europeans often observed but rarely understood: the dancing and drumming; the wearing of fetishes; and the recourse to spiritual adepts who kept them safe, identified the witches who sought to harm them, and helped them to regain health. Meanwhile colonial observers generally assumed that the enslaved populations were without any religious faith. Such comments as Knox's were common, and they generally implied that Africans were heathens in the sense not of pagans but of barbarous people subsisting without religion.

How far this was from the truth and how well captive Africans carved out a space for their own communal celebrations in the face of slavery is demonstrated by the evidence gathered at the African Burial Ground in New York City. Discovered during a construction project in Manhattan in 1991, the burial ground has yielded a rich archeological record of community practices. In use for most of the eighteenth century and possibly much of the seventeenth as well, the cemetery served as a place for community gathering. Joyous celebration was typical of West African and Caribbean funerary customs, and commentary by the white population of the city made clear that similar revelries marked the passing of colonial Africans.

Burial practices indicate the variety of cultural traditions at play in New York City in the African population. Many people were buried in coffins; almost all of them were shrouded and buried alone. Some were supplied with possessions. These practices all have African precedents. Not only were slaves poor; they were also not supposed to own anything but rather to be owned. For slaves to be buried with an object of any value therefore made a strong statement of defiance and of their continued humanity in the face of oppression. A number of women were interred with beads, sometimes tied about their waists, a common adornment practice in their homelands; some of the beads themselves were made in Africa. Almost 98 percent of the graves were oriented in an east-west direction, which suggests some Islamic influence as well. Great care was taken by the community with its dead, and this attention cemented community bonds as well as making a statement against the enslaved condition of the vast majority of African New Yorkers. They were not a people lacking in religious faith or community, despite the wishes and assumptions of their masters and mistresses.

Missionaries gave Native Americans only slightly more attention. By the late seventeenth century in New England the missions to the Indians organized under the 1649 Corporation for the Propagation of the Gospel were dramatically reduced. The missions were a casualty of King Philip's War and settler animosities toward all natives, even converts. Further south, clergyman Le Jau undertook a modest effort with Native Americans in South Carolina after he was stationed there in 1707. When four Indian "kings" visited London in 1710, they sparked a flurry of activity. The SPG sent another clergyman to the Mohawks in New York in 1712, where he succeeded in making converts. His mission built on the work of a Dutch Reformed missionary, who had converted a solid core, despite having been involved in a land swindle that also turned some Mohawks against him. The community's antiCatholicism fostered the SPG work, as it had that of the Dutch minister. This animosity had been fed by the fact that the French Jesuits won converts among their traditional enemies, so that Anglican Mohawks regularly warred against Catholic Indians living to their north. A Yamasee Indian dubbed Prince George by the English lived in England for years from 1713; while there he learned to read and was baptized by the Bishop of London. Upon his return to the Carolina region, he found his family dispersed by war and sold into slavery. There is no evidence that he communicated his new religious orientation to the native people of the region, although his benefactors had clearly hoped he would do so.

Officials remained optimistic that Indians would convert to Christianity, even while they failed to put much sincere effort into making that happen. Governor Alexander Spotswood of Virginia, for instance, hoped for a long-term cultural and religious conversion, referring to a 1714 treaty provision for Native Americans to send their children to be educated among the colonists as a way to make Christians of the next generation.[9] Few children ever participated in this project, and its apparent affect was negligible. The SSPCK received a 1717 bequest to fund missions among the Indians, which led to a sustained effort to promote missions in North America starting in 1730. The initial efforts in New England and Georgia had little impact. The Georgia mission addressed the spiritual needs of a Scottish Presbyterian settlement in that new colony, rather than those of the native population. The Society continued its work in subsequent periods, eventually funding ministers who did establish missions among Native Americans. David Brainerd and Eleazar Wheelock, for instance, would enjoy some renown in the later eighteenth century.

In the meantime, Europeans occasionally adapted to Native American practices. In order to facilitate diplomacy with various Indian peoples, colonial go-betweens and even imperial officials learned to participate in such rituals as the "At the Woods' Edge Ceremony." When journeying through the woods to a village, travelers moved "thro' dangerous places, where evil spirits reign, who might have put several things in [their] way to obstruct [their] Business."[10] A ritual cleaning would clear their minds and bodies, making the traveler ready to participate in the life of the village. Before a successful diplomatic exchange could take place, the ceremony prepared the visitors to participate after their journey to the treaty site. Numerous Europeans—especially those who worked as go-betweens—learned and routinely used these rituals in their travels through the Pennsylvania backcountry. No doubt colonial mediators often accepted the necessity for these observances without embracing the ideas about spirits and ritual cleansing that undergirded them, but the willingness to join in them nonetheless revealed the ways in which they negotiated the demands of a culture different than their own. In this way Native American understandings of the spiritual world and

the proper human relationship within it shaped some European lives. Such
ceremonial observances were far removed from the missionary work that was
intended to replace the native with the imported faith.

Alongside the new interest in missions, Protestants in the British Atlantic
world also embraced the reformation of manners and the rage for voluntary
societies that typically went with it. This European-wide movement emphasized godliness as one component of true religion. Rather than looking to the
interior experience of faith as the measure of Christian commitment, the
drive to reform manners asked for good behavior. Protestants had long believed that the sincere convert would manifest his or her new spiritual status
in a pious demeanor. A huge push now occurred to encourage exemplary
conduct. Voluntary societies took over disciplinary work that had once been
handled by church courts or by community watchfulness, and which was still
addressed by presbyteries where they were active. Support groups for various
constituencies sprang up, to encourage converts in their commitment to right
living. Young European American men in one location and enslaved Africans
in another met for prayer and mutual edification. Cotton Mather, who sponsored the meeting of Boston "Negroes," saw it as a way to teach proper
Christian comportment to the newly converted.

The bulk of the reform work aimed at improving manners occurred,
like the missionary outreach, within the ostensibly Christian community. In
England, reformers used the civil courts to prosecute the behavior of fellow
Christians that they found immoral, using the judicial system to handle
infractions that had once been punished by the Church of England's ecclesiastical courts. The new emphasis on acting as befit a godly person would
eventually meld into a dawning commitment to refinement and sensibility,
cultural trends growing over the course of the eighteenth century. Abhorrence of cruelty would also be a hallmark feature of this new emphasis. Small
group meetings fostered pious behavior and a godly experiential life throughout Britain, Protestant Ireland, and the mainland colonies. In a sense these
meetings set the stage for the early Methodist movement. Methodism began
as a reform movement within the established church, organizing intimate
meetings of believers (called "cells") for mutual edification.

An era of generally reduced coercion and heightened concern to act the
part of a good Christian fostered interdenominational cooperation. Unity
among Christians became something of a watchword after 1700, spurring
cross-confessional interaction. The idea that Protestants at least might find
common ground for working together had a long and checkered history.

James I had hoped to achieve unity among Christians. During the revolutionary era at mid-century, the splintering of the religious landscape led a number of churches—such as the Baptist, Independent (or Congregationalist), and Presbyterian—to join together in common causes. Prussian immigrant to England Samuel Hartlib and his Scottish associate John Dury (who reversed his friend's migration pattern by living out his last decades in Hesse-Kassel) advocated Christian unity from the 1630s, among other reforms. Theologians suggested that certain points dividing the different confessional traditions might be inessential and therefore open to varied interpretation. This argument had been used since the mid-seventeenth century in favor of a limited toleration. The drive to find common ground among the faithful gained credence as Christian leaders identified anti-Christian forces at work in their societies. Leaders, fearful that irreligion, atheism, and unbelief were on the rise, recommended cooperation among believers to fend off these threats. Cooperation was consistent with a broad trend toward liberalization of religion, which de-emphasized doctrinal differences in favor of a focus on piety. Clergy from different confessional camps worked together to spread Christianity and Reformed religion.

Dissenters from the Church of England, whether in Britain or the colonies, saw unity based on shared godliness as a means to defend their common interests against the dominant church. Father and son Increase and Cotton Mather, both clerical leaders in Massachusetts, actively promoted Christian union with their brethren elsewhere. In 1690 while in England to negotiate a new charter for the colony, Increase joined London Baptists, Congregationalists, and Presbyterians in signing a "Heads of Agreement" intended to serve as the basis of unity among those churches. Within the dissenter communities these efforts helped to counter the revitalized Church of England. Dissenters drew upon common cultural trends that favored toleration, experiential religion, and godliness, and that discounted religious bigotry and exclusionary gestures. The Moravians began migrating to the colonies during these years. With pre-Reformation roots, a heavy reliance on iconography, and a belief in the possibility of universal salvation, their opponents accused them of being Catholics in disguise. They initially supported ecumenism. The sect envisioned itself as an umbrella organization tying together all Christians around a concern for piety, literacy, and Christian education. Moravians never succeeded in uniting all believers but their liberal goals combined with their sectarian fervor did win them converts.

To an extent the liberal religious trend of this era was wedded to the idea that rationality ought to infuse religion and that its opposite represented a threat. In these early days of the movement known as the Enlightenment, these intellectual developments were not yet seen as challenging religion. Piety, toleration, and reasonable Christianity were seen as rational and sensible, the polar opposite of the feared and reviled religious enthusiasm. "Enthusiasm" was the term used for religious expressions that seemed too emotional or mystical. In the later seventeenth century, conservative supporters of traditional religions (especially the Church of England) had attacked enthusiasm, which they linked to the excesses of the mid-century revolution. They wanted to avoid repeating the situation in which uneducated men and women put forward their own religious ideas and cited otherworldly authority for them. Seeing such ideas as necessarily based on claims to private revelations (which they only sometimes were), conservatives cautioned that excessive emotionalism and giving one's self over to the spirit was bound to mislead. Better, they believed, for the uneducated to defer to their social betters for guidance on these matters rather than to follow their emotional and irrational leadings into strange and undoubtedly dangerous opinions. While liberal opponents of enthusiasm—such as John Locke in his *Essay Concerning Human Understanding* (1689) or the satirist Jonathan Swift in his *A Tale of a Tub* (1704)— rejected enthusiasm from a different angle than these conservative critics, all agreed that it ought to be forsaken.

Stories of religious excesses arising from private revelations circulated often enough to confirm opponents in their prejudices against enthusiasm. One such story came out of South Carolina. The tale began with a traveling preacher—described by a hostile observer as "a certain strolling Moravian, Dutch or Swiss Enthusiast"—who especially affected one family, named Dutartes, with his message. They soon withdrew from public worship and began to follow their own understanding of God's plan for them. One member of the extended family supposedly claimed to have received a revelation that his wife's first husband was about to be raised from the dead to be reunited with her. The dream instructed him to put her aside, to make room for the return of her first husband. Instead, he should take his wife's youngest sister as his new wife, she being a virgin. He managed to persuade his father-in-law of the truth of his revelation and was united with the younger Dutartes sister. No record survived to illuminate what either sister—the one cast off to await the return of a dead husband or the one who became the new sex partner of her former brother-in-law—thought of these arrangements. These irregular relationships came to light when the younger Dutartes woman became pregnant. As she was not legally married, her unborn child was considered a "bastard," a circumstance that brought her before the local court. The family adopted other illegal practices, refusing to pay taxes or bear arms, and when the authorities confronted them, a gun battle, arrests, and ultimately the execution of three men resulted. Two sons of the Dutartes patriarch—brothers to the women involved in the husband swapping—were slated for execution too, but they confessed their error and were reprieved after the first men executed failed to rise from the dead as expected. Once the story came out, the authorities did not try the young women involved, presumably because obeying the commands of the patriarch made them dutiful daughters and laid the responsibility on their father and husband. Such wild happenings confirmed critics in their belief that excess emotionalism in religion led to immorality and violence.[11]

Mysticism had appeal in spite of these denunciations, and not just for the reasons that its opponents feared. One mystical group, the Philadelphia Society, enjoyed a brief period of popularity in England around the turn of the century, before it came under attack as enthusiast. Inspired (as were some migrants to colonial North America) by the continental mystic Jakob Böhme (1575–1624), the Philadelphians' primary prophet, Jane Lead, attacked the reliance on reason. She advocated a firm dependence on revelation instead. Lead's revelations began with a dream in which a female Wisdom appeared, declaring, "Behold, I am God's Eternal Virgin-Wisdom, whom thou hast been enquiring after; I am to unseal the Treasures of God's deep Wisdom unto thee." Theologically Lead departed from the orthodox position and from many of her companions in supporting universal salvation, the idea that all would be saved.

She based that radical position as well as many of her other views on direct revelations, which claim violated both conservative views that God no longer sent revelations as well as emerging liberal religious ideas that reason ought to be the basis of belief. Lead and her co-religionists were eventually denounced through satire and ridicule, focusing on their supposed sexual licentiousness, their willingness to permit a woman to preach and teach, and the alleged silliness of their beliefs. These attacks came despite the group's emphasis on sober behavior and acceptance of those of other faiths. One critic wrote to a follower of Lead expressing his hope that "God [would] extricate you out of the snares of Enthusiasm and seducing Spirits wherein you are engaged."[12] With enthusiasm associated with the religious excesses of the mid-seventeenth century, advocates for rational religion, piety, and toleration depicted themselves as combating fanaticism. After Lead's death in 1704, Böhme-inspired mysticism gradually faded from public view in London.

The campaign of ridicule and suppression did not put an end to mystical or other religious approaches that would be characterized by some as enthusiastic. A number of communities of mystics were organized in colonial Pennsylvania in these years, including the Ephrata cloister. Like Lead's Philadelphians, the inspiration for this group came in part from Böhme. Palatinate migrant Conrad Beissel (1691–1768) was influenced by his ideas in Europe, prior to his migration to North America in 1720. In Pennsylvania, Beissel joined with some German Anabaptists (known as the Brethren but popularly called "Dunkers") who asked him to lead their congregation. His advocacy of celibacy split the group, and his supporters withdrew, eventually creating a community of monastic celibates. Members could also elect to live in family groups outside the cloister. Like the Labadists before them, they owned goods in common. Like other groups that would come on the scene later, most importantly the Shakers, they advocated a celibate lifestyle for at least some members. Their faith was mystical, and they presented God as combining male and female traits. Believers sought to achieve an androgynous state in their communion with the divine. Such ideas continued to circulate even if they seemed to run contrary to the dominant emphasis on piety, moderation, and reformation.

The trend toward moderation that opposed itself to enthusiasm and mysticism also furthered a decline in the strict Calvinism within the Atlantic world. In parts of New England and Scotland as well as in Protestant Ireland, Calvinism had been a hallmark religious position in the seventeenth century. Scots Presbyterians and New England Congregationalists had once underscored the sinful nature of humanity. They had been certain that all deserved damnation but that through the grace of God a limited number would enjoy salvation. This message had once served as the basis for tight-knit communities and effective political action. But over time this religious vision had not proved easy to sustain. Parents found it difficult to apply the implication of widespread damnation to their own children. Even though with every generation the church was to be made anew out of members who had experienced a conversion experience that indicated their hopes of salvation, in New England some churches began to emphasize descent from a converted church member as granting "the children of the church" a special status. In a subtle way, predestination was softened by a "puritan tribalism" that seemed to offer salvation to younger generations on easier terms.[13] This trend was far advanced in some churches, such as that of the elderly and revered minister Solomon Stoddard at Northampton, Massachusetts.

Rationalism undercut the strict Calvinist message in favor of a God who gave everyone the same chance and a view of human nature that accorded a greater support for human endeavor. Godly behavior and reformed manners did not necessarily contradict Calvinism (since the converted had always been expected to behave in a godly fashion) but promotion of those as goals in themselves suggested that anyone who could reform might be saved. For those who clung to the pure Calvinism of an earlier era, this shift seemed to move back toward the Roman Catholic emphasis on good works. Reformed Protestants had argued that human actions made no difference in salvation. Only the action of God in granting the sinner grace saved him or her. In conjunction with these widespread intellectual shifts, Ireland, Scotland, and New England witnessed an alteration of the Calvinist emphasis. Among Presbyterians in Ireland and Scotland, battle was joined over whether ministers had to subscribe to the Westminster Confession, which proponents saw as a way to underscore traditional doctrinal positions. The opposition spoke in terms of individual conscience, the importance of sincere belief, and the prospect for self-improvement on the part of the believers. A rising latitudinarianism—the tendency to accept a wide range of religious positions as equally worthy while at the same time rejecting skepticism about religion itself—created this new emphasis in many churches, and in this way was consistent with larger cultural changes. Opponents upheld doctrinal orthodoxy through subscription to their church's confession, or statement of doctrine. In both Ireland and Scotland church schisms ultimately occurred, with a Scottish Secessionist movement (1733) gathering those who wanted to return to a more primitive church with a stronger Calvinist inflection. In New England, open rupture over this issue did not occur prior to the 1740s, but the potential was there as well.

Awareness that the revealed aspects of religion were open to new challenges led some religious leaders to emphasize the mysterious nature of the supernatural world. Leading New England clergyman Increase Mather began collecting stories of supernatural occurrences toward the close of the previous century. In 1684 he published his *Essay for the Recording of Divine Providence,* based on accounts of apparitions, the timely deaths of sinners, and other "remarkable and very memorable events." He also preached a sermon series on angels that was published in 1696. Along with other ministers he was concerned to show that the unseen world existed. These learned men used early quasiscientific forms of research and documentation to prove their point. In Wales Edmund Jones toiled for many years during the eighteenth century to compile evidence of ghosts. He used rigorous standards of proof, thoroughly in keeping with Enlightenment criteria, gathering firsthand accounts from eye witnesses and analyzing the likelihood that his sources could have been mistaken. Using these techniques, he saw no contradiction with the fact that his goal was to demonstrate that spirits existed. Such efforts were intended to combat skepticism but to do so with the same tools employed by Christians who valued reason over revelation.

Some already feared that rationality in religion might go too far, with deism cited as one danger. The religious conservatives who opposed contemporary revelation and enthusiasm did so while trying to uphold the longstanding belief that the revelations contained in the Bible were entirely reliable. They based their arguments in favor of traditional religion on the faith that the Bible was the revealed word of God and should serve as a guide to all Christians. While deism held that God existed, it questioned other aspects of Christianity. Adherents to this view did not rely on sacred texts but on humanity's own rational capacities in order to understand the divine. Seeing their intellects as God-given, deists argued that what man could understand based on the information provided in the natural world was sufficient. The deists' God wanted people to develop their intellect, to pursue science, and to come to a better understanding of the natural world. Deism was not so much an organized religious movement as an intellectual trend. While still a teenager, Benjamin Franklin embraced deist views. In his voracious reading, he ran across deist authors who persuaded him of the truth of their insights. An extreme version of the prevailing accent on rationality, deism also partook of other cultural trends, such as sensibility and abhorrence of cruelty. One argument made against the traditional Christian view was that God would not be so cruel as to damn Indians who had never heard of him. The SPG devoted a number of its annual sermons to countering these deist arguments.

As compared to other parts of Europe, Britain and its Atlantic possessions were less affected by these widespread intellectual trends at this time. As scholar Kenneth Hylson-Smith observed, a widely embraced compromise between Newtonian science and the Church of England held the more extreme intellectual challenges at bay.[14] Bishop Joseph Butler published a major anti-deist document in 1736, *Analogy of Religion*. Despite criticisms, deist philosophers were more accepted in England than elsewhere in the British

Atlantic world. Scottish officials expressed fears of atheism and skepticism as early as 1696. John Toland, a deist respected in English philosophical circles, had to flee his native Ireland (to which he had returned) in order to escape prosecution. Along similar lines, the Dublin Presbyterian minister Thomas Emlyn was imprisoned for two years for questioning the doctrine of the Trinity. Such views would have been similarly ill received in other provincial capitals throughout the British Empire.

The opening decades of the eighteenth century witnessed a number of important shifts in religion. Some were broader than the geographical framework of the British Atlantic world: voluntary societies, reforming manners, mysticism, rationalism, and deism spread through much of northern Europe, circulating through England, Scotland, and the colonies as well. The changed nature of religious establishments—changed everywhere but Ireland, which bucked the trend by becoming more exclusive and officially intolerant—was a more narrowly British phenomenon, arising from the effects of the Glorious Revolution. Diversity, long a colonial reality, also became more widespread in the post-revolutionary era. As a beacon of Protestantism in an increasingly Catholic Europe, Britain and its colonies attracted a variety of Protestants who had been displaced on the Continent. Efforts to counter diversity shifted from coercion to persuasion in this era, with missionary societies originally aiming at converting the nominally Christian European populations throughout the British Atlantic to the Church of England or to Protestantism more generally. In England, Wales, Scotland, Ireland, and the colonies, loyalty to the official state church was seen as constancy to the crown, with Catholicism (and in Scotland the Episcopal faith) associated with disloyalty to the monarchy. Despite the fractured nature of "British" identity, the Protestant religion became a fundamental means whereby subjects could demonstrate their loyalty.

Protestantism was not truly British in the sense of broadly shared, however, as so much depended on local circumstance. In Ireland a person who defended the Episcopal church appeared to be a crown supporter, while Scottish Presbyterians in Ireland were suspect as the primary Protestant opponents of the Irish Episcopal church. Yet in Scotland, Episcopal leanings might be seen as a sign of Jacobitism (or support for the ousted Stuarts), while Presbyterian affiliation was a way to demonstrate loyalty to William and Mary as well as their successors. In the colonial environment, these divisions applied only insofar as Church of England adherence was still sometimes seen as entailing special dedication to the monarchy. With no organized Jacobitism in that environment, these political fissures were less salient. By 1735, however, the British Atlantic remained religiously complex and even fractured. At the same time, it was engaged in larger trends, such as sensibility and voluntarism, which helped to moderate at least some differences.

SEVEN

Revivalism and the Growth of Evangelical Christianity

THE MID-EIGHTEENTH CENTURY in the British Atlantic world witnessed religious ferment caused by revivals, an increase in evangelical religion generally, and unprecedented outreach across previously demarcated divisions. The groups most bent on converting others during this era of widespread evangelization were those that were outside of the traditional churches, especially those in interfaith groups, although well-established churches also gradually gained ground. Indians converted at a notable rate for the first time. More importantly, it became apparent that Native American sensibilities (in the contact zones) had been permeated by Christianity. Indians urging a return to traditional beliefs and lifeways revealed borrowing from Christian Europeans. African and African American slaves often heard the Christian message for the first time. Despite the ecumenical character of the initial impulse to spread Christianity, the ferment of mid-century ultimately tended toward an increase in pluralism and fragmentation. A wide variety of communities polarized over the religious issues raised by revivalism and the evangelical message. Evangelism spread Christianity more widely, appealed to new groups, divided some communities, and created a cultural ethos of revivalism that would continue to permeate the British Atlantic and its constituent parts for many years.

Religious change in this era was promoted successfully by two organizations that were not simply aiming to increase their own numbers. The Moravians and the Methodists each had a significant impact on the rise of evangelism in the period from 1730, and neither functioned fully or entirely as churches in this era. The Moravians underwent a revitalization. Their ostensible goal as they began to expand out from their new center on the continent of Europe was to reinvigorate existing Christian churches. They began their evangelical missions in the 1730s, with efforts in England, Ireland, the West Indies, Suriname, South Africa, and Georgia. They preached to African slaves, Native Americans, Hottentots, and their fellow Europeans. A 1749 act of Parliament declaring theirs to be an "ancient episcopal church," bolstered the group's freedom to establish missions throughout the British Atlantic. While the expansion was undertaken with the stated intention not to convert others to their way but to revitalize Protestantism more generally, in Europe Moravians gradually moved toward a conceptualization of themselves as a church, which might grow through adding new members. A tension therefore developed between the goal of creating a single religious confederation of all Protestant churches under Moravian leadership and building Moravianism up as a freestanding church.

The faith that the Moravians preached had ancient roots, extolled a distinctive combination of beliefs and practices, and offered an unusual lifestyle to believers. The remnant of the *Unitas Fratrum*, an old church that had been granted refuge by Count Nikolaus Ludwig von Zinzendorf in Saxony, the Moravians came under the influence of the pietist Zinzendorf who eventually took control of the community. They were also sometimes referred to as the Herrnhut Brethren after the name of their settlement in Saxony. Their faith was mystical, drawing on old Christian traditions that granted believers an emotional and even sensual spiritual experience. Dreams were therefore important to believers, one aspect of their faith that created a common ground with some of the Native Americans that the Moravians eventually sought to convert. Along with other radical groups, Moravians challenged the idea that God was male. They deemphasized the paternal aspect of the Christian deity and presented both Jesus and the Holy Spirit as female or as ambiguously gendered. This unusual conception facilitated union with the deity, a union that was further encouraged through rituals, litanies, and the contemplation of images of the side wounds of the crucified Christ.

Becoming a member of the church was a drawn-out process. An individual passed through multiple stages before achieving full membership: beginning with receiving permission "to stay" (freedom to be present within the community) and finally advancing to communicant (a participant in communion, the "love feast," and the absolution rituals that preceded it).[1] Moravian

Fig. 11. Moravian rituals included ceremonial foot washing intended to re-create instances of the practice from the Bible, including Christ washing the feet of his followers, the Apostles. Washing the feet of another was a sign of humility and hospitality. From David Cranz, *Kurze, zuverlässige Nachricht von der, unter dem Namen der Böhmisch-Mährischen Brüder bekanten, Kirche Unitas Fratrum* (1757), image 13. Courtesy of John Carter Brown Library at Brown University.

communities included two levels of membership, those who lived within gender-segregated, cloistered communities called "choirs" and those in open communities who resided in regular households. Believers treated sexual relations between married couples as a sacramental event, developing practices that linked sex to the spiritual union with God. Whereas other Christians suggested that avoiding sexuality allowed a greater focus on God or argued that sex was a necessary but potentially sinful act, the Moravians made eroticism central to their faith. These practices became the target of criticisms, with opponents presenting Moravians as debauched. Critics also falsely accused believers of advocating sex outside of marriage.

The Moravian influence spread rapidly from the 1730s until the 1750s, carried forward on the two prongs of ecumenical networking and conversion to the sect's own message. Spreading through Europe, it arrived in England by 1738 and in its first British colony, that of Georgia, even earlier (1735). The first sustained effort to convert African slaves to Christianity in the Caribbean was launched by the Moravians on the Danish island of St. Thomas. The earliest known writing by an African woman in North America was a spiritual memoir by a convert named Magdalena Buelah Brockden, written in the 1750s. Her unpublished account uses the imagery of the sinner enslaved to sin, which was widely employed among Christians at this time but must have had special meaning for this ex-slave.[2]

The Moravians also eventually converted numerous Indians in the Pennsylvania backcountry. Native converts saw the Moravian faith in part as a vehicle for pursuing their own traditions. They shared a common understanding of dreams as containing momentous messages, the idea that blood and suffering were spiritually significant, and the centrality of reciprocity within the community. Indian converts chose to live in their own households, often organized around female relationships that were frequently the basis of residential organization in their own communities as well, rather than in the gender segregated choirs in which some Moravians resided. Given this success among not only Africans and Indians but also Europeans, the leaders of other churches generally opposed Moravian plans for ecumenical union as a self-aggrandizing attempt to diminish other churches. Reaction against them from church leaders offered an indication of the great success of the Moravians, whose religious influence far outstripped their numbers.

Moravians contributed indirectly to the revitalization of other churches through their contact with John Wesley while the Church of England clergyman was visiting Georgia. Wesley attributed his call to preach a revitalized spirituality to his encounter with Moravians on a 1738 journey to North America. Upon his return to England, Wesley converted others to his new way of thinking and then he and other Methodist itinerants spread the word of God's grace, freely available to all, throughout Britain and Ireland. They advocated a spiritual discipline undertaken with the support of fellow believers organized in small communities. The idea of a new "method" to encourage spiritual commitment that first developed among a group of devout students at Oxford earned the movement its name. In these small religious societies, the Methodists reached out not just to Anglicans but to all Christians, regardless of church affiliation. Although in some ways a departure,

Methodism developed out of voluntary societies that supported missionary work and built on the tradition of interconfessional cooperation. It, like the Moravian movement, responded to widely felt spiritual needs. Wesley would of course become famous as the founder of the Methodist Church, but he himself had no intention of founding a distinctive church. His goal was much like that of the Moravians who influenced him: to work within an already extant church to reawaken the spirituality of members. Wesley conceived of the movement as taking place within the Church of England, supporting its mission by drawing people from the fringes into it. Only toward the end of his life did he approve, and then only grudgingly, the creation of an independent denomination. The Methodist Church would be a later development. At mid-century, Methodism is better understood as a movement of committed Christians, most of them formally within the Church of England.

As a movement, Methodism was notably successful within England and Wales as well as among Protestants in Ireland, far less so in Scotland. Its efforts differed in these locales. In England by the 1730s the Church of England was unable to service the entire population, in part because migration into the new northern industrial centers strained its resources. In these circumstances, Methodism reached out especially to the unchurched poor. Wesley also won elite converts. Notable among them was Lady Selina Hastings, Countess of Huntingdon (1707–91). She exercised the power of patronage over numerous chapels, appointing the men who staffed them. The Countess would eventually throw her support behind George Whitefield and other Calvinist Church of England clergy.

In Ireland, early Methodist successes were in southern port and market towns. With the British army outpost stationed there serving as one vehicle for spreading Methodism in Ireland, garrison towns played a key role. The movement also gained momentum among European Protestant minorities, such as the refugees from the German-speaking Palatine region who lived in an enclave in the south. Unlike in England, where they targeted the urban poor, Methodists in Ireland gave the Protestant gentry much attention. Later their efforts would move north, and successes there would increase the Protestant dominance of northern Ireland over time. As with other Protestant outreach in Ireland, the Methodists made little headway (or effort) among the Catholic majority, preaching in English and addressing mostly their fellow Protestants.

In England Methodists were sometimes attacked as Catholics in disguise, as the Quakers had been in the seventeenth century and as their contemporaries the Moravians were at this time. Critics of all these groups found similarities between them and Catholics upon which to base their claims. Anti-Methodist violence was tied to fears of Catholics and Jacobites, so that it reached its peak during the war years of 1739 to 1748. In the Methodist case, opponents pointed to the emphasis on sacraments and Wesley's support for the practice of celibacy on the part of itinerant ministers as proof of popish tendencies. But in Ireland Wesley engaged in the same anti-Catholic rhetoric as other Protestants, describing anti-Methodist mobs as bloodthirsty papists.

In Wales, Methodism succeeded most where it was presented with a strongly Calvinist message. To some extent, Methodism there appealed to those alienated from the established church or untouched by it, often due to rural isolation and a paucity of clergy. The Church of England ceased to give preference to Welsh clergy in Wales in the eighteenth century, and the Welsh reacted with reduced engagement in the church. Local commitment to a uniquely Welsh identity was encouraged by the circulating schools founded by Welsh Anglican minister Griffith Jones. Efforts to promote and maintain the Welsh language continued to enjoy success. Outreach in Wales touched the poor and remote parishes in the south, although Methodism appealed more to the middling sort there. Its efforts during this era laid groundwork that would be exploited by Methodists and other dissenting churches later. In Wales as in England, Methodist preachers were sometimes attacked. William Seward, who had worked as George Whitefield's publicist on his first tour of America, died in Wales in 1740 after a mob assaulted him.

In Scotland, Methodism enjoyed only limited success, and the little there was concentrated especially in Glasgow. The reasons are debatable, but it may be that bitter religious divisions within the Scottish Presbyterian Church already gave residents a sufficient variety of choices. The Wesleyan Methodist position did not differ much from one version of Presbyterianism already on offer. Scotland in this period generated such a variety of theological positions, religious styles, and political stances on religious issues that its inhabitants seemingly felt no need to turn to Wesley or others. George Whitefield was a popular preacher there, though his efforts ultimately did little to alter the religious landscape.

Not until the 1760s did Methodism come to the colonies. It arrived first in the Caribbean when a planter, converted on a visit to England, brought his newfound beliefs back to his Antigua plantation. Methodism's inauguration in North America occurred, as did so much else, via migrants. In this case Irish and English Methodists carried their faith with them as they moved out into the wider Atlantic world. In Ireland, Methodism spread among Palatinate refugees who had come from the Continent a few decades earlier. Upon arriving in North America, Methodists from both England and Ireland quickly began to broadcast their religious practices to others. They initially set up a system of household meetings in Maryland and New York. By the end of the decade, Wesleyan Methodist preachers began work in Pennsylvania. Methodism as a movement was transplanted into the colonies relatively late.

In Britain, revivalism was related to the early Methodist movement but not entirely coincident with it. The notable English revivalist, the "Grand Itinerant" George Whitefield, was initially associated with the Methodist movement. He made numerous tours throughout the Hanoverian British kingdoms and the colonies from the late 1730s until his death in 1770. He split with Methodism's founder, John Wesley, over theological questions, effectively leaving the Wesley-controlled movement to follow his own path. Other evangelical preachers worked outside of the Methodist tradition entirely. Congregationalists in England became caught up in the movement, which helped to revitalize their churches. Presbyterians from the Lowlands regions of Scotland worked to convert the Highlanders, who still tended to be Catholic, Episcopal, or unchurched. Indeed the largest evangelical movement within Scotland was this internal effort. The Church of England continued to work through its SPG to bring about conversions in Britain and, increasingly, in the colonies, efforts that remained largely distinct from the Methodist movement. On the Methodist side, organization largely proceeded without the excitement of large-scale revival. John Wesley, though he did preach to large crowds on occasion, favored small meetings and concentrated on local organizational efforts. Early Methodism and revivalism were related but largely separate phenomena initially, even though they would later come to overlap to a great extent in the early United States.

The foremost itinerant in North America was George Whitefield. Whitefield was a recently ordained college graduate when he first delivered electrifying sermons before large gatherings in London in 1736, earning himself the title of the "Boy Preacher." A protégé of John Wesley, Whitefield preached the necessity of "New Birth." This standard sermonic theme of Reformed Protestants advocated the need for a dramatic conversion experience that brought a person to a sense of her own sinfulness and God's great mercy in saving her in spite of her faults. When preached by Whitefield, this conventional idea took on enormous emotional power, profoundly moving audiences. In contrast to his mentor Wesley, who saw conversion as a process, Whitefield looked for a moment of crisis, which his preaching was intended to spark. Accepting a call to minister to a new orphanage in Georgia, Whitefield began to tour through North America and Britain in order to raise money for that nascent institution. The ostensible purpose of his tour was overshadowed by the more general impact of his preaching.

Like the Methodist movement he participated in and the Moravians who had influenced it, Whitefield claimed that he did not aim to make converts for the Church of England. Rather he urged those whom he touched to recommit to their own faith tradition. Not all of his fellow ministers believed that Whitefield's aims were innocently ecumenical. Some saw the message preached by Whitefield and others as potentially threatening to their own ministry. From the vantage point of his own Church of England, however, Whitefield seemed too general in his aims, for he was suspended for a time from his position for failing to use the Book of Common Prayer with its official liturgy. The formulaic prayer book was far from the style of a Whitefield performance. Although he repeatedly preached the same sermon, which became more polished with each delivery, his listeners thought that he delivered them extemporaneously. His engaging style gave the sense that he conveyed God's message directly to the hearts of his enthralled listeners.

The large crowds he gathered and the heightened religiosity encouraged by his presence made his visits major public events. Whitefield himself enhanced the excitement by advertising his successes in published journals that appeared in each locale well timed to anticipate an impending visit. Even before Whitefield arrived to deliver an electrifying sermon, communities were primed for his visit. The excitement of a Whitefieldian tour was captured in the account of Nathan Cole, a Connecticut farmer, who described the road to the place where Whitefield was scheduled to speak as so full of mounted riders that it appeared from a distance like a flowing river. Cole, who threw himself into the torrent to reach the appointed place in order to hear the great man preach, was profoundly changed by the experience. Even the secular Benjamin Franklin found Whitefield immensely compelling. Going to hear his friend preach out of curiosity, Franklin resolved not to be swayed. Finding himself swept up in the excitement, he attempted to borrow money from others in the audience in order to donate to the orphanage. The Quakers from whom he sought the loan told him that he was not himself and that they therefore must decline to lend him money. The skill of Whitefield's appeal was such that even the usually sensible Franklin was not immune, although his Quaker friends were less susceptible.

Whitefield was instrumental in fostering religious revival especially in New England, and he became a transatlantic symbol of evangelical revivalism. In Scotland, he identified the Secessionists, a splinter group that had recently left the established church, as most amenable to his message, but he ended up preaching with more success to those who had stayed within the church. His far-flung itinerant tours helped to transform the periodic revivals that congregations in many locations had experienced irregularly and in isolation into a widespread, interfaith event. His greatest achievement came early in his career, in the years straddling 1740, when he contributed to widespread revivals. As historian Charles Cohen observed, his brand of revivalism, "featuring itinerant preachers using an emotionally expressive homiletics to address cross-confessional and unaffiliated audiences—proved to be a mechanism admirably suited to recruiting Christians in a promiscuously Protestant environment in which religious identity was often shallow—in other words, on the Anglo-American periphery of Christendom."[3] Although Cohen was thinking of the colonies in particular, even in some parts of Britain, population growth and internal migration stretched the Church of England's ability to serve everyone. Dearth created a hunger for preaching and pastoral care that encouraged people to respond to Whitefield and to other traveling evangelicals. The Atlantic context particularly but not exclusively promoted Whitefield's successes, as he (and other revivalists) pulled in listeners looking for a spiritual home among the many options available to them.

Whitefield was not alone in traveling to preach in support of revival. American evangelists included Middle Colony Presbyterians, especially members of the Tennant family. These men built on the Presbyterian tradition of periodic renewal services as they evangelized that colonial religious community. James Davenport, the well-educated descendent of first-generation New England minister John Davenport, shocked the colonial religious establishment by preaching a radically egalitarian message and staging the burning of books and finery to symbolize believers' rejection of worldliness. He also converted people who might not have been reached by a moderate message. Among them was Mohegan Samson Occom (1723–92), whose conversion at the age of seventeen motivated him to go to school. He would later take up a career as a missionary to native peoples.

Colonists who had been lukewarm participants in services at their local churches found their spirituality transformed by the preaching they heard at the height of the Awakening. Many who had not sought full church membership before joined their local church. They also sought spiritual counseling from suddenly overworked pastors, purchased selections from the flood of books promoting the revival message, and flocked to meetings. The initial months of the Great Awakening (as the movement came to be called) were euphoric times, with Christians throughout the Atlantic basin cherishing millennial expectations and church leaders pleased to see a renewed commitment among their parishioners. That revival and a quickening of spiritual impulses were occurring everywhere at one time seemed an indication that a millennium was dawning that some Protestants believed was foretold in the biblical book of Revelation.

Although not especially successful as a revivalist preacher, Northampton, Massachusetts minister Jonathan Edwards emerged as a key figure in the revivals. Edwards had recently taken over the pulpit of his maternal grandfather Solomon Stoddard, replacing a man who had dominated his region and its religious life for decades. The young Edwards was dismayed by the spiritual condition of his new congregation and especially by what he viewed as lax admission requirements, which his grandfather had favored. In the late 1730s Edwards succeeded in bringing about a revival in the town, engendering fervor that swept young people and others who had been on its margins into the church. Criticism of the revivals and especially of their displays of emotionalism led Edwards to justify his efforts and their fruits. His published accounts of the awakening in Northampton, including *A Faithful Narrative of the Surprising Work of God in the Conversion of Many Hundred Souls in Northampton* (1737), with its ruminations on how God worked in the souls of believers, garnered attention among ministers who were similarly concerned with spiritual malaise in their churches. When Whitefield burst onto the scene a couple of years later, his work was interpreted in relation to the ideas that Edwards had already suggested.

Whitefield's tour and those of other evangelicals led Edwards to publish his further thoughts, providing revivalism with a theoretical underpinning. Like many other revivalists, Edwards also speculated about the coming millennium. He anticipated years of tumult before the dawning of a millennial age, and his own experience gave him plenty of evidence of strife. Edwards faced problems in his congregation—older members objected to his criticisms of the state of the church and to his methods for increasing membership. He was eventually driven out of his pulpit. But his ideas about conversion had a huge impact nonetheless. Edwards is considered the first American philosopher as well as the intellectual founder of a theological school that would foster revivalism later in the United States. In his own day, his writings were read from Boston to Scotland, opening a broad dialogue about the nature of conversion and the validity of the evangelical movement being encouraged by Whitefield and others.

The heightened concern for religion in the years 1730–65 fundamentally reshaped the British Atlantic world. The era witnessed two currents, the creation of more explicit transatlantic bonds and the regularization of specific church organizations. Whereas select groups of Christians (for instance those united by their dissenter status in relation to the Church of England) had previously worked to forge connections, the revivals created a sudden and intense sense of linkages that cut across confessional identity and ethnicity. The Great Awakening of the early 1740s was a transatlantic phenomenon, giving its supporters a sense of participating in a movement that united Protestants throughout the English speaking world. The Awakening was only the most dramatic aspect of a more general development toward increased religious outreach that spread beyond the supporters of revival.

Many churches and movements experienced this era as a time of organizational growth and the explication of goals. Continental European pietism helped to lay the groundwork for added attention to religious issues among the various groups it touched. It also spread directly through immigration to Britain and the colonies, bringing increasing numbers of adherents to the Middle Colonies in particular. Large-scale Lutheran immigration to North America began in the 1740s. This infusion of new members triggered efforts to institutionalize the church in the colonies, revitalizing a tradition that had been in the doldrums since the collapse of the small Swedish colony on the Delaware River a century earlier. Moravians made strides in these decades in converting members of groups who had not been touched by Christianity previously, visiting numerous European countries and American colonies and establishing new communities. Revivalism in the early 1740s ultimately contributed to the numbers of Baptists in North America. Awakening-era converts were not enlisted immediately in the ranks of the Baptist churches, but over time a minority of converts followed their newfound convictions into separatist Baptists churches. Revivals also gave a boost to the vitality of Presbyterian churches, especially in the Middle Colonies. Both Baptists and Presbyterians subsequently inaugurated missionary efforts in the American South that would, especially in the case of the Baptists' efforts, bring more Africans into churches. Methodist preachers who traveled through Britain and Ireland organized local cells that met regularly to support the spiritual growth of the participants. The widespread religious ferment, whether carried forward in energetic burst by revival preachers or in incremental steps by the organizational efforts of Methodists and those in other faith traditions, had a transforming effect on the mid-eighteenth-century Atlantic world.

Despite the hopes of revival leaders that the Great Awakening would unite all believers and even usher in the millennium, religious divisions were another feature of this era. One source of division was hostility toward preachers themselves. Itinerant preaching had long generated opposition. Visitors who gathered crowds and conveyed novel messages might be welcomed with open arms but they might also be viewed with deep suspicion. Preachers in Ireland were sometimes suspected of Jacobite tendencies—that they intended to bring the dispossessed Stuarts back to the throne. Even when opponents did not fear any particular political intervention on the part of preachers, they might still greet them with hostility. One Scottish critic of revival meetings labeled Whitefield "a Mountebank and a Damn'd Rascal, who was putting all the people mad: that he put on his black gown to fright people out of their wits, and that when he put on his black gown and black cap at night he frighted them terribly."[4] The unnamed man who made this denunciation wanted his laborers to stay home and not chase after revivalists like Whitefield. Not only did their latter-day gadding after sermons (to use the language that was once aimed at puritans) keep servants from their work; it also threatened true religion. This man equated true religion with learning the catechism and working hard in the station to which God had appointed an individual. He, like others, thought that revival and religious itinerancy challenged the established order.

The religious division characteristic of this era had various other sources as well: theological differences within movements; opposition to revivalism or to the spread of Christianity to heretofore largely untouched groups; and rivalries between alternative religious organizations. Just because the Methodists and Moravians saw their expansion in terms of ecumenical harmony did not mean that other churches felt comfortable with their agendas, by any means. As might be expected, heightened attention to matters of church and faith led to disagreements over a variety of issues. When Lutheran pastor Heinrich Melchior Mühlenberg (1711–87) criticized the Moravian movement by claiming that "The true church of Jesus Christ had never since the time of the Apostles had a more harmful, dangerous and sly enemy as the Zinzendorfian sect,"[5] his rhetoric demonstrated the hostility that rival churches might feel toward expansionist groups of believers with grand schemes for Christian unity.

One important disagreement that marred efforts at unity was over the availability of salvation. This issue divided the leading proponents of Methodism and shaped British revivalism as a result. John Wesley, in keeping with a more general trend within the Church of England, averred that all might be saved. This position was known as "Arminianism," after the sixteenth-century continental theologian Jacob Arminius, who argued against the predestination of his contemporary Calvinists, making a case for the human ability to elect salvation. The belief in the possibility of universal salvation was popular among Methodist converts in England and Ireland. In general, the Arminian or Wesleyan Methodists enjoyed greater success. There were exceptions, however. In Ireland, the Ulster Presbyterians responded instead to Calvinist evangelists, who preached limited redemption. Whitefield similarly embraced the Reformed position that only a few would be saved. Whereas Wesley put most of his energy into organizing the Methodist "connexion" by erecting numerous small local societies to support the faithful as they worked toward salvation, Whitefield conveyed his call to repentance as he masterfully preached to multiconfessional crowds. He then left the local pastors who supported his "heart religion" to deal with the resulting conversions.

Once Wesley and Whitefield agreed to disagree on this fundamental theological question, in the early 1740s, Whitefield's message became more consonant with Presbyterians, Congregationalists, and Baptists within the Reformed tradition. The Welsh favored the Calvinist version, and the Methodist movement there split into a vigorous Calvinist branch and a much weaker Wesleyan–Arminian one. In 1743 Whitefield and others organized the Joint Association of English and Welsh Calvinist Methodists, with the Welsh side of the association being the more vigorous of the two. Wesley's version of Methodism was more influential in England, leaving the Calvinist variation marginal there. Whitefield's message appealed widely to those with a penchant for Calvinism. His greatest successes occurred in those areas where this theological orientation was central to the local tradition. Wales, New England, and Ulster were all carried away by Whitefield's preaching.

The issues at stake between Wesley and Whitefield can be appreciated by looking at the biography of a singular woman, Selina, the Countess of Huntingdon, who accepted the theology promulgated by each man for a

Fig. 12. The English noblewoman Selina Hastings, the Countess of Huntingdon, patronized evangelical religion in England, Wales, and the colonies. Associated with John Wesley, George Whitefield, and other religious leaders, she found spiritual comfort elusive even as she tirelessly worked for her faith. James Fittler's 1790 line engraving is based on an earlier image by Robert Bowyer. Courtesy of the National Portrait Gallery, London.

time. An aristocratic woman with an unhappy marriage and a contentious family life, the countess searched unflaggingly for religious fulfillment. She briefly adhered to the Moravians, but had a falling out with them after a sister-in-law married a poor Moravian preacher and through her marriage captured an inheritance that would otherwise have gone to the countess's own offspring. She then aligned herself with the Wesley brothers (in 1741), and began giving religious instruction and planning a utopian community. Failing to find spiritual joy in the Methodist movement, she reversed her theological position, moving from John Wesley's idea that believers could achieve "sinless perfection" to the Reformed position that most people were justly damned and that human perfection in this life was unlikely. Her latest views matched her spiritual psychology, in that she often felt the anxiety that Calvinist preachers argued should be accepted as part of a Christian's life. The countess worked closely with Welsh Methodist Howell Harris for some years, and eventually named Whitefield (Harris's fellow Calvinist) as her chaplain. Her next project was a fruitless attempt to create a phalanx of godly aristocrats, converted by her and working for the cause. Next she established a college to train evangelicals in Wales (1768). In 1770, she inherited Whitefield's Georgia orphanage. She never succeeded in converting her own children, who resented her relentless proselytizing. One daughter described her as "righteous over-much."[6] Her patronage and position meant that gaining her support was a major prize for any man with a religious organizational agenda, but her almost desperate spiritual strivings offered insights into the experiences of many less socially illustrious converts.

Although one variation or the other appealed in many locations, neither Whitefieldian revivalism nor either variant of Methodism enjoyed much success in Scotland. Scotland ultimately followed its own path, which occasionally intersected with these larger trends but was not redirected by them. Scottish Presbyterians regularly gathered for communion festivals that were part of their worship calendar. These events occasionally launched revivals, as was the case in 1742 at Cambuslang in the southwest of Scotland. Extensive conversions there were largely orchestrated by local ministers, although Whitefield hurried to the region to participate when he learned of the glorious work afoot. He and others held large revival meetings in the mid-1740s. Leaders and participants in the Cambuslang revival were aware that they were contributing to a broad renewal of Christian commitment, having heard of the revivals first in Northampton and then elsewhere in America. Revivalists may have been concerned to find a middle way, between an orthodoxy that felt increasingly narrow and an elite rational Christianity heavily associated with the Enlightenment. The area around Glasgow, rocked by revivals for three years that involved some seventy ministers and fifty congregations, was a center of opposition to the elites of the so-called Moderate party but also engaged in its own version of the Enlightenment. Revivalism, with its ecumenical bent combined with an emphasis on experience, offered an attractive alternative.

Their revival was ultimately contained within the Scottish church, with its already well established communion season and tradition of periodic revival. The surge in 1742 contributed to the international movement but did not fundamentally alter Scottish practice or institutions. In the Lowlands in particular, the Scottish church already attended well to its communities' need for evangelical preaching. Unlike in some areas on the Atlantic periphery, the compulsion to embrace a drastic change was not widely felt. In addition, the commitment to predestination had not waned there to the extent that it had in some areas, so an impulse to recommit to that tradition was not prevalent. Divisions that had developed in the Scottish church tended to put the revivalists within the broad middle, where they explored Enlightenment, sought literacy, celebrated ecumenism, and valued experience. Revival some Scots embraced, albeit on their own terms, but Methodism made little headway in that kingdom.

The divisions within the Methodist ranks reflected the divide between revival supporters and opponents in New England and elsewhere, to the extent that these were differences of theology and religious style. Revival preaching emphasized experience and appealed to the affections—the goal of such preaching was to elicit an emotional response, a sense of the individual's unworthiness, and a conviction that God's mercy was the only hope. Although it was not a typical sermon for him, Jonathan Edwards's famous *Sinners in the Hands of an Angry God* (first published in 1741) well captures this aspect of the revival message. In it Edwards conveyed the dangers of sin with concrete imagery: the sinner was a loathsome spider whom God holds over the burning pit of hell. In another passage he likened sinful humanity to "unconverted men [who] walk over the pit of hell on a rotten covering, and there are innumerable places in this covering so weak that they will not bear their weight, and these places are not seen."[7] A successful revival caused believers to question their worthiness and to decide to throw themselves at God's feet. Tormented sinners lined up outside their pastor's study, seeking spiritual counsel. Some ministers worried that affected parishioners might commit suicide in their anguish, as indeed a handful did. Evangelical ministers thought the victims had succumbed to the temptations of Satan, at the same time that they appreciated the power of the emotions that preaching could elicit. Edwards and other revival supporters saw themselves as playing a thin edge, urging their fellows toward a powerful conversion while hopefully not pushing them over.

Revival opponents saw Satan as more prominently at work in the revivals, assessing the whole phenomenon as contrary to God's word. Many were persuaded that God did not act in these violent ways, but appealed to believers in a calmer and more reasonable fashion. These revival critics had been touched by the movement toward rational Christianity, which postulated that God worked through the person's intellect as much as his heart, offering a faith experience that was soothing, comforting, and, above all, reasonable. These Christians placed less emphasis on human failings and saw salvation as widely attainable. Ministers with this perspective were less alert to conversion as a moment of crisis, assuming that it might come as a gradual process. They emphasized the need to embrace free grace and to choose to act the life of a Christian convert. The awakeners—especially the more incendiary and leveling among them—struck these upholders of liberal Christianity as deluded and destructive. For their part, Calvinists objected to the idea that anyone could be saved. They viewed the perfectionism of an Arminian like Wesley "as not only eccentric but down-right popish," as one scholar put it.[8] To the extent that the British (non-Calvinist) Methodists built their movement incrementally, with sermon upon sermon preached in small gatherings by both men and women to their social equals, their modus operandi differed from the more electrifying celebrity preaching event featuring a Whitefield or a Gilbert Tennant.

The battle lines between these two camps—the supporters and opponents of revivals—were drawn quite clearly in New England, where a major reaction against the Awakening helped to bring the religious fervor to an end by 1742. If anti-revivalists favored a style of Christianity that fit poorly with the spirit of revivalism, they had refrained from attacking Whitefield when he first arrived. A broad spectrum of New England ministers in the 1730s would have liked to have seen a redoubling of religious commitment within their churches. Those who would eventually oppose the revivals often welcomed Whitefield's first visit. That his message minimized his Anglicanism had appeal. Clergy liked the fact that he sent their congregations back to their own churches for spiritual sustenance. After Whitefield's departure, however, when recent installments of his journal describing his visit appeared, his criticisms of what he viewed as the lukewarm commitment of specific clergy rankled. His hostile account of the state of religion at Harvard (which continued, as it had from its founding, to train prospective ministers) insulted these New England clergymen.

In the train of Whitefield's visits, too, lay preachers or more radical ministers like Davenport built on the excitement by preaching messages that were often more provocative than Whitefield's. Daniel Rogers, who orchestrated a major revival in his hometown of Ipswich in Massachusetts, reported on the emotional response to his preaching. "Some of them over come with the Love of [Jesus] even to fainting," and a fit of screaming "spread like fire . . . So [great] weep[ing] & Lamentation I never heard before."[9] These preachers began to criticize the spirituality of the clergy who did not enthusiastically support the revivals. Gilbert Tennant delivered one sermon, *The Dangers of an Unconverted Ministry* (1740), which became infamous. In it he argued, as did other preachers, that to be under the spiritual guidance of a minister who had not himself undergone a conversion experience was to risk damnation. Such allegations caused some converts to turn upon their ministers, eventually dividing congregations and spawning schisms between supporters and opponents of local religious leaders.

Throughout New England many congregations divided into pro- and anti-revival factions. In such cases, one usually retained the resident minister and the other either located a new, more conservative clergyman or recruited a revivalist minister or even a lay preacher to serve its needs. In the midst of these schisms there raged major arguments over which group could claim the designation "first church." Both sides claimed to represent tradition— understood by revivalists as the intense commitment of the first generation and by anti-revivalists as the established practices of decades of local worship. A *Boston Gazette* story conveyed the divisiveness of these developments in many towns in its report about Canterbury, Connecticut. According to an anonymous correspondent with the paper:

> Dec. 16, 1742. Canterbury is in worse confusion than ever. Their
> minister has left them, and they grow more noisy and boisterous so
> that they can get no minister to preach to them yet. Colonel Dyer
> exerted his authority among them on the Lord's Day, endeavoring
> to still them when many were exhorting and making a great hubbub,
> and ordered the constable to do his office, but they replied, "Get

thee behind me, Satan!" and the noise and tumult increased to such a degree, for above an hour, that the exhorter could not begin his exercise. Lawyer Paine has set up for a preacher . . . and makes it his business to go from house to house and town to town to gain proselytes to this new religion. Consequences are much feared.[10]

Such scenes were both unprecedented in many New England towns and an all-too-frequent occurrence after 1740.

Conservative ministers and laypeople were shocked by their opponents' apparent disrespect for clergy, the sense that uneducated laypeople (including women) could judge the spiritual worth of their betters, and the movement's violations of the spirit of reasonable Christianity. The leader of the anti-revival forces in New England was the energetic Charles Chauncy, minister of the First Church of Boston, who attacked the revivals as a species of enthusiasm. For Chauncy, enthusiasm denoted dangerously misguided emotionalism. The term was used to link the Awakenings to all manner of earlier radical movements. Amid these heightened tensions conservatives (known in New England as Old Lights and in the Middle Colonies Presbyterian community as Old Side) moved to suppress the revivals, lay preaching, and the more radical itinerant ministers. Authorities in several colonies put James Davenport on trial. After a number of confrontations, colleagues finally persuaded him to apologize for his more excessive statements. The laws that supported the established churches were used to harass those who had left their local churches to set up alternative "separate" meetings. Revivals that proponents hoped would reinvigorate spirituality across communities and throughout the Anglo-Atlantic world accomplished those goals but also exacerbated tensions within communities and churches as well.

The autobiographical account of a Connecticut woman who converted during the revivals suggested the tensions inherent in the revival's impact on communities and families as well as the motives that propelled some into the revivalist camp. Hannah Heaton had been attending a Separatist church (and therefore not her town's established church) for almost two decades since her conversion by George Whitefield in 1741 when she was hauled before the courts to answer charges of breaking the Sabbath. Hannah refused to pay the fine that was levied against her. Her husband, Theophilus, a lukewarm Christian who attended not her church but the non-revivalist town church, paid the fine over her objection. Hannah, who spent much time in pious reading, prayer, or recording her spiritual life in her journal, never succeeded in converting her husband. They occasionally fought over her unwavering attention to her spiritual life. On one occasion, Theophilus hid her spectacles so that she was unable to read. She interpreted this incident as a further sign that a godly person ought not to be yoked in marriage to one unconcerned with spiritual matters: "I wright these things to warn others to marry in and for the lord. Where there is no agreement in the things of god how can they walk together."[11] The two never were reconciled on this subject in thirty-eight years of marriage, a source of constant anxiety and distress to Hannah.

Opposition to evangelism arose not only from in-fighting over the shape and tenor of the Christian community among Europeans, but also from hostility to the very idea of evangelizing within certain communities. This period witnessed the first concerted push to convert African and African American slaves to Protestant Christianity. Older objections to this idea were renewed. Masters feared that converted slaves might feel that they were the equals of their owners, not just spiritually but in other ways as well. A few continued to worry that conversion would bring freedom, although that idea began to lose credence with mounting evidence to the contrary. Laws explicitly stated that conversion did not automatically emancipate the convert. Slave owners worried too that the literacy that was generally seen as part of a thorough Protestant conversion (since it facilitated Scripture reading) would make slave resistance both more likely and more effective.

South Carolina slave Philip Johns offered a case in point. He apparently told illiterate slaves that a printed text in his possession, possibly a millennial tract, contained God's instructions to revolt. Johns used the text—incomprehensible to those he sought to convince—as a sort of talisman, suggesting that it held its own power. Johns never succeeded in launching a revolt but instead was executed for his efforts in 1759. Of more widespread significance, however, was the fact that Protestant converts felt compelled to become literate, which was as true of slaves as it was of Scottish laborers or Native Americans. Once they did, they could not be duped by the claims of a Philip Johns: they acquired the power to read and decided about the import of written texts for themselves. It was this power in particular that masters feared.

In addition to worries about revolt, slave owners—especially in the southern mainland and the Caribbean—loathed the idea of filling their churches with their chattel. Where missionaries hoped to work with slaves, they had first to persuade masters to permit their efforts. Moravians in the British Caribbean (where Jamaica hosted their first mission, dating from

1754) and elsewhere fought an uphill battle to gain access to bonds people. Anglicans supportive of slave conversions also struggled with slave owners. In New York City only the wealthiest slave masters allowed their chattel to attend the school for "Negroes." They seemed to have sent slaves whose acquisition of polished manners and literacy would showcase their owners' wealth and piety. Even in Barbados, where the SPG owned a plantation and the slaves who worked it, opposition from other masters constituted one of the many challenges to the furtherance of that mission. The relatively small number of slave conversions in many areas—such as colonial South Caro-lina—may have been attributable in part to a sense among the masters that it was acceptable to convert only a select group among their slaves. Sometimes owners acquiesced to clerical outreach undertaken to those slaves who were creole (that is, American born), of mixed European and African ancestry, with artisanal skills. Bestowing the favor of literacy and Christianity on these slaves supported a more general effort to create an elite cadre within the slave community, a cadre that served as both a buffer from and a bridge to the wider community of enslaved Africans. Many of those evangelized as a result were relatives to their masters since enslaved mulattoes were often the chil-dren or siblings of their owners.

The only mission field where Africans might be evangelized without a struggle with masters was Africa, but British evangelicals did not yet labor much there. A missionary visited Sierra Leone for the first time in 1758, a rather inauspicious start to an effort that would later become significant. He did baptize a few mulattos, who were the offspring of European traders and local women. He also met the grandson of the Cape Mount ruler, recently returned from New York, where he had received an education and baptism. Whether this young man worked toward the conversion of his kinsfolk or others was not recorded.[12] The main focus until 1765—such as it was—occurred in the colonies.

Despite opposition from the masters, however, Christianity began to make serious inroads into the slave quarters by 1760. Even though the south-ern mainland colonies were less taken up with the Awakening of the early 1740s, some residents did convert. Among them were members of the wealthy South Carolina Bryan family, who supported Whitefield's efforts and orga-nized a missionary endeavor among their own slaves. In 1741 twelve of By-ran's slaves converted. This news inspired the English evangelist Anne Dutton to write a pastoral letter to the "Believing Negroes."[13] These early converts to the evangelical cause laid a foundation upon which later preachers, especially Baptists, would build. The Codrington Plantation in Barbados, though it had been owned by the SPG since the early eighteenth century, only launched a serious effort at catechizing its slaves in the 1740s. Some adults had already received baptism and nominal instruction by that time, and thenceforth the SPG ordered all children born on the plantation to be baptized. Two slave boys received extensive instruction and by mid-decade they were teaching basic literacy to the plantation's other children. These tentative steps did not impress all observers: Whitefield for instance commented "that seventy may have learnt to repeat their Creed, the Lords prayer & ten commandments in the Vulgar tongue & been baptized is probable enough. But that seventy are now *Believers in* X^t. I cannot help questioning."[14] Whitefield, looking for signs of rebirth in anyone—white or black—who was said to experience conversion, would not be easily impressed by rote learning, no matter how hard won. Moravian missions established in the West Indies and Georgia in the 1730s to Christianize Africans and their descendents began to show signs of success. Methodism arrived in the Caribbean in 1760. In that year a leading Antigua planter returned from Britain, where he had been converted by Wesley to establish a congregation on his plantation with at least ten of his own slaves as founding members. In both the Caribbean and the mainland, Christianity gained a foothold among the enslaved during this era of increased church activity and shifting spiritual messages.

Christianity furthermore made headway among Native Americans in various areas. Missionary efforts launched by British organizations like the SPG and SSPCK bore fruit from Suriname to New York, as native converts undertook the work of remaking Christianity into an indigenous faith. Moravian efforts in the backcountry of the mainland colonies did too, with native converts apparently preferring to remain in open communities (rather than cloistered choirs) that allowed them to reside in matrilineal households much like those they favored in their traditional villages. David Fowler (1735–1807), a Montauk, a Christian, and a schoolmaster, found the native peoples of western New York "rearly desirous to hear the Word of God; we have no Minister and yet we have a full Assembly every Sabbath."[15]

The religious renewal represented by the Great Awakening encouraged a number of colonial churches to support missionary efforts, so that the mid-eighteenth century saw a further increase in outreach to Native Americans. Jonathan Edwards, after he lost his pulpit at Northampton, preached for a time to both Indians and colonists in Stockbridge, Massachusetts, delivering sermons to his Native American congregation that carried the implications of the doctrine of original sin to radically egalitarian extremes. Comparing his native congregants favorably to their English neighbors, he preached "in a way that encouraged the lowly and humbled the mighty."[16] A few years later, when Rhode Islander Joseph Fish preached to the Narragansetts, he came up against theological divisions quite similar to those plaguing settler churches in the region. Fish's auditors wanted a more evangelical message than he was prepared to convey, clearly having had a taste of revivalism prior to his arrival in 1765. If he thought by going to preach to Indians he would escape the discord within colonial society, he was sorely mistaken. Fish dismissed his critics as "heathens," a label that obscured the fact that they were partaking of divisions common within the wider Christian community. Christianization of Native Americans, although not a priority for many colonists, had undoubtedly advanced by mid-century.

Hostility toward Native American conversion, while also evident in the European-American community, began to develop into a coherent critique among Indians. Nativism—a movement that sought to link Indian peoples across older tribal and linguistic divides by arguing that Native Americans had a distinct history and religious mission—surfaced clearly for the first time. Nativists blamed a wide range of troubles within Indian communities (including declining populations, poverty, and alcoholism) on the willingness to adopt imported European culture. When Indians used European trade goods and accepted European belief systems, proponents believed, they violated their traditions and denied their true natures. Only by reaffirming their commitment to native ways and weaning themselves away from dependence on Europeans could Native Americans be saved. These ideas had numerous central religious components. Native spirituality was one tradition that advocates sought to reinvigorate, although their version of it often contained vaguely Christian elements after centuries of contact. Nativitist leaders (beginning perhaps with a Delaware woman in the 1750s) posited separate creations for Indians, Africans, and Europeans to defend their analysis of the irreconcilable differences. Coming from distinctive origins, this theory suggested, the three peoples were to remain separate. Since Indians had failed to maintain this separation, they suffered for their violation of this cosmic scheme. Europeans interested in Indian origins had previously floated the idea of polygenesis (or multiple creations). This idea was officially considered a heresy in that it denied the single Christian Creation that led to the Fall and the doctrine of original sin. Nativists, suggesting that a return to tradition would solve a myriad of problems, urged their adherents to adopt this course. Others, such as those who fought against the settlers in King Philip's War, had rejected Christian tradition as one component of the European culture they attacked. But the Nativist message also showed strong signs of having been influenced by Christianity: prophetic visions that supported the movement were generally framed in terms of a single supreme deity and an afterlife in heaven.

Ironically the fluidity and flexibility of Native American culture had encouraged the absorption of aspects of European culture over the preceding centuries. Even calls to return to old ways demonstrated the alteration of tradition that had occurred in the intervening time. In fact the slow process of religious change that had incorporated Christian concepts into Native American cosmologies may have been similar to the way that the Protestant Reformation took hold only very gradually among Christians in Britain. What Felicity Heal referred to as "process of assimilation, by which a new language and ideology were to become normative, the stuff of everyday experience and exchange," with regard to the Reformation in sixteenth-century Britain might also be applied to the assimilation that occurred among Indians exposed to Christianity.[17] In addition, native tradition may have been especially syncretic, peculiarly open to and able to absorb new influences and ideas. As a result, the Nativist incorporation of Christian elements was consistent with that tradition in its very tendency to absorb some aspects of the imported tradition it overtly rejected. The introduction of Nativist ideas during this era have been labeled, by Gregory Dowd, as the Indians' own Great Awakening, in that native peoples awakened to a sense of community peril and a plan for addressing it.[18] Yet Indian identities and the ways in which they negotiated the various threads of belief and practice running through their lives remained somewhat fluid. Many ways existed to relate to the presence of European ideas and the alterations in native cosmologies, and Indian peoples inhabited a complex spiritual landscape.

During the mid-eighteenth century numerous European or European-American observers described Native American beliefs and practices, descriptions that convey the extent to which many communities and individuals remained largely untouched by the faith promulgated by Europeans. Mary Jemison, a captive adopted by the Seneca, later recounted practices current in that community in the 1750s, including an annual cycle of five ceremonies marking various transitional moments in the year. John Brickell, who traveled the Carolina backcountry, lamented that European men abandoned their

Christian upbringings to live with their native partners, leaving the children of these unions to be raised in their mother's traditions and therefore in ignorance of Christianity. He provided a detailed account of Indian "Customs, or rather Absurdities," while also noting that the native peoples kept much of their tradition hidden from outsiders. He noted the use of objects thought to bring protection in war, the observance of ritual feasts, the leadership role provided by "priests or conjurers," burial practices and beliefs about an afterlife current among the peoples he visited. Brickell published his ethnographic account in Europe to satisfy curiosity about American Indians, supporting a publishing practice with a long history by the time his account appeared in 1743.[19]

One man who lived as a captive among the Indians for four years recounted an instructive conversation. He heard that the plenty enjoyed by Europeans obscured their reliance on the spirit that provided food to people, whereas Indians "who are frequently out of provisions, and yet are wonderfully supplied" can better appreciate "that they are supported by the Ruler of heaven and earth." As Tecaughretanego explained, "Owaneeyo sometimes suffers us to be in want, in order to teach us our dependence upon him."[20] John Heckwelder learned that the Delaware "do not exclude other animals from their world of spirits, the place to which they expect to go after death." All "animated nature," including plant life, is part of "a great whole, from which they have not yet ventured to separate themselves." In this view, humans were "only the first among equals." He found "this abstruse subject" difficult to explain, supposing the Indians also considered it confusing.[21] These firsthand accounts from colonial observers, all dating from the 1740s and 1750s, demonstrate the continuity of religious beliefs and practices in Native America.

For a wide variety of individuals and communities within the British Atlantic world, the religious developments of this era created opportunities to pursue a collective enterprise in the interest of protecting the autonomy of traditional culture. Many Africans found the evangelical message far better suited to their own cultural tradition than had been the earlier variants of Christianity offered to their communities. Evangelical Christianity appealed in the slave quarters in part because it represented continuity with older religious traditions. Similarly Welsh converts during the revivals used them as a vehicle for expressing traditional culture—including local community bonds and the need for household worship—and for protecting and promoting the Welsh language. With Protestant outreach in Ireland occurring in

English only after a debate over whether to switch to the traditional Celtic language of the majority of the populace, Irish Catholics maintained their disinterest in Protestant conversion. Native Americans, whether they became Christians or embraced Nativism, worked through these choices to maintain a range of cultural practices. They demonstrated an ongoing commitment to the traditional prohibition against intra-clan incest whether within a newly adopted Christian framework or a Nativist one. Even the more general trends in the geography of revivalism demonstrated that communities renewed an older commitment to Calvinism by embracing the predestinarian message of the itinerant preachers. Religious change was simultaneously a vehicle for continuity and for innovation in a wide range of locations.

These changes brought a perplexing combination of division and unity in their wake. Divisions were obvious when rival religious traditions competed for ascendancy in a specific community or region. The Nativist trend within Indian communities exposed differences over how to respond to the cultural practices introduced by Europeans. Some Indians embraced the religious conversion that other native peoples were ostensibly rejecting. A once largely unified Congregationalist establishment in Massachusetts and Connecticut split in reaction to revival, marking off Old Light (or anti-revival) and New Light (pro-revival) positions. Similarly Presbyterians in the Middle Colonies struggled over whether to promote or oppose revival. Active religious organizations, such as the Moravians and the Methodists, earned the criticism of religious leaders unwilling to accept their claims that their outreach beyond the bounds of churches made no effort at conversion to an alternative church as evangelism and missionary outreach customarily did. Clergymen occasionally viewed the energetic evangelism of other churches as a threat. Church of England clergy did not applaud the revitalization of the dissenter community that evangelical activism heralded.

In American colonies where the Church of England was not legally established (as in the New England region), outreach on the part of the church continued to be viewed with suspicion. George Whitefield's ability to gain invitations into the pulpits of non-Anglican ministers—if only for a time—was remarkable. Churches initially opened to him were subsequently closed as the reaction against the Awakening built. Other Church of England efforts tended to be seen from the start as partisan campaigns on behalf of that particular church order. Colonists objected when missions seemed more bent on converting them to an alternative faith tradition within Christianity than on converting non-Christian Indians. When Boston minister Jonathan

Mayhew attacked the SPG in a tract published in 1763, accusing it of raising money under false pretenses, he voiced an animosity that dissenting ministers often felt as they watched the Church of England become more aggressive about evangelizing. The church became more heavily influenced by Central European pietism after mid-century, and this connection led some dissenters to pull back from pietism as a result.

Indian communities were sometimes caught between feuding Christian factions. Beginning in the 1760s, Church of England and non-conformist ministers got into a tug-of-war over Indian missions. The Mohawks were either Catholics—if they had been converted by French missionaries—or Church of England communicants. Those in the latter group were not especially tolerant of dissenting ministers when they encountered them. Samuel Kirkland found his mission to Mohawks and other native people questioned when he departed from the practice of making baptism freely available. He demanded some sign of religious commitment (beyond requesting baptism for a child) on the part of the parents. As representatives of the community noted,

> our first ministers were very fond of baptizing our children immedi-
> ately upon be[in]g desired. They taught us that Children should be
> baptized as soon as they made their appearance in our world, & that
> delays were dangerous, no matter what character the parents sus-
> tained . . . But you, Father, are not fond of baptizing our children.
> We have many Children among us yet unbaptized, & some have
> gone out of life, unbaptized. This we view as confining the word of
> god, & shutting up the way to Heaven, or making it very narrow.[22]

Their complaint resonated with those made by seventeenth-century Bermu-dans when their island churches similarly restricted its practices. A second objection had to do with the lavishness of the meeting house: the Indian faithful wanted to build a fine house, with a steeple, and thought that failure to do so would make them seem ungrateful to God, as dissenters (such as their new minister) were reputed to be. Some also asked for a Prayer Book service similar to the one they had first encountered in an Anglican mission. With a minister who was not a Church of England man, they were unlikely to get their wish.

While some of these divisions could be described as political (in that they were fights over who held authority and about which of a number of available options a group should pursue), other divisions were fundamentally theological. When Wesley and Whitefield split over their differing views on the availability of salvation, they acted out a much larger fissure within British Christianity. The Scots, who were relatively unchanged by international revivalism or by Methodism, were deeply engaged in similar debates within their own Presbyterian Church of Scotland. Schisms were frequent among the Scots in the eighteenth century—over theology and religious style (the Seceder movement of the 1730s, which arrived in Ulster in the following decade); over oath taking (the Burgher-Antiburgher split of 1747 that revolved around whether taking the oath upholding "true religion" was intended as support for the established church); the recurrent issue of patronage (flaring up again in the Moderate versus Popular party division in 1750s that reflected liberal religion and accommodation with the power of the state versus Calvinist orthodoxy and opposition to any accommodation); and other issues (the Independent tradition, a bone of contention in the 1730s). These splits revolved around as many political as religious questions, such as whether to take the oath or how to relate to the power of patronage. Profound differences also developed around the church's Calvinist heritage and how the contemporary faith ought to relate to it. Generally the traditionalists hailed from the poorer churches and those that were more isolated, while those partaking of the liberalizing trends of the era tended to be more educated and prosperous. This correlation was typical throughout the Atlantic world.

Clergy were more numerous in the liberal ranks, sometimes leaving disillusioned believers without amenable options within the establishment. The Presbyterian church in England drifted so far in a liberal direction (especially away from the predestinarian tenets of an earlier generation) that those within that church who clung to the older ways eventually joined with like-minded Scots (crossing ethnic lines that had previously prevailed) to uphold their theological traditions. Pro- and anti-revivalists in the colonies often also divided over the question of the availability of salvation and the value of reasonable Christianity. Charles Chauncy, who led the Old Light attack on revivals in Massachusetts, would end his days as a Universalist. Universalism, or the belief in universal salvation, was such an extreme position that Chauncy kept his interest in the idea secret for three decades (1752–82) before going public with his views. As Chauncy's trajectory may also suggest, these divisions related to variants in religious style as well. Rational Christianity favored a God who was a loving Father figure; such a deity worked through the intellects of his children, guiding them to the reasonable choice of faith. Evangelical Christians emphasized the sinfulness of man and the just judgment of an awe-inspiring God who saved some though all deserved his wrath. These profound divisions cut across confessional lines, causing vociferous debate and creating new enmities where friendships had once reigned.

Paradoxically, the period also beheld a new sense of unity, at least in some quarters. Revivalists enjoyed a sense that they were participating in an international movement. They wrote about their own experiences and read about the experiences of others in England, Wales, Ireland, Scotland, Central Europe, and throughout the American colonies. In England and Wales, evangelically minded Christians gathered regularly for "Letter Days," when the correspondence from all over the British Atlantic world (and occasionally beyond) was read aloud from a pulpit so that all could hear of the work of God in distant communities. Revivalists gathered to sing hymns that extolled the far-reaching effects of their movement. One, written for the occasion of a November, 1742, meeting in London began: "Great things in England, Wales and Scotland wrought, And in American to pass are brought."[23] The sense of connectedness, of participating in a shared experience with distant co-religionists, was furthered by the explosion of print. Relatively inexpensive publications made it possible for individuals in far-flung locations to read of the same events. John Wesley supported his efforts with a wide variety of print media, including sermons, biographies, and hymnals. Methodist hymnody—the first such publication appearing in 1737—would have a lasting impact on Protestant culture on both sides of the Atlantic. For a time revival promoters published their own periodical in Boston, *The Christian History* (edited by minister Thomas Prince), to document the widespread work of the Lord. George Whitefield's tours and his labors to promote them through his own publications also added to the conviction that something major was brewing.

Whereas the revivals appeared to be a grave source of division from the vantage point of Charles Chauncy's Boston study, within the broader framework of the British Atlantic world they also created a new sense of unity. By the eve of the American Revolution, only newly acquired Catholic Quebec and Grenada (both of which had until recently been French colonies) had not been caught up in the culture of revival, as Eliga Gould has observed.[24] Revivalists were not alone in feeling that they were part of a larger Christian community that was undergoing significant change. Christians supported widespread missionary endeavors and eagerly awaited the news of success among the Muskito or Iroquois Indians that came in missionary correspondence and periodical pulpit announcements aiming to raise funds. Nativism within the Indian community also promoted unity, an unprecedented pan-Indian effort drawing together a wide variety of people across tribal and linguistic barriers. Unity along one axis and disunity along another seemed to be a hallmark of this era.

All this interest in religion also helped spur a remarkable period of institutional growth in the churches. Much Methodist outreach within Britain itself sought to gather in the unchurched, particularly those who were previously left out by rural isolation (as in Wales) or by migration to growing cities that were underserved by clergy. The trend toward organizational expansion was most marked within the colonies, not surprisingly, given that churches there tended to be only incomplete copies of their older and more vigorous home institutions. Religious energy and religious rivalries contributed to the founding of a spate of colonial colleges in this period: six of the nine colleges with colonial beginnings were founded between 1746 and 1769.[25] These institutions trained clergy, usually for a specific church. For instance, the College of New Jersey (1746, later Princeton) was founded by Presbyterians, while King's College (1754, later Columbia) was, as one might expect from the name, Anglican. Only one, that in Pennsylvania (1755), boasted no religious affiliation. With the Society of Friends, the dominant religious group in the colony, uninterested in promoting a college-educated clergy, it was left to the unaffiliated Benjamin Franklin to launch the college. Ecclesiastical building took off during this period as well, so that the colonial landscape bore the imprint of vigorous Christian organizing (and funding) by the mid-eighteenth century. Not all the building was related even tangentially to changes in Christianity, however: the Newport Jewish community built the lovely Touro Synagogue in the early 1760s.

Churches became more organized and better able to staff their pulpits too. Lutherans today honor immigrant pastor, Heinrich Melchior Mühlenberg, as the individual responsible for founding American Lutheranism. A man of enormous energy and organizational skill, Mühlenberg found his work cut out for him in the Middle Colonies. There he dedicated decades to the work of founding and staffing churches and bringing them into some general conformity on belief and practice. The first American presbyteries date from the mid-eighteenth century as well. Indeed the energy that went into church organization and the building of places of worship has led Jon Butler to say that the American colonies only became Christianized at this time.[26] While this argument equated institutional church structures with religion and therefore overlooked much religious activity that had occurred in the preceding century and a half, it did give a sense of the high level of institutional building that took place in the middle decades of the eighteenth century.

John Wesley, although he welcomed revivals, thought they had little lasting effect (and that the hard work of local and small-scale organizing was necessary to "silently increase" the faith).[27] Nonetheless, revivals did revitalize existing churches. This effect was especially apparent among Congregationalists in New England and Presbyterians in the Middle Colonies. Although the end of the world which some revivalists anticipated failed to materialize, widespread Awakening enhanced a feeling of participation in an international Protestant community. The hegemony of the old Congregationalist establishment in New England was irrevocably undermined, as revivalist New Light churches provided an opening wedge for the Baptists who converted many after 1750. Baptists later evangelized in the South, where they, like the Methodists, helped to remake the region's religious complexion. Circulation of new ideas was spurred on by revivalism, as in previous decades it had been supported by migration. Southern black preachers converted by Baptist and other evangelists would eventually take up missionary work in the British Caribbean. Whereas England responded more vigorously to Methodist local organizing, colonies embraced revivalism. In America, in a later period, these two strands would be combined to create a powerful new movement, giving birth to the Second Great Awakening and the Methodist camp meeting. In the meantime, both Methodism and evangelism more generally encouraged cooperation and the creation of a shared evangelical culture.

EIGHT

Revolutionary Divisions, Continuing Bonds

AS IN THE LATE seventeenth century, in the later eighteenth century the British Atlantic world endured serious conflicts with implications for religion. The American, French, and Haitian revolutions all affected religious institutions and trends. Both the American and French revolutions were interpreted by conservatives as arising from irreligion. While the American conflict divided the British Empire, religious links built up over the previous century and three quarters continued to knit that world together. The division of the formerly British Atlantic into British and American political entities changed the institutional landscape, causing the creation of new churches. After the Revolution Britain recommitted its empire to the supremacy of the Church of England, even as that church's hegemony within England was further undermined. Transplanting the established church remained on the agenda, despite what might have seemed to be the lesson of the previous centuries. On the other side of the Atlantic, the long tradition of diversity pointed the new United States toward an innovative national policy separating church and state. Antipopery still flourished as a prejudice in some circles but, at the same time, the number of Catholics rose and their treatment improved markedly, in both the United States and England. Evangelism, such an important aspect of the recent history of the British Atlantic, continued to shape both polities. It circulated especially within the African diasporic community. Native peoples of the Americas meanwhile carried forward their negotiation between assimilation and separation from European culture and religion. Revolution may have split the Anglophone Atlantic community into two countries, but the cultural commonalities ensured that the religious connections and shared experiences carried on.

NEW FRANCE

NEWFOUNDLAND

NOVA SCOTIA
(ACADIA)

MAINE

NEW
HAMP-
SHIRE

MASSACHUSETTS
PLYMOUTH PLANTATION
MARTHA'S VINEYARD

NEW
YORK
(NEW
NETHERLAND)

RHODE ISLAND &
PROVIDENCE PLANTATIONS

PENNSYLVANIA

CONNECTICUT
NEW HAVEN

NEW
JERSEY

DELAWARE

MARYLAND

ATLANTIC

VIRGINIA

OCEAN

NORTH CAROLINA

BERMUDA

SOUTH
CAROLINA

GEORGIA

•UISIANA
Spanish)

FLORIDA
(Spanish)

*Gulf
of
Mexico*

0	150	300 Miles
0	150	300 Kilometers

p 5. Eastern North America before 1763

From the perspective of conservatives, the American Revolution reprised the very issues that had been at stake a century before in Bacon's Rebellion. As colonies moved fitfully toward separation and the creation of the United States, disloyal individuals, many of them religious dissenters, failed to respect their duty to God and King and instead participated in revolt. These analysts were correct insofar as they were describing their own position, for their loyalty to the monarch was predicated on their sense that God called them to uphold the social and political order. As Sir William Johnson—crown official, Indian agent, and partner to the Mohawk woman Molly Brant—put it, "In truth the Principal Dissenters have little or no Religion yet they have a particular aversion to ours, because it is interwoven with the Constitution, & the best Support to Monarchy, a form of Government against which they are all Strongly prejudiced." He shared with other Church of England men a view that "Members of that Church are the Surest Supports of the Constitution and the faithfullest Subjects of the Crown."[1] Often "High Church" in their attitudes toward the Church of England and its relationship to monarchy, these conservatives saw disloyalty as sinful as well as treasonous. In England and America, such people were the staunchest crown supporters. They opposed the American revolutionary cause and later, and for similar reasons, they abhorred the French Revolution with its attack on monarchy and the church.

For the most conservative of Church of England members, when war against the crown came, religious affiliation usually dictated allegiance. All members of the church might be expected to support the king, who was not only their political ruler but also the head of their church. Yet opponents of royal policy ignored their ecclesiastical links to George III in making their choices in the revolutionary struggle. Ministers in the established church had a more compelling reason to side with the monarch, as they had sworn an oath to the king when they joined the clergy. As their communities divided into patriot and loyalist camps, the decision to deny their oaths was reminiscent of that faced by their forbearers in the Glorious Revolution. Just as the non-jurors who refused to ignore their oaths to James II to support the new regime after 1688 had been in a minority in England and Wales in that earlier controversy, so too were the clergy who opposed the break with Britain a minority in this conflict. Still 25 percent of all colonial American Church of England clergy became loyalist rather than abandon their king in violation of their oaths. Other clergy would make their peace with the change, staffing the new Episcopal Church that would rise out of the ashes of the Church of England after the Revolution.

Church of England adherents were not the only ones who might choose to oppose the Revolution on religious grounds. Members of certain faith communities, especially those in a minority in a given area, sometimes supported the crown out of a conviction that the king's government protected them from interference from local majorities of other religious persuasions. Baptists in parts of New England, for instance, feared that if the colonies won independence Congregationalists in their new states would use the end of royal oversight to persecute minority churches out of existence. Baptist leader Isaac Backus negotiated assurances about the post-war ecclesiastical order before recommending that his co-religionists support the patriot cause. Such fears arose from memories of the time when the king had stayed the hand of local establishments that pursued policies hostile toward others— such as when Charles II put a stop to the execution of Quakers in Massachusetts a century before. Recent immigrants from the European continent to the Mid-Atlantic often had similar fears about what independence portended for their liberties. Yet, unlike with conservative Anglicans, their loyalism did not generally arise from any specific ideas integral to their faith. Rather they made a calculated decision about what political outcome would best protect their churches and communities. That Baptists in Virginia supported the Revolution on the grounds that its success would improve the position of their churches offered further proof that their stance was the result more of practical than of principled considerations.

For opponents of crown policy who ultimately supported the Revolution, allegiance did not follow simply from their religion (or any lack thereof). While loyalists claimed that the atheism, irreligion, or at least dissenter status of many revolutionaries determined their position on the conflict, patriots tended to be motivated by other issues in their support of the cause of American independence. They fought to defend liberties, as they said, and they worried that their society was under threat from government policies. Critics only gradually blamed the objectionable policies on the king, however, and far from being eager to throw off monarchy (as their opponents claimed), most of them hesitated to do so. Some early supporters of the protests against royal policy ultimately chose the loyalist side when the moment to break with the crown occurred. That many patriots were not in the end prevented from rejecting their allegiance to the king by the idea that loyalty was divinely ordained gave a modicum of proof to the arguments of their opponents. They were not motivated by the convictions that guided conservatives, which is not to say (as the conservatives did indeed say) that they were driven by religious views that propelled them to rebellion.

Religion could encourage disloyalty in at least two ways, however. The recurrent fear of popery, which also carried over from the late seventeenth-century conflicts, contributed to the revolutionary impulse. The 1763 British victory in the Seven Years or French and Indian War brought numerous French colonies, including Quebec and some Caribbean islands, under British control. With this sudden influx of French-speaking Catholic subjects, British authorities had to decide their status and that of their faith. Given the rhetoric identifying British national identity with Protestantism, a move to coerce these newly conquered Catholics into conformity to the Church of England would have come as no surprise. The fact that many of the Native Americans living in Quebec had been converted by Catholic missionaries created another incentive to suppress that church. As British official John Ogilvie remarked, "These Savages are extremely attached to the Ceremonials of the [Catholic] Church, & have been taught to believe the English have no Knowledge of the Mystery of Man's Redemption by Jesus Christ."[2] In addition, British authorities had recently dropped their policy of permitting the French Catholics in Acadia (conquered in 1713) to remain unmolested in their traditional faith. The decision to expel the Acadians in 1755 corresponded with an end to a laissez-faire policy regarding their Catholicism. Expulsion did not bode well for the future of French Catholic subjects, nor did measures intended to coerce religious conformity to the Church of England adopted in another newly conquered French colony, the West Indian island of Grenada.

When, in the Quebec Act of 1774, the British determined not to force conformity upon the newly conquered Québécois, the move dismayed the empire's most ardent Protestant subjects. The Quebec Act did not denote any decision on the part of officials to abandon the religious establishment for its imperial possessions. Instead it heralded a policy of conversion rather than coercion that they hoped would achieve the desired ends. Upper Canada (that section of the colony not already peopled by French Catholics) would have a Church of England establishment, and the goal was to bring those in Quebec into line through persuasive means. Still, antigovernment protests in England and Scotland as well as speeches in Parliament criticized the provisions of the act permitting Catholic worship and eliminating trial by jury. The combination suggested that French popery and despotism were to replace Protestantism and British liberty. The City of London petitioned against the act in part on the grounds that it allowed Roman Catholic worship, "without any provision being made for the free exercise of the Protestant religion which may prove greatly injurious and oppressive to his Majesty's Protestant subjects."[3]

Coming as it did in the midst of tensions over imperial policy in colonies south of Canada, the Quebec Act emerged as one of a number of issues that settlers criticized in their protests against the imperial government. New Englanders' hostility to the act was particularly vehement. Anti-Catholic rhetoric still resonated loudly in a region where colonists commemorated Guy Fawkes' Day under the sobriquet "Pope's Day." As the local name of the celebration implied, Bostonians had not softened the anti-Catholicism traditionally associated with the occasion. Many New Englanders had supported the French and Indian War as a campaign against popery and their colonies had sacrificed more of its male population to the war than any other colonial region. Expecting the war to strike a blow against popery, the settlers there objected strenuously to the new policy enshrined in the Quebec Act. Toleration of Catholicism and a plan to organize an Episcopal presence in the colonies caused non-Anglicans to conclude that a plot was afoot against their own variants of Christianity. A political cartoon entitled "The Mitred Minut" depicted bishops (denoted by the hat or "mitre" they wore) dancing on the Quebec Act while approving imperial officials looked on, one of them with Satan perched on his shoulder. Such images collapsed together British policies toward French Catholics with the introduction of bishops and associated all with the Devil's work. That popery and tyranny came to be associated in some minds with Britain's government instead of with Britain's foes did not bode well for resolving the brewing imperial crisis.

Millennial preaching that framed the conflict with the royal government in terms of the coming end of time helped some potential patriots to accept that confronting their monarch had become a necessity. Resistance was made easier when colonists believed that they faced a threat to liberties of cosmic proportions and that their battles had a divinely ordained purpose. Preachers, having depicted the war against the papist French in such terms, turned the same rhetorical strategies toward British policy makers as the conflict neared the breaking point. Whereas some clergy—particularly conservative Church of England ministers—preached the traditional political message of the duty of obedience to authority, others urged their hearers to follow their consciences. Framing the protection of liberty and of customary rights as a

The Mitred Minuet.

Fig. 13. Colonists, especially in New England, feared that the Quebec Act, in granting liberty to Catholics, demonstrated Britain's intention to destroy colonial liberties. In this 1774 engraving by Paul Revere, "The Mitred Minuet" (based on a cartoon in *Royal American Magazine*, 1774), bishops danced a minuet around the act while ministers, goaded by the devil,

community mandate, preachers rallied their congregations to oppose British policy. More importantly, once war began, the newly formed American identity could be understood in cosmic terms. Millennialist rhetoric represented one strand in the public discussion of liberty and the struggle against tyranny.

Religion was not the cause of the American Revolution. But it wound through the breach, affecting it in a variety of ways. Occasionally religious affiliation guided a person's position on the break with Britain. Ministers for or against the war preached sermons that steeled the resolve of their auditors to fight on their favored side. Conservatives who supported church and king often saw the conflict in religious terms, as their opposition to the rebellion combined religion and politics. Yet this did not amount to a religious cause for the war. Most people did not make their choices largely on religious grounds. Men and women who supported the cause of independence saw a more complex relationship between religion and resistance. They believed that the Revolution was caused by a host of problems, most of them constitutional, political, and social. That the two sides experienced the dynamic so differently was one more indication of the seriousness of the breach between them. It also demonstrates the many ways in which religion and politics intersected.

While the Revolution was not caused by religion and even individual political allegiance was rarely determined by religion, the consequences of the American Revolution for religion were enormous. On the most basic level, the revolutionary war affected various religious communities, among them native groups. In some cases, the disruption caused by war undermined the religious integrity of communities. The Cherokee would later recall the 1770s as the time when the traditional ritual calendar was severely abridged. After that decade, the Green Corn Ceremony became the predominant annual ritual, a change from early times when it had been only one of a number of festivals. The encroachments of the white community on Indian land, which redoubled after the Revolution ended British efforts to halt expansion, strained native communities. While such strains might result in a constriction of communal practices, as with the Cherokee, it might also spur a return to older ways. The Nativist movements that called for revitalization (often describing them in terms that incorporated Christian influence) continued as a powerful force among Indian peoples who endured regular contact with Europeans. Missionary Samuel Kirkland reported that in 1798 "ancient pagan sacrifice & religious festival of their forefathers [were] performed . . . after a total neglect of them for more than thirty years." A young man in a dream trance called the community to return to its previous practice of honoring the Great Tortoise who was "Upholder of the Skies or Heavens." Failure to do so explained the sufferings of the people, and only a return to these abandoned sacred practices would alleviate that suffering.[4]

The Revolution directly caused the persecution of some religious communities. Members of the Society of Friends generally tried to remain uninvolved in the fighting once the war broke out, since their commitment to pacifism precluded participation. Their position was not always easily distinguished from loyalism, since inaction might support the status quo. Especially in the Pennsylvania area, where Quakers were numerous and the British army maintained a major presence in the middle years of the war, Friends' pacifism became the object of patriot ire. New state governments imprisoned a number of Friends as alleged loyalists. Others chose to abandon the peace testimony to join the patriot war effort. These so called "Free Quakers" or "Fighting Quakers" were especially common in southern New England. Their fellow Quakers often drove them out of their local meetings for their violation of the peace testimony.

Meanwhile, North American residents feared Methodists and Shakers, who began arriving in the colonies just prior to the Revolution, as possible agents of the British. Methodism at this time was still officially a movement within the Church of England. That link alone was not sufficient to make participants unsavory, however, since Church of England members were involved in the patriot cause. Methodists organizing activities, which involved setting up small group meetings, did appear suspect, especially as they were launched in the Middle Colonies concurrent with the pre-war imperial struggle. John Wesley, although he warned members of the movement to remain out of the imperial political fray, exacerbated tension by publishing *A Calm Address to our American Colonies.* The tract advised those who were dismayed with Crown policy to back down. His intervention helped to earn the Methodist movement the wrath of rebels, and it set up Methodists for a difficult time during the Revolution itself. After the war the political issues would be sorted out. Then fear of Methodists declined, although occasionally a missionary's antislavery stance would still elicit hostility.

The so-called Shakers, members of the Society of Believers in Christ's Second Coming, arrived in North America just on the eve of the outbreak of war. A small group from England, the Shakers followed a woman named Ann Lee, or Mother Ann. Her followers believed that Lee was Christ come again, providing the symmetry of a female version of the deity to complement the male figure of Jesus. She advocated celibacy and communal ownership of all things. With its unusual beliefs and its female leadership, Shakers probably would have met initial opposition regardless of the existence of an imperial conflict. Suspicious communities accused Shakers who tried to organize meetings of spying for the British army, and mobs harassed movement members during the war. Shakers, too, would find a different welcome once these suspicions were allayed after the war.

The Revolution required a new religious settlement for those former colonies that joined together to create the new United States. Observers and even participants were surprised that the thirteen distinct colonies that, prior to the revolutionary crisis, seemed to have little in common were able to join in a shared polity. To draw this variety of people and polities together, a number of compromises were necessary. From 1775 through the writing of the federal Constitution of 1787 was a period of repeated negotiation. To create a united nation, the founders had to hammer out a series of agreements over issues as disparate as slavery, claims to western territory, debts, individual rights, and the shape of a new government. Among the problems confronting them was how to adapt the contradictory and complex legal situation of various religious groups that had prevailed in the British Empire to the new nation emerging out of the revolutionary struggle.

When the founders agreed to keep the federal government out of the affairs of the church, they resolved the dogged question of a new religious order by agreeing not to designate one. Refusing to erect a new establishment, the patriot leaders decided to leave religious choice a local and individual decision. To do otherwise would have created insurmountable difficulties. First, the diversity present in each state and across all the states made identifying one church that could be established by law an impossible proposition. The only serious contender, the Church of England, was tainted by its association with British monarchy. It remained, in any case, a minority faith in some areas. On the eve of the Revolution young Josiah Quincy Junior traveled from his native New England through the colonies to the south, and everywhere he went he remarked on the religious diversity he observed. He considered slavery and religious differences the two potential divisive factors that could prevent united action, as "areas of dangerous practical vulnerability" for the revolutionary cause.[5] A widespread awareness of this danger led many to conclude that any attempt to induce conformity or even favor one church over another would result in disaster.

Second, creating a national framework for endorsing a series of local establishments, while it might have satisfied the defenders of New England's Congregational orthodoxy, would have been wildly unpopular with minority faiths everywhere. At the time of the Constitution, two states had religious establishments that they had carried over from the colonial era. In both Connecticut and Massachusetts, some inhabitants had already objected to these legal supports for one church order. Congregationalist patriots promised local Baptists that they would not pursue a strengthening of the church-state relationship should the Revolution succeed, and those assurances had been critical to ensuring Baptist support for the cause of Revolution. Under the unregulated system created at the federal level, both states kept an established church—but did not use it to coerce dissenters—into the nineteenth century. Both establishments would eventually lapse in favor of the more open practices prevailing elsewhere.

Third, citizens opposed the idea of the state meddling in religion on principle. Deists and other enlightenment thinkers who favored individual freedom fell into this category, such men as the religiously unconventional Thomas Jefferson as well as his less daring colleague George Washington. So did believers of a more traditional Christian hue, since their faith communities thought—as the radical Roger Williams had a century and a half before—that mixing politics and religion was ultimately bad for religion and even for the prospects for individual salvation. A variety of Christian churches favored freedom of worship without any government involvement so that Christians could concentrate on the affairs of the spirit and on spreading their faith through persuasive preaching. Decoupling church and state thus had the approval of a wide swath of the new citizens of the United States, both conventionally religious people and less traditional thinkers.

For a variety of motives, therefore, the founders deliberately rejected any linkage between the church and the federal state—either government control of religion or religion's control of the state. In so doing, they discarded models that would have set broad religious boundaries. They had chosen not to follow early colonial laws in favor of limited religious liberty that listed basic Christian beliefs (such as the Trinity) that had to be accepted by all. Had they established parameters of this sort, drawing on local colonial precedents, the United States would have been legally defined as fundamentally Christian. Religious tests at the national level did not carry the day after 1776: after much debate, the founders rejected the suggestion that the new nation as a whole should be made explicitly Christian in a general way.

Religious conservatives worried about the implications of this decision.

"A Deacon Stone" was "much alarmed because there was no test." According to his opponent Jeremiah Libbey, writing to his like-minded friend Jeremy Belknap, "He thot it would leave the Bible, that precious jewel, that peal of great price, without any support, and that the Papists or men of no religion would get into office, and that the blood of all the martyrs would rise up against us." Libbey's contempt for Stone's worries was clear, indicating how divisive this disagreement could be.

With the views of Libbey and Belknap carrying the day at the federal level, a 1797 Senate treaty with the Barbary states confirmed the official position, asserting that "the government of the United States of America is not in any sense founded on the Christian Religion . . . [and] has in itself no character of enmity against the laws, religion or tranquility of Musselmen" (meaning Muslims).[6] The system they had established was predicated on the idea that it was better to leave belief and practice entirely to believers and practitioners. Those who shaped the federal constitution thought that such stratagems as doctrinal tests represented an unacceptable intrusion on personal belief.

How this separation would work in practice was a matter of continued discussion, and struggles over the details of its implementation began almost immediately. Those leaders who assumed that religion, and particularly Christianity, would enjoy an official role in the new government pursued this goal at the state level. Since the federal constitution did not speak to the decisions made by the states, they could make Christianity official within the state arena. For decades, Connecticut and Massachusetts maintained the privileged place of Congregationalism in their states against vocal opposition from dissenters and those who supported separation on civic grounds.

Much more widespread was the practice of promoting general religious principles. State constitutions that erected no establishment often endorsed Christianity generally. Delaware, taking an unusually definitive position on this issue, adopted the colonial-era policy of requiring state office holders to endorse Christian doctrine by taking an oath that they believed "in God the Father, in Jesus Christ His only Son, and in the Holy Ghost, one God, blessed forevermore; and I do acknowledge the holy scriptures of the Old and New Testament to be given by divine inspiration." Other states asked for less specificity from their office holders on the nature of their belief, an approach that allowed persons with a broader range of views to serve. Such was the case in Pennsylvania, where all had to acknowledge the existence of

God and a "future state of rewards and punishments"—a provision that would allow any Christian, Jew, or Muslim to qualify.[7]

In many instances, early leaders of the new nation promoted prayers at the beginning of legislative meetings. These gestures toward a shared commitment to religion and particularly Christianity were not limited to the states. The federal government occasionally endorsed broadly religious practices, such as declaring days of fasting or thanksgiving in response to worrisome or felicitous developments in the nation's circumstances. These particular public rituals had been common in many colonies and were adopted—although not without protests from the stricter advocates of separation—nearly as a matter of course. When newly elected President Jefferson did away with the practice of public days to offer thanks or to beg forgiveness, which his predecessor in the White House, John Adams, had employed, Levi Lincoln warned him that the move would be controversial. While Jefferson saw the elimination as consistent with the official policy of separation, leaders like Adams and Levi believed the ritual practice was unremarkable.

While few people advocated that government support a particular version of Christianity, most Americans expected religion, and especially Protestant Christianity, to flourish. The separation did not arise out of hostility to religion but rather out of a sense that government involvement in religion was bad for both religion and government. George Washington noted that he would oppose a Constitution that "might possibly endanger the religious rights of any ecclesiastical Society" or any act of the federal government that might "render the liberty of conscience insecure."[8] As James Madison explained in a letter dated from 1822, "We are teaching the world the great truth that Governments do better without Kings & Nobles than with them. The merit will be doubled by the other lesson that Religion flourishes in greater purity, without than with the aid of Government." Jefferson was perhaps the most unconventional religiously of all the founders, and he coined the phrase "wall of separation" to describe the agreement that had been hammered out vis-à-vis the relationship between church and state.[9] Yet he believed religion and the morality it encouraged were fundamental to a healthy society. His unconventionality came through when he invested an enormous amount of time cutting up the Gospels to eliminate passages he considered irrational accretions introduced by a human hand. The moral lessons woven amongst the miraculous and otherwise unlikely events were, he believed, a message to be heeded by all. His approach to Christianity was unusually heterodox, but Jefferson was not hostile to religion as long as it was left a matter of individual choice.

Many revolutionary leaders felt strongly that religious divisions were to be avoided. Rather than endorse one faith, and force all to conform to it, as had been the early modern solution to the problem of religious pluralism, these Americans thought that differences should be set aside. Thomas Jefferson approved of a sentiment he heard attributed to Quaker preacher Richard Motte, that "he did not believe there was a Quaker, Presbyterian, Methodist or Baptist in heaven . . . [for] in heaven, God knew no distinctions, but considered all good men as his children, and all brethren of the same family."[10] For Benjamin Franklin it was a matter of pride that an unaffiliated public meeting space had been built in colonial Philadelphia as one of his community projects. As he noted in his account of his life, the building was "for the Use of any Preacher of any religious Persuasion who might desire to say something to the People of Philadelphia . . . so that even if the Mufti of Constantinople were to send a missionary to preach Mahometanism to us, he would find a Pulpit at his Service."[11] This spirit of openness to the airing of all views (even non-Christian, in this case, Islamic, ones) was typical of the leaders of Franklin's generation. It informed their opposition to suggestions that the new United States be shaped into a Christian commonwealth and their support for the idea that all views should be heard. They had enormous faith—as befit the authors of a successful revolution based on Enlightenment principles—that individuals would find their own way to the truth and that the good that religion did would make it an important if unofficial aspect of community life.

The revolutionary experience and the creation of an American republic in which church and state were legally separated did not alter the British commitment to religious establishment and indeed may even have strengthened it. The British governed their empire, which began to expand into new directions after the losses in North America, with the centuries-old expectations about the necessity of a church establishment. In such new colonies as Australia and New Zealand, authorities established the Church of England as a matter of course. When a Canadian Constitution was hammered out in 1792, it reaffirmed the plan for a Church of England establishment for Upper Canada, that is, for the non-French sector. The Church sent bishops to the colonies to correct an earlier problem of institutional neglect in peripheral areas. When bishoprics were created for Canada (1787) and, later, the Caribbean (1824), a policy was finally implemented that had been contemplated as

early as the 1630s. The Revolution had been more than an interruption of
that policy. It had highlighted the need to control colonists more effectively
and suggested that a strengthened established church might assist in that
project. This strategy was consistent with the loyalist interpretation that the
American Revolution had been caused by lack of commitment to church
and king, a commitment that conservatives believed was fostered by proper
allegiance to the Church of England.

The plan to create a strong Church of England establishment in the
empire after 1783 succeeded only nominally better than the original attempt
in the period between 1607 and 1783. The metropolitan core of the empire
remained diverse, so Britons (not to mention Irish men and women) who
participated in colonization or imperial administration were unlikely to be
members of the church. The Scottish and later the Irish role in imperial
endeavors grew, giving their religious proclivities a larger impact than would
have otherwise been the case. The English too continued to adhere to a
variety of Christian options, adding to the complexity of the religious landscape. Upper Canada attracted dissenters, especially Methodists, although
not to the same extent as had been the case in the colonies that had joined
in the creation of the United States. Diversity would also distinguish New
Brunswick, which had previously been settled in part from New England
and therefore included a dissenter population uninterested in the Church of
England. Then, too, later British colonies such as Australia and New Zealand
attracted non-British migrants from Europe, who were by definition not
members of the British national church. Creating an empire dominated by
a Church of England religious establishment would continue to elude the
British.

The legal position of Catholics within Britain and Ireland underwent
change, moving against the general trend of strengthening the establishment.
During the last quarter of the eighteenth century, the numbers of Catholics
under British rule rose precipitously. Considering the importance of anti-
Catholicism in the history of that world, an upsurge in Catholics was an
event both surprising and dramatic. The numbers of Catholics in England
had probably been on the rise throughout the period since 1600, but the
notable increase throughout the British Empire that occurred in the late
eighteenth century began as a result of conquest. At the same time, the Revolution reduced the number of Protestants within the empire. The founding
of the United States in effect withdrew people from the British polity, almost
all of whom were of one Protestant persuasion or another. The tilt toward a

greater Catholic presence (although Catholics nonetheless remained an over-all minority) was made somewhat sharper as a result of the departure of Protestants from the political community at the heart of the British Atlantic world.

During the revolutionary era, the British government reduced the legal disabilities placed on Catholics. These changes were predicated in part on the pope's refusal in 1766 to recognize the latest descendant of James II as the rightful occupant of the British throne. With that policy shift, Catholicism ceased to be officially associated with support for the Stuart Pretender. Ameliorating legislation was passed in 1778 and 1782 and more would come in 1793, within the context of the French Revolution. The authorities softened the penal laws in Ireland (where they were most severe) in part out of a need to recruit Irish Catholics to support the revolutionary war effort. Both fear of Irish revolt and appreciation of the greater role the Irish could assume within Britain's empire encouraged the authorities to alter their legal place. Recruiting regiments among the Highland Scots—who were still often Catholics—further suggested the government's willingness to utilize its Catholic subjects in new ways. While Catholics within Ireland and Britain did not rise to the level of freedom of choice that their co-religionists in Quebec enjoyed, they moved in that direction somewhat during the 1770s and 1780s.

Anti-Catholicism did not vanish as a result of these shifts. The governor appointed in Newfoundland in 1763, Sir Hugh Palliser, made a sustained effort to prevent Irish Catholic emigration to the colony, and future governors continued his policy. In Ireland itself, the political contexts for improving the situation for Catholics was more fraught with difficulties than was the case in the more religiously homogenous Quebec. There resident Protestants were an organized, suspicious, and powerful minority. A predictable backlash against Catholic gains occurred in Ireland, with conservative advocates of the Protestant Ascendancy again winning the upper hand over liberal Protestants in the 1780s.

Anti-Catholic agitation dogged the efforts to improve the plight of Catholics in Britain as well. Anti-Catholic riots in Scotland in 1779 and in England in 1780 culminated in the week-long Gordon Riots in London in June 1780. The last of these resulted in hundreds of deaths as well as the destruction of much property. Even outside of Ireland, where the situation was especially tense, Protestant Britons were far from united in support of relief for Catholics. At this time, hostility toward Catholics drew upon older associations between Catholicism and absolutism. Fears that George III displayed authoritarian tendencies helped to fuel the anti-Catholic frenzy in London. The Gordon Riots echoed colonial fears that favorable treatment of Roman Catholics in Quebec indicated the government's intention to undermine liberties.

While the official role of religion in the new United States was a matter for constitution writers (at both the state and the federal level), other ecclesiastical issues had to be worked out within the churches themselves. The Church of England underwent profound changes. It lost its legal place as the established church in every location, as those new states that had previously had colonial Church of England establishments all voted to have no established church whatsoever. More importantly, the Church of England in America had to give up its connection to the monarchy. It had in effect to figure out how to be an independent American church. This change involved abandoning its identity as a national church as well as its more obviously problematic tie to the British monarchy. Bishops remained the distinctive feature of the church once it broke with Britain, and the new church's name—the Episcopal Church—underlined that characteristic. The Episcopalians organized as a denomination in the United States, adopting a new constitution in 1789. They took over the old Anglican church buildings, employed the ministers who were willing to stay on in a new American church, and revised the liturgy to suit their changed political circumstances. Former colonists who had been Anglicans could become Episcopalians, which was the most familiar of the available options. As the Church of England had formerly done in many colonies, the Episcopal Church offered a spiritual home to social elites in the new United States.

The transformation of the Church of England into the Episcopal Church of America fueled the development of a separate Methodist Church. Methodism began as a movement within the Church of England, and its founder, John Wesley, hoped it could retain that unofficial character. By the 1780s, events were driving it into a separate existence in Wesley's native England as well as in America. Separation from the Church of England was essential to Methodism's continued existence in the new United States, since that church would no longer be part of the religious landscape there. John Wesley agreed to the separate ordination of ministers in 1784. A superintendent (later called a bishop) was set over the United States churches, while another was given charge of the Methodists residing in the remaining British colonies. The creation of a Methodist and an Episcopal church structure in the post-revolutionary era established two denominations that would have a significant impact on the religious environment of the United States.

Migration directly spurred by the American Revolution complicated religion in the British Atlantic as well, and it gave a huge boost to the presence and significance of African-diasporic Christianity. By the time of the Revolution the conversion of the black population of the North American colonies had made great strides. The use of biblical names for slave children was on the rise by the late eighteenth century, marking a shift from African naming practices that had previously prevailed. Although masters often named the slaves they purchased from slave ships (showing a predilection for classical names such as Caesar or Pompey), the children born to slaves seem more often to have been named by their parents. Hence when use of African-day names declined and biblical names rose, it can be taken as an indication of the shifting priorities of slave parents. After 1800 biblical naming would surge upward, with a special emphasis on Old Testament monikers particularly for their sons.

The extent of the Christianization of African Americans in the Anglophone Atlantic was indicated by the sudden appearance of numerous black authors writing and publishing in English. Although not the first persons of African dissent to so publish—that distinction goes to young slave poet Phillis Wheatley—these African American authors participated in a rising trend. Their published works laid claim to Christianity as their own faith. Simply by demonstrating their personal literacy and piety, these writers made a case against slavery. They proved that Africans were as capable as any others of participating fully in society. In this way, religious conviction helped to moderate the growing importance of race, pointing to a way around the barriers between Africans and freedom. These authors often explicitly presented the Christian religion as a faith that militated against slavery, and they condemned ostensibly Christian masters for holding people in bondage. Despite Old Testament examples of slavery, future minister Lemuel Hayes concluded that the Bible did not justify the institution. In 1776, he wrote that Christ's appearance on earth had taken the curse off Ham, a biblical figure understood to be the forbearer of later slaves, and that contemporary slavery therefore had no religious justification. Olaudah Equiano, the most famous of such writers in the late eighteenth century, similarly struggled with this question. Citing the same evidence as Hayes and many other Protestant theologians, Equiano finally concluded that Africans were as able to enjoy freedom as any people. They could participate fully in Christian life. Such biblical exegesis

on the part of literate Africans was only one more indication of the Christianization of a large swath of both the free and captive African population. In
many cases too, they used Christianity just as masters had long feared, to
criticize the institution of slavery itself.

Migration patterns further scattered religious groups, in particular
spreading the Christianity of the African diaspora. Loyalists left the United
States in sizeable numbers when the British defeat ensured the independence
of the new nation. While a few of them went to Britain itself, more resettled
elsewhere in the empire. Migrants traveled to Upper Canada and Nova Scotia
in large numbers, adding to the English-speaking and Protestant population
of the Canadian colony. Others, particularly white loyalists who carried their
slaves with them, went to island colonies. Slavery became explicitly illegal
within Britain with the 1772 Somerset decision. Owners who wanted to keep
their slave property could not migrate there. Canada did not offer large-scale
slave owners a viable option either, as the climate was not conducive to labor-
intensive agriculture. Some slaves were imported there by their loyalist owners, where they would shortly be included in the provisions of a gradual
emancipation law that would bring them eventual freedom. The islands were
attractive to slave owners who wanted to keep their chattel and to employ
them profitably.

Slave-owning refugees, in migrating, brought not only their own religious proclivities to the islands but also those of their slaves. Slave preachers
who had been converted to Christianity in the late colonial period on the
mainland took up ministries among slaves and free blacks of the island colonies. Four hundred white families with their slaves came to Jamaica in the
aftermath of the war. Among the latter group were a number of influential
preachers. When Methodists arrived in the Bahamas in 1800, they found the
colony to be exclusively Baptist, the result of the work of black preachers
who came with the loyalist migration. These Methodists set to work among
their fellow whites, so that the Bahamians would be largely divided between
black Baptists and white Methodists in coming years. Statistics for Kingston,
Jamaica, in the early nineteenth century suggest that, while whites apparently
avoided the Baptist church in favor of the Anglican, Methodist, and Presbyterian churches, blacks joined both the Baptists and Methodists in sizeable
numbers. Migration of slave preachers fueled slave and free black conversions
in these locations. African American preachers were able to accomplish in a
short time what almost two centuries of ostensible European commitment to

Fig. 14. Olaudah Equiano escaped from slavery and went on to become an author and abolitionist. *The Interesting Narrative of the Life of Olaudah Equiano, or Gustavus Vassa, the African, Written by Himself* (1789) demonstrated that an African-born former slave could become a pious Christian. Evidence as to whether Equiano was actually born in Africa is ambiguous, but he clearly used that claim (true or not) to help make his point about how slavery (not the nature of Africans) degraded its victims. By the time this frontispiece was engraved, depicting Christians with a book in hand was a standard trope. From the 1789 edition of *The Interesting Narrative of the Life of Olaudah Equiano, or Gustavus Vassa, the African, Written by Himself.* Courtesy of John Carter Brown Library at Brown University.

Christianization had not: the widespread conversion of slaves in the British Atlantic colonies.

The British also evacuated large numbers of ex-slaves in the wake of the Revolution, individuals who similarly took their religious orientation to other locations within the British Empire. Much to the chagrin of patriot slave owners, British officials (beginning with Lord Dunmore, royal governor of Virginia) offered freedom to any slave of a rebel master who ran away to British troops. Lord Dunmore's Proclamation (1775) and that of General Henry Clinton issued four years later offered slaves a means to escape to freedom. After the war, the British made good on their promises by evacuating hundreds of ex-slaves to Nova Scotia. Others went to England. The evacuees (whether slave or free) were in certain cases already Christian. Others used the opportunities presented in their new homes to become involved in Protestant churches. While ex-slaves joined a variety of different denominations in Nova Scotia, African American worshippers, regardless of affiliation, followed a typical pattern. Within their chosen denominations, they eventually created independent religious communities with their own leadership and cultivated a sense of separation from other churches in the area. One case involved an African American ex-slave ordained in the Huntingdon Connexion, the English offshoot of the Methodist movement organized by Selina, the Countess of Huntingdon, that had already sent one black preacher to the colonies. John Marrant and another preacher came to Nova Scotia in 1785 to begin proselytizing there. Separate black churches and congregations became an important component of the religious admixture in Nova Scotia until the early 1790s, when Nova Scotian refugees would migrate again, this time to the British colony of Sierra Leone in Africa.

As blacks in Nova Scotia were founding their independent churches or organizing quasi-independent congregations, their counterparts in the new United States were establishing separate black churches. The first of these had been in South Carolina (Silver Bluff, 1773). The slave preacher there, a man by the name of David George, had been born in about 1743 to an enslaved couple in Virginia. Nothing is known of his parents' religious inclinations, but the fact that they gave him the name David—a biblical reference to the boy who confronted Goliath and went on to become a king—offers a clue that they were themselves Christians. David ran away from their master at the age of nineteen, going to live as a slave first with the Creeks and then with the Natchez Indians. The latter sold him to a white master in Silver Bluff. On his plantation, George married and began attending Baptist meetings organized by a former slave George Liele, who lived in the area. The two men gathered a church in 1773, the first to have an exclusively African American membership. Inspired by his conversion with a desire to learn to read, George got the plantation's white children to teach him, using a spelling book he had acquired. When the British marched into the area in 1778, George joined them. During the war, he preached to other blacks and resided in Savannah. At the end of the war, the British evacuated him, his family and many others to Nova Scotia. There George continued his ministry, eventually participating in the sponsored migration to Sierra Leone.

Other churches followed that erected in Silver Bluff. In Philadelphia, African Americans had joined the white-dominated Methodist church, but they eventually fell out with the church over its treatment of them. The breaking point came after the blacks in the congregation, who had helped to raise funds and build a new church, were consigned to seats in a gallery. Walking out of the church led by Richard Allen, the African American members formed the African Methodist Episcopal Church in 1793. Besides its reference to the African descent of the founders, the name indicates Methodism's origins in the Episcopal Church as well as a continuing commitment to the Episcopal structure. The first A.M.E. bishop was not appointed until 1816, by which time a number of independent black churches within the Methodist tradition had joined together to create this ecclesiastical apparatus. Other African Americans organized private religious meetings as Christianity spread through the slave quarters and believers met in secret to listen to black preachers and to worship together. This "invisible" church involved unknown numbers of African Americans in the autonomous practice of Christianity.

African American Christianization was related to a further growth in evangelical outreach. Christianity moved rapidly through the slave population in the American South after the Revolution, continuing a trend that had gotten underway before 1776. It would spread more slowly among slaves in the British Caribbean, where the masters' opposition remained vigorous. Because of their ability to move undetected through the slave community, Christianized slaves brought to the Caribbean by loyalist masters had a greater impact than did missionaries sent out from England. They did not need to seek masters' permission to preach, as they could gain access without that permission. Slaves, as well as their free counterparts, were apparently more effective at converting their fellows than were white missionaries. As John Leland, a white Virginia Baptist, noted, slaves "seem, in general, to put more confidence in their own color, than they do in the whites. When they attempt to preach, they seldom fail of being very zealous."[12] Largely as a result of their work, by 1800 a third of all the slaves in the British Leeward Islands were Christian. Not only might their preaching be more readily received by their fellow slaves, but they were less obvious targets for white mobs that attacked Methodists and other missionaries in the late eighteenth century.

An upsurge in mission work built upon that which had begun prior to the Revolution but was given added impetus by revolutionary ferment that encouraged hopes for positive change. Evangelical Christians in both Britain and the United States launched new missionary efforts in the post-revolutionary period, increasing the preaching to slaves along with that to other groups. Evangelizing in the new United States, Caribbean islands, and Nova Scotia took off at this time. British slave masters would not actively encourage the Christianization of their chattel until the 1810s or even the 1820s, but they confronted many more requests from missionaries to permit the work from the 1780s on. By 1791 work to convert Antiguan slaves had proceeded to such a point that one observer remarked that their morality had been notably improved. This comment may have meant that the slaves were observing Christian marriage customs to the extent that their servile condition made that possible.[13] The Methodists were especially successful in making converts, not only in the United States but also in colonial locations. Conversions in Nova Scotia as well as in Caribbean and North American slave quarters were driven in part by this renewed attention to missionary activity.

Evangelical outreach was at times greeted with hostility, especially when preachers worked among the enslaved. The only black missionary to work in the colonies as they verged on revolt was David Margate. The first African preacher sent out by the Huntingdon Connexion, Margate came close to death at the hands of a Georgia lynch mob in 1774. He not only publicly opposed slavery; he also claimed to be a second Moses who "should be called to deliver his people from slavery."[14] Christianized slaves used the Old Testament story of the Jews rescued from captivity and led to the Promised Land as a parallel to their situation and their hopes for freedom, but they realized the wisdom of making those connections quietly. Slave spirituals that referred to these ideas could be sung in the presence of masters without invoking ire. But Margate publicly challenged the slave order and cited Moses' work as a model for his own, in direct provocation of the masters. Outrage at his statements was allegedly exacerbated by the fact that he had sexual liaisons with a variety of slave women during his brief stay in the colony.

Even preachers who did not explicitly articulate a critique of slavery might make slave owners nervous. Whites in Richmond, Virginia, who came out to hear Methodist itinerant John Littlejohn, left the meeting in alarm when blacks in the crowd "with strong cryes and tears called for mercy."[15] The expressive spirituality of African American worshippers seemed strange and even offensive to these non-Africans, coming as they did from a different religious tradition. Violent opposition was offered to Methodist preachers as they began their ministry in the Caribbean. The concerns that preaching to slaves would spark rebellion—which had become standard by the time the Methodists arrived in the 1770s—fueled suspicions against this faith. The government of Saint Vincent prohibited preaching by anyone within a year of arrival on the island, legislation that was intended to stop Methodist itinerants. The crown later disallowed this law. Mobs attacked Methodist superintendent Thomas Coke in Jamaica in 1789. Anti-Methodist agitation continued in the Caribbean through the 1790s and into the next century.

Adding to their potential for unpopularity, various religious groups or individuals became involved in abolition. Opposition to slavery had been articulated using religious and ethical arguments since the seventeenth century, but an organized anti-slavery movement had only emerged in the eighteenth century. African-descended free men agitated for an end to the institution in publications and from their pulpits. Slave preachers speaking to their fellow bonds people could criticize slavery when they met in secret, usually at night away from the slave quarters. Otherwise slaves referred to their desire for freedom metaphorically, often citing Moses leading his people out of slavery in the Old Testament book Exodus. Among whites, members of the Society of Friends were the first group associated with this cause, and they were active in northern colonies and later states in opposition to slavery. In Britain Quakers agitated against slavery and the slave trade. In the post-revolutionary era their movement gained adherents among evangelicals who added considerable political traction to the movement. Under the leadership of Thomas Clarkson who was allied with parliamentary leader William Wilberforce, this movement would first succeed in ending British involvement in the slave trade (1807). Only well into the nineteenth century (1833) would it finally culminate in an end to slavery in the British colonies. Opponents of slavery and the slave trade would find themselves unwelcome by slave owners in colonies and states where slavery continued as an important institution.

Masters' long-held fears that Christianization would lead to slave rebellious-
ness seemed to gain confirmation as missionaries became associated with abo-
litionism in their minds. As the association between evangelical preachers
and abolition gradually took shape, it did nothing to hurt the reputation of
missionaries among slaves.

The first British colony in Africa was born at this intersection of anti-
slavery and evangelical sentiment. The colony of Sierra Leone would provide
a new home for poor blacks living in England, for ex-slaves living in Nova
Scotia, and eventually for other groups of African or Afro-Caribbean peoples.
Among them were Maroons from Jamaica, who had lived independently of
British control in their own autonomous communities since the 1650s; they
were exiled after an uprising in 1795–96, in the aftermath of which the British
sought to eliminate their presence altogether. Another group was the so-
called "liberated Africans" taken off of slaving ships once the British navy
began seizing slave cargoes as part of its commitment to end the slave trade.
Nova Scotia blacks, learning of an early version of the settlement project
(known as the Province of Freedom), sent a delegate to England to negotiate
a place for them in it. Sierra Leone was at first company-run with humanitar-
ian goals. At its inception, it was comparable to the earlier effort in Georgia,
which was to have been a haven for poor whites from Britain and for religious
refugees from elsewhere in Europe. Eventually the state would take over man-
agement of the colony. The evangelicals engaged in its founding were also
involved in missions to Australia and India at the same time.

With Sierra Leone, Europeans in Africa moved away from a top-down
model of conversion. Beginning with the Portuguese efforts centuries earlier
in the Kongo, missionaries had worked to convert leaders on the assumption
that their subjects would follow. In the new approach used in Sierra Leone,
Christian blacks from North America were expected to serve as agents of
the conversion of the African population. Since the Nova Scotian migrants
continued in their habit of removing themselves from the larger culture to
create exclusive religious communities, their impact on the general population of the area was less than the colony's organizers hoped. As the colony
filled up with Africans, Afro-Caribbean Maroons, and other new arrivals, the
privileged place of the Nova Scotia community within the colony eroded.
Some would participate in a revolt against the government in 1800 as a result.
Their departure from Nova Scotia, meanwhile, resulted in the collapse of the
autonomous black chapels there after 1792. The institutional basis of black
Christianity would be rebuilt later, when the remaining Nova Scotia blacks

converted in large numbers to the Baptist faith in response to the preaching of minister Richard Preston.

While many former slaves were evacuated out of the new United States by the British, a smaller number of Native Americans were relocated elsewhere in the British Empire. This removal similarly spread Christianity to other locations. Mohawks, who had been important allies of the British during the Revolution, received land in Canada. The most sustained Church of England mission among native peoples had been aimed at the Mohawks, and with some success, so much so that dissenting ministers were irritated to learn of the converts' dedication to the church and to its Book of Common Prayer. When the British lost the revolutionary war, authorities agreed to grant Mohawk leader Joseph Brant and his people a large tract of land in Grand River, near Niagara on the Canadian side of the newly established border. In erecting a town for the resettled Mohawks and others who joined them, the British officials had both a church and a school built for their use. Without a resident minister, the church did as many underserved Anglican settlers had long done: they appointed one of their number to read the service each Sunday. In the case of the Mohawks of northern New York, religious conversion and loyalty to the monarchy went hand in hand, just as conservative defenders of church and crown asserted that they ought. It was in that spirit and to escape the juggernaut of expansion in the new United States that they migrated to Canada.

Evangelical work among Indians rose measurably, making more advances in native communities and continuing the struggle over the choice between Christianity and tradition. The mission to the Cherokees dated from this period. It was given added impetus by a policy of George Washington's presidential administration to work toward assimilation of Indians. A portion of the community living in Georgia entered the church in these decades. They also developed a syllabary for their spoken language, which allowed Cherokee speakers to read using a limited number of syllable sounds, each represented by its own symbol. Expected, like the Indians of southern New England in John Eliot's time, to adopt both civility (that is the trappings of European dress, agricultural practices, and the like) and the Christian faith, some Cherokees appeared to have gone far down that road. With extensive land holdings, the wealthier members of the community even worked their land in the European manner, using slave labor to do so, just as did their white Georgian neighbors. Their efforts to combine elements of European culture with their own traditions had limited usefulness for them in the end, as they would still lose their land in the removals of the nineteenth century.

The effort to combine the old with the new was also visible among Indians at Oquaga on the Susquehanna River. While attending a Christian school and worship services, they also secretly kept an Indian elder to teach the children their own traditions. J. Hector Saint John de Crevecoeur, when he visited the settlement, was surprised to find European living among the Indians there in order to be healed.[16] Christian missions might erode differences between Indian and European culture, but the communities, each with their own traditions of healing and worship, continued to be differentiated.

The experience of Samson Occom underscored the tensions that native peoples faced. A teenage convert to Christianity, he became literate in order to pursue his new religious conviction more fully. After receiving an education from Eleazar Wheelock, who was then training European boys for college admission in his home in Connecticut, Occom worked as a school teacher, a preacher, and a missionary in the employ of the New England Corporation. He traveled to England to raise funds for an Indian college. Well received there, he accumulated many honors. He even met the king, who presented him with a psalter. The money Occom raised was to have been used for an Indian school in his own southwestern Connecticut. Wheelock instead opened Dartmouth College in New Hampshire, focusing his efforts mainly on the education of colonial youths. With this betrayal, Occom wrote to his former mentor, "Your having so many White Scholars and so few or no Indian Scholars, gives me great Discouragement. I verily thought once that your Institution was Intended Purely for the poor Indians. With this thought I Cheerfully Ventured my body & Soul, left my Country, my poor young Family, all my Friends and Relations, to sail over the Boisterous Seas to England, to help forward your School."[17] Solicited by Occom, British donors had continued their support for missionary work among the Native Americans, and again the colonists, this time in the person of Wheelock, failed to pursue that goal. Prejudicial treatment at the hands of the settler community, with which Occom had struggled all his life, eventually caused him to despair of ever improving relations with the Europeans. Although he never wavered in his commitment to Christianity, Occom decided late in life to move his community from southern Connecticut to upstate New York. There he arranged the purchase of a tract of land that he thought would be safe from white encroachment and established a separatist Indian community. His choice of religious assimilation combined with physical

Fig. 15. Samson Occom, a Mohegan born in Connecticut, became a minister and missionary. To raise money for an Indian college planned by his mentor Eleazar Wheelock, he traveled to England in 1766–67. His portrait, painted in England by artist Mason Chamberlin, showed him with a book to denote his learning and piety; this 1768 mezzotint by Jonathan Spilsbury was based on that portrait. Courtesy of the National Portrait Gallery, London.

separation was only one of the various ways Native Americans could respond to the options presented by their situation. Some native peoples attempted separation on all levels while others chose complete integration. None of these possible paths promised sure success.

The French and Haitian revolutions, although they occurred outside of the British Atlantic, also had a major impact—both directly and indirectly—on religion there and in the United States. The French Revolution began in 1789 with the calling of the National Assembly. Like the English parliament in 1640, it was summoned to address dire financial needs faced by the government.

During the initial phase of the Revolution in France, British as well as American public opinion was optimistic that the Assembly would bring much-needed reforms. Observers on both sides of the Atlantic believed that France was moving toward constitutional change that would put an end to absolutism without necessarily eliminating monarchy altogether. Since French absolutism had been depicted as the inveterate enemy of British liberties during nearly a century of wars between the two countries, the prospect was greeted with almost universal acclaim. In England, nonconformist minister Richard Price published *A Discourse on the Love of Our Country* (1789) in favor of events in France. Speaking before a society dedicated to commemorating the Glorious Revolution of 1688, Price preached a sermon linking that event to both the American and French revolutions, praising all three. The subsequent publication of his sermon indicated the continued support in certain circles for the French Revolution. In Ireland the Revolution was heralded among Protestants, especially those outside the Church of Ireland establishment. Ulster Presbyterians were especially strong supporters, seeing the fall of both the Roman Catholic Church and the monarchy in a positive light. In the United States, urban artisans and others who generally favored Enlightenment philosophy—Jefferson prominent among them—similarly supported the French Revolution. They endorsed the skepticism toward organized religion in some circles throughout the British Atlantic, the United States, and France itself. These groups welcomed the 1790 Civil Constitution of the Clergy, reforms that put the church under the control of the state and thereby outside of the Roman Catholic hierarchy. To the extent that Catholicism had been implicated in French absolutism in the minds of critics, such a reorganization seemed a vindication of the criticisms of France that had been frequently expressed since 1688.

For all its appeal to the secular-minded proponents of Enlightenment, the French Revolution initially sparked millennial expectations in both Britain and America. A general upsurge in religious prophecy occurred in this era, not only in the British Atlantic but more broadly. "Amid the unprecedented assault on Christianity and unparalleled social and political upheavals, many in Europe turned to Scripture, and especially to scriptural prophecy, in the search for meaning behind the events."[18] Numerous individuals stepped forward to make religiously inspired predictions of future events.

In England, Joanna Southcott (1750–1814) was a famous example. A woman of humble origins but more illustrious ancestors, Southcott worked as a servant in various households. At the age of forty-two, she began hearing a voice that conveyed warnings. To demonstrate the veracity of her prophecies, she would mail her predictions to clergymen. She hoped that when events that she had predicted subsequently transpired, they would corroborate her prophecies. These ministers did not cooperate but rather told her to cease her prophesying. Her fame grew, however, as some predictions came true, and she obeyed the voice when it told her to publish her views. She gathered supporters who moved her to London and promoted her work. Her prophetic career continued for years and won her numerous adherents. Her prophecies were at times directly relevant to the unfolding Revolution across the Channel. Southcott finally predicted that she would give birth to a savior. She died at age sixty-four alleging herself to be pregnant with a baby who was by that time overdue. Her followers kept a box of her prophecies that was to be opened in the future, as a small core group upheld her vision. Southcott's career indicated the continued interest in prophecy, female religious leadership, and speculation about the end of the world in some circles.

Other prophetic voices were raised on the both sides of the Atlantic. Prophets in the United States were part of the evangelical upsurge, even as they took its language and its central concerns in a different direction by emphasizing end times. In America prophets tended to be more democratic and less learned than in Britain. Whereas the latter often kept with an older tendency toward careful exegesis—using their learning to plumb the meaning of biblical text and relate it to current events—the former focused on getting a message to the people.

As the French Revolution's radicalism became apparent, conservatives and many moderates reacted against its excesses. Monarchy was abolished in 1792, and Louis XVI was executed early the following year. With the Reign of Terror launched that year, the Revolution became increasingly violent. More refugees fled France, for other places in Europe, for the United States, and for France's colonies. Conservatives in both Britain and the United States abhorred the excesses in France. Responding to Price's *Discourse on the Love of Our Country*, Edmund Burke published *Reflections on the Revolution in France* (1790). Selling thirteen thousand copies in just a few weeks, Burke's *Reflections* offered the consummate expression of the conservative position in favor of political and religious tradition. He and other conservatives interpreted the Revolution in France as part of an attack on religion generally. They feared deism—a belief in a distant God accompanied by a skeptical attitude toward those aspects of religion that could not be proven—or atheism—disbelief in God altogether. Either view, they assumed, would overturn the social order. As the British entered another series of wars against the French state, they articulated their fight as support for king and country, which became a conservative rallying cry. Reactionaries attempted to suppress atheism and even nonconformity, especially in England and Ireland.

The Atlantic dimension of the French Revolution included revolt in the French Caribbean, which complicated the reaction to the Revolution for some, while affirming it for others. In the colony of Saint Dominique (later Haiti), slaves and free persons of color rose up against the island's ruling class, seeking freedom and equality in 1794. Radicals who opposed monarchy, slavery, and a church establishment saw the French and Haitian revolutions as positive goods, endorsing all aspects of the attack on traditional hierarchies. Thomas Jefferson, a man well-known for his radical sensibilities, could not, however, endorse the revolution in Haiti. Deeply complicit in the slave system—he was himself the owner of many slaves, including some of his own offspring—Jefferson was compromised by that complicity. He could not support a slave revolution fought in the name of the liberty and equality of the French Revolution, which he otherwise supported, since it meant an end to slavery. Jefferson found himself in the odd position of arguing for periodic revolution to end tyranny in government—famously saying that the tree of liberty needed to be regularly fed by the blood of patriots—but opposing revolution aiming to end the tyranny of slaveholding. Many of Jefferson's political opponents found it easy to be consistent on the other side of the divide, opposing both the French and Haitian revolutions for their excesses and for overturning the traditional order. New Englander John Adams, who would be Jefferson's political rival in the election of 1800 and who criticized the excesses of the French, was so staunch an opponent of slavery that he approved of the Haitian cause. The regional divisions that would lead ultimately to civil war in the United States were hinted at in this odd constellation of opinions among the two men.

Scholars have declared the 1790s key to the shape of religion in modern Britain. The number of dissenters and evangelicals in the population expanded. In Ireland, Ulster Protestantism emerged as the political force it would heretofore be. The United Irishmen, organized in 1795, aimed at political reform and Catholic liberation. Parliamentary leader William Pitt feared an Irish Catholic and Protestant alliance against British rule in the 1790s and granted Irish Catholics concessions to counter it. As events developed, Britain would find itself opposing France in the company of the papacy, a historic shift that helped further ease hostility toward Catholicism within Great Britain. Roman Catholic schools, colleges, and religious houses that had been located on the European continent since the Reformation in England and the conquest of Ireland returned during this period to England, another indication of the relaxing relations. Over the course of decades of war, the French eventually invaded Ireland in the hopes of launching an attack on Britain from there. After centuries of worry that Ireland would be used as a beachhead for a European Catholic invasion of England, when invaders did arrive the Irish understood them in precisely those terms. To the dismay of the French, who were well along in their secular Revolution at the time, the Irish they encountered in the isolated region where they landed thought of them as religious crusaders. Little wonder—given the poorly executed landing and the lack of communication among the ostensible allies—that the invasion failed. Religion could only effectively serve as the basis of civil insurrection or alliance if the participants fought for shared goals.

Concerns about atheism similar to those that animated the British were expressed in the United States. American politics (especially around the election of 1800 and the struggle between Federalists and Jeffersonian Republicans) became infused with rhetoric of the dangers of atheism and radicalism. The new Universalist religious movement embraced the belief that salvation was available to all and created a liberal alternative to traditional Christianity. Although not atheistic, Universalism frightened many conservatives, who objected to its rejection of many standard Christian tenets. As one speaker at the Massachusetts constitutional convention supposedly warned, under the new constitution, "a Turk, a Jew, a Roman Catholic, and what is worse than all, a Universalist, may be President of the United States."[19] Conservatives who opposed Jefferson on the alleged grounds that he was an atheist also strove to remake the United States as a Christian nation. Thomas Paine's deist tract *Age of Reason* became their whipping horse. They advocated public religious practices, such as prayer before legislative sessions, in reaction to the more secular tendencies of the new government. In that sense the battles of this era continued the revolutionary era's fight over whether to separate church and state and what such a division would mean in practice. During this time, millennial thinking became more focused on religious solutions than political ones, a shift from the 1770s when political change seemed to support millennial hopes. This shift toward finding resolutions in the religious sphere gave added impetus to evangelical missionary work as well as support for social reform.

The American embrace of evangelism—captured in the upsurge in revivals around 1800—had its British counterpart. The so-called Second Great Awakening in the United States began in New England in the 1790s, spreading out from there to engulf the new nation. This upsurge in revivalism was accompanied by a renewed interest in evangelical missions. First in 1798, the General Association of Connecticut formed the Connecticut Missionary Society "to Christianize the Heathen in North America, and to support and promote Christian knowledge in the new settlements within the United States."[20] Its purpose was remarkably like that of the eighteenth-century evangelizing organizations in Britain which had found the choice between converting their fellow Britons and heathen a difficult one. Other organizations would follow, some of them patterned on British precedents, such as the Bible societies that undertook printing and distributions of Bibles (beginning in England, 1804, followed by Philadelphia, 1808). In Britain the numbers of dissenters from the Church of England rose steadily as a result of evangelicals efforts. This rise then sparked a veritable explosion of missionary societies (including the Baptist Missionary Society, founded in 1793; the London Missionary Society, 1795; and the Church Missionary Society, 1799). Lowlands Scots founded the Society for the Propagation of the Gospel at Home in the same decade, aiming once again to convert the Highlanders. The Welsh Sunday School movement was founded in 1789. American missionary efforts were given added impetus in this era as well.

Although not entirely traceable to the French Revolution, of course, these developments were fueled by it in a number of ways. The more optimistic views about the potential for politics to change the world for the good that came in the wake of the American Revolution took something of a beating, at least in certain circles, with the excesses of the French Revolution. Except for the most secular minded, those working for change then turned toward religion as a more promising arena. The French Revolution's attack on religion also encouraged many to rally to the cause of traditional Christianity, even as it softened animosity toward Catholicism in some British and American circles.

The French and Haitian revolutions again increased the number of Catholics in Britain and its colonies as well as in the United States. Émigrés left France beginning in 1791 and Saint Dominge in 1794, traveling to other locations in Europe or the wider European Atlantic world. Not every émigré retained his or her Catholicism. Some joined other churches in their new homes. The Episcopal or African Methodist Episcopal churches attracted some of those who came from Haiti to the mid-Atlantic region of the United States. Remaining within the Catholic Church was the norm for these migrants, however, at least initially. Britain received refugees, including large numbers of priests and over thirty bishops, all of whom had refused to sign the Civil Constitution of the Clergy demanded of them in France. London became an émigré center, with eight chapels built by 1800. Prior to the French Revolution, none existed other than those attached to embassies of various Catholic countries. Other British towns also saw an influx of French Catholics. Their growing presence changed the nature of Catholicism in Scotland. The Catholic churches there embraced a more sophisticated and continental style of worship, with such innovations as singing during Mass. Émigrés, including priests, also traveled to the United States. Marylander John Carroll, who had charge of the newly organized Catholic Church in the United States, employed French émigré priests throughout the states. In both Britain and the United States, immigrant priests ministered to the resident Catholics as well as to the émigré population. They also worked in schools. The practice of using Catholic religious to staff New World schools, started by the Spanish colonizers centuries before, thus came to the Anglophone region of North America.

Similarly the British Caribbean received additional French-speaking Catholics after the revolution in Haiti drove out people who took up residence in neighboring colonies. The arrival of Catholic refugees revived the Catholic Church in Jamaica and other island colonies with an influx of members. Staffing these island churches proved difficult. Priests were repeatedly recruited from Spanish colonies to work among Catholics resident in the British Caribbean. Permitting Spanish priests to sojourn to British Caribbean colonies and work openly among their fellow Catholics marked a dramatic change from the forced exile of not only all priests but also all Catholics from

Spanish Jamaica when the English conquered it in 1655. Catholic masters and their slaves immigrated to the United States when Haiti first erupted in rebellion. Opposition to continued immigration developed not because they were Catholic but because of fears that an influx of slaves with experiences of revolution in the Caribbean would foment revolt in the United States.

Louisiana, which was in the 1790s a Spanish colony with a large number of French settlers, received refugees from the islands. Shortly it would be returned to France (1800), and three years later it became part of the United States with the Louisiana Purchase. With this, the United States would absorb a largely French-speaking and Catholic population. It included recently arrived slaves from Haiti who were followers of a hybrid folk religion known as Vodou. Negotiating the Catholicism of their masters in the context of their own West African beliefs, Haitian slaves created a synthesis that emerged as Vodou. In the Vodou tradition, spirits saturate the world. Created by the Christian God, these spirits assist him. Devotees participate in rituals—using drumming, dancing, and trance states—that encourage the spirits to protect and support them. Their ritual calendar closely follows that of Roman Catholicism. With the migration out of Haiti at the time of the revolution, these practices were exported to Louisiana and elsewhere by the refugees who left the island. Just as after the French and Indian War, when numbers of French Catholics came under British rule, French émigrés and later Haitian ones increased the religious diversity in Britain, the British Atlantic generally, and the new United States. Wherever Haitian slaves were taken, they added the component of Vodou to the religious mix as well.

The French Revolution and the plight of French priests and laypeople helped to change attitudes toward Catholicism. Public appeals to raise funds in support of the émigrés noted the common Christianity of the host and refugee communities. Whereas earlier rhetoric made much of divisions within Christianity, these appeals envisioned a shared identity. The presence of French Catholics, while occasionally greeted with hostility, tended to soften animosities. As Britain embarked upon another series of wars against the French (and eventually against that nation's new ruler, Napoleon), it also entered an alliance with the Holy See that further improved relations with Catholicism's leaders. The last of the Catholic Relief Acts was passed in 1793, again reducing civil penalties against Catholics in Britain and Ireland.

These concessions and the increase in the Catholic population changed the experience of Catholics. Migration from Ireland to England accounted for a portion of that increase, but conversion of formerly Protestant Britons contributed more. Catholics in Britain outnumbered Methodists in the 1790s. Although the Methodists would soon surpass them, the Catholic population continued to grow in coming years. John Bossy estimates that 80,000 English Catholics in 1770 would rise to 750,000 by 1850.[21] Sometimes the periphery showed greater toleration of Catholics than the center, as when the Leeward Islands passed legislation to eliminate all civil penalties on Catholics in 1798. The act was eventually disallowed by the crown. Throughout the British Atlantic, however, larger numbers of Catholics and greater toleration of their presence was a hallmark of this era.

The Haitian Revolution also brought with it increased fears of revolt, fears that had long been tied to religious considerations. Like the American Revolution, the rupture in Haiti was not primarily shaped by religion. The early phases of the uprising drew upon Vodou practices, some rebels used fetishes—or collections of objects imbued with spiritual power—to protect them, and Vodou meetings may have provided a locus for organizing. Yet the revolt itself cannot be attributed to religion, despite masters' fears that religious instruction and Christianization would encourage rebellion. The example of a revolution in Haiti and the creation of the first free black republic in the Atlantic world could combine with religious ideas in a heady brew that might foster revolt. When Gabriel, a literate and highly skilled slave in Richmond, Virginia, worked to organize a revolt of slaves and free blacks, he drew upon Christianity and the ideas about liberty circulating through the Atlantic world in equal measure. While elite slave artisans like Gabriel himself may have found the language of rights most appealing—and so directly utilized Haitian along with other revolutionary examples—the plantation slaves they sought to recruit were more attuned to biblical language. Christianity had become widespread among Virginia's African population, so that it provided a persuasive language that could be used to many purposes. Gabriel—whose own name indicated the faith of his parents and invoked the powerful figure of the angel Gabriel—referred to himself as "Daniel" when confronted by men who would later betray him to the authorities. His hearers would have understood the allusion to the Old Testament Daniel, whom God protected while he was among lions.[22]

Even if religion was only nominally implicated in Haiti, slave owners still responded with increased attention to religious messages if they feared that these might trigger revolt. The head of the SPG, Bishop Shute Barrington, scoffed at the idea, saying, "What connection subsists between instilling the genuine doctrine & precepts of the Gospel into the mind of the untu-

tored African, rendering him by that means a better slave, a better man, &
more contented with his condition than he was before, & the unexampled
atrocities produced by French Atheism, & French Republicanism in the Island of St Domingo . . . I am at a loss to conceive."[23] Despite his dismissive
comments, fear of sparking another Haiti caused the SPG to postpone reform
on its Codrington Plantation in Barbados. Such fears also increased hostility
toward evangelical groups. In 1800 Methodist leader Francis Asbury was
warned not to visit Charleston, South Carolina, where his public opposition
to slavery made him unwelcome. Religion and revolution continued to be
seen as a potentially explosive mixture, and the Haitian case did nothing to
allay those associations. That Christianity might inspire slaves to revolt was
by 1800 a truism among slaveholders. Despite mounting evidence that such
was not always the case, some still worried that it might do so.

The quarter century before 1800 politically fragmented the British Atlantic world. The American Revolution and the departure of most of the North
American colonies from the British imperial orbit meant that the English-
speaking Atlantic was no longer encompassed within a single political unit.
Rather, it was divided between the new United States and a somewhat
shrunken British Atlantic empire. Political separation had important consequences for religion, in particular the separation of church and state in one
entity and the recommitment to the mutually supporting relationship of
church and state in the other. By sparking a loyalist diaspora, it also brought
trends that were well underway in those mainland colonies that were exiting
the empire to colonies that would remain within the British Atlantic system.
Again the circulation of people and ideas created new connections and
planted new options in a number of locations. Evangelism and reform remained important in both Britain and the United States. If the former became a more significant aspect of American religious culture over time,
religiously inspired reform played a central role in both cultures.

The religious history of the two entities often proceeded in tandem despite the political split, as the importance of missionary societies and anti-
slavery campaigns attested. The on-going British commitment to empire (and
expansion into new areas in this era) fueled the need for missions. The work
of transplanting specific versions of Christianity to areas brought under British control continued, with missions expanding their role. Christians in the
United States would follow the British example in this, creating numerous
missionary societies to service its own populations and eventually the peoples
of distant lands as well. The political context for anti-slavery differed in Brit-

ain's realm and in the United States: in the former, it pitted reformers in Britain against slave owners in colonies, but in the latter, it divided slave masters and reformers within the nation. As northern masters agreed to give up their slaves—usually only very gradually—the United States would become divided regionally over this question, setting up a situation that would have unforeseen consequences in the nineteenth century. Perhaps because in the British case opposition was centered in the more powerful (and geographically separate) metropole, anti-slavery would succeed more rapidly there, with the slave trade abolished in 1807 and slavery ended in the colonies in 1833. Participation in the international slave trade by the United States would end in the same year that the British involvement in the carrying trade ceased (1807), but slavery itself would flourish for decades after the 1833 abolition in the British realm. As northerners took on the role that the British imperial center had wielded, their lack of authority over the slaveholding south meant they could not succeed through legislation. Finally a bloody Civil War would end the institution in 1865. British Christian reformers would lead the way in colonizing Africa with black Christians whom, it was hoped, would spread the faith to Africans. The United States would follow the lead of Sierra Leone with its own project in Liberia in 1821. Despite their separation the two continued to develop common solutions to their comparable problems.

The French and Haitian revolutions also brought similar changes to both nations. It increased the numbers of Catholics in the populations of Britain, its colonies, and the United States, and encouraged greater tolerance for an active Catholic presence. The institutional church in all those locations was bolstered by the influx of priests who left France and later Haiti in this era. In the United States, Ireland, and Britain, reactions to the Revolution exacerbated tensions over atheism, freethinking, and other forms of radicalism. Fear of slave revolt and a tendency to connect the prospect of revolt with religion was common in both the United States and the British Caribbean colonies. Subsequent slave revolts would also be linked to religion. Denmark Vesey's slave conspiracy of 1822 was thought to have religious links, as did the so-called "Baptist Revolt" on Jamaica in 1831. Fears that had long guided masters' hostility to Christianization continued to play out in the nineteenth century, even as many whites became convinced that Africans everywhere should be converted. The United States may have gone its separate way politically, but its religious character and concerns, having been originally forged in the British Atlantic world, continued to have much in common with this world.

CONCLUSION

The British Atlantic World in Perspective

THE CIRCULATION OF peoples throughout the British Atlantic world brought together many different religious traditions. The meeting of western European Christianity, West African traditional beliefs, and Native American spirituality only began to capture the extent of the ideas and practices in circulation. Atlantic African Muslims, Mohawk and Kongolese Catholics, Sephardic Jews, and an enormous variety of European Christians further enhanced the complexity of the religious scene. Believers transplanting a wide range of organized church alternatives especially from Protestant Europe into Britain, Ireland, and the Atlantic basin. This diversity and the multiplicity of encounters it engendered changed religions and believers' understanding of their faiths, as traditions blended or clashed, and individuals negotiated the various options presented to them.

By 1800, monotheism and especially Christianity had reached deep into North America, carried by European-descended believers, embraced by recently converted slaves and freed persons of color, and taken up by Native American peoples. While monotheistic institutions and practices had not been transplanted in precisely their Old World forms, the variations that had been translated into the wider Atlantic world spread Mediterranean monotheism well passed its original boundaries. By 1800, indeed, Christianity and Islam were both becoming global religions, penetrating far beyond their long-established geographies. Both Africans and Native Americans had begun to remake Christianity into faith traditions of their own. Despite the expectations of those who sought to convert them, they did not simply drop their old ways, ties, and perspectives, entirely transforming themselves into new persons. The rhetoric of Christian conversion assumed drastic change, but incremental shifts and gradual blending had been the case since the Protestant Reformation first began to remake English Catholics into Protestants centuries before.

When charting the effect of expansion, we naturally look first to the places Europeans moved into, yet the impact was not limited to those areas. Rather religion in Europe itself was also transformed as part of this process. Atlantic settlements became sites of unprecedented religious diversity, challenging expectations that such diversity would lead to social and political collapse. If some conservatives understood the American Revolution to prove that maxim, others had come to perceive the possibility that persons of different faiths might live side by side in relative harmony. A transatlantic religious trend like evangelism arose out of the strife of a religiously divided Europe, speaking to the need of Protestants of different stripes to find common ground and to spread the faith to non-Christians in various missionary outposts. British Protestants learned to become missionaries in the Atlantic world, a surprisingly long and slow process given the rhetorical commitment to outreach from the first. British abolitionists who extolled publications by African Christian men to prove the injustice of slavery and the educability of the peoples of West Africa thereby participated in the creation of an inclusive Atlantic Christian community. In these ways and more, the religious encounter changed thinking and forged new practices in Europe as well as elsewhere.

The Protestantism of the British Atlantic fundamentally shaped its development. The Christianity that had been brought to the New World after 1600, and in particular to the British Atlantic world, had itself already been fragmented, so the diversity that prevailed should come as no surprise (though it occasionally did so). As the leading edge of expansion out of the British and Irish archipelago, the English transferred their various iterations of Protestantism and their residual Catholicism as well as opening the way for Scots Presbyterianism, Irish Catholicism, and other local variations. As Britain increasingly became a refuge for European Protestants the variety of faiths present expanded further, to include many forms of German Protestantism, French Huguenots, and others. Protestants in Europe, although proportionally fewer in number than Catholics, were more inclined to leave home during these centuries than their Catholic counterparts, and they thereby transferred the complexity of the European Protestant scene to the British Atlantic. If Protestantism generally had more difficulty launching itself into the African American and Native American communities than Iberian Catholicism did, it did eventually make inroads, fostering a vibrant African American faith by 1800 as well as some strong strides among Indians. The diverse and predominantly Protestant nature of the British Atlantic world is traceable to the unpromising beginnings of an early English movement into the Atlantic basin after 1600.

Surveying religion from an Atlantic perspective offers a number of advantages. On this scale, we can see the shaping but ultimately limited role of legal structures that dictated the relationship of church and state and defined dissent. It is possible to chart the spread of specific faiths—including sixteenth-century Protestantism, seventeenth-century Quakerism, and eighteenth-century Methodism—and of shared religious cultures, such as that of evangelism. Religion participated in and responded to major political events, including the five political revolutions (that of the 1640s as well as the Glorious, American, French, and Haitian). We can also discern that the questioning of old Christian verities, like the beliefs in God's role in daily life or in the existence of a supernatural world, was an Atlantic-wide phenomenon. Other broad changes include the weakening or destruction of religious establishments, the increase in diversity, especially within Protestantism, and the shifting emphasis on the confessional divide between Catholic and Protestant. All these trends had a wide impact, more easily appreciated from an Atlantic perspective.

Anti-Catholicism was an Atlantic-wide phenomenon. Arising out of the torturous Reformation in England and fueled by repeated wars against Catholics, opposition to popery spanned the entire period under scrutiny here. The English and later British sense of national identity was built in large part around being Protestant in opposition to Catholic Spain and subsequently Catholic France. Communities feared Catholic attacks, from the Gunpowder Plot of 1605—which helped cement loyalty to James I—to the borderland wars with French and Indians in North America. A wide variety of religious groups were tarred with the brush of popery, so that at different times Quakers, Labadists, Moravians, and Methodists found themselves objects of such suspicions. Often not especially worried about the actual practicing Catholics among them, the Protestant faithful feared papists and particularly Jesuits in disguise that they believed to be hidden within their midst. Signal political events, most notably the Glorious Revolution, arose from fear of Catholics. If by the time of the American Revolution, the North American rebels could enter an alliance with the Catholic French, fears still lingered, and French forces never traveled far enough north during the war to enter formerly puritan New England, where antipopery continued with most force. Out of its Protestant identity, the British Atlantic defined itself against Catholicism into the late eighteenth century.

Elites often feared that religion would become a source of resistance to authority, and to some extent those fears were played out. The Irish had many reasons to remain Roman Catholic, but surely one was that the latest English invaders were Protestant and hoped to impose Protestantism on them. The English worried that Catholic Ireland would be used as a beachhead for an invasion from the Continent. It was so used twice, once by James II when he was attempting to retake his kingdoms from William and Mary and again by the French during the late eighteenth-century wars pitting the British against revolutionary France. In the first instance religion functioned as authorities feared, providing a common ground upon which could meet invading forces and resident supporters. In the second, with devout Irish Catholics uncomfortable with secular French revolutionaries, it did not. Native Americans also rallied around their religious traditions in an effort to thwart the incursions of European Americans into their lands. The well-documented Nativist movements of the eighteenth century represented religious hybridities at the same time that they fomented resistance. Africans used their own religious systems (whether traditional West African, Muslim, or Roman Catholic) brought with them from Africa when they organized to resist enslavement. This might occur on a small scale, as when cruel masters were identified as witches and treated accordingly, or on a large scale, as when the Stono rebels used Marian imagery. Once Protestantism began to spread in the slave quarters and among free Africans, it too sometimes showed its potential as a tool to criticize injustice. This liberation theology was central to Gabriel's Rebellion (1800). Religion could be useful as a source of resistance, providing a language with which to criticize oppression and a sense of protection and justification from a higher power.

Religion could also be called in to bolster loyalty to the status quo. The approved message preached to slaves often presented Christianity as a faith of meekness and acceptance, which may be one reason why it at first made little headway in that community. The Church of England and its cult of Charles the martyred king also served as a rallying point for loyalty to monarchy, in the colonies and in England, Wales, and Ireland. For those who chose to remain in the British Empire at the time of the American Revolution, religion often supported that decision. It operated in a similarly conservative way during the French Revolution, as British subjects joined together in support of king and country, abhorring the irreligion they saw at work in the violent upheavals in France. The political implications of religion were potentially flexible, able to support radical resistance or conservative accommodation.

Religion was intimately intermingled with the signal events that shaped and reshaped the Atlantic world. The Elizabethan vision of a Protestant empire fueled early English expansion in Ireland and later into the Americas. Conflicts over religion encouraged migration into the Atlantic basin in the 1630s and helped to bring about wars, rebellions, and regicide in England, Scotland, and Ireland in the 1640s. Fears of predatory Catholicism was a key issue in the Glorious Revolution, with ramifications in England, Scotland, Ireland, Maryland, New York, and Massachusetts. The confessional divide between Catholic and Protestant became increasingly tangled up with questions of loyalty in Ireland and, with variations, in Scotland as well. Another divide, between Protestant dissent and Church of England adherence, was more important in the colonial context. Religious diversity proved a basic feature of colonial society south of New England (and in Rhode Island within New England itself), and that diversity undermined the commitment to religious establishment altogether. Religion fostered transatlantic ties and shaped culture dramatically in the evangelical movement of the eighteenth century. Conflicts in the late eighteenth-century empire and in the two polities— British and American—that emerged from the American Revolution had significant religious components. Both radicalism and the conservative backlash of the 1790s pivoted on the relationship of church and state, the liberating potential of religion, and the nature of belief. Religious faith—both individual belief and its collective expression—are key to understanding the history of the British Atlantic world.

Looking ahead, we can see that the circumstances set into motion by the expansion of England into the wider Atlantic world continued after 1800. Churches persisted in their work both at home and in the wider world. The imperial authorities appointed Church of England bishops to serve the remaining colonies, two centuries after organizing a New World episcopate was first proposed. Following one in Canada in 1787, two bishops were assigned to the east and west Caribbean in 1824; another, seated in Nova Scotia, soon followed. If British leaders had learned to accept religious heterogeneity, many remained committed to the hope that the shared experience of Protestant worship in a state church would bind the polity and further its goals. The empire carried the church with it, even if the authorities had discovered that they needed to expect less from and invest more in the Church of England than they had originally assumed.

Christian outreach through missions, begun in earnest in the previous century, expanded after 1800. Residents of the United States would employ models developed at the imperial center during the colonial period, creating their own missionary organizations to serve within and eventually beyond their own borders. Books continued to be important carriers of religious culture, as the early nineteenth-century explosion in cheap print made available large numbers of inexpensive religious publications. The close relationship of Protestant mission and empire prevailed, demonstrated in 1816 with the Anglican ordination of a Miskito Indian leader in Belize whom the British authorities also crowned King George Frederick in a ceremony staged to endorse his leadership within his community. The Church of England concern for the souls of non-Europeans would take on even stranger manifestations. During the years that a young Khosian woman from Southern Africa was being exhibited throughout England, her body on display as an oddity for paying crowds, she was also instructed in the catechism of the Church of England. In Manchester in 1811 the "Hottentot Venus" was baptized. We do not know what Sara Baartman thought of her conversion or her experience as a public curiosity, but among the British she served as a symbol of the exotic at the same time that she—rather contradictorily—participated in a ritual affirming the common humanity of all persons. Scots Presbyterians became more active evangelizers in the nineteenth-century Atlantic, inaugurating missions in the Caribbean and Guyana in the early decades. Institutional Christianity maintained efforts to increase its reach that it had developed over the previous centuries in the British Atlantic.

Catholicism, which had long been in an awkward position, would continue its recent growth. In the nineteenth century Catholicism within English culture would become more visible and more influential, until by the 1830s a remarkable rejuvenation was under way. The Roman Catholic Church in Ireland experienced institutional changes as well, with official and popular positions coming more into line in 1830. Whether for this reason or as part of the ongoing resistance against the imposition of an alien form of Christianity, the work of Protestant missionaries in Ireland, launched with energy after 1820, proved largely unsuccessful. When the Irish began migrating to the United States in subsequent decades, they remained overwhelmingly Catholic. In a development dripping with irony, they would remake once puritan and staunchly antipapist Boston into a largely Catholic town.

African diasporic Christianity exerted its influence ever more widely. Protestantism first made serious inroads into North American plantation slave communities in the 1760s and in Caribbean slave communities in the 1770s; by 1815 it was well on its way to becoming the dominant religious tradition among Africans in North American and the British Caribbean. Nothing short of a mass movement, carried along by the circulation of converts and ideas, could have propelled this campaign forward with such rapidity. African conversions to Christianity, especially Protestantism, proceeded apace in the British Caribbean, elsewhere in the British Empire, and in the new United States. The movements of populations occasionally transferred black Christians into new locations where their preaching was again well received. Evacuations by the British after the War of 1812 took freed slaves to Trinidad, where a Baptist church was established as a result of their efforts. When English Baptists first arrived to preach in Jamaica in 1814, they were surprised to find already converted Baptist slaves worshipping there. Once the British started seizing newly enslaved Africans off slave ships plying the Atlantic, they dropped them in various locations. From 1811 the Bahamas received a large number of so-called "liberated Africans," and missionaries would find this community ripe for evangelizing when they began to work there some years later. Protestant Christianity slowly made headway in West Africa. African American converts who settled in Sierra Leone and later Liberia brought the Protestant message as did missionaries sent out from Europe or North America, both black and white. While the evangelization of Africans and African Americans carried on, so too would the tendency for communities of Christians to split along color lines. Even the Moravians, who had maintained biracial religious communities far longer than many churches, divided into black and white churches in North Carolina and elsewhere in the early nineteenth century. The African Methodist Episcopal Church (AME) would be the most famous of the independent black churches, but it was joined by numerous others.

Missionary work was still associated with slave revolt in the minds of some nervous masters. In 1822 Charleston, South Carolina masters executed both slaves and freemen accused of conspiring to revolt. Evidence they collected of the conspiracy showed how they thought religion could be used to encourage slaves to rise up. The following year, slaves in the South American colony of Guyana did rebel, and the white British Baptist missionary who had been preaching to them was condemned to die for having sparked the Demerara Revolt of 1823. He would be remembered as a Christian martyr. A rebellion in Jamaica in 1831 was, similarly and predictably, blamed on preaching. Indeed it was dubbed "the Baptist Revolt" by planters who saw Christianity at the center of the uprising. Christian slaves frequently gathered in secret to pursue their own worship separate from their masters and overseers, and masters fear that such meetings would be seatings for conspiracy. Even if Christianity itself was no longer suspected of directly fostering revolt, it presented an area of slave life that masters did not always feel confident they could control.

Native Americans still worked to reconcile tradition and the new faith and culture brought to their shores by invaders. Nineteenth-century missionaries working among Indian peoples expected culture accommodation to white ways as part of the conversion process, attempting to introduce various European-American practices not obviously related to religion, such as sedentary agriculture. Missionary schools for native children attempted to eradicate languages as well, with the idea that language carried culture and conversion would succeed better if the other culture was eliminated. Indian Removal from the eastern states in the early nineteenth century signaled the unwillingness of white citizens to live among native peoples (as well as desire for their prime farmland in states like Georgia). The new reservation system echoed the Praying Indian Village practice of the seventeenth century, with their emphasis on separation as well as conversion. The Cherokee people of the southern states, who converted to Christianity, sent their children to Christian schools, and developed a written version of their language, tested the limits of white willingness to accommodate Indian peoples outside the reservation system. The government seized their lands and banished them to a reservation in what would later become the state of Oklahoma. The lesson of the Cherokee—many of whom died along the "Trail of Tears"—seemed to be that the offer of acceptance for converts was a chimera.

Evangelical religion and periodic revival remained important on both sides of the Atlantic as well. Widespread awakening became a regular feature of life in the United States and in other parts of the English-speaking Atlantic world. The so-called Burned-Over District in upstate New York, site of much revival activity, also gave rise to a new religion, the Church of the Latter Day Saints, which combined elements of traditional Protestant Christianity with new revelation recounting New World biblical history. Conveyed in the Book of Mormon, this new faith soon spread widely within the United States and in Britain itself. Missions to Britain were so successful that after ten years, the church had more British than American converts. Many British believers migrated to the United States, participating in the building of a Mormon colony in Utah. Like Judaism, Islam, and Christianity, Mormonism relied heavily on its sacred books—in the Mormon case, both the Christian scriptures and the newly revealed Book of Mormon. Unlike the others it had both Mediterranean and American roots, creating a new version of an old faith adapted in some ways to the New World. The Book of Mormon sacralized the American landscape, as indeed Native Americans had done long before Joseph Smith. The Latter Day Saints offered only one especially dramatic example of a dynamic process of integration and adaptation that had been going on for centuries in the British Atlantic.

As with the widespread appeal of the Church of the Latter Day Saints and many other developments, the British and United States areas of the Atlantic participated in common trends despite their political rupture. Methodism in both the United States and Britain split over political and economic differences in the 1830s, with division in the United States focused on slavery and in Britain on tensions over class. Catholicism remained a powerfully appealing minority faith throughout the Anglophone Atlantic. When the United States bought a huge tract of land from France in the Louisiana Purchase, it absorbed large numbers of Catholics (including French, Spanish, Native American, and African) into the expanding United States. This absorption presaged later expansion into the Spanish Southwest on the part of the United States but it also gave a taste of the trend that the British Atlantic had been participating in for a time, in which Catholic populations (such as that in Quebec) had to be accommodated into a predominantly Protestant polity. As the United States was figuring out how to incorporate Catholics— the numbers of whom would keep rising over the course of the nineteenth century through the twin trends of immigration and conquest—the British were further easing restrictions on their own Catholic populations. If the United States and Britain would part ways on the subject of slavery—with the British ending it in their colonies in the 1830s while the southern United States remained committed to slavery and its expansion—this division has to be understood in the context of a transatlantic abolition movement that drew heavily on ties of religious community in organizing against slavery. The formerly united British Atlantic had been pulled asunder but the cords that bound it together remained strong.

The expansion of Europe and the movement of people, ideas, and goods it engendered had a strong religious component. In 1600 European leaders knew, based on a century of Protestant Reformation and battles over religious allegiance, that church and state had to work hand in hand. They also felt that expansion into other areas of the globe was justified by the fact that they sent out, along with ships, colonists, and trade goods, the one true faith, and that it was a faith those in distant lands would eagerly embrace. Their expectations about the workings of church and state as well as their assumption that their faith would be easily conveyed and enthusiastically welcomed were challenged in the experience of founding colonies, conquering peoples, and managing slaves. The movement into the wider world—the Atlantic and beyond—was full of unintended consequences. Although not by anyone's design, religion spread, men and women were converted, faith communities were created or relocated, and cultural differences were confronted and, occasionally, overcome. Far-distant individuals participated in similar experiences and developed a sense of connection and common purpose. British Atlantic political boundaries in 1775 encompassed three continents and many faiths. Despite the remarkable variety in this world, however, it was united by common bonds. Those were not sundered by revolutions, wars, or emancipation movements. They would continue to cement together people and communities sharing a religious culture.

SUGGESTIONS FOR FURTHER READING

THE SCHOLARSHIP ON religion in the British Atlantic world is vast and diffused. Most scholarly works take up one faith tradition in a specific location (such as Methodists in North America), explore one event (religious revivals of the mid-eighteenth century), or present the life story of one believer (the Countess of Huntingdon). Many books that are not primarily concerned with religion provide insights and details not available elsewhere. Preparing this book involved gathering much far-flung information and molding a narrative that connected events, people, and trends that generally had been treated in isolation. Readers who would like to explore this history in greater depth may consult the books recommended here. The list is merely suggestive of the recent scholarship, indicating starting points for further exploration.

A few works offer a broad-ranging treatment of some aspect of this history. Sir John Elliott compares British and Spanish New World empires (including religion) in *Empires of the Atlantic World: Britain and Spain in America, 1492–1830* (2006). Coverage of Christianity throughout Africa over the centuries can be found in Adrian Hastings's *The Church in Africa, 1450–1950* (1994). For general treatment of the colonies that would become the United States, see the first half of Jon Butler, Grant Wacker, and Randall Balmer, *Religion in American Life: A Short History* (2003); also helpful are Patricia U. Bonomi's recently revised *Under the Cope of Heaven: Religion, Society, and Politics in Colonial America* (2003), and Butler's provocative and engaging *Awash in a Sea of Faith: Christianizing the American People* (1990). On theological trends in the same geographical area, see E. Brooks Holifield, *Theology in America: Christian Thought from the Age of the Puritans to the Civil War* (2003). My own *The English Atlantic in an Age of Revolution, 1640–1661* (2004) places religion in the mid-seventeenth .century in an Atlantic context. For an early attempt to present the history covered in this book, see my essay "Religion," in *The British Atlantic World, 1500–1800*, edited by David Armitage and Michael J. Braddick (revised edition, 2009).

Topical works with a broad geographic reach abound. W. R. Ward's well-regarded *The Protestant Evangelical Awakening* (1992) places revivalism in a transatlantic and multinational context, as do Susan O'Brien's "A Transatlantic Community of Saints: The Great Awakening and the First Evangelical Network, 1735–1755," *American Historical Review* 91 (1986): 811–32, and a more recent effort by Ward, *Early Evangelicalism: A Global Intellectual History, 1670–1789* (2006). Thomas S. Kidd, in *The Great Awakening: The Roots of Evangelical Christianity in Colonial America* (2007), focuses on North America. Susan Juster contrasts prophecy in Britain and North America during the American revolutionary era in *Doomsayers: Anglo-American Prophecy in the Age of Revolution* (2003). Catherine Brekus's *Strangers and Pilgrims: Female Preaching in America, 1740–1845* (1998) follows the phenomenon of women's preaching across various religious groups.

Africa and religion in the transatlantic encounter are treated by John Thornton in *The Kongolese Saint Anthony: Dona Beatriz Kimpa Vita and the Antonian Movement, 1684–1706* (1998) and by George E. Brooks in *Eurafricans in Western Africa: Commerce, Social Status, Gender and Religious Observance from the Sixteenth to the Eighteenth Centuries* (2003). Linda M. Heywood and John Thornton make the case for the major impact of central Africans on the culture of the black Atlantic in *Central Africans, Atlantic Creoles, and the Foundation of the Americas, 1585–1660* (2007). Robin Law's history of a West African slaving port, *Ouidah: The Social History of a West African Slaving "Port," 1727–1892* (2004), demonstrates how little concern for missionary outreach prevailed in such outposts for much of the period. Sandra E. Greene's "Religion, History and the Supreme Gods of Africa: A Contribution to the Debate" is thought provoking (*Journal of Religion in Africa* 26 [1996]: 122–38). In *Shrines of the Slave Trade: Diola Religion and Society in Precolonial Senegambia* (1999), Robert M. Baum locates religion in one African community in a context reshaped by the Atlantic slave trade. Rosalind H. Shaw addresses this transformation in *Memories of the Slave Trade: Ritual and the Historical Imagination in Sierra Leone* (2002).

For Europe, understanding the Reformation is essential. Felicity Heal's *Reformation in Britain and Ireland* (2003), and the still more expansive survey by Diarmaid MacCulloch, *The Reformation: A History* (2003), are indispensable. Eamon Duffy's work suggests the tenacity of allegiance to English Catholicism during the Reformation; see *The Stripping of the Altars: Traditional*

Religion in England, c. 1400–c. 1580 (1992) and *The Voices of Morebath: Reformation and Rebellion in an English Village* (2001). The Welsh variation is revealed by Glanmor Williams in *Wales and the Reformation* (1999). Placing the Reformation within Scotland in its political context is Jane E. A. Dawson, *The Politics of Religion in the Age of Mary, Queen of Scots: The Earl of Argyll and the Struggle for Britain and Ireland* (2002). For England, see Ethan H. Shagan, *Popular Politics and the English Reformation* (2003). The European Counter Reformation is intelligently handled in R. Po-Chia Hsia, *The World of Catholic Renewal, 1540–1770* (1998). Allyson M. Poska's *Regulating the People: The Catholic Reformation in Seventeenth-Century Spain* (1998) shows the Counter Reformation's impact in one location.

The complexity of the religious situation in the three kingdoms and later Britain and Ireland can be explored in various works by John Morrill; his "A British Patriarchy? Ecclesiastical Imperialism under the Early Stuarts," in *Religion, Culture, and Society in Early Modern Britain: Essays in Honour of Patrick Collinson*, edited by Anthony Fletcher and Peter Roberts (1994), is especially incisive. Also see Brendan Bradshaw's "The Tudor Reformation in Wales and Ireland: The Origins of the British Problem" (in *The British Problem, c. 1534–1707*, edited by Bradshaw and Morrill [1996]) and C. S. L. Davies, "International Politics and the Establishment of Presbyterianism in the Channel Islands: The Coutances Connection." *Journal of Ecclesiastical History* 50 (1999): 498–522. David Hempton's *Religious and Political Culture in Britain and Ireland* (1996) is also worthwhile.

England's religious history has received much study. Various books by Patrick Collinson remain the starting point for understanding the early puritan movement. Michael Questier's *Conversion, Politics and Religion in England, 1580–1625* (1996) offers a noteworthy addition. A recent work by Ann Hughes makes comprehensible the fears of religious conservatives in revolutionary England: *Gangraena and the Struggle for the English Revolution* (2004). Alexandra Walsham explores the debate over toleration in *Charitable Hatred: Tolerance and Intolerance in England, 1500–1700* (2006). Andrew Lacey's *The Cult of King Charles the Martyr* (2003) looks at that phenomenon in England. For the period after the Glorious Revolution, see Craig Rose, *England in the 1690s: Revolution, Religion and War* (1999). Tony Claydon argues that far from being insular, English Protestants envisioned themselves as part of an international movement in *Europe and the Making of England, 1660–1760* (2007). Also see Stephen H. Gregg, " 'A Truly Christian Hero': Religion, Effeminacy, and Nation in the Writings of the Societies for Reformation of

Manners," *Eighteenth-Century Life* 25 (2001): 17–28, and Paula McDowell, "Enlightenment Enthusiasms and the Spectacular Failure of the Philadelphian Society," *Eighteenth-Century Studies* 35 (2002): 515–33, for close studies of the later period.

Welsh history is often subsumed by English history, but the religious situation there was distinct and fascinating. In addition to the works of Glanmor Williams, see Stephen Roberts, "Religion, Politics and Welshness, 1649–1660," in *"Into Another Mold": Aspects of the Interregnum*, edited by Ivan Roots (revised ed., 1998). David Ceri Jones's *"A Glorious Work in the World": Welsh Methodism and the International Evangelical Revival, 1735–1750* (2004) offers an excellent account of Welsh revivals. For a welcome addition, see Richard C. Allen, *Quaker Communities in Early Modern Wales: From Resistance to Respectability* (2007).

The religious culture of Ireland is insightfully explored by Raymond Gillespie in *Devoted People: Belief and Religion in Early Modern Ireland* (1997). The Reformation era has been studied by a number of scholars, including Samantha A. Meggs, *The Reformations in Ireland: Tradition and Confessionalism, 1400–1690* (1997); Mary Ann Lyons, *Church and Society in County Kildare, c. 1470–1547* (2000); and Alan Ford, *The Protestant Reformation in Ireland, 1590–1641* (revised ed., 1997). Also see the essays in Alan Ford and John McCafferty, editors, *The Origins of Sectarianism in Early Modern Ireland* (2005). S. J. Connolly's *Religion, Law, and Power: The Making of Protestant Ireland, 1660–1760* (2001) is also helpful.

Scotland's religious history is illuminated by Margo Todd in *The Cultures of Protestantism in Early Modern Scotland* (2002) and by Clare Jackson in *Restoration Scotland, 1660–1690: Royalist Politics, Religion and Ideas* (2003). T. S. Smout's "Born Again at Cambuslang: New Evidence on Popular Religion and Literacy in Eighteenth-Century Scotland" (*Past and Present* 97 [1982]:114–27) treats the major revival there. Anne Skoczylas's *Mr. Simson's Knotty Case: Divinity, Politics, and Due Process in Eighteenth-Century Scotland* (2001) underscores the impact of the Enlightenment, while Jeffrey M. Suderman makes a compelling case for the importance of Enlightenment Christianity rather than hostility between the two, in *Orthodoxy and Enlightenment: George Campbell in the Eighteenth Century* (2001).

Turning to the Americas, on Native American/European encounter, see Daniel K. Richter, *Facing East from Indian Country: A Native History of Early America* (2001), and his "'Some of Them . . . Would Always Have a Minister with Them': Mohawk Protestantism, 1683–1719," *American Indian Quarterly*

16 (1992): 471–84; Neal Salisbury, " 'I loved the Place of my Dwelling': Puritan Missionaries and Native Americans in Seventeenth-Century Southern New England," in *Inequality in Early America*, edited by Pestana and Sharon V. Salinger (1999); David J. Silverman, *Faith and Boundaries: Colonists, Christianity and Community among the Wampanoag Indians of Martha's Vineyard, 1600–1871* (2005), and Karen Ordahl Kupperman, *Indians and English: Facing off in Early America* (2000). Works by Gregory Evans Dowd explore the Nativist movement of the late eighteenth century; see most recently his *War under Heaven: Pontiac, the Indian Nations, and the British Empire* (2002). Barbara Alice Mann makes the richness and complexity of one version of native religion more understandable in her *Iroquoian Women: The Ganto Wisas* (2000), and essays in Kenneth M. Morrison's *The Solidarity of Kin: Ethnohistory, Religious Studies, and the Algonkian-French Religious Encounter* (2002) are also helpful. Christian missions are explored in Kristina Bross's *Dry Bones and Indian Sermons: Praying Indians in Colonial America* (2004), and Laura M. Stevens, *The Poor Indians: British Missionaries, Native Americans, and Colonial Sensibility* (2004). For the mission in early New England, see Richard W. Cogley, *John Eliot's Mission to the Indians before King Philip's War* (1999).

African American Christianity has recently received close study. Sylvia R. Frey and Betty Wood consider the Christianization of Africans in the British colonies and the early United States in *Come Shouting to Zion: African American Protestantism in the American South and British Caribbean to 1830* (1998). Christianity's role in a northern enslaved population is sensitively presented by Leslie M. Harris, *In the Shadow of Slavery: African Americans in New York City, 1626–1863* (2003). Biblical themes are explored by Phillip Richards, "The 'Joseph Story' as Slave Narrative: On Genesis and Exodus as Prototypes for Early Black Anglophone Writing," in *African Americans and the Bible: Sacred Texts and Social Textures,* edited by Vincent L. Wimbush (2000). The discussion of Catholicism's possible role in the Stono Rebellion is carried forward by Mark M. Smith, "Remembering Mary, Shaping Revolt: Reconsidering the Stono Rebellion," *The Journal of Southern History* 67 (2001): 513–34. For religion in Gabriel's Rebellion, see James Sidbury, *Ploughshares into Swords: Race, Rebellion, and Identity in Gabriel's Virginia, 1730–1810* (1997). The encounter with Moravians is the subject of John F. Sensbach's *A Separate Canaan: The Making of an Afro-Moravian World in North Carolina, 1763–1840* (1998). The post-revolutionary black diaspora has been considered in many recent works; see in particular Cassandra Pybus's *Epic Journeys of*

Freedom: Runaway Slaves of the American Revolution and Their Global Quest for Liberty (2006). While focusing on the modern period, Jeffrey E. Anderson's recent study *Conjure in African American Society* (2005) explores how European, Native American, and African traditions might combine.

Scholars have long been fascinated by the religious settlement of the American Revolution. Helpful recent efforts include Frank Lambert's *The Founding Fathers and the Place of Religion in America* (2003) and James H. Hutson's collection of essays, *Forgotten Features of the Founding: The Recovery of Religious Themes in the Early American Republic* (2003). Edwin Gaustad's work, *Faith of Our Fathers: Religion and the New Nation* (1987), revised as *Neither King nor Prelate: Religion and the New Nation, 1776–1826* (1993), remains illuminating.

Regional studies of American religion include Robert Olwell, *Masters, Slaves and Subjects: The Culture of Power in the South Carolina Low Country, 1740–1790* (1998), and Rhys Isaac's prize-winning *The Transformation of Virginia, 1740–1790* (1982). David D. Hall's *Worlds of Wonder, Days of Judgment: Popular Religious Belief in Early New England* (1989), and especially the brilliant chapter on Samuel Sewall, explores popular religion in New England. Thomas Kidd's *The Protestant Interest: New England after Puritanism* (2004) focuses on antipopery in the eighteenth century. Joyce D. Goodfriend offers insight into early New York in "Recovering the Religious History of Dutch Reformed Women in Colonial New York" (in *Women and Religion in Old and New Worlds*, edited by Susan E. Dinan and Debra Meyers [2001]). The Caribbean has been little studied with regard to religion, but Arthur Dayfoot's recent survey begins to fill the gap: *The Shaping of the West Indian Church, 1492–1692* (1999). Karen Ordahl Kupperman's account, *Providence Island, 1630–1641: The Other Puritan Colony* (1993), corrects the sense of New England as either unique or isolated, while the older work by J. Harry Bennett, Jr., *Bondsmen and Bishops: Slavery and Apprenticeship on the Codrington Plantation of Barbados, 1710–1838* (1958), explores the Church of England's failure to catechize the slaves bequeathed to it by one pious planter.

For individual churches and faith traditions, much has been written. A number of excellent recent works have been produced on Methodism; see especially Dee E. Andrews, *The Methodists and Revolutionary America, 1760–1800: The Shaping of an Evangelical Culture* (2000) and David Hempton, *Methodism: Empire of the Spirit* (2005). The long history of the Church of England (with some attention to other churches) has been surveyed in Kenneth Hylson-Smith's *The Churches in England from Elizabeth I to Elizabeth*

II, 3 volumes (1996–98), covering the years 1558–1998. The Church of England in the American Revolution has been oft considered; see especially Nancy L. Rhoden, *Revolutionary Anglicanism: The Colonial Church of England Clergy during the American Revolution* (1999), and Peter M. Doll, *Revolution, Religion, and National Identity: Imperial Anglicanism in British North America, 1745–1795* (2000). I have written *Quakers and Baptists in Colonial Massachusetts* (1991). A recent addition to Baptist historiography, and one that illuminates various other issues along the way, is Monica Najar's *Evangelizing the South: A Social History of Church and State in Early America* (2008). Carla Gerona's *Night Journeys: The Power of Dreams in Transatlantic Quaker Culture* (2004) looks at Quaker dreaming and dream exchanges with Native Americans. Rebecca Larson explores how women Friends who served as ministers managed to balance their various roles in *Daughters of Light: Quaker Women Preaching and Prophesying in the Colonies and Abroad, 1700– 1775* (1999). William Lamont presents the fascinating tale of one obscure sect in *Last Witnesses: The Muggletonian History, 1652–1979* (2006). Bertrand Van Ruymbeke places French Protestants in the Atlantic context; see his *From New Babylon to Eden: The Huguenots and Their Migration to Colonial South Carolina* (2006). Raymond Hylton follows the same group into Ireland in *Ireland's Huguenots and Their Refuge, 1662–1745: An Unlikely Haven* (2005). An account of the Moravians that emphasizes their transatlantic expansion and the erotic nature of their mysticism is Aaron Spencer Fogelman's *Jesus Is Female: Moravians and Radical Religion in Early America* (2007). For the Ephrata brethren in the British Atlantic, see Jeff Bach, *Voices of the Turtledoves: The Sacred World of Ephrata* (2003). Patrick J. Griffin's *The People with No Name: Ireland's Ulster Scots, America's Scots-Irish, and the Creation of the British Atlantic World, 1689–1764* (2001) puts Presbyterianism in its primary transatlantic context. Those interested in the early Mormons will find that Richard Bushman's books on Joseph Smith, including the recent *Joseph Smith: Rough Stone Rolling* (2005), offer an accessible introduction.

For non-Protestant monotheistic traditions, Roman Catholicism within both Britain and Ireland has been explored by Michael A. Mullett, in *Catholics in Britain and Ireland, 1558–1829* (1998). For England see also Michael Questier, *Catholicism and Community in Early Modern England: Politics, Aristocratic Patronage and Religion, c. 1550–1640* (2006). Frances E. Dolan's *"Whores of Babylon": Catholicism, Gender, and Seventeenth-Century Print Culture* (1999) studies Catholicism and gender within England, while her stimulating "Gender and the 'Lost' Spaces of Catholicism" (*Journal of Inter-*

disciplinary History 32 [2002]: 641–65) considers the issue of space. One Atlantic context for Catholicism is limned out by Amos Megged in *Exporting the Catholic Reformation: Local Religion in Early Colonial Mexico* (1996). The late eighteenth-century migration of French Catholics can be followed into one region in Kirsty Carpenter's *Refugees of the French Revolution: Émigrés in London, 1789–1802* (1999). Islam in Britain is the subject of Nabil Matar's *Islam in Britain, 1558–1865* (1998); its place in early Atlantic history is explored in Sylvaine A. Diouf, *Servants of Allah: African Muslims Enslaved in the Americas* (1998).

On witchcraft see, for England, James Sharpe, *Witchcraft in Early Modern England* (2001); for Scotland, Lizanne Henderson, "The Survival of Witchcraft Prosecutions and Witch Belief in South-West Scotland," *The Scottish Historical Review* 85 (2006): 52–74. How the encounter reshaped some aspects of witchcraft belief can bee seen in Matthew Dennis, "Seneca Possessed: Colonialism, Witchcraft, and Gender in the Time of Handsome Lake," in *Spellbound: Women and Witchcraft in America*, edited by Elizabeth Reis (1998); and in John Thornton, "Cannibals, Witches, and Slave Traders in the Atlantic World," *William and Mary Quarterly*, 3d ser., 60 (2003): 273–94. The Salem trials have been the focus of a cascade of books; the recent effort by Mary Beth Norton (*In the Devil's Snare: The Salem Witchcraft Crisis of 1692* [2002]) ably narrates the events, although her emphasis on Indian fears works best to place the events in a regional context.

Biographies offer a way to get at individual experience. Among those I found engaging were Elaine G. Breslaw's provocative *Tituba, the Reluctant Witch of Salem: Devilish Indians and Puritan Fantasies* (1996); John Coffey's learned *Politics, Religion and the British Revolution: The Mind of Samuel Rutherford* (1999); and Boyd Stanley Schlenther's able *Queen of the Methodists: The Countess of Huntingdon and the Eighteenth-Century Crisis of Faith and Society* (1997). Richard L. Greaves, author of many important works on mid-century radicalism, explores the life of one Irish Friend in *Dublin's Merchant-Quaker: Anthony Sharp and the Community of Friends, 1643–1707* (1998). An especially sympathetic treatment of James VI and I is offered by W. B. Patterson, *King James VI and I and the Reunion of Christendom* (1997). David William Voorhees demonstrates the religious aspect of Jacob Leisler's role in "The 'Fervent Tale' of Jacob Leisler," *William and Mary Quarterly*, 3d ser., 51 (1994): 447–72. Two scholars offered competing images of George Whitefield: Harry S. Stout, *The Divine Dramatist: George Whitefield and the Rise of Modern Evan-*

gelicalism (1991), and Frank Lambert, *"Pedlar in Divinity": George Whitefield and the Transatlantic Revivals, 1737–1770* (1994). The brief biographies compiled in the recently revised and expanded *Oxford Dictionary of National Biography* provide a treasure trove of information on the religious lives of hundreds of individuals involved in the British Atlantic world.

NOTES

INTRODUCTION

1. James H. Merrell, "The Indians' New World: The Catawba Experience," *William and Mary Quarterly*, 3d ser., 41 (1984): 537–65; Colin G. Calloway, *New Worlds for All: Indians, Europeans, and the Remaking of Early America* (Baltimore, 1997).

2. John Thornton, "Cannibals, Witches, and Slave Traders in the Atlantic World," *William and Mary Quarterly*, 3d ser., 60 (2003): 279.

3. Rolena Adorno has insightfully explored the way fear shaped the early encounter in her essay, "The Negotiation of Fear in Cabeza de Vaca's *Naufragios*," in *New World Encounters*, ed. Stephen Greenblatt (Berkeley, 1993), 48–84.

CHAPTER I

1. [John Lok], "The Second Voyage to Guinea," 1554, in Richard Hakluyt, *The Principal Navigations* (Glasgow, 1904), 6: 167; Leo Africanus, *A Geographical Historie of Africa* (London, 1600), 293.

2. Kenneth M. Morrison, "The Cosmos as Intersubjective: Native American Other-Than-Human Persons," in *Indigenous Religions: A Companion*, ed. Graham Harvey (New York, 2000), 23–36.

3. Robin Law, *Ouidah: The Social History of a West African Slaving Port, 1727–1893* (Athens, Ohio, 2004), 88.

4. James E. Seaver, *A Narrative of the Life of Mary Jemison* (Canandaigua, N.Y., 1824), 163–67.

5. William Bosman, *A New and Accurate Description of the Coast of Guinea* (London, 1705), 456, 466.

6. Thomas Harriot, *A Brief and True Report of the New Found Land of Virginia* (London, 1590), 26.

7. Ulli Beier, comp., *Yoruba Myths* (New York, 1980).

CHAPTER 2

1. Michael Graham, "The Scottish Reformation," in *A Companion to Tudor Britain,* ed. Robert Tittler and Norman Jones (Malden, Mass., 2004), 300.

2. David Daniell, "Tyndale, William (*c.* 1494–1536)," *Oxford Dictionary of National Biography* (New York, 2004).

3. James VI & I, *Basilicon Doran,* ed. James Craigie (Edinburgh, 1844), 1: 74.

4. Eamon Duffy, *The Stripping of the Altars: Traditional Religion in England, c. 1400–c. 1580* (New Haven, 1992).

5. Felicity Heal, *Reformation in Britain and Ireland* (Oxford, 2003), 253.

6. John Gee, *The Foot out of the Snare* (London, 1624), 41.

7. Nicholas Canny, "Early Modern Ireland, 1500–1700," in *The Oxford History of Ireland,* ed. R. F. Foster (New York, 1989), 116–19.

8. David Knowles, *The Religious Orders in England,* vol. 3: *The Tudor Age* (Cambridge, 1959), 353.

9. Patricia Seed, *Ceremonies of Possession in Europe's Conquest of the New World, 1492–1640* (New York, 1995), 71.

10. Robert Ricard, *The Spiritual Conquest of Mexico* (Berkeley, 1966), 91.

11. Bartolomé de las Casas, *Brevísima Relacion de la Destruccion de las Indias* (1542), reprinted as *The Devastation of the Indies: A Brief Account,* trans. Herma Briffault (New York, 1974), 29.

12. *A Particular Discourse concerning the greate necessitie and manifolde commodyties that are like to growe to this Realme of Englande by the Westerne Discoveries lately attempted, written in the yere 1584, by Richarde Hackluyt,* known as the *Discourse on Western Planting,* reprinted in the *Collection of the Maine Historical Society,* 2d ser., 2 (1877): 13.

13. Sir Walter Ralegh, "Of the Voyage for Guiana," in *Sir Walter Ralegh's Discoverie of Guiana,* ed. Joyce Lorimer, Hakluyt Society 3: 15 (Burlington, Vt., 2006), 253.

CHAPTER 3

1. Later published as Johannes Campanius Holmiensis, trans., *Lutheri Catechismus, Öfwersatt på American-Virginiske Språket* (Stockholm, 1696).

2. The nine were Virginia (1607), Bermuda (1613), St. Christopher (1624), Barbados (1627), Nevis (1628), Providence Island, Massachusetts Bay (both 1629), Montserrat, and Antigua (both 1632). The same could be said of the failed attempt at Roanoke (1584).

3. "Articles, Instructions and Orders," November 20, 1607, in Alexander Brown, *The Genesis of the United States,* 2 vols. (Boston, 1897), 1: 67–68.

4. The first organization was chartered by Parliament in 1649 as the Corporation for the Propagation of the Gospel in New England.

5. John Rolfe to Sir Thomas Dale, in Ralph Hamor, *A True Discourse of the Present State of Virginia* (London, 1615), 65.

6. P[erceval] W[iburn], *A Checke or reproof of M. Howlets untimely schreeching in her*

Majesties eares, 15 vols. (London, 1581). Wiburn's original spelling is "whotter sorte of Protestants."

7. *Archives of Maryland,* vol. 1 (Baltimore, 1883), 244–47.

8. David D. Hall, *The Faithful Shepherd: A History of the New England Ministry in the Seventeenth Century* (Chapel Hill, 1972), 72.

9. Muriel Sedley Gurdon to Margaret Winthrop, April 4, 1636, *Winthrop Papers,* vol. 3: *1631–1637* (Boston, 1943), 243.

10. *Proceedings and Debates of the British Parliaments Respecting North America,* vol. 1: *1542–1688,* ed. Leo Francis Stock (Washington, D.C., 1924), 207–8.

11. *The Diary of John Evelyn,* ed. E. S. de Beer, 6 vols. (Oxford, 1955), 3: 150.

12. The Rhode Island law code of 1647 refers to granting liberty about differences "touching the truth as it is in Jesus." *Records of the Colony of Rhode Island,* vol. 1: *1636–1663,* ed. John Russell Bartlett (Providence, 1856), 156.

13. Instructions to the ministers of Curaçao, 1638, quoted in Cornelis Ch. Goslinga, *The Dutch in the Caribbean and on the Wild Coast, 1580–1680* (Assen, the Netherlands, 1971), 368.

14. David J. Silverman, "Indians, Missionaries, and Religious Translation: Creating Wampanoag Christianity in Seventeenth-Century Martha's Vineyard," *William and Mary Quarterly,* 3d ser., 57 (2005): 141–74.

15. Daniel K. Richter, "War and Culture: The Iroquois Experience," *William and Mary Quarterly,* 3d ser., 9 (1983): 528–59.

16. Carla Gardina Pestana, *The English Atlantic in an Age of Revolution, 1640–1661* (Cambridge, Mass., 2004), 193.

17. Richard Ligon, *A True & Exact History of the Island of Barbados* (London, 1657), 47.

18. J. G. Stedman, *Narrative of a Five Years' Expedition against the Revolting Negroes of Surinam* (London, 1796; reprint ed., Barre, Mass., 1971), 364.

19. "Father Antoine Biet's Visit to Barbados in 1654," ed. Jerome S. Handler, *Journal of the Barbados Museum and Historical Society* 32 (1967): 61.

CHAPTER 4

1. Morgan Godwyn, *The Negro's and Indians Advocate* (London, 1680), 33.

2. Charter of the Royal African Company of England, 27 September 1672, *Collections of the Virginia Historical Society,* n.s., 6 (1887): 36–53.

3. Warren M. Billings, *Sir William Berkeley and the Forging of Colonial Virginia* (Baton Rouge, 2004), 74.

4. *Memorials of the Discovery and Early Settlement of the Bermudas, 1511–1687,* vol. 2: *1650–1687,* ed. J. H. Lefroy (1877–79), 291, 569.

5. T. H. Breen and Stephen Innes, *"Myne Owne Ground": Race and Freedom on Virginia's Eastern Shore, 1640–1676* (New York, 1980), 87.

6. Jaspar Danckaerts, *Journal of a Voyage to New York and a Tour in Several of the*

American Colonies in 1679–80 by Jaspar Dankers and Peter Sluyter, trans. and ed. Henry C. Murphy (1867; Ann Arbor, 1966), 268.

7. John Oxenbridge, *A Seasonable Proposition of Propagating the Gospel by Christian Colonies in the Continent of Guaiana* (London?, 1670).

8. John Griffiths, *A Journal of the Life, Travels and Labours in the Ministry* (London, 1779), reprinted in *The Friends' Library* 5 (1842): 345.

9. Sydney E. Ahlstrom, *A Religious History of the American People* (New Haven, 1972), 198.

10. William Penn, "Preface to the First Frame of Government," in *A Collection of Charters and Other Publick Acts Relating to the Province of Pennsylvania* (Philadelphia, 1740), 10.

11. Christopher P. Magra, "Faith at Sea: Exploring Maritime Religiosity in the Eighteenth Century," *International Journal of Maritime History* 19 (June 2007): 96.

12. Charles II, "The Declaration of Breda," in *Documents of the English Reformation,* ed. Gerald Bray (Minneapolis, 1994), 545.

13. David Ceri Jones, *"A Glorious Work in the World": Welsh Methodism and the International Evangelical Revival, 1735–1750* (Cardiff, 2004), 42.

14. *Vestry Book of Christ Church Parish,* in *The Old Dominion in the Seventeenth Century: A Documentary History of Virginia, 1606–1700,* rev. ed., ed. Warren M. Billings (Chapel Hill, 2007), 387.

15. William Hooke to John Davenport, 2 March 1663, in "A Censored Letter: William Hooke in England to John Davenport in New England, 1663," ed. A. G. Matthews, *Transactions of the Congregational Historical Society* 9 (1902): 266.

16. Donald B. Cooper, *The Establishment of the Anglican Church in the Leeward Islands* (Stillwater, Okla. 1966), 21, 29.

17. Peter E. Pope, *Fish into Wine: The Newfoundland Plantation in the Seventeenth Century* (Chapel Hill, 2004), 288.

18. John Ruston Pagan, *Anne Orthwood's Bastard: Sex and Law in Early Virginia* (New York, 2003), 134.

19. Charles II, "The Charter of the Governor and Company of the English Colony of Rhode Island and Providence Plantations in New England in America, 1663," in *Records of the Colony of Rhode Island,* vol. 2: *1664–1677,* ed. John Russell Bartlett (Providence, 1857), 5.

20. Raymond Gillespie, "Catholic Religious Culture in the Diocese of Dublin, 1614–1697," in *History of the Catholic Diocese in Dublin,* ed. James Kelly and Dáire Keogh (Dublin, 2000), 139.

21. Danckaerts, *Journal of a Voyage,* 147, 309.

CHAPTER 5

1. Unsigned preface to Mary Rowlandson's *The Soveraignty and Goodness of God* (Cambridge, 1682), A2.

2. Jaspar Danckaerts, *Journal of a Voyage to New York and a Tour in Several of the*

American Colonies in 1679–80 by Jaspar Dankers and Peter Sluyter, trans. and ed. Henry C. Murphy (1867; Ann Arbor, 1966), 383; and Jill Lepore, *The Name of War: King Philip's War and the Origins of American Identity* (New York, 1998), 43.

3. Increase Mather, *A Brief History of the Warr with the Indians in New-England* (1676), reprinted in *So Dreadfull a Judgment: Puritan Responses to King Philip's War, 1676–1677,* ed. Richard Slotkin and James K. Folsom (Middletown, Conn., 1978), 86.

4. "William Hubbard and the Providential Interpretation of History," *Proceedings of the American Antiquarian Society* 52 (1942): 15–37.

5. Louise A. Breen, "Praying with the Enemy: Daniel Gookin, King Philip's War, and the Dangers of Intercultural Mediatorship," in *Empire and Others: British Encounters with Indigenous Peoples, 1600–1850,* ed. Martin Daunton and Rick Halpern (Philadelphia, 1999), 101.

6. These were Natick, Hassanamesit, Punkapoag, and Wamesit.

7. "A Narrative of the Indian and Civil Wars in Virginia, In the Years 1675 and 1676," in *Tracts and Other Papers relating principally to the Origin, Settlement, and Progress of the Colonies in North America,* comp. Peter Force (Washington, D.C., 1836; reprint ed., Gloucester, Mass., 1963), 1: 8.

8. Berkeley, "Declaration and Remonstrance," 29 May 1676, in *The Old Dominion in the Seventeenth Century: A Documentary History of Virginia, 1606–1700,* rev. ed., ed. Warren M. Billings (Chapel Hill, 2007), 272.

9. "Proclamations of Nathaniel Bacon," *Virginia Magazine of History and Biography* 1 (1893–94): 58.

10. Berkeley to Henry Coventry, 3 June 1676, in *Old Dominion in the Seventeenth Century,* ed. Billings, 272.

11. [Thomas Matthews], *The Beginning, Progress, and Conclusion of Bacons Rebellion in Virginia,* in *Tracts and Other Papers,* comp. Force, 9.

12. Ibid., 12; Berkeley, "Declaration and Remonstrance," 271; "A True Narrative of the Rise, Progresse and Cessation of the Late Rebellion in Virginia," in *Narratives of the Insurrections,* ed. Charles M. Andrews (New York, 1915), 110, 111; "A Narrative of the Indian and Civil Wars in Virginia," 26; Ludlow to Sir Joseph Williamson, 28 June 1676, *Virginia Magazine of History and Biography* 1: 184.

13. "The Declaration of the Gentlemen, Merchants and Inhabitants of Boston and the Country Adjacent, April 18, 1689," in *Narratives of the Insurrections,* ed. Andrews, 175.

14. J. F., *The Declaration of the Reasons and Motives for the Present Appearing in Arms of Their Majesties Protestant Subjects* ([London,] 1689), 6.

15. Elaine G. Breslaw, *Tituba, the Reluctant Witch of Salem: Devilish Indians and Puritans Fantasies* (New York, 1996).

CHAPTER 6

1. W. R. Ward, *The Protestant Evangelical Awakening* (New York, 1992), 299.

2. James Kelly, "The Impact of the Penal Laws," in *History of the Catholic Diocese in Dublin,* ed. Kelly and Dáire Keogh (Dublin, 2000), 152.

3. Sydney E. Ahlstrom, *A Religious History of the American People* (New Haven, 1972), 224.

4. Leigh Eric Schmidt, *Holy Fairs: Scottish Communions and American Revivals in the Early Modern Period* (Princeton, 1989).

5. The last extant colony to gain an Anglican church was apparently New Hampshire in the 1730s; by that time the Church of England was officially established in Jamaica, Barbados, the four Leeward Island colonies, South Carolina, Virginia, Maryland, and New York. Those without Anglican establishments were North Carolina, Delaware, New Jersey, Pennsylvania, Connecticut, Rhode Island, Massachusetts, and New Hampshire. (Georgia was not yet founded, while Maine was under the control of Massachusetts.)

6. Hans Werner Debrunner, *Presence and Prestige: Africans in Europe, A History of Africans in Europe before 1918* (Basel, 1979), 68.

7. Randy J. Sparks, *The Two Princes of Calabar: An Eighteenth-Century Atlantic Odyssey* (Cambridge, Mass., 2004); Terry Alford, *Prince among Slaves: The True Story of an African Prince Sold into Slavery in the American South* (New York, 1977).

8. Donald B. Cooper, *The Establishment of the Anglican Church in the Leeward Islands* (Stillwater, Okla., 1966), 39.

9. *Journals of the House of Burgesses of Virginia, 1712–1714, 1723–26,* ed. H. R. McIlwaine (Richmond, 1912), 79–80.

10. James H. Merrell, *Into the American Wood: Negotiators on the Pennsylvania Frontier* (New York, 1999), 20.

11. Bertrand van Ruymbeke, *From New Babylon to Eden: The Huguenots and their Migration to Colonial South Carolina* (Columbia, S.C., 2006), 142–44.

12. Paula McDowell, "Enlightenment Enthusiasms and the Spectacular Failure of the Philadelphian Society," *Eighteenth Century Studies* 35 (2002): 519, 524.

13. Edmund S. Morgan, *The Puritan Family: Religion and Domestic Relations in Seventeenth-Century New England,* rev. ed. (New York, 1966), 161.

14. Kenneth Hylson-Smith, *The Churches in England from Elizabeth I to Elizabeth II,* 3 vols. (London, 1997–98), 2:29.

CHAPTER 7

1. Beverly Prior Smaby, *The Transformation of Moravian Bethlehem: From Communal Mission to Family Economy* (Philadelphia, 1988), 22–23.

2. Katherine M. Faull, trans. and ed., *Moravian Women's Memoirs: Their Related Lives, 1750–1820* (Syracuse, N.Y., 1997), 77–78.

3. Charles L. Cohen, "The Colonization of British North America as an Episode in the History of Christianity," *Church History* 72 (2003): 553–68.

4. T. C. Smout, "Born Again at Cambuslang: New Evidence on Popular Religion and Literacy in Eighteenth-Century Scotland," *Past and Present* 97 (1982): 118.

5. Aaron Spencer Fogleman, *Hopeful Journeys: German Immigration, Settlement, and Political Culture in Colonial America, 1717–1775* (Philadelphia, 1996), 119.

6. Boyd Stanley Schlenther, *Queen of the Methodists: The Countess of Huntingdon and the Eighteenth-Century Crisis of Faith and Society* (Durham, N.C., 1997), 25, 60.

7. Jonathan Edwards, *Sinners in the Hands of an Angry God* (New York, 1769), 8.

8. John Walsh, "'Methodism' and the Origins of English-Speaking Evangelism," in *Evangelicalism: Comparative Studies of Popular Protestantism in North America, the British Isles, and Beyond, 1700–1990*, ed. Mark A. Noll et al. (New York, 1994), 22.

9. Thomas Kidd, ed., *The Great Awakening: A Brief History with Documents* (Boston, 2008), 71.

10. The December 1742 issues of the *Boston Gazette* are apparently no longer extant, but this story was printed in Ellen D. Larned, *Historic Gleanings from Windham County, Connecticut* (Providence, R.I., 1899), 22.

11. Barbara E. Lacey, ed., *The World of Hannah Heaton: The Diary of an Eighteenth-Century New England Farm Woman* (DeKalb, Ill., 2003), 253.

12. P. E. H. Hair, "Christian Influences in Sierra Leone before 1787," *Journal of Religion in Africa* 27 (February 1997): 14 n. 40.

13. Stephen J. Stein, "A Note on Anne Dutton, Eighteenth-Century Evangelical," *Church History* 44 (1975): 489.

14. J. Harry Bennett, Jr., *Bondsmen and Bishops: Slavery and Apprenticeship on the Codrington Plantation of Barbados, 1710–1838* (Berkeley, 1958), 82.

15. David Fowler to Eleazar Wheelock, January 27, 1766, in *The Letters of Eleazar Wheelock's Indians*, ed. James Dow McCallum (Hanover, N.H., 1932), 99.

16. Rachel Wheeler, "'Friends to Your Souls': Jonathan Edwards' Indian Pastorate and the Doctrine of Original Sin," *Church History* 72 (2003): 765.

17. Felicity Heal, *Reformation in Britain and Ireland* (New York, 2003), 253.

18. Gregory E. Dowd, *A Spirited Resistance: The North American Indian Struggle for Unity, 1745–1815* (Baltimore, 1992), 13.

19. *The Natural History of North Carolina* (Dublin, 1743), 301, 335, 379–83.

20. "An Account of the Remarkable Occurrences in the Life and Travels of Colonel James Smith," in *Tragedies of the Wilderness*, comp. Samuel G. Drake (Boston, 1842), 227.

21. John Heckwelder, *Account of the History, Manners, and Customs of the Indian Nations, Who Once Inhabited Pennsylvania* (Philadelphia, 1819), 247–48.

22. Walter Pilkington, ed., *The Journal of Samuel Kirkland: 18th-Century Missionary to the Iroquois, Government Agent, Father of Hamilton College* (Clinton, N.Y., 1980), 74.

23. Susan O'Brien, "A Transatlantic Community of Saints: The Great Awakening and the First Evangelical Network, 1735–1755," *American Historical Review* 91 (1986): 811.

24. Eliga H. Gould, "Prelude: The Christianizing of British America," in *Missions and Empire,* ed. Norman Etherinton (New York, 2005), 32.

25. Joining Harvard, William and Mary, and Yale were Princeton (1746), Columbia (1754), Pennsylvania (1755), Brown (1764), Rutgers (1766), and Dartmouth (1769).

26. Jon Butler, *Awash in a Sea of Faith: Christianizing the American People* (Cambridge, Mass., 1990).

27. Walsh, "'Methodism' and the Origins of English-Speaking Evangelicalism," 33.

CHAPTER 8

1. Johnson to Dr. Samuel Auchmuty, April 26, 1770, in *The Papers of Sir William Johnson* (Albany, 1931), 7: 584–85; and to Daniel Burton, October 8, 1766, ibid., (1927), 5: 388.

2. Peter M. Doll, *Revolution, Religion, and National Identity: Imperial Anglicanism in British North America, 1745–1795* (Cranbury, N.J., 2000), 81.

3. Philip Lawson, *The Imperial Challenge: Quebec and Britain in the Age of the American Revolution* (Buffalo, 1990), 135.

4. Walter Pilkington, *The Journal of Samuel Kirkland: 18th-Century Missionary to the Iroquois, Government Agent, Father of Hamilton College* (Clinton, N.Y., 1980), 364.

5. Daniel R. Coquillette and Neil Longley, *Portrait of a Patriot: The Major Political and Legal Papers of Josiah Quincy Junior*, vol. 3: *The Southern Journal (1773)* (Boston, 2007), 41.

6. Libbey to Belknap, 22 February 1788, *Collections of the Massachusetts Historical Society*, 6th ser., 4 (1891): 390. Article 11, Treaty of Peace and Friendship, trans. Joel Barlow, ratified by the Senate, 10 June 1797, http://www.yale.edu/lawweb/avalon/diplomacy/barbary/bar1796t.htm

7. Edwin S. Gaustad, *Faith of Our Fathers: Religion and the New Nation* (San Francisco, 1987), 114.

8. George Washington to the United Baptist Churches of Virginia, May 1789, in *Papers of George Washington*, Presidential Series, ed. Dorothy Twohig (Charlottesville, 1987), 2: 423.

9. James Madison to Edward Livingston, 10 July 1822, *The Founders' Constitution*, vol. 5: *Amendment I (Religion)*, Document 66, http://press-pubs.uchicago.edu/founders/documents/amendI_religions66.html. Thomas Jefferson to the Danbury Baptist Association, 1 January 1802, in *The Writings of Thomas Jefferson*, 20 vols., ed. Andrew Lipscomb and Albert E. Bergh (Washington, D.C., 1905), 16: 281–82.

10. Thomas Jefferson to William Canby, 18 September 1813, in *Writings of Thomas Jefferson*, ed. Lipscomb and Bergh, 16: 281, 13: 377.

11. Benjamin Franklin, *Autobiography of Benjamin Franklin*, ed. Louis P. Masur, 2d ed. (Boston, 2003), 114–15.

12. John Leland, "The Virginia Chronicle," in *The Writings of John Leland*, ed. L. F. Greene (New York, 1969), 98.

13. Dale Bisnauth, *History of Religions in the Caribbean* (Trenton, N.J., 1996), 109.

14. Boyd Stanley Schlenther, *Queen of the Methodists: The Countess of Huntingdon and the Eighteenth-Century Crisis of Faith and Society* (Durham, N.C., 1997), 91.

15. Sylvia R. Frey and Betty Wood, *Come Shouting to Zion: African American Protestantism in the American South and British Caribbean to 1830* (Chapel Hill, N.C., 1998), 123.

16. Colin G. Calloway, *New Worlds for All: Indians, Europeans and the Remaking of Early America* (Baltimore, 1997), 31.

17. Alan Taylor, *The Divided Ground: Indians, Settlers, and the Northern Borderland of the American Revolution* (New York, 2006), 63.

18. Stewart J. Brown, "Movements of Christian Awakening in Revolutionary Europe, 1790–1815," in *The Cambridge History of Christianity*, vol. 7: *Enlightenment, Reawakening and Revolution, 1600–1815*, ed. Brown and Timothy Tackett (Cambridge, 2006), 582.

19. John Sullivan to Jeremy Belknap, February 26, 1788, *Collections of the Massachusetts Historical Society*, 394.

20. Sydney E. Ahlstrom, *A Religious History of the American People* (New Haven, 1972), 423.

21. John Bossy, *The English Catholic Community, 1570–1850* (New York, 1976), 298.

22. James Sidbury, *Ploughshares into Swords: Race, Rebellion, and Identity in Gabriel's Virginia, 1730–1810* (New York, 1997), 78.

23. J. Harry Bennett, Jr., *Bondsmen and Bishops: Slavery and Apprenticeship on the Codrington Plantation of Barbados, 1710–1838* (Berkeley, 1958), 108.

INDEX

Aberdeen, Scotland, 111
abolition of slavery, 241–42, 255, 257, 264
absolutism, 146, 161, 233–34, 246. *See also* tyranny
Acadia, 171, 222
act concerning religious toleration (Maryland), 76
Act of Union, 12, 164
Adams, John, 230
Adis, Henry, 119
Adopting Act, 168
Afonso I, 15
Africa, 57, 176, 242; missions in, 60, 62, 207; trading posts in, 12, 101, 173. *See also* Kongo
African: as category of persons, 29–30; names, 235
African Americans, 102, 145; conversion and, 89, 95–96, 103–4, 172, 178, 206–8, 236–37, 240, 262; evangelical Christianity and, 211, 236–37, 262; preachers, 217
African Burial Ground, 175–76
African Methodist Episcopal Church, 239, 251, 262
Africans, 112, 259; converted to Catholicism, 98; converted to Christianity, 6, 14; in England, 96; enslaved, 5, 95–96, 101, 172; "liberated," 242, 262
African traditional religion, 8, 16, 17, 20, 56, 97, 99, 153, 175; in 1500, 18, 20–25, 27–29; imported, 96–97, 101, 175
Africanus, Leo, 17
afterlife, beliefs about, 9, 23–25, 27, 70, 210, 211, 229–30
Allen, Richard, 239
All Souls Day, 24
Anabaptism and Anabaptists, 35, 162, 182
ancestors, 18, 19, 20, 24, 28, 29

Andover, Massachusetts, 151
Andros, Sir Edmund, 144, 152
angels, 18–19
animals: in Christian belief, 28, 29; in Native American belief, 26, 28, 211, 225–26
Anomabo, 173–74; in West African belief, 18, 28
Ansah, William, *Royal African: or, Memoirs of the Young Prince of Annamaboe*, 173, 174
anti-Catholicism, 222–23, 232, 246, 258–59; in colonies, 73, 74, 88, 122, 144, 146–48, 223; declining, 218, 233, 252–53; in England, 44–45, 50, 79, 141, 233, 234; as a motive for expansion, 9, 63, 73; among Native Americans, 176; in Scotland, 38, 47; unifying force, 128, 192; and war with France, 160–61
Anthony (slave), 96
Antigua, 110, 192, 208, 240
Antwerp, 42
Armada, Spanish, 63
Armagh, Ireland, 51
army, British, 191
Arminianism, 199
Arminius, Jacob, 199
Ashbridge, Elizabeth, 112
Ashbury, Francis (bishop), 254
Asia, 57
Askew, Anne, 44–45
atheism: accusations of, 138, 221; fears of, 151, 156, 179, 185, 248, 249
Atlantic, British: defined, 12; significance, 13–14, 258–59
Augsburg, Peace of, 38, 53
Australia, 231, 242
Azores Islands, 15

Baartman, Sara, 261
Bacon, Nathaniel, 135, 136, 137, 138

Bacon's Rebellion, 129, 135–38, 150, 220

Bahamas, 236, 262

Baltimore, 2nd Baron (Cecil Calvert), 75, 88–89, 122

Baltimore, 3rd Baron (Charles Calvert), 147

banishment, of unpopular religious groups, 85, 118–19, 163; on pain of death, 90, 118–19

baptism, 15, 70, 78, 123, 137, 207; adult, 35, 81; emancipation and, 96; mass, 58; as sacrament, 34; of slaves, 101, 172; withheld, 85, 102, 103, 213

Baptist: churches, 83, 109, 116, 197, 236, 262; Missionary Society, 250; Revolt, 255, 263

Baptists, 81, 142, 167, 179, 199; American Revolution and, 221; converting African Americans, 197, 207–8, 217, 236–37, 242–43

Barbados, 95, 98, 116, 120, 173; Quakers in, 103, 104, 110; religious policies in, 77, 87, 96

Barrington, Shute (bishop), 253–54

Battle of Killiecrankie, 142; of the Severn, 76, 88–89

Baxter, Richard, 87, 101, 121

Beissel, Conrad, 182

Belknap, Jeremy, 229

Benin, 20

Ben Israel, Menasseh, 91

Berkeley, Sir William, 101, 125, 133, 135

Bermuda, 88, 102, 110; religious policies in, 85, 87, 113, 213

bewitchment, 137, 153

Bible, 7, 5, 6, 132, 229; in Gaelic, 87; as guide, 35, 56, 106, 184; in Indian language, 94, 130; Jefferson, 230–31; King James Version, 42; study of, 51; symbol of Protestantism, 63; translation, 41–42, 130; vernacular, 36, 41, 42, 47, 51, 61

biblical: language, 253; literalism, 107; naming, 235, 238

Biet, Father Antoine, 98

bishops, 37, 39, 42, 53, 67; AME, 239; in colonies, 75, 260; eliminated, 45, 80; Glorious Revolution and, 141; opposed, 76, 87, 223. See also kirk

Bishops' Wars, 78, 113

Böhme, Jakob, 181, 182

Boleyn, Anne, 41

Book of Common Prayer, 42, 43, 63, 125, 213; proscribed, 80; read aloud, 75, 115, 243; required, 77, 194

Book of Martyrs. See Foxe, John, Actes and Monuments

Book of Mormon, 263

books, 52, 63, 113, 123, 196; burning of, 195; circulating, 7, 83, 261; as symbol, 63, 86, 237, 245

Bossy, John, 253

Boston, 144, 156, 178, 215, 261

Boston, First Church of, 205

Boston Gazette, 204

Brainerd, David, 177

Brant: Joseph, 243; Molly, 220

Brattle Street Church, 165

Brazil, 73, 91

Breda, Declaration of, 118

Brent, Mr., 137

Brent, Margaret, 121

Bricknell, John, 210

Brockden, Magdalena Buelah, 190

Bryan family, 207

Bunyan, John, Pilgrim's Progress, 116

Burgher-Antiburgher split, 214

burial, 23, 24–25, 94, 176

Burke, Edmund, Reflections on the Revolution in France, 248

Butler, Jon, 216

Butler, Joseph, Analogy of Religion, 184

calendar, 16, 19–21, 56, 201, 252

Caliban, 69

Calloway, Colin G., 1

Calvert family, 147, 148, 163, 166. See also Baltimore, 2nd Baron; Baltimore, 3rd Baron

Calvin, John, 35, 39

Calvinism, 35, 39, 68, 82, 212, 214; shift away from, 68, 164, 182–83

Calvinists, 191, 192, 193–94, 199, 214

Cambridge, University of, 82

Cambuslang, 201–2

Canada, 222–23, 260; Constitution of, 231–32

Canary Islands, 15

Canny, Nicholas, 52

Canterbury, Connecticut, 204

Cape Mount (Africa), 207

capital punishment, 181; for adultery, 91; for disobedient sons, 90; for Jesuits, 44; for Quakers, 90, 118–19; for witchcraft, 26, 151

captives, war, 95–96, 161

captivity narrative, 132, 134

Caribbean, 65, 95, 101, 236; established church in, 113, 120, 170, 260; Moravians in, 188,

190, 206–7, 208; other groups in, 105, 108, 162, 241, 261; Quakers in, 103, 110, 118

Caribs, 105

Carolina, 109, 110, 162, 210; religious policies in, 113, 118, 120. *See also* South Carolina

Carroll, John, 251

Cart and Whit Act, 119

catechism, 47, 53, 198, 261; new emphasis on 57; translations of, 51, 60–61, 67

Catherine of Aragon, 36

Catherine of Braganza, 139

Catholic Relief Act, 252

Catholics, African, 1, 57, 173, 175; conflated with Indians, 147, 148, 158; in disguise, 179, 191–92, 258; in Dutch colonies, 89; English, 8, 43, 47, 48–50, 68; in English colonies, 68, 74, 76, 84, 115, 162, 166; expansion and, 222–23; increasing numbers of, 232, 255; Irish, 51, 53, 64–65, 68, 191, 212, 257; Scottish, 47, 48–50, 67–68, 162, 193; treatment of, 84–85, 120–22, 142, 162–63; in the United States, 251, 261; Welsh, 48–50, 121. *See also* Maryland

celibacy, 40, 48, 51, 71, 182, 192, 227

Channel Islands, 52, 79, 113

chapels, 141, 191, 242, 251

chaplain: army, 82, 171; naval, 101, 115

Charles I, 89, 90; death of, 79, 98, 133, 137; as martyr, 98, 125, 126, 259; religious policies of, 68, 74, 76–79

Charles II, 80, 98, 101, 139; religious policies of, 112, 113, 114, 121, 169, 221

Charles the Martyr chapel, 125

Charleston, South Carolina, 254, 262

charter, 63, 101, 118, 155, 165; revocation of, 140, 143, 144, 148, 152

Chauncy, Charles, 205, 214–15

Cherokee, 225, 243–44

Chesapeake region, 23, 110, 172

Child, Robert, 165

Christendom, concept of, 30, 31

Christian: church, early, 45, 54; nation, United States as, 229, 231, 249–50

Christianity: evangelical, 13, 218, 242, 249, 257; liberal, 179, 203, 214; rational, 160, 180, 202, 203, 205, 214; slavery and, 96, 102, 206, 235

Christians, renegade, defined, 96

Christmas, 21, 56

church courts, 42, 68, 178; eliminated, 45, 80, 81, 117; opposed, 76, 85–87

church: admission requirements, 133, 149, 165, 196; membership, 85, 93, 133, 196; membership, slaves and, 102–3; yard, 24–25

Church Missionary Society, 250

Church of England, 36, 42–43, 52, 111, 118, 184; advocates of, 74, 81; Africans baptized in, 96, 174, 261; and American Episcopal Church, 227, 234; as basis of unity, 44, 45, 68, 136, 259–60; collapse of, 79, 80, 84; conformity to, 68–69, 148; efforts to expand, 84, 165, 169, 218, 222, 231–32; efforts to reform, 69, 73; Elizabethan, 42–43; established in colonies, 68, 73, 113, 115, 129, 149, 166, 282 n.5; fear of, 143, 144; institutional weakness of, 6, 8, 74–75, 77, 115; loss of coercive power in, 159, 163, 166–67, 169–70; members, 108, 115, 122, 162, 213, 236; and Methodism, 190–91, 226; Native Americans baptized in, 70, 176–77; nature of, 36–37, 40, 53, 68; proscribed, 80, 81, 84–85; restored, 98, 100, 113

Church of Ireland (Protestant), 50, 51, 53, 66, 68; Charles I and, 77, 78; after Glorious Revolution, 160, 163, 167–68; during interregnum, 80, 87; Restoration-era, 113

Church of Scotland. *See* kirk

Civil Constitution of the Clergy, 246, 251

civil war, 82; in England, 78–79; in Maryland, 88–89; in Scotland, 38; in the United States, 255; in Virginia, 135–38

civility, 72, 92, 93–94, 106, 243, 263

Clarendon, Earl of (Edward Hyde), 115

Clarendon Codes, 115–16

Clarkson, Thomas, 241

clergy, 69, 80; called by congregation, 76, 171; Church of England, 74–75, 103, 113, 118, 212, 220–21; dismissed, 81; educated, 216; educated, opposed, 81, 82, 107; New England, 8, 76, 133, 203–4; shortage of, 102, 171

Clinton, Henry, 238

Codrington, Christopher, 171

Codrington Plantation, 172, 207, 254

Cohen, Charles, 195

Coke, Thomas, 241

Cole, Nathan, 194

Columbia University (King's College), 216

Commission for the Propagation of the Gospel in Wales, 87

Committee of Safety, 146

communal living, 109, 227
communication: across cultural barriers, 60; across linguistic barriers, 58, 60–61
communion: host, 77; plate, 75; ritual, 168, 188, 201; withheld, 85, 87
community watchfulness, 90, 178
confession: of accused witches, 155, 156; doctrinal, defined, 183
conformity, 49, 77, 82, 118, 166, 170
Congregational: church order, 76, 80, 85, 88, 89–90, 94; establishment, 99, 107, 124, 129, 143, 228, 229; establishment, undermined, 151, 164, 165, 212
Congregationalists, 122, 171, 182, 199, 217; in England, 108, 116, 142, 167, 179, 193
Connecticut, 87, 140–41, 145, 165, 194, 205, 244; Missionary Society, 250; religious policies in, 89, 107, 114, 228, 229
conspiracy, 44, 139, 147, 152
conversion: to Catholicism, of Protestants, 68; of elites, as strategy, 47, 52, 57; experience, 182, 204; forced, 57, 63; as a goal of expansion, 59–63; nature of, debated, 193, 194, 197, 203; process, 7, 8, 62; to Protestantism, of Catholics, 89, 139; to Quakerism, 14, 155; relation of, 71, 85, 194
Coode, John, 147
Corporation for the Propagation of the Gospel, 69, 92, 244
cosmology: Christian, 18–19, 24–25; Muslim, 70; Native American, 18, 27, 29, 70, 210, 211; West African, 27–28
Counter Reformation, 43, 53, 57, 121
covenant renewal, 133–34
Covenanters, 80, 88, 113, 164
Cranmer, Thomas, 43
Crashaw, Richard, 68
Crashaw, William, 68
creation, dating of, 51. See also origin stories
Crevecoeur, J. Hector Saint John de, 244
Cromwell, Oliver, 79, 83, 84, 88–89, 91, 122
Cromwell, Richard, 79
cruelty, 178; Spanish, 58–59, 89
Curaçao, 67, 89, 161

dance, 97, 101, 175
Danckaerts, Jaspar, 122
Dartmouth College, 244
Davenport, James, 195, 204, 205
Davenport, John, 195

death, 16, 23–25; rate, 74, 95; ritual death, 95; rituals surrounding, 20, 22–24
Declaration: of Indulgences, 141; and Remonstrance, 136; of Right, 141
declension, 132
deism, 160, 184, 185, 228, 248
deities, multiple, 27, 28
deity: androgynous, 182, 188; female, 27, 188, 226–27; supreme, 18, 27, 28, 61, 210; supreme, rejected, 30
Delaware: people, 209, 211; place, 229; River, 67, 105, 197
Demerara Revolt, 262
Denmark, 161, 190
discipline, 39, 40, 45, 178; congregation responsible for, 76; English and Scottish contrasted, 45; as goal, 85, 87, 168; Scotland and, 47; lack of support for, 151
disease, 75, 131, 135, 139; explaining, 9; Native Americans and, 8–9, 95, 104, 105
dissenters, 119, 150, 170, 212, 232, 249; American Revolution and, 220; legal status of, 115, 142, 166–67
diversity, 108, 123, 218; in colonies, 1, 6, 12, 73–74, 83, 98, 100; in England, 8, 81–82; among Native Americans, 29; in the new United States, 231; within Protestantism, 35, 45, 257; among three kingdoms, 8, 66, 67–68, 100; in three kingdoms, 81–82, 83, 117
divorce, 83, 93, 107; Henry VIII and, 36, 37, 41
Doeg, 137
Dominicans, 58, 60–61, 74, 89
Dominion of New England, 114, 141, 143–46, 164
Dorchester Church, 86
Dowd, Greg, 210
dreams, 21, 70, 188; prophetic, 180, 181, 225–26; sharing of, 21–22, 111–12, 190; and witches, 25
Dublin, 52, 185
Duffy, Eamon, 48
Dundee, 1st Viscount of (John Graham of Claverhouse), 141
Dunkers, 182
Dunmore, Lord, Proclamation of, 238
Dury, John, 179
Dutartes family, 180–81
Dutch: colonies, 7, 13, 67, 89; in New York, 145; as Protestant alternative, 5, 6, 13, 67

Dutch Reformed Church, 67; in Curaçao, 89; members, 122, 176; slaves in, 103
Dutch West India Company, 67, 146
Dutton, Anne, 207

East Anglia, 88
Easter, 21
East Jersey, 111
ecumenism, 170, 179, 190, 194, 198, 202
Edict of Nantes, Revocation of, 108
Edinburgh, 47, 78
Edward VI, 36, 42, 43
Edwards, Jonathan, 196, 202, 208; *Faithful Narrative of the Surprising Work of God*, 196; *Sinners in the Hands of an Angry God*, 202
Edwards, Thomas, *Gangraena*, 83
Eikon Basilike, 79
ejectors, 81, 87
elect, concept of the, 35. *See also* predestination
Eliot, John, 92–95, 105, 106, 123, 130, 243; *The Christian Commonwealth*, 106
elite, 41, 52, 108; Africans, 173, Catholic, 47, 49; as focus of conversion efforts, 47, 57, 191; Protestant, 47; Quaker, 110; role in Protestantization, 52; in United States, 234
Eltie, 123
Elizabeth I, 36, 37, 38–39; personal faith, 42–43, 45, 77; religious policy of, 42–43, 44, 49
Emlyn, Thomas, 185
emotionalism, 180, 196, 204
Empire: British, 13, 218, 233, 243, 260–61; French, 161
England, 92, 93, 108, 109, 188; visit to, 70–71, 72, 173
Enlightenment, 202, 231, 246; religion and, 164, 180, 184; religious freedom and, 6, 228
enslavement, justified, 95–96
enthusiasm, 180, 205
Ephrata cloister, 182
Episcopal church: ancient, 188; form, 39, 53, 68, 167
Episcopal Church (American), 220–21, 234
Episcopalians, in Scotland, 67–68, 164, 169, 193
Equiano, Olaudah, 235, 237; *The Interesting Narrative of the Life of Olaudah Equiano, or Gustavus Vassa, the African*, 237
eschatology, 90, 247

ethnography, 70, 96, 211
European, as category of person, 29–30
evangelical religion, 187, 211, 215. *See also* Christianity, evangelical
Evelyn, John, 81
Exclusion: Bill, 140; Crisis, 139
expansion, Iberian, 15, 56–57, 62–63

faith follows ruler, 38, 52–53, 101
Faneuil, Peter, 162
Fanti, 173
Fawkes, Guy, 50, 141, 150
fear, 10, 43, 152, 158
Fendall, Josias, 139
Fifth Monarchists, 90–91, 115, 125
Fish, Joseph, 209
Fisher, Mary, 120
Florida, 69, 92, 105, 122, 175
Foster, John, 86
Fowler, David, 208
Fox, George, 102, 103
Foxe, John, 44–45, 46; *Actes and Monuments*, 44, 65, 91
France, 52, 141, 173; Scotland and, 37, 38, 54; wars with, 128, 142, 159
Franciscans, 60–61, 74
Frankfurt am Main, 146
Franklin, Benjamin, 184, 194, 216, 231
French colonies, 13, 74, 92, 94
French Prophets, 160

Gabriel's Rebellion, 253, 259
Gante, Pedro de, 58
Garzia, John, 163
George, David, 238–39
George, Prince (Yamasee), 176–77
George III, 220, 233
George Frederick, King (Miskito), 261
General Association of Connecticut, 250
Geneva, 35, 38, 39, 48
Georgia, 177, 240, 263; Moravians in, 188, 190, 208
German settlers, 108, 109, 162, 257
Germantown, Pennsylvania, 104
Ghana, 27, 173
Glanvill, Joseph, 154
Glasgow, 202; University, 164
Glorious Revolution, 139, 140, 141–42, 150; in colonies, 143–50, 152, 158; impact of, 128, 159, 169, 185

God, 18, 28, 105, 123, 131; belief in, 97
godliness, concept of, 179
Godwyn, Morgan, 102, 105
golden rule, 104
Good, Dorcas, 153
Good, Sarah, 153
good works, 40
Gookin, Daniel, 134
Gordon Riots, 233, 234
Gorges, Sir Ferdinando, 75
Gorton, Samuel, 84
Gould, Eliga, 215
Grand River, Canada, 243
Graunt, John, *Truth's Victory against Heresy*, 117
Great Awakening, 196, 210, 217; Second, 217, 250
Green Corn Ceremony, 225
Grenada, 215, 222
Guatemala, 60
Guernsey, 113
Guinea, 17
Gunpowder Plot, 9, 50, 141, 258
Guyana, 261, 262
Guy Fawkes Day, 50, 223

Hadley, Connecticut, 136
Hakluyt, Richard, 63
Half Way Covenant, 133
Hans, 105
Harriot, Thomas, 22, 27, 70
Harris, Howell, 201
Hartlib, Samuel, 179
Harvard College, 123, 131, 171, 204
Hayes, Lemuel, 235–36
Heads of Agreement, 179
Heal, Felicity, 210
healers, 21, 25, 26, 97
heathen, concept of, 61, 129, 135–36, 157, 175, 209
Heaton, Hannah, 205
Heaton, Theophilus, 205
Heckwelder, John, 210
Henry VIII, 36, 40–41, 42, 43, 55
heresy, 42, 43, 98
Herrnhut Brethren, 188
Hesse-Kassel, 179
High Church, 166–67, 220
Highlands, Scottish, 40, 47, 51, 121, 163; residents of, 87, 141, 193, 233

Hispaniola, 58
Hispanophobia, 44, 59, 73, 150
Holy Fairs, 168–69
Hottentots, 188
Hubbard, William, *Narrative of the Troubles with the Indians in New-England,* 133
Huguenot church, 162
Huguenots, 52, 108, 162, 257
Huntingdon, Countess of (Selina Hastings), 191, 199–201, 238; Connexion, 238, 240
Hurons, 106
hybridity, 9–10, 61–62, 107; examples of 94, 97, 153, 252; slaves and, 101, 103
Hylson-Smith, Kenneth, 184
hypocrisy, charges of, 90, 119

iconoclasm, 47, 48, 55, 80; Native Americans and, 129–30, 157
iconography, 179
identity: British, 161, 185; confessional, 88; English, 45, 146, 150; Protestant, 63–64, 65, 259
illness, 21; mental, 157; witches and, 25
Independents. *See* Congregationalists
India, 242
Ipswich, Massachusetts, 204
Inquisition, 42, 63
instruction, religious: Celtic language, rejected, 212; as goal, 87, 170, 177, 179; of Native Americans, 104; of slaves, 102, 104, 172, 208
interconfessional cooperation, 178, 187, 191
Ireland: conquest of, 44, 51, 52, 53, 64; diversity in, 81, 109, 188; invasion of, 259; and Glorious Revolution, 128, 142; migration to, 51, 64, 74, 108, 162; reconquest of, 81–82, 142; Reformation in, 42, 50; religious situation in, 52, 64, 182, 185, 198
Irish, 79, 150; characterized, 64; migrants, 12, 64, 76, 233
Iroquois, 20, 26–27, 94–95, 216; Great League of, 20
irreligion, 179, 218, 221
Islam, 5, 28, 29, 58, 99, 176; conversion and, 58, 96; toleration of, 229, 231

Jacobites, 163, 185, 198
Jamaica, 122, 172, 241, 242, 263; diversity in, 91, 110, 206, 236, 251, 262; religious policies in, 87, 89, 113, 121, 172

James V (Scotland), 37

James VI and I, 64, 66; religious policy of, 67–69, 77; in Scotland, 39, 39–40, 47

James VII and II, 114, 128, 160, 259; Catholicism of, 139–40; religious policies of, 121, 169

Jamestown, 69, 135

Japhet, 107

Jefferson, Thomas, 228, 230–31, 246

Jemison, Mary, 210

Jesuits, 44, 74, 75, 122; as missionaries, 9, 60, 94, 176

Jews: Christian millennialism and, 91, 92–93, 95; in colonies, 91, 100, 108, 120, 216; England and, 30, 91, 115; in Europe, 16, 29; excluded, 76; expulsion from Spain of, 7, 16, 57; forced conversion of, 57; in Ireland, 167; migrants, 12–13, 16; Sephardic, 57, 67, 91

Johnson, Sir William, 220

Johns, Philip, 206

Joint Association of English and Welsh Calvinist Methodists, 199

Jones, Edmund, 184

Jones, Griffith, 192

Judaism, 5, 28, 91

Keith, George, 111, 171

Kendall, John, 115

Kiddermister, England, 87

kidnapping, 69, 153, 173. See also captives; captivity narrative

King's College, 216

kirk, 38–40, 68, 158; bishops in, 47, 67, 113, 163–64; Charles I and, 78–79; shifting nature of, 87, 142, 151, 164–65, 214

Kirkland, Samuel, 213, 225

Knox, James, Commissary, 175

Knox, John, 37, 39

Kongo, 1, 57, 175; Portuguese in, 15, 57, 98, 242

Labadists, 109, 122, 182, 258

Lancaster, Massachusetts, 132

land, 93, 129, 135, 139

landscape, sacred, 26, 56, 264; African, 18, 23, 27; Catholic, 8, 19, 54–56, 62; Native American, 29, 129

language, 60–61, 263; Algonquian, 92, 130; Cherokee, 243, 263; discussed, 93, 211–12;

Gaelic, 51–52, 87; Latin, 61; vernacular, 51, 60–61; Welsh, 51, 113, 170, 192, 211

las Casas, Bartolomé de, 58, 59, 89; Brief Account of the Devastation of the Indies, 58

Latimer, Hugh, 36

latitudinarianism, 183

Laud, William (archbishop of Canterbury), 77–78, 83, 113, 167

Lead, Jane, 181–82

Lee, Ann, 226–27

Leeward Islands, 113, 114, 143, 240

Leisler, Jacob, 146–47, 149; Leislerians and, 146, 149

Le Jau, Francis, 173

Leland, John, 239–40

Lent, 21, 56

Libbey, Jeremiah, 229

Liberia, 255, 262

liberty: of conscience, 84–85, 112, 116, 118, 183; and Protestantism, 45, 146, 150, 161; religious, 6, 99, 149, 162, 228

Liele, George, 238–39

Ligon, Richard, 96, 97

Lincoln, Levi, 230

Lincolnshire, England, 55

literacy, 47, 105, 179, 207; biblical, 41, 61, 71; converts seek, 206, 239; Protestantism and, 7, 65, 86. See also books

Littlejohn, John, 241

liturgy, 37, 77, 138; changes in, 40, 41, 42, 234; set, 45, 58

Locke, John, An Essay Concerning Human Understanding, 180

London, 141, 179, 215, 223; bishop of, 41, 114, 171, 175, 177; Great Fire of, 121; Missionary Society, 250; religious groups in, 68, 81, 84, 115, 247, 251

Long Island, 122

Louis XIV, 160

Louis XVI, 248

Louisiana, 252; Purchase, 252, 264

Low Church, 166–67

Lowlands, Scottish, 47, 202

loyalist, 236, 254, 259

loyalty, 136, 144, 158, 260; Church of England and, 125, 185, 220, 232, 243; religion and, 63, 74

Ludwell, Philip, 138

Luther, Martin, 15, 35, 55

Lutheranism, 35

Lutherans, 67, 108, 162, 197, 198

Madeira Islands, 15
Madison, James, 230
magic, 21, 25
Maine, 109, 110
Makemie, Francis, *Truths in a True Light*, 150
Maneto, 105
manumission, 102; conversion and, 96, 175; fears that conversion required, 103, 173
mariners, 112
Marrant, John, 238
Margate, David, 240
Maroons, 242
marriage: civil versus religious, 85; clerical, 42, 48; between natives and settlers, 70–21, 201–11; as sacrament, 34; of slaves, 103, 240
Martha's Vineyard, 93, 94, 105, 106, 109, 134
martyrs, 43, 47; Charles I as, 98, 125; Ralegh as, 64; missionaries as, 105, 118–19, 262; stories of, 36, 44–45, 50, 65, 98
Mary I (England), 36, 37, 38, 42, 43; marriage of, 44
Mary I (Scotland), 37–39, 53
Mary II, 121, 128
Maryland, 74, 75–76, 109, 110; Glorious Revolution and, 143, 147–48; Protestants in, 121, 139; religious policies in, 68, 85, 118, 166
Mary of Guise, 37
Mary of Modena, 139, 141
Mason, Captain, 137
Mass, 34, 37, 61, 121; available, 68, 76; defined, 20, 21; proscribed, 38, 42, 49; resumed, 43; singing during, 251
Massachusetts Bay Colony: Church of England and, 68; Glorious Revolution and, 128, 140, 143–45, 165; religious composition of, 73, 82, 112, 122, 125; religious establishment in, 89, 114, 228, 229; religious policies in, 87, 90, 118–19, 124
masters, 97, 151; slave conversion and, 95–96, 206
Mather, Cotton, 92, 178–79
Mather, Increase, 129, 148, 156, 179; *An Earnest Exhortation to the Inhabitants of New-England*, 132; *Essay for the Recording of Divine Providence*, 183
Mather, Richard, 86
Mathias, Gabriel, 174
Matthews, Thomas, 137
matrilineal family structure, 190, 208
Maule, Thomas, 155

Mayhew, Jonathan, 212–13
meeting house, 213
Melanchtlon, Philip, 35
Mennonites, 109
merchants, 162, 165
Merrell, James H., 1
Methodist: camp meeting, 217; cells, 178, 193, 198; Church, 191, 234–35; itinerants, 190; movement, 178, 1990, 208, 258
Methodists, 192, 198, 212, 232; African American, 208, 240; during American Revolution, 226; English, 191, 193, 253; Irish, 191, 193; Welsh, 191. *See also* African Methodist Episcopal Church
Mexico, 60, 62
Middle Colonies, 104, 111, 195, 216, 226; diversity in, 110, 159, 162, 221
Middletown, John, 88
migration: American Revolution and, 235, 236–37, 254; attempt to limit, 74; and diversity, 73, 197, 221, 256; internal, 108, 191, 195; of ministers, 74–77; Native Americans and, 104, 106; of Old English, 50, 51, 76; other revolutions and, 247–48, 251–52; to Protestant Atlantic, 6, 8, 108, 119–20, 161–62; of puritans, 73, 74, 77, 90, 132, 260; of Scots, 12, 53, 64, 108, 119–20, 183; of Welsh, 7, 12, 108, 110
Milbourne, Jacob, 149
militia, 175; duty, 110, 118
millennialism, 95, 160, 196; and revolutions, 82, 90–92, 224–25, 247
Miller, Arthur, *The Crucible*, 155
Miskito, 216, 261
missionary accounts, 92, 93–94; societies, 185, 254. *See also names of specific organizations*
missions, 69, 70, 261; in Africa, 57; in Britain, 70, 193, 216, 263–64; British, 171, 176–77, 240, 244, 261; to colonists, 159, 212–13; in early New England, 92–95, 134; English, 13, 91, 105; French, 92, 213; Iberian, 33, 57–58, 59–62, 69, 73; to Native Americans, compared, 69, 71, 105; to Native Americans, planned, 69, 70, 92, 105; among slaves, 240. *See also* conversion; *names of specific organizations*
Moderate Party (Scotland), 214
Mohawks, 123, 161, 243; mission to, 171, 176
Mohegan, 195, 245
monarchy: composite, 12, 67; divine right, 29,

79, 136, 138; hereditary, 140; religion and, 88, 98, 136, 221–22

Monmouth, Duke of (James Scott), 139

Montauk, 208

Montserrat, 74, 76, 120

Moravians, 162, 179, 188–91, 201, 262; characterized, 192, 258; choir system of, 188, 190, 208; missions, 190–91, 197, 206–7, 208; opposed, 198, 212

Morgan, Henry, 122

Morgan, William, 51

Mormonism, 263–64

Morris, Lewis, 120

Mosaic government, 106; law, 91

Motte, Richard, 231

mourning, 20, 23; wars, 23, 94–95

Muggleton, Lodowick, 81, 115

Muggletonians, 81, 115

Mühlenberg, Heinrich Melchoir, 198, 216

Murdock, Kenneth, 133

music, 48, 215

Muslims: in Africa, 16, 17, 98; beliefs, 70; in colonies, 98; conversion of, 101; enslaved, 98, 101; in Europe, 16, 57; expulsion from Spain of, 8, 16, 57–58; slavery and, 95–96

Myles, John, 109

mysticism, 180, 185; examples of, 28, 160, 181–82, 188

Nantucket, 134

Narragansett Bay, 70, 93

Narragansetts, 209

Natchez, 238

Natick, 134

Native Americans, 6–7, 89, 92–95, 112, 188; characterized, 69–70, 135–36; conversion of, 93–95, 100, 123, 172, 190; enslaved, 104, 177; interred, 131, 134; in King Philip's War, 129–31, 132; thought to be Jews, 91, 92–93

Native American traditional religion, 5, 56, 70, 105, 153; characterized, 17, 61–62, 92, 211; and clans, 47, 212; maintained, 5, 94, 99, 106, 127; prior to contact, 18–23, 26–29

Nativism, 209–10, 212, 216, 225–26

negotiation, 9–11, 31, 62, 100, 106, 218, 256

neophytes, 58, 93

Netherlands, 6, 7, 67, 74, 141, 160, 161

Nevis, 110

New Bohemia, 109

New Brunswick, 232

New England, 13, 110, 122, 177, 195; Calvinism in, 182, 199; puritan, 8, 88, 121; Way, defined, 144

Newfoundland, 110, 115, 170

New France, 9, 94, 105, 161

New Hampshire, 165, 244

New Haven, 87, 89, 119

New Light (Congregationalist), 212, 217

New Mexico, 69, 92

New Model Army, 81, 82, 84

New Netherland, 13, 67, 103, 108, 145, 146

Newport, Rhode Island, 216

New Spain, 60, 73

New Testament, 41, 51

New York, 108, 113, 118, 244; City, 175, 207; Glorious Revolution in, 145–46, 148–50; missions in, 171, 176, 208

New Zealand, 231

Nicholson, Francis, 145, 149

Nigeria, 27

nonconformists, 53

non-juror controversy, 166, 220

North Carolina, 27

Northampton, Massachusetts, 183, 196, 201, 208

Nova Scotia, 236, 237, 240, 242, 260

Nurse, Rebecca, 155

Oates, Titus, 139

oath, 101, 110, 166

Obeah, 97

obedience, political, 63, 223–24; to God, 70

objects, sacred, 18, 129, 175; amulets, 18, 21; Bible as, 94, 129–30; criticism of, 62; crucifix, 43; graves and, 23, 94, 176; medals, 89, 94; relics, 19, 48, 55, 94; talisman, 206; totem, 19

Occom, Samson, 195, 244–46

Old Lights (Congregationalists), 205, 212, 214

Old Side (Presbyterians), 205

Old Testament, 28, 91, 106, 235, 240, 241, 253

Oquaga, 244

orders, religious, 21, 34, 43, 51, 249; disbanded, 37, 40, 41, 48, 55; and expansion, 71, 74, 92

ordination, 171, 261; opposed, 76

origin stories, 16, 20, 26–29, 70, 105

Outer Banks (Carolina), 70

Oxenbridge, John, 105, 119, 120

Oxford, University of, 41, 190

pacifism, 110, 111, 226
pagan, as concept, 17, 30, 175
Paine, Thomas, *Age of Reason*, 249–50
Palatines, 162, 167, 182, 191, 193
Palliser, Sir Hugh, 233
papacy, 64, 65, 249
parish, as unit of organization, 85, 87
parliament, 92, 140, 188, 222; English Revolution and, 79–81; Cavalier, 112, 119
Passion Play, 61
Patronage Act, 164, 214
Payne, Francis, 102
Penn, William (father), 96
Penn, William (son), 111, 124–25, 140, 162; First Frame of Government, 111
Pennsylvania, 96, 177, 229–30; diversity in, 124–25, 140, 162, 182, 193; Quakers in, 104, 110, 111; University of, 216
Pernambuco, 91
persecution, 46, 49, 226; of Anabaptists, 35; of Baptists, 124; of Catholics, 44, 68, 121, 163, 170, 233; defended, 90; of native Christians, 123; of Protestants, 36, 44; of Quakers, 90, 118–19, 124, 226
Peru, 60
Peter, Hugh, 74, 82–83, 91, 93, 98
Philadelphia, 239; Society, 181–82
Philip, King, 131
Philip II, 44
Phipps, Sir William, 149, 155, 156
pietism, 197, 213
pietists, German, 109, 127
piety, 179, 180
pilgrimage, 19, 55
Pilgrimage of Grace, 55
piracy, 56, 73
pirates, 122; Barbary, 96
Pitt, William, 249
Plymouth Plantation, 7, 109, 131, 165; religious policies in, 87, 89, 114
Pocahontas, 70–71, 72, 92
polygenesis, 209
pope, 34; and American missions, 60; and Henry VIII, 36, 37; Pius XII, 62
popery, defined, 38
popish: defined, 45; Plot, 121, 139
Popular Party (Scotland), 214
population: colonial, 100; slave, 172
portrait, 70, 96, 174
Portugal, 57, 73, 74; colonies, 13, 60, 73, 89; expansion, 15

possession, 105, 156; defined, 153
poverty, 209; vows of, 51
power, spiritual, 9, 10, 16, 17–19, 28, 95
prayer, 205; extemporaneous, 45; the Lord's Prayer, 155; meetings, 178, 196; Native Americans and, 93
Praying Indian Villages, 93–94, 106, 134–35, 263
preaching, 132; banned, 77, 104; extemporaneous, 81, 194; importance of, 43, 77, 82, 87; itinerant, 198, 205; lay, 82, 83, 172, 180; message of, 81, 132, 202; role of, 40, 47, 48, 223–24; slaves and, 236–37
predestination, doctrine of, 35, 39, 47, 109, 182, 202
Presbyterian Church: expansion of, 168, 169, 197; form, 39, 45–47, 52, 67, 69, 78; in Scotland, 48, 69, 142, 156; and Westminster Assembly, 80–81
Presbyterian, clergy, 150, 165, 185
Presbyterians, 83, 183, 195, 199, 257; in colonies, 177, 217, 236; English, 108, 142, 179; Scots, 53, 87, 113, 182, 183, 201
presbytery, 39, 45, 67, 120, 178, 216
Preston, Richard, 243
Pretender, 141, 233
Price, Richard, *A Discourse on the Love of Our Country*, 246, 248
priesthood of all believers, 35, 56
priests, 21, 34, 251, 255; banned, 49, 163; in colonies, 76; and English Reformation, 40, 41; lack of, 122–23; missionary, 50
Prince, Thomas, *The Christian History*, 215
Princeton University, 216
Proctor, Deliverance, 155
Proctor family, 155–56
prognostication, 21–23, 97, 111–12
prophecy, 82, 83, 90, 107, 247
Protestant: Ascendancy, 167, 233; Associators, 147, 148; divisions, 35, 66–67; expansion, 5, 56, 65, 67, 73; migration, 6, 159, 161–62; revitalization, 188; unity, 150, 160, 197
Protestant Reformation, 8, 12, 31, 33, 34–35; attempted in Ireland, 42, 50–52, 54, 64–65; in Channel Islands, 52–53; compared, 41, 48; effect on encounter, 56, 264–65; in England, 33–37, 40–43, 54; as process, 40–43, 47, 49–50, 210; in Scotland, 35–40, 45–48, 54, 67–68; in Wales, 37, 42, 54
"Protestant Wind," 141

Providence, doctrine of, 12, 90, 131–33, 137–38
Providence Island Colony, 73, 96, 120
Prussia, 179
puritan, 198; in colonies, 73, 74, 84; defined, 45, 74; tribalism, 182
puritanization, 87–88

Quakers, 14, 81, 83, 122, 166, 169; beliefs, 107, 112; as dissenters, 142, 167; executions of, 33, 118–19; "Free," 226; migration of, 109–10, 120, 258; ministers, 110; missionaries, 84, 90, 102, 120; persecution of, 116, 118–19, 124, 221; slavery and, 103–4, 241–42; witchcraft and, 155
Quebec, 1, 92, 105, 122, 161, 215, 233, 264; Act, 222–23, 234
Quincy, Josiah, Junior, 227

Ralegh, Sir Walter, 63–64
Radicalism, 107; during interregnum, 81–83, 84
Randolph, Edward, 144
Ranters, 107, 111
rationalism, 184, 185
rebellion, 55, 135–36, 169, 175; slave, feared, 242, 253–55, 262; slave, religion and, 97, 259; slavery and, 102, 104
Rebellion, Irish, 79, 150; Stono, 175, 259
Reeve, John, 81, 115
reformation of manners, 160, 178, 183, 185
Reformed, 162, 193; sensibility, 94
regicide, 79, 82–83, 90, 98, 124; guilt for, 125–26, 133, 137, 158; regicides, 119, 136
religion: absence of, alleged, 97, 175; and conquest, 6, 57–58, 62–63; defined, 11–12, 30; and enslavement, 17, 235; and expansion, 72–73, 129, 131, 257–58; importance of, 12, 15–16, 17, 31, 157; politicization of, 44, 63, 99; and social and political system, 29, 125–26, 138
Remonstrants, 165
republic, English, 79, 98
republican thought, 140
Requirimiento, 58
resurrection, 25, 181
Restoration, 80, 98–99, 100, 106, 112
revelation, 107, 180
Revelation (book), 90, 116, 196
revival, 13, 193–96, 202, 215–16, 250; opponents of, 203

Revolution, 218, 258; American, 6, 13, 136, 218–26, 246, 257; English, 67, 98, 100, 106, 124, 133; French, 13, 233, 246–48, 259–60; Glorious, 121, 141–50, 246, 260; Haitian, 246, 248–49, 253–54
Rhode Island, 94, 141, 145, 209; religious groups in, 84, 107, 109, 110; religious policies in, 85, 118, 124–25, 165
Richmond, Virginia, 241
ritual, 19–21; African, 16; anti-Christian, 25–26; cannibalism, 95; ceremonialism, 166; Christian, 9, 16, 19, 188–89; church, approved, 77; days of thanksgiving or humiliation as, 88, 230; festivals, 19–21; gift exchange, 20; Moravian, 188–89; Native American, 16, 18, 19–20, 177; sign of the cross, 78; of transition, 21, 34; Vodou, 252, 253
Roanoke, 22, 70
Rogerenes, 107
Rogers, Daniel, 204
Rogers, John, 107
Rolfe, John, 70–71, 72
Rolfe, Rebecca. See Pocahontas
Roman Catholic: expansion, 5, 33, 56–60, 73, 74; practice, Church of England and, 36, 137; succession, opposed, 140, 150
Roman Catholic Church, 17, 19, 34, 251, 261; attempt to eliminate, 40, 163; contrast with, 42, 74; in Maryland, 68, 75–76, 124; mission status within, 75, 163
Roman Catholicism, 1, 16, 43, 54, 264; Iberian, 13, 56–57, 257–58; intercultural marriage and, 71; Irish, 51, 121; and Reformation, 43, 49, 53, 62
Rotterdam, English church at, 82
Rowlandson, Mary, 132, 134
Roxbury, 92
Royal African Company, 101
royalism, 88, 116
royalists, 112, 126, 33

Sabbath: legislation, 88; observance, 78, 107
sacraments, 34, 137; altered, 40; Confession, 21; Confirmation, 34; defined, 34; eliminated, 49, 56; Eucharist, 26, 34; Extreme Unction, 34; reinstated, 43; unavailable, 76, 122
Saint Christopher (island), 76, 108, 110
Saint Thomas (island), 161

Saint Vincent (island), 241

saints, 19, 23, 54, 55, 56, 62; days 21, 56; Saint Anne, 19; Saint Swithun, 55; Saint Teresa, 68; as spiritual intermediaries, 28, 48

Salem, 85, 119, 151, 152–56

salvation, 34, 35, 58, 199; limited, 40, 109, 199; universal, 68, 82, 179, 181, 190, 214

Sassamon, John, 131

Satan, 28, 223, 224; Native Americans and, 61, 94, 105; witches and, 25, 88, 152, 153

Savannah, Georgia, 239

Saxony, 188

schism, 204; Keithian, 111; in Scotland, 164, 168, 214

Schluter, Peter, 122

school, 60, 170; charity, 170; circulating, 192; hedge, 170; Indian, 263; master, 208; for "Negroes," 207

Scotland, 13, 109, 128, 151, 162; and Glorious Revolution, 141–42, 163, 164–65

Scottish Society for the Propagating of Christian Knowledge, 170, 177, 208

Secessionist movement, 183, 195, 214

Seneca, 19, 210

sensibility, 178, 184

separation of church and state, 6, 218, 227–29, 230, 260

separatists, 14, 74, 84, 205

servants, 152; indentured, 112; religious instruction of, 102

Sessarakoo, William Ansah. See Ansah, William

sexual licentiousness, 181, 189, 241

Seward, William, 192

Shakers, 226–27

Shakespeare, William, *The Tempest*, 69

Shattuck, Samuel, 119

shrines, 18, 19, 24, 48, 54–55

Sierra Leone, 1, 207, 238, 239, 242, 255, 262

Silver Bluff, South Carolina, 238, 239

Simson, John, 164

sin, 24, 40, 132–33; introduced, 28; freedom from, 83; original, 209

skepticism, 184, 185, 246

slave population, 101, 102, 103

slave trade, 12–13, 95, 101, 172, 255; effect on beliefs, 24; opposed, 104, 241

slavery, 227; effect on religious practice of, 23, 97; as metaphor, 146, 149, 190

slaves: African, 8, 13, 95–98, 100, 108, 110; Native American, 153

Sloughter, Henry, 149

Smith, Joseph, 264

Smith, Samuel, 102

Society for the Promoting of Christian Knowledge, 170

Society for the Propagation of the Gospel at Home, 250

Society for the Propagation of the Gospel in Foreign Parts, 171, 173, 184, 193, 207, 208, 253–54

Society of Friends, 103, 110. See also Quakers

Somerset decision, 236

South Africa, 188

South America, 153

South Carolina, 171, 173, 180, 207. See also Carolina

Southcott, Joanna, 247

Spain, 63, 64, 74, 142

Spain: colonial religious policy, 6, 7–8; colonies of, 13, 15, 58–63, 73, 94; in colonies, 89

spectral evidence, 156

spirit: African concept of, 18, 27; Holy Spirit, 188; Native American concept of, 11–12, 17–18, 177

spirits, 252; of the dead, 23, 24, 184; household, 18; water, 29

Spotswood, Alexander, 177

Squanto, 14

Stafford, 1st earl of (Thomas Wentworth), 78

Stockbridge, Massachusetts, 208

Stoddard, Solomon, 183, 196

suicide, 25, 203

Surinam (English), 91, 119, 120

Suriname (Dutch), 13, 67, 105, 162, 188

Susquehanna River, 244

Swansea Baptist Church, 7, 8, 109

Sweden, 67, 197

Swedish settlers, 108

Swift, Jonathan, *A Tale of a Tub*, 180

synod, 120, 168

Tangiers, 125

Tecaughretanego, 211

Tennant, Gilbert, *The Dangers of an Unconverted Ministry*, 204

Tennant family, 195

Test Act, 167

testamentary statements, 102

Thanksgiving, 20

theology, discussed, 104

Thirty-Nine Articles, 40
Thomas, John, 115
Thornton, John, 9
three kingdoms (England, Scotland, and Ireland), 12, 66, 141; complex religious situation of, 66, 68, 169; complex religious situation exported, 73–74
Tituba, 153
Toland, John, 185
toleration, 150, 179, 180, 181–82; in colonies, 75, 118, 121, 167, 253; defined, 124; under Muslims, 57; opposed, 84–85, 223
Touro Synagogue, 216
Trail of Tears, 263
transplantation, 7–9, 31, 61, 254, 256; Catholic versus Protestant institutions, 74; difficulty of, 75, 171; ease of, 76, 99
Trinidad, 262
Trinity, 18, 62, 185; belief in, required, 76, 228
tryers, 81, 87
Turtle Island, 26
Tyndale, William, 41–42
tyranny, fear of, 79, 140, 144, 146, 223

Ulster. See Presbyterians, Scots
unbelief, 179
uniformity, religious, 7–8, 68, 123–24; as goal of Charles I, 74, 77, 78–79, 113
Unitas Fractrum, 188
United Irishmen, 249
United States, 227, 240, 251; Constitution, 227; treaty of (1797), 229
Universalism, 214, 249
Ussher, James, 51
Utah, 264

Veneer, Thomas, 91
Vesey, Denmark, 255
vestments, clerical, 75, 77; opposition to, 76, 81
vestries, 103
violence, popular, 227; against Catholics, 38, 141, 233; against Methodists, 192, 240, 241
Virgin Mary, 55, 62, 175, 259; as Our Lady of Guadalupe, 62; of Remedios, 62
Virginia, 73, 116, 125, 133; Bacon's Rebellion and, 135–38; native conversion and, 68–72, 177; religious policies in, 75, 77, 113, 169; slaves in, 95, 101, 102, 105, 253
Virginia Company, 73, 90

Vodou, 252
voluntary societies, 178, 185, 191

Waldensians, 162
Wales, 52, 92, 184, 199; established church in, 68, 113, 170; puritans in, 87
Walloons, 108
Wampanoags, 94, 109, 131, 134
war: between Britain and France, 128, 158, 159, 160–61; among Native Americans, 104; between Native Americans and colonists, 13, 129, 152, 258; against pagans, 58; religious, 36, 38, 53
War: Bishops', 78, 113; King Philip's, 129–35, 176, 210; Nine Years, 160; of Spanish Succession, 160
warming pan controversy, 141
Warwick, 2nd Earl of (Robert Rich), 82, 84
Warwick, Rhode Island, 84
Washington, George, 228, 230, 244
Welsh Sunday School movement, 250
Wesley, John, 190–92, 203, 215, 217, 235; A Calm Address to our American Colonies, 226; George Whitefield and, 193–94, 199–201, 214
Westerly (Rhode Island) Seventh-Day Baptist Church, 107
Western Design, 83, 87, 88–89
West Jersey, 110, 111
Westminster Assembly of Divines, 80; Westminster Confession, 183
Westphalia, Peace of, 53
Wheatley, Phillis, 235
Wheelock, Eleazar, 177, 244, 145
Wheler, Sir Charles, 114
White, John, 22
Whitefield, George, 191, 192, 198, 200, 208; publishes journal, 194, 204. See also Wesley, John
Wilberforce, William, 241
William III, 121, 160
William and Mary, 159, 166, 185, 259; Glorious Revolution and, 140–42, 144, 146, 147
William and Mary, College of, 169, 171
Williams, Eunice, 161
Williams, Roger, 70, 84, 93, 228
Winchester, 55
Winthrop, John, 112
witchcraft, 9, 13, 19, 21; beliefs, 25–26, 88, 150; official view of, 25–26; prosecutions, 88, 128, 151–55; scares, 151–57, 158, 164

witches, 25, 69, 150–51; protection from, 97, 259

women, 49, 121, 176; as daughters, dutiful, 181; as first human, 70; preaching, 82, 123, 181; as religious leaders, 110, 181–82, 226–27, 247; spiritual power and, 26–27, 28; wise, defined, 26; witchcraft and, 152, 153

Wood, William, *New England's Prospect*, 70

Wood's Edge Ceremony, At the, 177

Wouter, 123

Yale College, 165, 171–72

Yamasee, 176

York, 55

Yoruba, 27

Yucatan, Bishop of, 62

Zinzendorf, Count Nikolaus Ludwig von, 188, 198

Zwingli, Huldrych, 35

ACKNOWLEDGMENTS

This book grew out of an essay I wrote for *The British Atlantic World*. I thank David Armitage and Michael Braddick for the initial invitation to contribute to that volume. At a stimulating gathering to discuss the project hosted by the International Seminar on the History of the Atlantic World at Harvard, various participants urged me to write an expanded version of my essay in order to present this complex story in more detail. Years later, this book responds to that suggestion.

Many scholars have helped me along the way. Numerous people graciously answered my wide-ranging and often obscure questions: Leslie Alexander, Bob Baum, Chris Brown, Colin Calloway, David Cressy, Matt Goldish, Ray Irwin, Wim Klooster, Robin Law, Allan Macinnes, Charlene Mires, Lucy Murphy, Jeani O'Brien, Lisa Poirier, Neal Salisbury, (Mary) Katharine Simms, Philippa Mein Smith, Alan Taylor, Dale van Kley, and Peter Williams. I was fortunate to have helpful readings of all or part of the manuscript from a varied collection of scholars. Michael Braddick, John Coffey, Drew Cayton, John Cinnamon, Fran Dolan, David Fahey, Raymond Gillespie, Eric Hinderaker, E. Brooks Holifield, Ray Kea, Dan Richter, and Sharon Salinger, as well as an anonymous reader for the press, made suggestions that saved me from many errors and prodded me to think more deeply. Authors of many books and articles made this book possible through their scholarship; I regret that each of them cannot be acknowledged here.

Others also helped. Amy Bergseth, Catherine (Cat) Schmierer, Blake Vaughan, and Joe Wachtel provided research assistance at Miami University. Liz Smith, in the Department of History, typed up a thirty-page bibliography from my often only semi-legible note cards. While collecting images to include in the book, I called upon Matthew Bailey at the National Portrait Gallery (London), Georgia Barnhill and Cindy Brennan at the American Antiquarian Society (Worcester), Susan Danforth at the John Carter Brown

Library (Providence), and Steve Tabor at the Huntington Library (San Marino). I am grateful to all of them, but especially to Cindy and Steve, who saved me in the midst of a last-minute crisis with cheerful alacrity. Don Pestana, who loves maps, helped me figure out those that appear here. At the University of Pennsylvania Press, Bob Lockhart welcomed this volume. Working with him has been a pleasure.

I have talked about this book in a number of venues, occasions that provided opportunities for thinking through ideas and issues. In 2004 I was able to teach a course on "Religion in the British Atlantic World" at Miami University, where my students' questions and suggestions pointed me toward additional aspects of the story. I presented a paper on missionaries to the Australia New Zealand American Studies Association meeting in Launceston, Tasmania, in July 2006. The History and Religious Studies departments at the College of William and Mary graciously hosted talks in fall 2006. The American Cultures Seminar at Miami discussed a chapter in the spring of 2007. At the University of Michigan conference "Religion and Empire in the Early Modern Atlantic" in the fall of 2007, I gave a keynote address; preparing that talk and engaging in the stimulating conversations at that meeting permitted me to reconsider the bigger picture as I concluded work on this volume. I thank everyone for their suggestions.

My father was a modest man, so I suspect he might not have chosen to have one of my books dedicated solely to him. Ever his independent-minded daughter, I nonetheless dedicate it to his memory with love.